ALSO BY SILVANA PATERNOSTRO

In the Land of God and Man

MY COLOMBIAN WAR

SANTA MAR

El Rod

BARRANQUILLA
Puerto Colombia
PNN ISLA DE SALAMANCA
Pueblo Vie
Playa Turipana
SOLEDAD
MALAMBO
Sabanagrande
Galerazamba
Baranoa
Sitionuevo
Santo Tomás
ATLÁNTICO
Varela
Ponedera
Pta. Canoas
Luruaco
SABANALARGA
Repelón
Pivijay
CARTAGENA
I. de Tierrabomba
Villanueva
Manatí
Campo de la Cruz
Turbaco
Cerro de San Antonio
Bahía de Cartagena
Calamar
Ega. San Antonio
I. del Tesoro
I. Barú
Arjona
Isles del Rosario
Mahates
Ega. Sapayán
I. Grande
Pta. Barbacoas
PNN CORALES DEL ROSARIO
Pta. Barú
Carrato
Pta. Comisario
María La Baja
SFF
San Juan Nepomuceno
Pta. La Salina
LOS COLORADOS
Tenerife
Arigu
I. Mucura
I. Tintitipan
San Jacinto
PLATO
Islas de San Bernardo
Pta. I. Mangles
San Onofre
MAGI
San Bernardo
I. Salamanquilla
I. Palma
CARMEN DE BOLÍVAR
DE MORROSQUILLO
Tolú
Ovejas
San Pedro

MY COLOMBIAN WAR

A JOURNEY THROUGH THE COUNTRY I LEFT BEHIND

SILVANA PATERNOSTRO

HENRY HOLT AND COMPANY NEW YORK

For
my Colombian-born godson

Henry Holt and Company, LLC
Publishers since 1866
175 Fifth Avenue
New York, New York 10010
www.henryholt.com

Henry Holt® and 🛡® are registered trademarks of
Henry Holt and Company, LLC.

Distributed in Canada by H. B. Fenn and Company Ltd.

Portions of this book have been published in *Colors,*
The New York Times Magazine, and on Slate.com.

Library of Congress Cataloging-in-Publication Data

Paternostro, Silvana.
    My Colombian war : a journey through the country I left behind / Silvana Paternostro. — 1st ed.
        p. cm.
    Includes index.
    ISBN-10: 0-8050-7605-0
    ISBN-13: 978-0-8050-7605-9
        1. Colombia—Description and travel. 2. Paternostro, Silvana—Travel—Colombia.
3. Colombia—History—1974– I. Title.
F2264.2.P38 2007
986.1—dc22   2006049708

Henry Holt books are available for special promotions and premiums.
For details contact: Director, Special Markets.

First Edition 2007

Maps by Jeffrey L. Ward
Designed by Kelly Too

Printed in the United States of America
10 9 8 7 6 5 4 3 2 1

I see you once again,
City of my childhood, horribly lost . . .
Sad and happy city, I am here dreaming once again . . .

I? But I am the same one who lived here once and returned,
And came back here again and returned.
And here I am once again?
Or are we all the I's that were here,
A string of person-beads threaded by memory,
A string of dreams of me dreamt by someone outside of me?

I see you once again,
With a heart more detached, with a soul that belongs less and less to me.

—Fernando Pessoa, "Lisbon Revisited"
Translated by Miguel Falquez-Certain

The author wishes to note that certain names and details in this book have been changed to protect the privacy of individuals who generously shared their stories.

CONTENTS

MY COLOMBIAN WAR

Map of Colombia

Caribbean Sea

76°   72°   68°

12°   12°

Sierra Nevada de Santa Marta
Santa Marta
Barranquilla   Caracas
Cartagena
Valledupar

PANAMA
Serranía de Perijá
8°   8°

VENEZUELA

Chigorodó

Magdalena River
SANTANDER   ARAUCA
Medellín
Pacific
Ocean   BOYACÁ
CHOCÓ
CUNDINAMARCA
Santa Fe de Bogotá
4°   4°

COLOMBIA
The Andes

0°   0°

Quito

ECUADOR   BRAZIL

AMAZONAS

0 Miles   200   400
0 Kilometers   200   400   Amazon

4°   4°

© 2007 Jeffrey L. Ward   76°   72°   68°

PERU

THE MAPS

Many years later, facing the map of Colombia I've hung on the kitchen wall in my New York City apartment, I recall that distant time when I kissed Luis good-bye before leaving for school in America, never thinking that my life from that day on would continue without him and outside of my country of birth. I left in 1977, a fifteen-year-old girl who knew nothing about the world outside of a narrow enclave of family and friends where I had been made to feel special. Reluctantly, I left my American-style school in the loud and chaotic coastal city of Barranquilla, where I had just been crowned Popularity Queen, for the quiet and manicured streets of suburban Detroit, where I would live with Colombian friends of my parents and attend the all-girl Academy of the Sacred Heart. If the first few months were difficult, mostly because I missed the attention bestowed upon me back home, I soon turned my back on the place where I was from.

At first, I returned to Colombia for short family visits, but after my parents settled in Panama in 1979, where my father worked as a banker, the visits became less frequent. It was only when they returned in 1986, this time to Bogotá, the capital high in the Andes, that I was faced with Colombia again. By then, I had already found the insatiable need to tell stories—real stories—and all my attention was directed toward how to become a journalist. I was determined to write in English about Latin America. In those days, the war of drug lord Pablo Escobar with the Colombian government over an extradition treaty grabbed the attention of newspaper editors, but I was more interested in what was happening in Central America, the focus of Washington in those Cold War days. In 1989, Escobar ordered the explosion of a commercial airplane in midair (killing 197 people) but instead of investigating his story, I chose to travel to Nicaragua—left-wing rebels were to me more interesting than drug lords.

I kept in touch with my family through letters and phone calls and the infrequent short visit but I didn't like going back, though I'm not exactly sure why, and the thought of returning to live there, despite my father's many pleas, felt like I would be entering a long tunnel. I had become fully immersed in a new life, where being from Colombia was mostly a nuisance. All it meant to me was a green passport that was viewed with suspicion everywhere: First as a curious young traveler and later when I became a freelance journalist writing for American publications, it meant complications and restrictions. I could not travel on a whim or rush to a breaking story. I spent hours standing in lines in front of consulates begging them to let me visit their countries and paying hundreds of dollars for permits and unflattering pictures taken in corner shops. But getting permission to visit was winning half the battle. Airport customs officials around the world all treated me the same way when they saw my passport: I was strip-searched in Miami, Houston, and New York; thoroughly questioned in Frankfurt, Rome, and Geneva. In Athens, I was held up for three very long hours by two menacing men insisting on an explanation of why I was carrying not one, but two, bottles of contact lens solution. "So I can see" did not seem to be a satisfactory answer. I was the only person awakened on a night train from Florence to Paris. The knock was forceful. The voice was intimidating. "Open the door. Please open the door. *La signorina* from Colombia, please open the door." These moments were annoying at the very least; they were also humiliating and scary. But they did not stop me from traveling. As the world opened in front of me, even if suspiciously, I closed my door on Colombia.

In 1997, exactly twenty years after I had left, I came to realize that the place of my childhood was disintegrating and a series of events, some news related, others personal, made me want to play closer attention. In April 1996, I had attended a three-day writing workshop given by Gabriel García Márquez in the colonial city of Cartagena where I listened to *el maestro* with complete attention. But something else was triggered when I learned about the stories that my Colombian colleagues were covering and how they were doing so. Rubén Valencia, from Cali, traveled for three days by car, boat, and scooter to write about the massacre of eighteen people inside a billiard hall in a town called Chigorodó where a twenty-year-old hit man had already killed eighty-three people; Wilson Daza lived for twenty days in a square in Medellín with young hit men, drug pushers, and prostitutes; Edgar Téllez was investigating the country's president and his links to drug cartels. Envy, guilt, and alarm suffused my thoughts. One night at dinner, I met a young woman from Apartadó, close to where Rubén had been reporting the massacre. She too had a story about collective killings. Her uncle, who served as the mayor of the small town, was accused of killing left-wing rebels. For her safety, she had moved to Cartagena where she worked as a waitress. Colombia is in trouble, I realized as I scurried back to the safety of my Greenwich Village apartment. I had no idea where Chi-gorodó or Apartadó were located, but from then on, I slowly started to put my hand back on Colombia's doorknob, unsure if I was capable of turning it or not.

A year later at a film screening, I ran into Max Rosenbaum, a photojournal-ist that I knew but not well. He was part of a posse of journalists who covered Latin America. A mutual friend, a documentary filmmaker, was showing his latest work, a journey into the Brazilian Amazon and the effect that the global concern for saving the rainforest was having on the indigenous population (not good). Max and I spoke that night, half in English, half in Spanish, exchanged phone numbers, and agreed to meet to see if there were stories we could do together. It was obvious we were both curious and attracted to each other. I don't know if he knew that I liked his commitment to tell the stories of Latin America, and that I was drawn to American storytellers, especially those who worked in Latin America as journalists and photographers.

I admired the group's unbalanced all-encompassing lifestyle dedicated to reporting stories of U.S. foreign policy in faraway places. Their lives were made up of clothes that came out wrinkled from duffle bags, apartments that pro-vided basic shelter, far from prime real estate, and relationships that were as unstable as the countries they covered. I was starting to realize that telling sto-ries is not a job; it's an addiction. Ask anyone who does it.

When I found out that Ryszard Kapuscinski, a Polish journalist and master of literary journalism, was speaking at The New School on Max's birthday, I invited him over without telling him why. When he arrived at my house that night, I announced a surprise celebration. "I need to blindfold you to take you there," I told him. I covered his eyes with the brown scarf he had given me and led him by the hand. Asking where I was taking him every step of the way, he found himself in the last place he would have expected—in a seat at a uni-versity's auditorium on Thirteenth Street and Fifth Avenue. Once he was in his chair and Kapuscinski was sitting at the dais, I revealed my surprise.

"Let's do a story in Colombia together," I whispered in his ear as Kapuscinski spoke.

The visit to Cartagena in 1996 had left me curious and hungry and I had started doing what I call "a little research," similar to what happens when you start developing a crush on someone. I was now reading the magazines that my parents had religiously been sending since I left and that, until recently, had gone unopened. I leaned over and told Max, very sure of myself, that what was happening in Colombia was easy to explain: There are landowners who have a lot of land; there are Marxist rebels who want to take the land from landowners; and there are paramilitary that fight the guerrillas for the landowners. Then I told him about a farm my grandfather had in northern Colombia where we could go and tell that story. I knew little about what was happening there, other

than what my mother told me during our weekly phone conversations, mostly
that *la guerrilla* had taken over the region, kidnapping someone we knew here
and there, killing cattle, burning pastures. She never mentioned the paramilitary in her conversations, but "I'm sure we'll find them," I said to Max. "There's
never one without the other."

It was decided. We would go there, to the region where the farm is, and talk
to rebels and paras. No one had done that story. "We will go talk to both sides.
We can definitely do it," I said naïvely. "I'm sure they'll talk to us. We are American journalists. With my Spanish and the fact that I'm from there but I'm not
really and I don't live there, it'll be easy for us to really understand what's going
on." This would prove to be the most out-of-touch statement I could have ever
made.

The allure of going back to Colombia to report had more than a journalistic component. With Max, I saw a chance for my two identities—the girl
from Colombia and the New York City–based journalist—to come together. I
yearned to find a way to resolve my internal schizophrenia.

When I found out a few months into our research that Colombia's minister
of defense would be talking at the Americas Society, the little sister to the
Council on Foreign Relations, the most exclusive of American think tanks, I
called Max to give him the details. "I will meet you there for sure," he said.

It was on a cold November evening that I made my way up Park Avenue to
the mansion with the fancy address and the imposing white columns where
Latin American heads of state, government officials, historians, and authors
come to speak to a select audience. The organization was founded in 1970 by a
group of businessmen led by David Rockefeller. Originally known as the Center for Inter-American Relations, its mission statement argued that "ignorance
of our neighbors is neither sensible nor safe, neither smart nor neighborly,
neither good economics nor good manners." I was nervous walking there, as I
was going to hear about Colombia in a very formal setting for the first time.
Colombia, up to that moment, was mostly where I had grown up and where
my parents lived. What will Colombia be here? I wondered as I climbed the
marble staircase.

The crowd consisted of a dozen or so people, the men in suits and ties, the
women in suits and pearls. They were bankers, lawyers, representatives of
important multinationals; many were those who manufacture agricultural
machinery like John Deere or who deal in commodities from Colombia. They
were here for the insider perspective on Colombia, hoping to figure out whether
the country was an investment risk or an opportunity, whether they would be
selling fewer or more Caterpillars. When Max finally showed up, an embroidered
cap on his head and a tattered bag full of cameras on his shoulder, I was relieved.

Gilberto Echeverri, a prominent industrialist, had a long-standing public service career, having served as minister and ambassador. He had gained notoriety when he served as mayor of Medellín, known to the world as the home of Pablo Escobar. Echeverri embraced the huge task of erasing the wake of violence left behind by Escobar and worked incessantly to bring civility to a city that in a decade had gone from having the most beautiful orchids in the world to breeding the highest number of teenage killers. Echeverri was a hero, my father had said on the phone when I told him I would be attending this talk, happy and mystified by my sudden interest in Colombia. My father was right when he described him as unassuming and incredibly personable; Echeverri was the antithesis of the image of a Latin American military man. Wearing a blue suit instead of a uniform, the minister opened his talk with the standard welcoming remarks, delivered in English but with the singsong of a Medellín accent.

After a ten-minute overview of Colombia's basic stats that could have been lifted from the *Encyclopedia Britannica,* Minister Echeverri mentioned that he had just arrived from Washington, where he had a very productive meeting at the State Department. The minister then revealed his real presentation, an agenda that centered heavily on Washington's War on Drugs, so popular then, before it was replaced after 9/11 by the War on Terror. Echeverri produced and held up a map of Colombia. "These are the Andes," he said, passing three fingers up the spine of the laminated mounds, one over each of the three cordilleras, the mountain range that splits like a three-pronged oyster fork. Down here are Putumayo, Caquetá, Guaviare, Vaupés, and the Amazon, he said, pointing to the big, bright green area right underneath the mountains. "All jungle," he said. "It is impenetrable. Anything can be happening there and we wouldn't know it." I stared at the map and realized how unfamiliar I am with the geography of my birthplace. I had no idea half of it was jungle. "We know that this is where the drug traffickers have their laboratories. Finding them here, however, is more difficult than finding a needle in a haystack."

Echeverri then covered the map with a plastic transparent sheet adorned with red dots, turning the big green blanket into a red-polka-dotted one. "This is where they are," he said, explaining that each red dot indicated a cocaine laboratory. The minister continued with his show-and-tell, taking another plastic sheet, this one covered with blue dots, and placing it on top of the other. The blue dots, representing the rebel camps, aligned perfectly with the red-dotted cocaine labs. "We have also identified the main rebel camps," he said. Max and I looked at each other across the table, both thinking: Washington and the Colombian government have conveniently found a way to fight left-wing rebels. After Vietnam and the Contra wars of Central America, Washington had decided that fighting rebels in foreign lands was a bad idea, a move that could invoke a media nightmare as had happened with El Salvador and the Iran-Contra scandal. We understood the reasoning behind the geography lesson: If the rebels were considered drug traffickers, if they started calling them narco-guerrillas instead of plain guerrillas, then it would be okay to fight them.

I looked around the room. The crowd was bored. The minister disappointed the audience, who had come to hear about economic forecasts, not about an Amazonian place riddled with armed Communist rogues producing cocaine. The man next to me shrugged his shoulders as if to say, "Colombia has always had both. So what? You've wasted our time."

But to Max and me it had been a very productive two hours. We exchanged conspiratorial glances. Finally, we might do a story, together, in Colombia. Yes!

"Colombia is poor. Our country is very poor. Our soldiers are poorly equipped," the soft-spoken minister continued, starting to sound like a late-night infomercial about how fifty cents a day, the cost of a cup of coffee, can help send a child in Latin America to school. At the end of his speech, Echeverri delivered the punchline and announced that thankfully, by Christmas, in little over a month, Washington would be sending the first batch of equipment to help Colombian soldiers hunt down the narco-rebels. He seemed especially excited about the night-vision goggles. "Those kids cannot see anything without them." The infrared light will save lives.

After the talk, Max and I went up to the minister. When I told him I was from Colombia, he smiled with grandfatherly affection and asked me, "From where?" After pleasantries, I asked him in my Colombian voice, in Spanish—which is different from my reporter's voice, in English—if he would take us to see the soldiers using the goggles for our story. His smile grew wider. *"Claro,"* he said, turning into the most accessible Latin American military officer in history. "Can I try them on?" I asked. "I want to see how they make you see in the dark." He handed me a card with his assistant's cell phone. "Come down," he said. "I hope to see you both there." He patted Max on the back.

"You are shameless," Max said, not fully understanding the dual identity that has allowed me to get into places that a full-blooded gringo reporter could not enter in Latin America. "Is that so wrong?" I responded. "It will get us there. Sometimes you've got to wear blindfolds and other times it's infrared goggles."

Max and I spent the next months writing pitches to magazines and grant proposals to foundations. But we found no takers. It was as easy to think that we might have had a story as to forget that we didn't. The life of freelance journalism is made of that: looking for ideas that can become stories. If the story about the United States sending military equipment to help track down narco-rebels did not work, it was time to find another one that did. Max went to cover the revolution in Zaire, and I went to Cuba to cover the preparations for Pope John Paul's visit.

TWO YEARS PASSED BEFORE I SAW A MAP OF COLOMBIA AGAIN. WHEN I DID, sparked by a newspaper report in June 1999 about the rebels' close proximity to the capital, where my parents lived, Colombia became my obsession. If I was going to face my country, I'd better get to know it. I had never looked closely at a map of Colombia. The minister's map had been the closest I had gotten. I remembered buying one at a supermarket during one of my more engaged return trips, and on a Kerouac-inspired whim, I thought that it would be interesting (or fun, or both) to drive from the coast to Bogotá, an idea that I soon abandoned. The roads were terrible, the trip would take days, and it was not that safe, I was told by the few friends I invited to go with me. Upon my return to New York, I stashed the map in a cigar box where it stayed through many Junes.

The time to face it had come. I stretched the map out on my living room floor, glanced at it without really knowing what I was looking at, walked it over to the kitchen, and taped it on top of a framed poem by Charles Baudelaire on the wall that Viktor, a Romani, gave to me in the midst of the Balkan wars. Viktor and I met in Vienna in June 1993 at a symposium about the rights of street children, during the World Conference on Human Rights, where 7,000 participants representing 171 countries and 840 nongovernmental organizations gathered to celebrate and reassess the Universal Declaration of Human Rights. Viktor explained how he would go into Belgrade and Zagreb and take children out of the war zone and into safe houses in Milan and ran into trouble with the Italian police. He was lobbying at the convention for the children, asking that the Italian government protect them and not send them back, even though he was taking them in without proper passports.

Viktor and I became fast friends, spending the three days of the conference together, choosing which panels we would attend and planning to meet afterward when our interests separated us. In between, we strolled the ringed streets of Vienna. We sat on a bench and listened to musicians while Viktor read my palm, because "all gypsies can do it," and played me an invisible saxophone. He combed my hair as he told me stories of war. Before he left to go back inside the belly of Yugoslavia, he handed me "À Une Passante" ("To a Passerby"), Baudelaire's poem. He had illustrated each verse with a woman who looked like me, except she had blue hair. I framed it and hung it on my kitchen wall, wondering at times how he was doing now that Yugoslavia no longer exists.

The street about me roared, deafening.
Tall, slender in deep mourning, majestic in her grief,
A woman passed—with imposing hand

Gathering up a scalloped hem—
Agile and noble, her leg like a statue's.

A lightning flash . . . then night!—Fugitive beauty.
Whose gaze has suddenly given me new life,
Will I see you again before the close of eternity?

I covered Viktor's gift with my map and wondered what happens to those whose work pertains to war when the fighting ends. I located the places I had visited on the map, the ones I can find with ease: Bogotá, the cold capital; Medellín, where I went on a family trip at age thirteen; Santa Marta and Cartagena, near my native Barranquilla and where I had spent many vacations by the sea. The rest of the country is unknown to me, a mystery. I found the area where El Carmen, my family's farm, lies but I had to search hard to find it. When I did I was surprised by how far it is from Barranquilla and how close it is to Venezuela. I also searched for Chigorodó and Apartadó, places that evoked death.

FROM THAT DAY I HAVE STARED AT THE MAP AS IF BY DOING SO I WOULD GET TO know it faster, better. I start my days by looking at it while I wait for my coffee to be ready. I do it without my glasses on so that it is blurry and I watch it take on the form of a doll my nephew Felipe once made out of Play-Doh. He gave the doll all the basic body parts but, as happens when a child molds clay into figures, they were somewhat deformed, a bit off. Colombia, like the doll, has a tiny head and an overstretched neck. It has two arms, one a short stump and the other skinny with one long bony finger. Instead of legs, the doll has a mermaid's tail.

The more I look at the map pasted over the Baudelaire poem, the more the doll takes on a life of her own. She fights hard to survive with all the abnormalities with which she was created. Each one of those deformed organs has built its own defense mechanism, its own immune system. Each one of those parts is independent and fierce. It has to overcompensate for what is missing. Colombia does the same thing. Colombians like to say that it is a country of regions, instead of body parts. But like my deformed doll, each region, or part, fights another, tooth and nail, to survive. The result is tragic.

Every morning when I face my map of Colombia, I assign a body part to each of the regions. First, the head, bald and too small, and the neck, long like a giraffe's, is what Colombians call "the Coast." This is where I come from. It is the extension of land that borders the Atlantic Ocean and shares mountains, a long extension of soft hills, like a mini-Andes, with Venezuela. It is called, I learn, the Serranía de Perijá. It is amid those foothills that El Carmen, the family farm, lies. It is here, my family tells me, where *la guerrilla,* who always chose mountains, have settled.

Then there are the disproportionate arms. The left one, the stump, is hunched up higher as if it were recovering from the blow it received in 1903, when Teddy Roosevelt chopped off the beautiful, muscular, and healthy arm to create Panama. Roosevelt "took Panama," as he told Americans—an amazing vein in that arm that would make everything in the world move much faster and make America more powerful. Colombia lost its arm and the Panama Canal became known as the center of the world, the heart of the universe.

Colombia was left with the underarm, the region known as Chocó, with its forgotten impenetrable rainforest—a perfect place for drug labs and armed rogues to hide. Extending south, down the rib cage, the nooks and crannies, the jungles and rivers of the Pacific Coast emerge. That entire underarm and rib cage are closer to the laws of nature, far from the rule of law. On the shoulder sits the gulf of Urabá, where I found Chigorodó on my map. When Rubén Valencia went to investigate the massacre in the tiny town, all he found was an eerie silence and a source who identified himself as an angel.

"What kind of angel?" Rubén had asked him.

"An angel with a white wing and a black wing," came the answer. The angel demanded to know what side Rubén was on before he would agree to an interview. Rubén left the town by dawn.

The doll's left breast houses the valleys of Central Magdalena, where the land is rich, and where cattle roam on big estates. The lords of these lands, the owners of the animals, are men who believe in self-defense against the rebels who've gone to the sierras. And they have sworn to take revenge and "eliminate" anyone who dares to want to change how things have been working since the Spanish left more than two hundred and some years ago.

The right breast has a similar affiliation to its other rich neighbor. Venezuela with its oil-inflated economy is prepared, like Panama on the left, to facilitate and to buy anything and hire anyone. This side has a very long and skinny arm that droops to the side, almost to the hip, and it has one bony finger, like a witch's, that tickles and prods, always creating tension between them. Colombia, Brazil, and Venezuela engage in a blurry ménage-à-trois, forming a triangle of love and constant dispute.

Continuing from the neck down, there's the heart, the center of it all. This is the capital of the country, the seat of government, and everything that is reminiscent of the authority once held by Spain's Reino de Castilla y Aragón. The country's heart is cold and formal, characteristics embodied in the children born of Santa Fé de Bogotá's blood, a city that insists on being royal and remote. This is where the air is chilly and the oxygen sparse, nearly ten thousand feet high and more than five hundred years baroque. The heart is selective, choosing to let inside only those with sophistication or connections to riches. The men and women who live in Colombia's heart discuss matters in clubs that aspire to be like London's. Dressed in tweeds and ties, the men from the capital, known as *cachacos*, copy the upper-class Brits. They would like to blackball the *paisas*, the *costeños*, the *vallenatos*, anyone from any other region. But the men from these regions insist on coming in; after all, they grew up in a land where fighting is the only way to survive.

When I explain my Colombian map-doll to Max, he disagrees. He tells me that no, Bogotá is more brain than heart. It is rational and educated, not emotional. I listen because unlike me, Max went to Colombia, after Zaire, and since 1997 he has been taking pictures of Colombia, traveling the roads I only get to see hanging on my kitchen wall.

"The heart," he says, standing in front of my map one day, placing his finger between Barranquilla and Santa Marta, "is the Sierra Nevada de Santa Marta."

His finger rests on a purple mound, a big rugged triangle in the shape of a heart. From the arid Guajira and the delta of the Magdalena, the Sierra Nevada emerges, sixteen thousand feet tall, so tall it has snowy peaks and pointy glaciers on the southern side that turn into the plains of Valledupar. The Sierra is another place I had forgotten about. I made trips to the Sierra when I lived in Colombia, and listening to Max I realized the magnificence of the mountain that to me had simply been a fun place to pick blackberries and get frightened by the possibility of tarantulas. The Sierra I now see is one enormous piece while the Serranía de Perijá is a long strand of rounded hills that sit like a horse's spine, separating Colombia from Venezuela. In both of these mountain ranges is where danger lurks. It is here, in the Sierra Nevada and in the Serranía, that armed men—some claiming social justice; others clamoring for protection and revenge—came and settled while I was away.

Under Bogotá lies the underbelly, that green blanket the minister referred to as the home of narco-guerrillas and where Washington would soon send in military equipment to help vanquish them. The bottom half of my map, like the minister's, is a blank slate of foreign territory, cities I have never heard of and places with the cacophony of far away as if they were located on distant continents. I recall learning they were not even considered states, which in Colombia are called departments, because they were not developed enough to be given such ranking. It's where the pink dolphins swim, where the shamans take hallucinogens, and where the San Agustín sculptures built in pre-Columbian years attract adventurers and anthropologists from everywhere. It is the Colombia of the Discovery Channel, not the Colombia where I once lived. I remember the minister pointing at the gut as the theater of war. In the next few years, U.S. soldiers will be coming to Tumaco on the Pacific Ocean and Saravena and Puerto Inírida on the border with Venezuela—these are tiny names on my tourist road map.

As I start reading from the piles of books accumulated over the years since I left, tome after tome sent to underscore my father's insistence that I am a Colombian, I start to look for what I want to know. When did this war that has become my obsession begin? The more I read the more it seems to me that Colombia has been at war since it broke away from Spain, since the days of the seminal Battle of Boyacá where Simón Bolívar vanquished the Spaniards in 1819. The Spanish Crown might have been kicked out but the internal struggles of a newly liberated land had brought about an endless dispute for power that, to me, continues to today. The reason for this seems to be simple. There were two currents of thought that sprang out of emancipation. One was a conservative line, based on the legacy of monarchical Catholic Spain. The Conservatives, who called themselves *Conservadores,* wanted to keep practicing what the Spaniards had imposed, to continue the rule of the landed and of God in government. The other was a more Liberal line, influenced by the Enlightenment and by republican France rather than by the Vatican and the kingdom of Spain. They called themselves *Liberales,* and they advocated commerce and masonry and wanted the Jesuits out of their newly formed country. The Republic of Colombia began as a Conservative nation but the Liberals were augmenting in force. Instead of finding a place for both ideologies to coexist and share power, the two bands only saw each other as enemies. Differences had to be resolved on the battlefield. I read all about the battles of Peralonso and Palonegro outside of the rich coffee-producing region of Santander, located in the right rib cage of my map. I read about how in 1899 Santander was hit by the decrease in the price of coffee and the high expenditures of a country run by an eighty-four-year-old Conservative president who was too sick to even sign his name. Santander was the cradle of liberal thought and the Liberal residents claimed the Conservative governments were bankrupting the nation. A war broke out with Conservatives fighting on the side of the army, mostly as paid conscripts, against the Liberals, a volunteer army of about eight thousand men. They fought so hard that a few months into it, the government had to decree a state of emergency in Santander. The army went in to arrest anyone who was "disaffected from the government," meaning anyone with Liberal sympathies. This only intensified the Liberals' outrage and for three consecutive years, day in and day out, from 1899 through 1902, *Liberales* and *Conservadores* literally hacked one another to pieces, leaving the country in ruins and with a toll of eighty thousand dead from a population of four million. (The weapon of choice was the machete.) For its length, it is known as the War of One Thousand Days, *Mil Días.* Documents from those years bear testament to the hate between the two factions, a hate that carries on today.

The Conservatives won the war and Colombia lost Panama. Historians note the truce between the Liberals and the Conservatives was signed first aboard the *Wisconsin,* a U.S. vessel anchored in the Caribbean—raising the eyebrows of those who believe Roosevelt helped out in order to secure Panama—and then in a Colombian hacienda known as Neerlandia, located in the coastal state of Magdalena. But the hard-line Liberals were not ready to give up, and branched out into agitated rebel armies to continue their fight to "be free or die." This moment marks the beginning of my family's Conservative lineage. My great-great-great-grandfather, a Conservative general, fought the Liberals and attended the ceremony in Magdalena.

Colombia's history marks the next war, forty-three years later when the story repeats itself. By 1946, the Liberals and the Conservatives were at it again. This time, the country became engulfed in a period simply and starkly known as La Violencia (The Violence) where now, with even more ferocity, the armies of both sides immersed the country in another bloodbath. This time, the Conservatives had rebel armies known as the Chulavitas—named after a black bird—that arrived in the small towns dressed in black. Their purpose was to massacre all Liberals or whomever sympathized with one. Corpses appeared, floating down the river. Liberals had the same panache for the macabre. Liberal rebel leaders took such names as Black Blood and Vengeance. Both factions reveled in killing methods, inventing new ways and even coining names for them: The Necktie Cut, when the tongue is cut out and left to hang like a tie on the chest; or the Monkey Cut, decapitating the body and leaving the head on the victim's lap; or the Vase Cut, when the limbs are cut and inserted into the body trunk like flowers in a vase. To keep Liberals and Conservatives from killing one another during Catholic masses—which they, as practicing Catholics, must have needed to attend often to be forgiven for these horrors—some churches had two entrances: a red side for the Liberals and a blue one for the Conservatives.

To end the continuing violence in the countryside, the leaders of the two parties, represented by men in tweeds and ties in Bogotá, decided to sign a truce similar to the treaty signed in Neerlandia. It was called the National Front and its hallmark, not in negotiation or compromise, was in taking turns controlling the government. From 1956 until 1970, the two parties took turns: The first president was a Conservative. Four years later a Liberal followed him. This went on for sixteen years: four presidents, two Liberals and two Conservatives. The country appeared to have calmed down but the primary reason that the fighting had subsided had more to do with the establishment of a strong military. The country smiled with superficial civility in the cities; but in the countryside the army and the Chulavitas hunted down Liberals while followers of Black Blood and Vengeance, turned into Communist guerrillas thanks to the times, hunted down Conservatives in the name of Karl Marx, Ho Chi Minh, Jesus Christ, and Che Guevara. The National Front was just that—a front of false civility.

In a place called Marquetalia, a tiny hamlet of coffee growers where the population consisted mostly of armed Liberals, followers of the rebel forces in the Violencia days, who lived off their parcels of land, a group of rebels started calling *their* territory "independent republics." Conservative congressmen grew nervous and in June 1964, the government sent in the army. The Republic of Marquetalia was destroyed in an air raid. (Many claim it was here that the United States tested napalm before using it in Vietnam.)

The leader of the Republic of Marquetalia was a young man named Pedro Antonio Marín whose land burned and whose animals died in the attack. He swore to keep fighting. He strengthened his troops, and taking the name of a murdered union leader, he became Manuel Marulanda Vélez, also known as Sureshot, and formed the Revolutionary Armed Forces of Colombia, known today by its Spanish acronym, the FARC. Every day from that day onward, Marulanda has continued to fight the Colombian army tooth and nail. The FARC is the same rebel army that Minister Echeverri referred to as the narco-rebels, the one that Washington was going to help hunt down by sending infrared night goggles. On my kitchen map I look for Marquetalia for a few minutes without success. As I search, I realize that like the Colombian soldiers, I too am going to need special glasses to find the places of war in Colombia. The places I'm learning about—Chigorodó, where the paramilitary attacks occur; Marquetalia where the army bombed; San Vicente del Caguán, where the narco-rebels roam free—were never meant to be places known to the world. They are in the middle of nowhere. I find Marquetalia is to the left of the capital. Like a navel, it leads into everything that is green on my map, and was dotted on the minister's map, the unknown jungle where Colombian soldiers would get lost if it weren't for Washington's night-vision goggles.

The landed now had to fight the FARC, and to do that they created self-defense units. Not only did they become legal, the government encouraged them. They slowly gave birth to what is known today as the AUC, Autodefensas Unidas de Colombia, the Spanish name for the Self-Defense Forces of Colombia, the other violent side of Colombia's coin. Just as Manuel Marulanda is the oldest guerrilla in Latin America, a man who at 80 is still raising his armed fist against oligarchic Colombia, 86-year-old Ramón Isaza Arango is the oldest paramilitary chief in Colombia.

Isaza took up arms in 1978, fifteen years after Marulanda, for exactly the same reason that the peasant leader did in 1964. He lost a handful of hens, hogs, and "two calves." Marulanda blames the army for the destruction of his property; Isaza blames the FARC's Ninth Front. Twenty-eight years later, he recalls how the fight began, speaking from his stronghold, a hamlet in Antioquia. "A peasant came to tell me that twenty rebels were coming for me," Isaza told a reporter from *El Tiempo*, Colombia's main newspaper. When the rebels entered his *finca* and shot his animals, Isaza grabbed his eight rifles and handed them to eight of his workers and fought back. They waited for the rebels to show up and ambushed them. "We were born here," Isaza said, "and here they will see us die."

The only reality Colombia has known since its inception is war. A few wars have been given names as if they had ended but the countryside has never stopped bleeding. Colombia has a war going on in her head and neck; a fight in her abnormal arms. It has a brain for a heart and a heart for a brain and a furious and fierce gut. It has bloody breasts and brutal mounds. In each region all three—the FARC, the AUC, and the army—are both represented and fully equipped to fight one another. Colombia is not fighting one war. It is fighting a war in each of its body parts. In each region, the FARC and the AUC operate under a never-ending rain of drug profits to buy land and arms and influence. Add a big check of American dollars for the Colombian military into the mix, and the map in my kitchen is transformed into a bloody landscape.

Turn to a map of Colombia now; identify the regions, the mountains, the jungle, and the rivers. It will be easier to understand how the war works, how the rebels fight the paras and the paras fight the rebels, and how the army interacts. The FARC and the AUC have fronts and blocs. The army has battalions. From the head to the tail, each region has fronts, blocs, and battalions fighting as hard as they can, using every river, every hamlet, and every mountain.

In 1997, Colombia believed that by calling the FARC narco-rebels and by inviting the interest and support of the United States, the Colombian government could kill two birds with one stone. But it was the arrival of those night goggles that was the prelude to a more violent and more protracted war, one that has made the map bloodier, one that has resulted in the methods of killing only becoming more horrible. The FARC specializes in bombs made from kitchen gas tanks filled with nails, glass, and feces. The paras' preferred weapon is the chain saw. "It makes it easier to bury the dead. The graves can be smaller," Max explained.

In 2002, when the night goggles had turned into a $1.3 billion military package, the FARC kidnapped Gilberto Echeverri. He was held captive for more than a year. When the army sent in a team of seventy-five soldiers and five U.S.-donated Black Hawk helicopters to liberate him in the mountains of Antioquia, the minister was killed. The FARC soldiers and the former minister in captivity must have heard the army helicopters, those Black Hawks that Washington had promised him, at very close range. At the end of the battle, Gilberto Echeverri was dead.

Each side has its version of the story. The government accused the FARC of killing the minister as retaliation for the army's attempt to rescue him, saying that he was found with a coup de grace shot behind his back or close to his ear. During a televised address that day, Colombia's president promised to "fortify our decision to defeat terrorism" and that "in this moment of pain, Colombia cannot surrender." The FARC countered that the minister died "during the confrontation between the FARC and the fascist army," adding that they had repeatedly warned that the lives of hostages would be at risk if the government tried to rescue them.

That day, like every day in Colombia, the dance of death resumed: the government called the rebels "terrorists" and the FARC in turn called the army "fascist." But that's what Colombians have been doing; they have been catcalling and killing since the day Colombia was born. During the War of One Thousand Days: killed for being a Liberal, killed for being a Conservative. During La Violencia: killed for being a Liberal, killed for being a Conservative. During Pablo Escobar's war: killed for being with Pablo, killed for being against Pablo. Today: killed for being FARC, killed for being AUC, killed for being landed, for being a journalist, killed for being a union leader, a human rights lawyer. Killed. Will this war ever end? What will this one be called in history books?

GROWING UP COLOMBIAN, ONE SOON LEARNS THAT IDENTITY IS DEFINED BY two things: region and political orientation. One of the first platitudes one learns growing up is that Colombia is a country of regions just like knowing very early on if your family is Liberal or Conservative. Mine is a Conservative family from the coast. That makes me a *costeña* from a Conservative family. Like partisan politicos, Colombians make it a point to embrace only what comes from their own region. The rest is treated with disdain and little tolerance. For *barranquilleros*, for example, the people from Medellín, who are called *paisas*, are boring, ruthless, and workaholic. Those *cachacos* from Bogotá will always be cold, haughty, and hypocritical. A columnist wrote recently that the *cachacos* and the *costeños* are like Cain and Abel. The people from Cartagena are seen as lazy and out of touch, resting on their colonial laurels. Those from the department of Santander, who fled to the north to escape The Violence, are seen as aggressive. In Barranquilla they are called foreigners, and are looked upon with suspicion even as everyone comments how they are entrepreneurial and hardworking. The rest of the regions see *costeños* as *alegre*, which means "happy" but they really mean "loud." Lately, they're also being dubbed as "the most corrupt."

Sadly, it seems no one was interested in joining forces to improve the health of the doll, in giving it a better life. Not the *costeños* in the north or the *caleños* on the Pacific or the *vallenatos* in the foothills of the Sierra or the *santandere-anos* near Venezuela. Everyone is pretty satisfied with this arrangement of atrophies. Colombia is a fiefdom of dysfunction under one flag. It's like being married and having children but not talking to your family or caring for each other, as if fighting keeps the union together.

I focus on where I come from: the head and the neck of Colombia. The coast is like a soccer player ready to hit the ball with his head, ready to do a *cabezazo*, as my brother calls that move. Like when Carlos "El Pibe" Valderrama, our local soccer hero, cannot find the ball with his legs and stretches his neck to bounce it up and send it off into the air. Sometimes I look at the head and it turns into a fist, a raised fist, a Black Power kind of fist. Head or fist, it's a feisty creature, reaching out, blasting into the Atlantic, wanting to reach those Caribbean islands and convince whoever wants to *negociar*, to do business and make deals, that they are a force to be reckoned with, and that the Colombian coast will welcome them.

In the 1800s, English pirates, French adventurers, charlatans, and anarchists in search of Arcadia, Italian bon vivants and German builders heard their call. Spanish schooners anchored on the bays, with all their curves and caves that made hiding perfect. Everyone came to the coast for an adventure. Some stayed. Many left but not without having paid the pearl searchers, young boys who in those first days dove deep into the ocean and, for a coin, handed all of the pregnant oysters to men from far away. The Andes turned a blind eye to the Caribbean bacchanal, busy drafting laws that they would never care to apply.

The coast has always yearned to get closer to the Florida Keys than to the heart of the Andes that borders the interior and serves as their shield from the ways of the *costeños*. There is nothing more different than a person from the coast and one from the Andes, both groups will insist. *Costeños* dance and speak like Caribbeans, having more in common with a Cuban or a Puerto Rican than with their formal Andean fellow men. *Costeños* respect *contrabandistas* more than they care about lawyers and statesmen from the capital. *Costeños* would rather listen to the African drums of a Carnival street band than to the harpsichords of an erudite salon.

I grew up in Barranquilla, on the Atlantic coast and on the mouth of the Magdalena River, Colombia's Mississippi, without ever knowing I lived in a city with a river that could take me into the interior of Colombia, an example of how little I know of where I come from. Now with the map taped to my wall, I am ready to set out, pen and paper in hand.

I start by meeting with the compatriots I find in New York: I meet Miguel, another *costeño*. He told me that he too left Barranquilla to travel and saw London and the Thames, Florence and the Arno, Paris and the Seine, and realized that Barranquilla is the only city in the world that was built with its back to the river. I meet Nereo, Colombia's "eyes," a pioneer photojournalist who walked the country, the entire thing from head to toe, from 1945 until the early eighties and now spends six months out of the year in New York. I invite him over for Chinese food every time he is around. Nereo has navigated the Magdalena many times, and his work has given me all kinds of imaginary boats for my kitchen map. In his photos I have seen the steamboats responsible for keeping Colombia integrated. I have seen priests giving masses and blessing marriages in canoes along the river. Everything moved and still moves through the Magdalena River. It is the main thoroughfare, the artery that runs through the entire country, like an open wound. Through the Magdalena, Colombians deal drugs, get to school, and fight a war. The rebels search out paras and the paras look for rebels up and down the river. Colombia, I learn, has its own heart of darkness.

One of Barranquilla's most popular songs is about a man who becomes a caiman, a smaller crocodile that inhabits the banks of the Magdalena River. *Se va el caimán / se va el caimán / se va para Barranquilla.* (The caiman is leaving, the caiman is leaving, it's leaving for Barranquilla.) Legend talks of a man from a hamlet near the river who was suffering from unrequited love. To get the attention of the woman he was in love with, he turned himself into a caiman. Unfortunately, he was never able to turn himself into a man again. Rejected and now humiliated, he left his hometown. There is a caiman-man in every Colombian; people are leaving just like the caiman-man left. Sometimes they leave because of heartbreak, sometimes in search of the big city. Most of the time they leave because they are forced out by a war they are not fighting.

BOOK ONE

La Costa Atlántica

Caribbean Sea

Riohacha

Santa Marta

Sierra Nevada
de Santa Marta

GUAJIRA

Barranquilla

ATLÁNTICO

MAGDALENA

Cartagena

Valledupar

Magdalena River

CESAR

Lake
Maracaibo

VENEZUELA

Apartadó

Chigorodó

COLOMBIA

ANTIOQUIA

Magdalena River

0 Miles   100   200
0 Kilometers   100   200

Santa Fe de Bogotá ★

© 2007 Jeffrey L. Ward

1

MIAMI INTERNATIONAL AIRPORT
MAY 2002

The Miami airport is where the tug begins. Walking the long corridor that runs from the food court to the gate area is where the gringa in me starts struggling with my inner Colombian. It is here, at the airport, where the transformation began as I learned to run these terminals, as I went from Colombian to American and back again. I walk past the drugstore where, as a child on family vacations, I spent my last American dollar on Bazooka bubble gum before boarding the plane. A few yards down I encounter the bathroom where, as a college student returning to the University of Michigan after Christmas break, I ran to change from summer clothes into heavier winter attire. It was here where I turned into my American self: I had never had to wear a coat on the coast of Colombia. It is here where I started doing things on my own, from buying a book with sex scenes—Scott Spencer's *Endless Love*—to forgoing the flight that my parents had booked for me to hang out with my childhood friend, Allegra, who was already married and living in Miami, which is like living in Barranquilla, except with better roads and better stores.

As I walk toward the gate, I remember the time when I planned to meet Sam at the duty-free shop so we could spend the day together instead of taking our connecting flight back to school. I also remember the time when I heard my confusion voiced out loud for the first time. I was waiting outside for Allegra to pick me up when a young man wearing a janitor's jumpsuit and mopping the floor made comment after comment in Spanish, the kind we call *piropos,* flatteries. I struggled to ignore them. "Look at her," he finally said in Spanish. "Pretending she is a gringa with that Latin face of hers."

Going to Colombia is not easy for me. After almost twenty-five years of living outside of Colombia, I still define myself as Colombian when asked where I am from. But am I really? When does one stop being what one was born to be? I wonder as I sit at the gate waiting for the plane for Bogotá to board.

Colombia is having presidential elections next week and I have been hired as a "fixer" for the *Wall Street Journal.* My job is to accompany a staff reporter, who has never been to Colombia before, and help him navigate the list of sources and the safety of the streets. I took the job the instant it was offered. I stopped working as a fixer more than a decade ago but I couldn't resist the temptation. Whenever I am offered a job there I take it no matter what, especially since I put that map on my wall. My recent trips under professional auspices have made it harder to separate my American self from my Colombian self, to divide the journalist in me from the daughter and the sister. During college, I thought of Colombia as a place of familial obligations; now I think of it as a war zone where my family lives. It might be that my journalistic ambitions are a way for me to protect myself from where I come from, a way of clarifying and exposing the ugly reality that surrounds and threatens my family. Or maybe I accept those assignments as an excuse to see them.

Between 1999 and 2000, news editors became increasingly interested in Colombia and so I've gone back with some regularity. It all goes back to the minister's visit to the America Society in New York City. By August 1999, the gift of the night goggles had turned into Plan Colombia, a $1.3 billion military aid package, a move that opened the door for news stories about Colombia. "It is the recipient of the United States government's third largest military package" is the sound bite I now repeat as a mantra to make my Colombia assignments materialize. "The third," I say. "After Israel and Egypt." After I mention those two countries, editors want to know why the United States is being so generous to such a rogue country, still known as cocaine country and now known as the home of the intransigent FARC rebels. Plan Colombia opened the doors for news stories about Colombia for a sliver of time, but those doors were closed by 9/11. Now, however, with Hugo Chávez next door in Venezuela and the extensive military aid on the table, the financial paper has decided that the country's election merits at least a story, even one written by someone who has never been there. Still, I am glad the *Journal* needs me.

I am full of doubts and trepidations, angels and demons talking at the same time. It's all about how I feel about this place I still call home. So I am thankful to be distracted by a handsome young American who sticks out in the crowd of mostly *cachacos* waiting to board the plane. His nervousness is palpable to me—perhaps because I am also nervous, but also because he cannot sit still. His clothes also make him stand out among the formal *bogotanos.* The men wear tweed jackets and suits, mostly blue and gray, and he is dressed in a loud brown and white short-sleeved tropical shirt.

I watch him closely as he approaches other passengers. *"Hola,"* he says, *"tengo que practicar mi español,"* but he is not having any luck engaging anyone. A group of businessmen give him the silent brush-off, not even pausing in their conversation to look at him, perhaps thinking he's just another gringo who wants to practice his pidgin Spanish. Clearly agitated, he approaches a man sitting alone. Politely, he also turns him down. Again and again, he tries to start a conversation but none of the passengers waiting for the American Airlines flight to Bogotá, Colombia, takes his bait.

Granted, these post–September 11 days are not particularly good for chatting with strangers. I've chosen to sit a few rows away, making sure I am in the outer circle of Colombians, as if that would differentiate me from them, pretending that I am not traveling to Colombia. I want to be the last one to board. Still, I try hard to overhear their discussion. "How paranoid and rude they've become," the man closest to me says, referring to the brusque manner of American immigration officials these days. But there are moments for light conversation too. The well-seasoned group in business suits and refined ties like to ask one another where they've dined. I hear Nobu mentioned a few times.

I cannot keep my eyes away from the American. He paces, he smiles, he tries to act calm but it's not working. I would do anything to have him talk to me. He is handsome but that is not why I've decided to focus on him. I want to tell him that *bogotanos* are reserved around those they don't know; they are polite, sometimes even too formal, and usually circumspect. He'd be better off striking up a conversation with me. We *costeños* are much more open than they are. I could tell him that *cachacos* are like Boston Brahmins and *costeños* are more like Texas cowboys. I am determined to find out why this young man is on his way to Bogotá. I have a hunch that our trips may be connected.

Although September 11, Afghanistan, and Iraq took the spotlight away from Colombia, the money Washington promised in 1999 did get there, the billion that would put Colombia on the news map arrived. Though the narco-rebels were eventually obscured by Osama bin Laden and Saddam Hussein, the United States did send in three counternarcotic training teams to the jungles of southern Colombia and added the FARC and the right-wing AUC to the terrorist list. By the time I boarded the flight to Bogotá, more than a dozen Huey helicopters had been sent to fumigate coca fields and the Department of Defense had turned a few Cessna planes into flying spies. By installing them with FLIRS, the acronym for Forward Looking Infrared Radars, a step up from the goggles, Washington was helping the Colombian government identify cocaine laboratories so that they could be destroyed and also helping hunt down terrorists. By 2002, four hundred military personnel were stationed in Colombia. It was conceivable that the young man at the gate could be one of them. I was right to jump on a plane if just to be another reporter's lackey, hoping for a moment like this.

I started going back to report in August 2001, and I soon began to understand what it was like to live there, a daughter's duty I had not fulfilled. The more I learned, the more I visited, the more I felt my brother's words of so many years before echo in my mind. "Easy for you living in New York," he would say angrily when I pontificated about what needs to be done in Colombia. "You come live here and see what it's like." I am sure that he—or any Colombian who knows me—would not believe me if I told him that I am haunted by Colombia.

I WANT TO SIT NEXT TO THE OVEREAGER AMERICAN. I WANT TO SIT WITH SOME-one who, like me, feels like an outsider. Once on the plane, I trade my seat for the middle seat next to him. It doesn't take him long to introduce himself.

"Hola, me llamo Charlie," he says, smiling. *"Colombiana?"* he asks.

I nod my head yes. "Going home," I say, fully aware that it's not how I've made it sound. But I know that if I say I am going to Colombia as a Colombian who works in American journalism, my new friend would not be as talkative as I want him to be, so I decide to keep my cards very close to my chest.

"So," I say, checking out the back of his neck, "why Bogotá?" He has a buzz cut. I believe I may have found my U.S. military personnel. I feel some guilt but Charlie is just happy to be finally talking.

"Moving there," he tells me. I ask him from where. "From North Carolina." I smile because that can only mean one thing: Camp Lejeune, home to forty-seven thousand marines. That is where new recruits live and train while they wait to be sent abroad. On a mission. That could mean anything from guarding an embassy to pushing paper in an office, to actual training. And fighting.

He asks the flight attendant for a scotch. "Military?" I ask.

"Yep," he replies. I could not have asked for more. I feel like I'm on a plane to Saigon in 1964, or Central America in the eighties. Finally, someone was using straightforward war language with me about Colombia, words straight out of covert operations and front-page scoops. I could be talking to the young men in Vietnam out of Michael Herr's *Dispatches.* This is better than flying to Baghdad or Kabul, I say to myself, because everyone knows marines are in Iraq and in Afghanistan; no one has yet heard of them in Colombia. He can be my next story. Will the *New York Times Magazine* want it? Maybe it's best for *Rolling Stone.* I wonder if my friend's friend is still an editor there.

I hang onto Charlie's every word like a cardiologist listening for a heart murmur. But it is hard to keep up with the jargon. He uses words like "joint patrol" and "riverine." Is he purposely enticing me? He reaches under his seat and from his black bag he takes out a file. "I shouldn't show you this," he says, a caveat directed more to himself. I see photocopies of papers that look totally ordinary, instruction sheets explaining what to do in the new country, like materials handed out to me during my orientation week at the University of Michigan. I nod as he talks and I try to read upside down, making it a point to memorize as much as I can make sense of from my seat. I remember two acronyms: JPAT and MILGRP and make a mental note to find out what they mean the moment we land.

"Did you want to come to Colombia?" I ask him.

"I've volunteered," he tells me.

"You volunteered to come to Colombia," I repeat. "Why would you do something like that? Colombia," I tell him, "is dangerous."

Colombian men his age, I tell him, would do anything to be him: twenty-four, handsome, and living in the United States. Many take great risks, especially now, to move there. I met a married hotel clerk who is working two jobs to accumulate five thousand dollars to pay for a fake tourist visa. "No one wants to be in Colombia. Why did you volunteer to do something so dangerous?"

"Because I want to kill each and every motherfucking drug dealer with my own hands." I had forgotten that Colombia still has that image: the place where drug dealers come from.

The legendary and ruthless cocaine lord Pablo Escobar put us on the map. Most of the world by now knows his story: a boy with an absent father and no money who hated the discrimination and the difficulty of achieving upward mobility for someone average—neither rich nor poor—in Colombia; a blood-thirsty teenager who started robbing graveyards and who by the time he was thirty-three controlled the world's largest drug-trafficking empire making the Fortune 500 billionaire list and having thousands of Colombians on his payroll, killing for him.

When I arrived in the United States in 1977, my classmates at the Academy of the Sacred Heart liked asking me if I knew Juan Valdez, the only thing they had heard about Colombia. The mustachioed coffee grower with a poncho, a gentle face, and a donkey that was created by a Madison Avenue advertising agency sold the idea to America that Colombia grew the richest coffee in the world, but Juan Valdez soon lost to the popularity of Pablo Escobar. Thanks to Pablo, Colombia went from being America's purveyor of coffee to becoming its prime supplier of cocaine. Soon, everyone had heard about Colombian "marching powder," and I was approached with all types of jokes and comments about the larger than life legend.

A Robin Hood, a corrupt drug dealer, a vicious killer, Pablo Escobar built hospitals and schools for the poor. He built himself a house as big as a national park and with as many exotic animals as a zoo. He imported giraffes, hip-popotamuses, and elephants from Africa and he extended his largesse to the people. The grounds of his entertainment park, known as Hacienda Nápoles, were open to the public. There he met with senators and partied with beauty queens. He also installed a reign of terror. Depending on whom you ask, Pablo Escobar directly killed somewhere between one thousand and four thousand

people, from presidential candidates, ministers, and judges to other drug dealers and girlfriends.

In 1989, Colombia was ready to sign an extradition treaty with the United
States. This would allow the United States to come arrest Escobar. That was his
biggest fear. To prevent that treaty from being signed, he ordered planes to
explode in midair. He killed magistrates and judges, kidnapped journalists and
politicians. He made it known that he preferred a grave in Colombia to a day in
a cell in the United States. At that time, my feelings were exactly the opposite of
Don Pablo's: I didn't want to spend one day in Colombia. I was by then a journalist reporting on Latin America, but I took little notice of my country's role
in global politics. When news of the rising violence reached me, nothing about
it felt particularly close to me or interesting to me as a reporter, except for a few
absurdities. There were so many murders at one point that Colombia passed a
law making it illegal for people driving motorcycles to wear helmets and for cars
to have dark-tinted windows. That way criminals could be more easily identified. Not that it mattered: In Colombia, 99 percent of crimes go unpunished.

The violence of those days had a name; everyone blamed it on Pablo. But
the drug lord was killed in 1993 and yet ten years later Colombia's violence still
persisted. As Charlie and I descend on Colombia, it holds the highest kidnapping
rate, the highest murder rate, and the highest crime rate in the world. Colombian
writer Fernando Vallejo, whose novels and essays capture the Escobar-induced
culture of killing in his native Medellín, has said that Colombia is, and has always
been, a country of killers and that it should change its name to Violencia. But
don't tell that to Colombians. They are furious at Vallejo's proposition.

Colombians might kill one another but they all agree on one thing: the great-
ness of Colombia, and the importance of never, ever, saying anything bad for
Colombia's image, especially abroad. I grew up hearing great things about my
country: It produces the richest coffee in the world, the most beautiful orchids,
emeralds the size of apples; it is the longest-standing democracy in Latin
America; it has a strong economy; and it is the only Latin American country
that never defaulted on its foreign debt. It also has a great "rumba," meaning an
amazing capacity to party. It has a raucous Carnival, a fabulous Miss Colombia
pageant, more than 365 fairs a year with young ladies wearing bathing suits
and crowns. Colombia even has a Queen of Sugar and a Queen of Coal. And if
that were not enough, Colombians will remind you that a study conducted by
the University of Leicester in England—led by psychologist Adrian White, in
case you doubted its legitimacy—found Colombians to be the happiest people
in the world. "The quality of life here is better than anywhere else," a well-
known and well-traveled writer once told me over dinner. His bodyguards
were waiting outside the restaurant and yet to him Colombia is bar none the
best place to live. I hear this from all Colombians. So why have I left it behind?

———————

I DIDN'T HAVE TO PUSH HARD TO FIND OUT WHY CHARLIE WANTS TO KILL DRUG dealers. Charlie tells me that he was born in St. Louis, in a "rough area," he says proudly. That's where his mom, Sue, "a stunning beauty," met his father. But that was not where he grew up. He was raised by a very nice family outside New Orleans. Charlie's parents divorced when he was three and Sue went to live in the South. The trouble started when Sue remarried. "She would always find guys to marry her," he says, and it's impossible to miss his hurt. "She just went from one man to another, always getting what she wanted. A lot of the time that was drugs." By the time he was seven, his mother was unemployed. She rented out the extra bedrooms in her house to "whoever could pay, preferably men with drugs."

Charlie tells me he preferred the silence of the library to the chaos of his home, so he spent a lot of time there after school. One day, a classmate, Todd, invited him to dinner at his parents' house. There Charlie saw family life for the first time: He had a dinner conversation with a mother and a father, and home-cooked food was passed around. Charlie wanted to be invited back every night. "Better than living with a bunch of coke heads," he tells me, sipping on his scotch. The two boys became so close that Todd asked his parents to adopt him. As Charlie puts it, "He knew about my mom." Rick and Dawn, a teacher and a nurse, said yes to their son's request and they fought in court for his custody. "They are my parents," he says. As for Todd: "There's no friendship there. We're brothers."

No matter how much he loves his adopted family, Charlie is on his way to Colombia because of his biological mother. Charlie wants to kill drug dealers because he is the son of a drug addict. He might not say it, the tough man that he is, but Charlie feels drugs robbed him of her care. By his emotional reasoning, if Colombian drug dealers didn't exist, Sue would have been there for him. Charlie wants to avenge what drugs did to him.

But just like Washington's support for Plan Colombia, Charlie's war has nothing to do with Colombia. And just like Plan Colombia can never bring peace to the country of my birth, he will not be able to kill every motherfucking drug dealer. Most likely, he won't even get close to one. But I don't tell him that. I'd rather he continue telling me how he came to be on this flight.

This is not the first time he is going abroad as a marine. He had been on an exercise operation in Croatia, part of an assault platoon that was training to hunt down war criminal Slobodan Milošević. Charlie loved everything about it: being stationed off the coast of Yugoslavia, being in choppers, and organizing raids to blow up "the object." "We were ready to go, but it never came to fruition," he tells me. "We drilled, we practiced, but it was called off."

He liked being abroad so much, he tells me, that when he returned from Croatia to Camp Lejeune, he went straight to the language lab. He knew that was a shortcut to get a foreign posting. Perhaps he would learn Russian. But when he saw a flyer on the bulletin board calling for volunteers "to prepare riverine troops to do drug interdiction," he switched to Spanish. All that the job required was the ability to either speak Spanish or have a thousand hours' worth of Spanish lessons. He signed up immediately. He thought the job meant tracking down meth labs in the desert or fighting cocaine on the Mexican border. Never did he imagine he would be going to Colombia.

He cannot believe how lucky he is. Charlie wonders—and asks me—what it will be like. I shrug my shoulders, but he refuses to let my coyness get in the way of his excitement. He says that it is uncanny that he is going to Colombia because when he was eight he wrote a report on drugs for school and remembers seeing pictures of the Colombian jungles in *TIME* magazine. I tell him I remember the story. It was a cover story in 1986, and the cover depicted two AK-47 rifles crossed over a mound of cocaine to suggest a skull and bones. "Amazing," he insists.

"And my Spanish is going to be perfect. I hear the girls are beautiful and I will have to follow my teacher's advice and find myself that dictionary with the long dark hair. That's the only way to really learn." Charlie is charming, handsome, smart, funny—and American. I am sure he will find many willing guides and teachers. I am sure he will have a chance to *practicar* his *español*. Charlie is coming to my country to fight, to have a good time, to learn a language, to flirt, to get paid good money. He gets an extra few hundred dollars a month for speaking the language and for being in a war zone, he tells me.

"Want to play a game?" he says as the plane is ready to land. "Come up with the title for the movie about your life."

"You go first," I say. He knew so little about me and I didn't want to tip my hand. I didn't want to explain that I was not really as Colombian as he thought.

He didn't flinch. "Oh, that's easy," he says smiling. "Mine would be called *How Did I End Up Here?* I want Ray Liotta to play me. I love that guy."

I CHOSE NOT TO TELL HIM HOW I GAVE UP ON MY COUNTRY AS HE GAVE UP ON HIS mother. And that like him, I too, was going back to fight a personal war in that country. I get his e-mail address and tell him that he should keep a diary, thinking selfishly that maybe he will one day let me read it. He says that's a good idea and that he would do so but by the time the doors of the plane open and the cold of the Andes night seeps into the cabin, Charlie, the talkative plane companion, turns into the young man on a mission. He flashes a smile, and rushes out.

2

SHELTER ISLAND
JUNE 1999

My friend Diana has invited me to spend Memorial Day weekend at her friend's house in Shelter Island, the perfectly kept rustic hideaway spot in eastern Long Island. A weekend of marsh and mist, barefoot walks, and barbecues is just what I need, she insists. I had broken up with a boyfriend of one year, and Diana, always one to encourage "moving on," insisted I escape the city. "You need to get out," she had said to me. "You're coming. Period."

The host, an English screenwriter with a sailboat and a life filled with traveling adventures, welcomes Diana and me with double kisses and rosé wine. His house has a shabby elegance: a house that feels lived in, with oversized couches and paperback books with bent covers forgotten between the cushions.

The other guests are an exuberant couple and their eight-month-old girl, and we are soon interacting with the buoyancy and the normalcy of a life filled with chores and activities. We come and go all day long—into town to buy the fresh vegetables for dinner, to the lake for a swim, to go visit neighbors. Diana was right. This is good—keep moving, be distracted, and be around people. I am happy Diana insisted on bringing me, I think to myself as I go up the stairs after dinner to my bedroom.

But the pangs of breakup are back by morning, so when Kim says that she is "dying" to go swimming but can't because she needs to stay with her baby daughter, Lucy, I offer to look after the little one. Alone, I turn down the volume on the TV set, and with baby in tow I plop myself on the couch staring at nothing, wanting to be swallowed by the huge down-filled cushions. I feel paralyzed, thinking I would never again be interested in writing another story. The possibility of another kiss seems forever away, impossible. Playing with Lucy's toes consoles me.

I turn my head toward the muted TV, surprised by the dateline popping up on the screen. It reads: Bogotá, Colombia. Men in camouflage, holding rifles, run across the screen so fast that I can't decipher if they are soldiers or rebels, the guns Kalashnikovs or Galils. A tire burns in the middle of a street—the quintessential media image of war. I walk toward the set and turn up the volume. My parents are in Bogotá right now.

According to CNN, the FARC, the rebel group that has vowed to take over since 1964, has taken a small town just two hours away and has announced they are marching toward the capital. Carrying explosives and AKs, they've killed eight police officers and a civilian. The army, the report continues, is fighting back. In thirty-eight years, the rebels have never attacked so close to Bogotá. I hold on to Lucy's tiny thigh for support.

For all these years, rebel armies like the FARC and the smaller ELN, the National Liberation Army, have been taking over the tiniest hamlets and towns in the countryside provinces of Colombia. The places they attack are so small they are not even pueblos but *caceríos*, which comes from *casas*, as Nereo defines it to me. It is "what the word implies, a *cacerío* is nothing but a row of houses in the middle of nowhere," he says. The FARC's actions are more targeted toward the government and toward those civilians who compose what they refer to as the exploiters of the people. Landowners make that cut and my mother's family is one of them. The ELN is constantly blowing up electric towers and the oil pipeline. Their actions—which include kidnapping for money and killing those who oppose them, especially those with ties to the paramilitary—have been limited to the countryside. Rebels marching into Bogotá is an entirely different ball game.

A million images flash through my mind: Fidel Castro and his bearded posse on horseback entering Havana after Fulgencio Batista fled the island on New Year's Eve in 1959; the Sandinista rebels with their female *comandantes* riding the fire truck into Managua in 1978. Will there soon be a photograph of the FARC commanders marching into Bogotá to add to the catalog of revolutionary memorabilia? Will Max take it? I knew the names of at least a handful of the revolutionaries who had fought with Fidel in the Sierra Maestra, and I could point out Violeta in the Sandinista victory picture from Nicaragua but I cannot for the life of me recognize the faces of any of the FARC leaders. I know the leader is Manuel Marulanda, who is known as Tirofijo, Spanish for "sureshot," a name that conveys violence more than social justice.

My romantic ruminations about revolutions quickly fade. The pictures of rebels holding fists of victory, the photos that I had admired (and even bought in Havana) of the young women in their berets and their raised rifles become threatening images. This time my thoughts were not about the dazzling talk of universal brotherhood, but about my father and how he likes to listen to opera while watering the potted bonsai tree my sister gave him one Christmas, and how my mother takes a silver platter from the safety vault when she serves lunch for her friends. For the first time, I think about El Carmen, the place my family calls *la finca*, a farm that makes my mother and everyone with her surname an enemy of the people—at least the enemy of FARC. If the rebels take over Colombia, they will expropriate it because that is what revolutions do. El Carmen is large, almost as large as Shelter Island, large enough for my grandfather to be called a *terrateniente*, a landowner, a word deeply fraught with consequences in the context of the story flashing on the screen.

I stand up and walk to the TV set in this paradisiacal slice of American life; of liberal American life; of liberal New York American life; of liberal elite New York American life, a place where I have chosen to live, far, very far, from where I was born. I wonder if the people vacationing in Shelter Island who will sit with me at dinner tonight will ever be put in my position, scared by the threat of takeover. It sure feels different to romanticize a group with guns when your family is caught in the crossfire. I switch the set off.

THE TRUTH IS LIBERAL AMERICA CAPTIVATED ME EARLY ON. I ARRIVED AT THE University of Michigan at sixteen in 1978 and registered as a political science student. I had no idea I was entering, a bit precociously, one of America's bedrocks of student activism. In fact, I had chosen the university pretty much by default. When Sister Cherry, the college counselor at Sacred Heart, told me I could graduate early and asked me what I wanted to study, I said political science without missing a beat. I was afraid to say that I really had no idea. Thankfully I remembered the issue of *Hola,* the Spanish gossip magazine that served as a guide to young ladies in Barranquilla that Princess Caroline of Monaco was studying political science at the Sorbonne in Paris. I had seen a picture of the long-haired brunette princess coming out of her student apartment wearing jeans and holding books under her arm, and I had wanted to be her. This was my chance. If Princess Caroline was a student of political science, I would be one too.

That fall, I wore my dark hair long and my designer jeans to class. And although I loved living with the bustle of student life in the red buildings with ivy growing on the walls (images I had only seen in *Love Story*), registering for classes, going to the university bookstore to buy my course books, and trying to make it to cafeteria dinners at the unheard-of early hour of five thirty, the truth is I was a lost puppy. Nothing felt familiar.

I had spent the summer carefully choosing my courses and I was sure that a class on American foreign policy was imperative. I was already envisioning it. Like Princess Caroline, who was being groomed to represent her own small country, I too would learn how to become a representative of Colombia at my university. My life was set. I would study hard, return, and become a diplomat.

I'd host banquets and go to balls, and dine with other dignitaries. That was the only meaning foreign relations had for me then.

"Fuck USA policy," the professor of American foreign policy says, stunning me with his lecture a few weeks into my first semester in the fall of 1978. "Fuck our policy toward Iran." In those days, Washington supported the shah of Iran who had just imposed martial law after squelching a student protest with army tanks, killing 89 demonstrators, and my professor was telling us that it shouldn't have. I had never witnessed such strong opinions in a classroom. The instructor's scraggly beard and his jeans with a hole on the knee had already been a surprise—a style of dress I did not associate with grown men, much less professors—but his cursing outright scared me. My classmates smiled, signaling their approval. I sat mute, confused by his choice of words and at his anti-Americanism. Up until that day, schooling had been a passive exercise.

As time went by I started to notice that students participated in class and I didn't. My classmates engaged in lively conversations, even confrontations, about their country's involvement in foreign wars. They discussed Korea, Pearl Harbor and the Allies, Vietnam. I was becoming self-conscious, realizing that I had little to contribute to the discussion. I had never thought about Colombia like they thought of their country. And I had definitely never thought about war, even if my country had had its share.

I knew the United States as the provider of all things good, the notebooks with pink pages, the pop songs and the platform sandals from Miami to the teachers who came down to my American school to teach me Mother Goose rhymes in nursery school and calculus in ninth grade in a language that was not mine but considered better than mine. My mother could not help me with my homework because she did not speak a word of English. "It's the best thing you can possibly know," she would repeat incessantly.

It was the American things, and our developing English, that had differentiated my best friend, Allegra, and me from the majority of the other girls in Barranquilla. We loved wearing our Miami-bought clothes and showing off our knowledge of the lyrics of American songs when we were at parties. We were the ones who could sing along as we danced. "Kung Fu Fighting" and "Seasons in the Sun" and "Get Down Tonight" were our favorites, though we missed all the drug and sexual connotations in the slang. We lip-synched to "Do the Hustle" belting out, "chew the hot dog," with complete confidence. No one could tell we had the wrong words.

College life could not have turned out more different than my life in Colombia. Maybe this is all a mistake, I started to think, as the weeks passed and the reading assignments started to pile up and I had to write papers expressing "my thoughts," an unknown and scary concept, in a language I did not even speak that well. My mother had told me that I could go back home if

I didn't like it, back to Barranquilla where I belonged, where I had a big bed-room with a pink desk and a bathroom with a marble bathtub, not the bland dorm room with the communal shower. I thought of going back to Barranquilla where I had more friends and cousins, and maids to make me the food I liked whenever I wanted it—definitely not at five thirty. If I had told my parents that the teacher swore, surely they would have forced me to leave.

One night I had to go see a required film for the class with that professor. I was not yet sure he was doing something legal, swearing and teaching us to be critical. I walked inside the auditorium in the East Quadrangle unaware of the reaction a documentary film could unleash. *Hearts and Minds,* about the U.S. involvement in Vietnam, left me unable to move from my chair for hours. I sat in silence knowing that I could never be able to forget what I had just heard, and seen. Gen. William Westmoreland smiled after he said that his feeling for America soared when, during a memorial service for four American soldiers killed in combat, he saw the determined looks on those paying respects. The Vietcong might have killed a few but his American boys, "They're a bloody good bunch of killers." I also heard him say to a classroom of American children that the Oriental doesn't put the same high price on life as a Westerner.

I heard Randy Floyd crumble—and I with him, as he recalled his missions. "During the missions, after the missions, the results of what I was doing—the result of this, this game, this exercise of my technical experience, never really dawned on me. The reality of the screams or the people being blown away or their homeland being destroyed. This was not a part of what I thought about. I dinged in on one of them and I nailed him, you know, and the Aussie with me confirmed I dinged him and I felt good and I wanted war and it wasn't that I wanted war for politics or anything like that. I couldn't have cared if they were whatever. I just wanted them because they were the opposition—they were the enemy!"

I heard the conviction and the power of opposition in Floyd's voice when addressing the Congress: "The Vietnamese were all considered less than humans. Inferiors, we called them gooks. Their lives weren't worth anything to us. Because we'd been taught to believe that they were all fanatical and all VC or VC sympathizers, even the children. Many of us, however, began to under-stand through our personal experiences in Vietnam the depth of the lies and deceptions practiced on us and the American people by our country's leaders. It was they who trained us to kill without question and to defeat our enemy, the Vietnamese. They concocted such phrases as 'kill ratio,' 'search and destroy,' 'free fire zones,' 'secure areas,' and so on to mark the reality of their combat pol-icy in Vietnam."

I took in the words of Father Chan Ti, a South Vietnamese priest who spoke straight into the camera. "People can be arrested at any moment by an organization and then tortured in inhuman ways, in all the prisons and above all the police stations, and then imprisoned for years and years without trial. Their only crime is loving their country. They had the courage to tell the truth. They asked for the liberation of political prisoners; they asked for an end to the war. They asked for peace, for national reconciliation and all that is considered a crime by the government of Diem."

The priest wore the same black tunic under a white round collar that I had seen on the Colombian priests who came over to my parents' house. I had received communion from their hands and they taught my mother things that she would then repeat to us, like give your old clothes and toys to the poor. I even shared secrets with them at confession. In my experience, what priests said was the word of God, lessons to be followed. So I took the Vietnamese priest's words to heart as I sat in the darkness of the auditorium jumping from emotion to emotion: "When a Vietnamese works for peace and liberty, he is considered a Communist." Based on what I was hearing from Father Ti, a Communist was a good thing.

"It is an honor for the Communist to have to work for peace and justice. So it is the government which gives validity to being a Communist because they continue to say that the people who work for justice and for peace are Communists. You see?" To a sixteen-year-old girl, unaware of Stalin, Communism sounded beautiful, and right.

The other thing that surprised me about *Hearts and Minds* was that Vietnam reminded me of Colombia. The countryside of Vietnam, lush and tropical, felt more familiar than the university's arboretum with its autumn leaves. The peasants in their flip-flops and their cries of despair felt less foreign than my fellow classmates sitting in the theater with me.

After seeing *Hearts and Minds* I learned the importance of critical thinking, and how works like films and books shine light on different points of view. I let go of my plans to be like Princess Caroline.

When the gang returns from their afternoon swim, I tell them what I had seen on television, creating an interest that I am not sure I'm ready for. When more dinner guests arrive, including a documentary maker, someone asks me, "Could it be the next Cuban Revolution?" I don't answer. I only feel that Colombia has re-entered my life, a different button has been pushed, one that makes me feel uncomfortable discussing my country as summer evening conversation. I find myself unable to explain Colombia as I have in the past, with the usual storyline about revolutionaries and oligarchs and the role of the United States. I am surrounded by smart, thoughtful people; people much like Peter Davis, the man who made *Hearts and Minds* and won an Oscar for it in 1972. This is a conversation I am used to having. I have canned answers, deep analysis, even jokes about how I perceive Colombia and the United States's involvement in my country. But tonight as we sit outside for dinner I am mostly uninterested in participating. For the first time I feel something close to resentment as the wine is poured, the stars shine, and no one is worried about a rebel platoon coming over the hills of Shelter Island tonight.

WHEN I RETURN TO MANHATTAN, I DIAL MY PARENTS' PHONE NUMBER IN Bogotá. My father answers, and from the tone of his voice I can picture him sitting in his favorite green leather chair, a blanket warming his legs, reading a history book—most likely about Colombia. A faint aria comes through his voice as he says *hola hijita,* hello my child.

"*Papi,*" I ask, "what is happening?" mentioning what I had seen on television. He laughs like he used to when I awoke him in the middle of the night as a child to tell him that I was scared. He would explain how the iron bars in all our windows, the machete under the watchman's mattress, and the gun by his night table protected us from all danger. I always tried without success to explain that it was the fact that we needed all those things that kept me so petrified. "*Aquí no entran, mi amor,*" he says now about rebels entering Bogotá, the same way he would tell me that the *ladrones,* the house thieves, would never be able to break into our house.

My father, a through-and-through Colombian, takes a serious tone to tell me that "our army is strong and is getting stronger." My father believes in Colombia in a way that I don't. This is how he tells me that he wishes I were more involved in Colombia, more knowledgeable about Colombia. He wished that I lived there, that I wrote for the Colombian papers, that I became part of the country where I was born, where he was from. I have told him that I cannot. At times over the years, this difference has led to awful fights, provoked us to say very hurtful things to each other. If I say Colombia is violent, he thinks I am betraying my country. If I say that the economy is fueled by narco-money, he says, "*Eso no es así,* Silvana," that is not so. He has called me a traitor, a person who does not care about family. I tell him that nationalism is dangerous, that it stinks of violence and that the Colombia he defends is to me a failed country. It would be nice if it were different; it would be great if Colombia really were the best place in the world to live. But how can that be if the institutions are corrupt, if people have a narco-price, if the military has been accused of flagrant human rights abuses, if the revolutionary army believes in involving the civilian population in their war with the state, and if the paramilitary believes that any amount of violence is acceptable if it is used to kill a rebel-sympathizer?

My father and I have had nasty fights, but I don't get into an argument this time. I just ask him if he thinks it's time for him to go to Miami, the place where everyone in Latin America escapes to when things like this happen. "This is my country, Silvana. I am not going anywhere. My life is here. Grand-mother's life is here. Your mother's life is here. Your family's life is here. I am Colombian. I am not from Miami." As I hang up, I feel queasy, questioning the choices I've made. They all add up to having turned my back on Colombia. My father's conviction about where he belongs lingers, making me feel homeless. I am only a resident in the United States and as such there are ways I still feel that indicate I am not fully American. I have by now lived in the United States longer than I have in Colombia, but without citizenship, I am not allowed to vote. I can, however, vote as a Colombian; I could go to the consulate on Forty-third Street, between Fifth and Madison, on Colombia's election day and cast my right as many of my compatriots do, but I don't.

Looking for consolation, I call Julia, a Colombian friend who works as an editor for *Newsweek* to see if she had seen what I had seen. "It's bad," she says and reads an Agence France Press wire story about the attack over the phone. An army official refers to the five-day offensive as the "largest" and "most demented" rebel attack in forty years. The rebels bombed banks, assaulted police barracks, and blew up bridges and electric towers on their way to Bogotá. The story points out that more people are being killed in one month of fighting in Colombia than have died so far in the Gulf War. "We are engaged in a non-declared conflict," the general is quoted in the story, "worse than the Gulf War." As concerned as we are about our country, neither Julia nor I had heard the name of the town nor were we sure where it was in relation to Bogotá. Colombia is terra incognita to her too, even though she votes.

Julia tells me that she too had called her family, alarmed by the news. But like my father, no one in her family feels that things are bad there. No one is moving, she says. We spend an hour on the phone pontificating about our fam-ilies and how "clueless" and "in denial" they are in not seeing the danger under their own noses. I remind her of Alexis de Tocqueville's line about "how the happy and the powerful don't go into exile." Violence aside, our families lead very comfortable lives. That is where I fail. I prefer to live without violence and in less comfort. But neither Julia nor I knows exactly where the FARC has attacked and it is in search of this town that I will look for the map I soon decide to hang on my wall.

I wonder how they are able to live in Colombia. I suppose there are ways to forget about the violence. There is the frantic support of the daily soccer and beauty pageants. I know they live comfortable lives, even if words like "kid-napped" and "killed" are words used often in family conversations. Or maybe they are stronger than I am?

SOON AFTER THE FARC ATTACK IN JUNE 1999, WASHINGTON APPROVED PLAN
Colombia, and with it, Colombia became certifiable current-affairs territory.
Everyone, including newspaper editors, college professors, other freelance journalists, and many of the well-informed people I would meet socially and pro-
fessionally, started talking about Colombia differently. The jokes about drugs
that I had always endured—"Are you related to Pablo?" or "A Colombian party,
ha?"—turned into more pointed questions: Who are these FARC guys? Are
they good guys? Are they bad guys? Do you think U.S. aid is a good idea?

By August 1999, Colombia had a new president, one the United States liked—
the reason my friends had voted for Andrés Pastrana. Colombia had even made
the opinion pages of the *New York Times*. "Colombia's Struggles, And How
We Can Help," was the title of an op-ed written by then secretary of state
Madeleine Albright. In it, she called Colombia, the "most troubled country" in
South America. "To turn the tide," she wrote, "President Pastrana must wage a
comprehensive effort. And he needs—and deserves—international support
that focuses on more than drug interdiction and eradication. . . . We will do all
we can to help them."

Although an ally in the fight against Communism, Colombia was never a
priority for Washington during the Cold War years. In the eighties it stopped
being a friend, and turned into a drug-fueled foe. Every year, it was decertified
as a country that didn't cooperate in the fight against drugs, a distinction that
came with consequences. To punish Colombia, the United States stopped
allowing the entry of flowers from Colombia. Colombia's previous president
Ernesto Samper wanted to enter the United States but his visa was revoked.
Accused of receiving drug money in his presidential campaign, he was labeled
persona non grata by Washington.

In less than a year, things took a radical turn. To indicate the change in attitude, President Clinton invited Andrés Pastrana to the White House.

Now that the FARC is a known enemy, Colombia is more than a drug-
running country. It is once again a friend, and even more so—it is a friend in
need. The magnitude of the aid package the government puts together invites
scrutiny: Congressmen want to know why the money is needed and where it's
going. The international human rights community, also, is suddenly interested.
So are college campuses. In November 2000, I am invited to Bard College to
speak at a one-day conference. As I enter the auditorium, I notice students that
remind me of the type of activists I had encountered for the first time at the university in Ann Arbor, except these have more piercings. In those days I saw signs
calling for the United States to disinvest in South Africa and to keep out of El
Salvador. Today I see students carrying a sign that reads U.S. OUT OF COLUMBIA.

I smile. Even if they think Colombia is spelled like the university, Colombia is now on the radar. For an entire day, theories are thrown out for discussion: Is this another Vietnam or El Salvador, or is it more like the Balkans? After a day of pondering, everyone was at a loss for a conclusion. It seems the conflicts in those other places were somehow easier for the academics and the experts to grasp. Perhaps the other conflicts fit into some binary model of good versus evil. Colombia defies comprehension. It is assumed that as a Colombian, I have insights into this conundrum; so they question me. And I pause to consider an answer but all I come up with is what little I know about the country I still claim as my own.

I COULD HAVE TOLD CHARLIE, OR THE STUDENTS AT BARD WHAT I THOUGHT: Colombia is a beautiful country with an awful history and a terrible present. I am a bad Colombian for telling you this. Colombians are at war with one another. Liberals and Conservatives will drag one another through mud; the FARC throws cylinder bombs at AUC sympathizers with disregard for the children who get caught between their hate; AUC members will chop off the heads of FARC militia with electric saws and play soccer with them. Colombia holds records that Colombians would prefer go unnoticed. I am a bad Colombian for pointing out things that we should sweep under the carpet. Colombians might be at war with each other but they all agree on one thing. You must never speak badly about Colombia. It's a mortal sin equivalent to breaking the commandment that prohibits taking God's name in vain. I am told that the dirty laundry must only be washed at home. I have been accused of being the person "who sells our problems abroad. Let's talk about the good things we have," they tell me, like Shakira.

No need to mention that there are so many massacres in the countryside and so many threats to small farmers that entire hamlets have disappeared or sit totally abandoned. People move from town to town and without anyone noticing it, two million people have had to abandon their homes, making Colombia the country with the highest current rate of internal displacement. The world is aware of Rwanda and Darfur but not of Colombia. Thanks to Colombia's great damage control and PR efforts, we don't yet have George Clooney or Angelina Jolie coming to visit our refugee camps.

History books talk about La Violencia, a time in our history just fifty years ago that bore us the phenomenon of violentologists, people who specialize in studying violence. "It is not because we are poor that we are so violent," one of the country's top intellectuals once explained to me. "Peru is as poor and they don't come near us when it comes to violence." A Spanish friend once told me that Colombians are so good at everything they do, that they have proven to be the best at killing. And yet, between 1999 and 2002 I did not receive any infor-mation about the history or the causes of the country's unraveling; instead I was inundated with chain e-mail messages with titles like "Why Believe in Colom-bia?" The reasons are many: Colombia had 583 species of amphibians, 14,000 species of butterflies, and 1,815 species of birds. Why not concentrate on these numbers instead, the messages suggest—records that indicate Colombia as third, second, and first in the world in these areas respectively. There is more: We are also the main growers of roses, orchids, carnations, and, of course, our famed coffee. Ours are the most beautiful in the world. Colombians invented contact lenses for babies. Our Amazon is the lung of the world. We are, these messages state soberly, the third largest manufacturers of "sensual" lingerie. Indeed, we have García Márquez, an artist whose round images are recognized around the world, a world-famous racecar driver, a handful of rock stars who play Madison Square Garden. As Colombia disintegrates, many Colombians, from the president to the street lotto seller, have taken to wearing bracelets with the Colombian flag around their wrists as a way of saying we are proud and we have faith in you. I have refused to wear the many I have been given.

My father was right. The FARC didn't take over. But it was after I saw the rebels' almost-takeover of Bogotá while I was resting in Shelter Island that I put up the map in my kitchen and I have lived with the obsession of Colombia ever since. By the end of that summer, my Colombia—my grandparents, my uncle, and the farm, everything that was a part of me but had not been in so long—consumed my thoughts. I wanted to meet Colombians. I wanted to learn the words of the *vallenato* songs I had never cared for. I wanted to feel what it was like to be Colombian. I saw Colombia everywhere. A normal night of watching a movie at home became a Colombian conundrum: As I watched Omar Sharif as Doctor Zhivago, I remembered how easy it was to know that Doctor Zhivago was fighting on the right side and that it was beautiful and romantic. Where was Colombia's Doctor Zhivago? Going to the theater, to the movies, watching a simple music video, the obsession took over: *Coriolanus,* Colombia; *Uncle Vanya,* Colombia; *Lion King* with my now nine-year-old nephew, Colombia; *The Leopard,* Colombia. I was fighting ideas, ghosts, and my own demons. During a night of insomnia, the video for REM's "Losing My Religion" came on TV. Again, Colombia—in it I saw an angel with huge wings in a corner, fighting his duality. I jumped out of bed and scribbled "Losing My Country" on a Post-it, and stuck it to the refrigerator door.

When at last I decided to return to Colombia, I went to write a story for the *New York Times Magazine.* I wanted to show that Colombians do not and can-not think that they are the happiest; that they cannot think their quality of life is the best money can buy. Experts talk about a forty-four-year-old conflict where thirty thousand people die every year and two million people are left displaced. I hear about how barbaric the rebels are and I hear about an armed conflict but I don't hear what I want to hear. I don't hear what needs to be said. Colombia, they continue to insist, is a happy place, the best place in the world.

To them, Colombia might not be at war. But I am at war with Colombia.

I am going back because there is a war, brutal war, a war full of horror. I am going to tell them that each and every one knows it, allows it, and hides it. Everyone has blood on their hands. I want everyone to plead guilty.

3

BARRANQUILLA
AUGUST 2001

For two hours, I've been sitting at the gate with a book in hand, trying to read, but I can't stop myself from playing the profiler. Really I'm watching everyone, wondering if people I know are on the flight, hoping they are not. The plane from Miami to Barranquilla is boarding and the process is as loud and laid-back as I remember it. The gate feels more like someone's living room with a party of good friends going at full blast. Waves, kisses, and *aja*, in English it would sound like "a-ha," the crutch word that means "hello," "sure," and "maybe" are exchanged at disco-level decibels. When I'm working I prefer to act as a fly on the wall, and I worry that running into a friend of my mother's or an old schoolmate would interfere. My anxiety also reflects a deeper concern, one that I've been struggling with ever since I received my assignment—this is my first attempt to report on Colombia and I'm determined to get this right. I've decided to explain the larger conflict in Colombia by telling the story of my mother's family's land, arguing that this land overtaken with the violence of guerrilla and paramilitary forces is a microcosm of the country as a whole.

I look around the boarding gate, profiling the other passengers. There's an executive returning from a business trip and a man of more stature, a business owner not an employee, sitting next to each other: the first type sits with his legs crossed, the latter with his legs uncrossed, spread widely, taking up as much room as he feels he needs. I can tell which are the families with immigrant relatives in the new Miami developments of Kendall and those who have the fancier condominiums on Brickell Avenue. I spot a woman with stilettos, shinier replicas of Manolo Blahniks, and peg her as one of the women who makes a living taking a dozen of the same pair to sell to friends at a profit. She is called *la contrabandista,* the word literally means "smuggler," but in Barranquilla, bringing in undeclared goods to sell for a profit is a decent profession, with no ignominy attached to the moniker. In Barranquilla a *contrabandista* provides a service, as essential and as banal as dentistry. Women smugglers bring suitcase after suitcase filled with anything from nail polish to wedding gowns to sell to those who don't get to travel to Miami, and for most everyone in Barranquilla things are better if they come from Miami.

Turning to look at the two families a few seats away, I notice a little girl asking for help dressing her new Barbie. I wonder if she wakes up at night, like I used to, scared for her life that "someone"—I never knew exactly who—was going to hurt her. But someone whose face is so familiar it could have been my own mother snaps me out of my thoughts. Daisy, my friend Patricia's mother, sits next to me and says hello, jumping into a conversation without acknowledging my twenty-five-year absence. "How is your grandmother?" she asks me. "She had the flu last week when I saw her at mass."

In my bag I have the essentials of my trade: my laptop, a cheap tape recorder, a ten-pack of ninety-minute audiotapes, a couple of the spiral notepads I like to take notes with, and an envelope with the logo of the *New York Times* that holds the standard letter of assignment that reporters carry when doing a story and is used as a form of introduction to request interviews. I told my editor that this time the letter was also a way to hide my true identity. If I showed the letter in Colombia saying that Silvana Paternostro was writing a story for the *Times Magazine,* it could save me a lot of trouble.

I was born and baptized Silvana María Paternostro Montblanc. All legal documents identify me with a total of four names. Following the Spanish-inherited custom, everyone uses first the father's, then the mother's last name. It is a system that allows for an instant genealogy, so what was once useful to separate those like us with the good names from the *corronchos,* Barranquilla's term for the riffraff, *costeño* language for the hoi polloi—she is the daughter of so and of so—today is a tool for rebels to target their intended prey. When I get to Colombia, I plan to drive from Barranquilla to the family farm, to finally go on the road, and if I have my full name anywhere in sight, my odds of getting there without being kidnapped or threatened are slim. My uncle had warned me about the dangers of my second last name and how, no matter what I said at a rebel checkpoint, that was the only thing that mattered. He probably thinks that after his explanation, I would abandon my idea.

WHEN WE ARE CALLED TO BOARD, EVERYONE GETS UP AT THE SAME TIME. BARranquilleros don't travel quietly nor do they travel lightly. Shopping bags and stuffed backpacks slow the process of boarding. But no one is in a hurry. I scan my fellow passengers' faces looking for signs of anxiety or resignation, something that would indicate what going home feels like when home is a country at war. No one here seems to share my apprehension. They seem to feel more preoccupied with the hazards of flying, bracing against each bump of turbulence and clapping when the plane lands. They are happy to be going home.

Less than three hours later we land in Barranquilla and disembark, automatically shifting into the arrival routine: baggage, customs, and finally, release. As if a switch had been activated during landing, people walk faster, speak louder, and push each other, suddenly in a rush. The first stop is at the immigration office and an official stamps my passport without looking up. "How was Miami?" he says. To him, there is nothing extraordinary about my entering Colombia—it's practically the only place in the world where my arrival isn't noted with suspicion or doesn't involve special documentation, like my Green Card everytime I enter the United States. I walk into the luggage room with the conveyor belt of contraband-stuffed bags hissing like a cobra. Everyone is calling for a baggage handler, grabbing them even as they pace around in their smoky blue uniforms. It's crucial to get the right one. And the right customs official too: the ones who don't go through the bags, keeping the stuff you spent hours, days, even months finding in the malls of Florida.

I stand to the side again and watch as the baggage handlers jockey for the good clients, the passengers with the most suitcases. "All taken," Daisy tells me as a nearby handler ignores her request for help.

"*Claro,*" she continues, "they look at us as if we are nothing. They only want to help those who bribe them, the ones who have ruined them with their fat tips."

The handler is busy with someone else's luggage. "This one, chief, right? I know it's this one, *patrón.* I know your bags. I know this one is yours." The men don't look back as they push Daisy's suitcase aside and grab the two overstuffed bags next to hers. As a child I overheard how important it was to bring something, usually a bag of Three Musketeers or Milky Ways, to leave at customs. I guess now that is not enough.

I have witnessed this scene since the day I was born. The power of the few and the servility of the many remains unchanged. There will always be those who hover around moneyed pockets like bees around honey. These men are willing to lift more than their body weight for a few dollars. A man whose face I recognize but whose hair has gone gray and whose body has shrunk since I was last here passes by, shuffling his feet. He is carrying a suitcase on his back and two on each arm. There is no bribe big enough for him to shed the drab gray uniform and move on to a better life. But the game continues, its rules intact.

After the baggage exercise, there is still one more hurdle to overcome. An armed guard patiently checks each baggage ticket at the exit. He patiently checks each one as everyone shoves the others trying to get out. On the other side of the glass doors, the faces of expectant relatives glisten in the tropical humidity. I stand in a stupor, paralyzed at the familiar chaos. Knowing what to expect doesn't stop me from wanting to scream at my compatriots, to demand that they stand in a straight line and wait their turn. A wheel from a wayward suitcase drags across my foot. "Don't sweat it," says its handsome owner. I immediately recognize him as a fellow student from my high school who graduated a few years ahead of me. "You are not in the United States anymore. *Aquí lo que cuenta es la viveza.*" Here, he says, what matters is to be sly. He gives me a patronizing look that makes it clear: Queuing up and waiting for your turn have no place here; that's gringo stuff. Here what matters is staying alert, being cunning, taking advantage, surviving. *Juega vivo.* Play alive. Kill before you are killed. I remember how the boys at school would push one another around and scream at the slower kids, *bobo el último.* Last one's a fool.

4

SEEING YOU AGAIN

The car suddenly brakes, giving the right-of-way to an old man in his donkey cart slowly crossing to the other side of the road. I do not know if I am seeing through the eyes of the journalist or the eyes of the girl who always found this road to the airport dangerous and ugly. Smoke billows from smoldering garbage along the road, wafting an acrid smell of burnt plastic toward the car's open windows. I roll my eyes, sighing deeply. I remember my father's comment every time I had turned my face into a frown at my surroundings. "The stork made a mistake," he would announce. "She dropped Silvana in the wrong B. She was not supposed to be delivered here. She was on her way to Brussels and now she has to deal with Barranquilla." It is fair to say I was not a well-adjusted creature of the Caribbean, but *papi* would quickly deflate my pretensions. "You are not a *belga*, dear. You are from Barranquilla." Instead of my dad's gentle teasing, Colombia treats me rudely. As I leaf through the issue of *Semana,* the leading newsweekly that I find in the backseat of the car, trying to hide my discomfort, I encounter a cartoon of a young man scribbling graffiti: *And you? Why haven't you left for Miami?*

One out of every five Colombians is leaving, according to recent polls, but I have decided to come back, though I am not sure why. Is it out of concern or conceit? None of my childhood friends remain. Emma called from Miami to chat, saying she was "waiting for the rain to stop," which meant she had left Colombia for a spell when things got "a bit too dicey." Not too long after, David, who I've known since nursery school, told me over dinner in Soho, "The situation is not good. Nothing serious," he said "it's just not prudent being there right now." "Nothing serious" sounded like delusions of a silver lining to me. Twelve people, many of whom he knew, had been taken by rebels that Sunday afternoon while they were enjoying boat fishing at El Torno, a channel near Barranquilla. He might have gone along, had he not been in Europe on a business trip. That week, he took an apartment around the block from me and enrolled his daughter in a New York City school.

And so I arrive in Barranquilla, the Caribbean coastal city of Colombia where I was born and where I lived during the first fifteen years of my life, unclear about what it is I'm looking for and determined to act as an American journalist on assignment. As such, I should be staying at the Hotel El Prado, the city's prime hotel with its architecture similar to the grand Art Deco palace hotels in the south of France. During previous visits, staying in one of the cabanas was one of the highlights of coming to Barranquilla. This time I forego the pleasure of walking up and down the palm tree courtyard. Instead I choose to take one of the rooms in my grandmother Cristina's new apartment, half a block from my uncle's house—it's best to be nearby if I'm going to focus on getting to El Carmen.

As I walk inside my grandmother's home I remind myself that I am here as the journalist who writes in English and who embraces American liberalism wholeheartedly. I insist on this invisible armor because to admit that I am here for any other reason—to reclaim my past, to re-create memories, even to simply see my family—is terrifying. I spend the rest of the afternoon setting up shop: laptop on desk hooked up to the Internet, television on and set to CNN (I'm surprised and pleased that my grandmother's house has all these modern amenities). In a matter of hours I turn her house into a news bureau, like I've done before in hotel and rented rooms in Managua, in Panama City, in Rio de Janeiro, and in Mexico City. Once I'm done, I decide to cross over to check on my uncle and tell him that I'm here, that he should start planning our trip. When I had gotten the assignment a few months ago in New York, he agreed to help and even suggested he would come along. "I haven't been there in a very long time and I really would like to go," he had said; "there's no way of knowing. Conditions change all the time. You just have to come and we will assess it when you're here." I think it's his way of not saying no outright to his favorite niece. It is hard to get him to concentrate on what I'm telling him on an international phone call; I am asking him to go there with me "for this article I'm doing for the *New York Times,*" words that are as hard for him to grasp as it is for me to understand the way he has had to conduct his working life.

I walk outside and the balmy air envelops my body and frizzes my hair. Tree branches sway releasing yellow petals that fall to the ground, that explains the tree's name, the Golden Rain. I am caught off guard. I've returned to make sense of the strife that has plagued my country but as I walk the half-a-block distance to my uncle's I can almost convince myself it is 1977, when danger was the last thing I needed to worry about.

It's seven o'clock on the streets of Riomar, a neighborhood referred to as a number-six barrio. (Neighborhoods in Colombia are ranked and taxed by numbers from one to six, one being the poorest; six being the most affluent.) Riomar is where I grew up and where most of my family still lives. The evening's routine is about to begin. Cars, some brand-new, some very old, drive up to the garages attached to the lines of well-kept houses. Behind the wheels are the social and economic pillars of the city, men and women returning home after the day's work. They honk the same way my father used to do, two short beeps that announce to the household's gardener, maid, or watchman—usually standing by—that the patrón, the master, has arrived.

I pause to watch employer and employee interact. Their exchange is laid-back, informal, and full of warmth, just like I remember it. I continue on crossing in front of a house with a tall pine tree in the front yard. The climate in Barranquilla cannot breed pines but *barranquilleros* like to show off their status by importing foreign plants and trees. And so I pass a row of houses with perfect lawns and transplanted foliage growing amidst the native hibiscus and the coconut palm trees. Boys too young for facial hair and men stooped over with age make a living—if you can call making a few dollars a day a living—watering, pruning, planting, and fertilizing whatever type of garden is fancied by the *doña* of the house. In a few months, during Christmas time, the pines will even be covered with snow, fake white powder brought in from the North and so many lights and props that people from the poorer parts of town bus in to see the spectacle. Some houses have real-life Santa Clauses waving from fake chimneys added for the season. Others have them handing out candy to visitors.

I stand in front of a two-story house because the gardener has left the servant's entrance open and I can peer into the kitchen, catching sight of two maids preparing dinner. Hearing voices behind me, I keep walking, not wanting to be caught standing there, as if I were snooping. Three maids, two very young ones and an elderly one, in their aproned uniforms and flip-flops, chat away, it's unclear to me if they are talking about the family they work for or soap opera story lines as they walk miniature French poodles on thin gold-leather leashes. War changes everything and war changes nothing, I think to myself as I move on. Not the flowers, not voices, and not the breed of dogs—we also had two poodles, a black one and a gray one, and maids who walked them.

The night grows dark, the street unlit, and I feel a body bump into mine.

"Pardon me," I say, startled.

"Madame," a man materializes in front of me speaking directly into my face. "I am looking for work. I'll do anything. Please give me work. I can cut grass. I can paint. Anything." He has the clothes of a beggar, in contrast to his energy and his disposition to work. I ask him where he is from, noting his unfamiliar accent. He is from Chigorodó, he tells me, and I recognize the name because it is the town where Rubén Valencia went to investigate why eighteen people had been killed and he was stonewalled—"by that angel" he had told us—at every attempt to find out what had happened. (When I return to New York I look it up on my kitchen map and find it on the left shoulder. I highlight it with a blue marker.)

The beggar arrived in Barranquilla a few months ago, he tells me, after walking for three days, "escaping violence, *doñita,* escaping the horror." The guerrilla had killed his father and his two sisters right in front of him. To prevent the rebels from coming into his house, to protect his wife and three children, he had to use his sisters' bodies to barricade the front door. "No one, *doñita,* no one should have to endure that." He tells me he lives near the old cemetery in a tent where hundred of displaced families like his are camping out; that there is a good priest, who is trying to help them but that the camp is teeming with impatient, hungry families. I want to ask him his name, thinking that I should go there, report his story. But I surprise myself when I don't. I just listen. A few weeks later I read in the paper that there are more than 840 families, totalling 33,000 people, living there, as a result of forced displacement.

He tells me he walks these streets every day because "this is where they hire." If there is work to be had anywhere, it is here, he says. But the *patrones* don't trust him because he has an accent; he is from "the interior" of the country. *Costeños* think the populace there is more violent and are always reminding themselves and others that "here we are people of peace." There are no rebels here, *barranquilleros* claim, insisting that their fortune is due to the fact that "here the rich and the poor dance together. Come to carnivals, you will see."

The War of One Thousand Days, and La Violencia, and Operation Marquetalia, all of Colombia's theaters of war, have been fought far from Barranquilla. Whoever is not from here is called a *forastero,* a foreigner, as if they come from another country. They are the knife-wielding, baby-snatching killers of the kind that populated the horror stories of my childhood, the ones the maids would invoke at dinner time to get me to eat my vegetables, the ones that would leave me so petrified as I lay in bed that I was too terrified to move to even wrap myself more tightly with my pink covers.

Compassion wins out every so often he says and a *patrón* will give him a day's work, or a meal, or scraps and old clothes that a man can take back to his family. A resourceful type, he describes how he goes through the garbage at construction sites where he finds things to sell to recyclers, pointing at the pipe in his hand.

"Give me some work," he pleads again.

"I wish I could," I say, making an effort to hide my fear. Colombia still petrifies me. I see a potential killer in everyone's gaze. As I look at this man, I feel the same sinking sensation in the pit of my stomach that I felt as a child at dinnertime.

The same panic emerged a few days later on this same street when another man, this one much older, approached my two nephews and me. He too was looking for work. "Let me cut your grass, *señora.*" And he too held objects that threatened me: a machete and garden scissors, even if they were so rusty they could have been rescued from a Spanish galleon from the bottom of the sea. I handed him a five-thousand-peso bill, the equivalent of two dollars, the amount he would have made if one of these households had hired him for a day of gardening. He told me he wishes he didn't have to beg but he needs to feed his five children. He took the bill, kissed it, blessed the air, and with a smile he turned to my six-year-old nephew: "You are luckier than my children."

WHY HAVE I RETURNED TO FACE THIS? WHY DO I WANT TO GO TO EL CARMEN, a place I have never been interested in, where armed groups have labeled anyone from our family as the enemy? For having my mother's name alone I could be kidnapped. I could die, shot like a dog with rabies or in the crossfire of a liberation attempt, and no one would know the truth, like what happened to Gilberto Echeverri or later to Consuelo Araujo, a former minister of culture, a classmate of my aunt Cecilia. I heard Consuelo was killed because she couldn't keep up with her kidnappers as she was taken into the hills—the Perijá hills behind El Carmen. I have heard about Gregorio, a seventy-two-year-old distant uncle, who was taken and escaped by some miracle after being held for seventy or so days. I have heard of the absurd tragic fate that befell a distant cousin who died on his way to meet his father for lunch during a vacation from medical school in London. He had been shot trying to avoid running into a rebel checkpoint.

I've spent all this time keeping Colombia's volatile existence at bay, listening quietly when my mother called with news of kidnappings and killings. I had never felt close to or paid much attention to my mother's extended family, the Montblancs. To me they were boring and provincial. To the rebels they are landowners, not a good thing in Marxist terms. To my mother, they are her family, the people she grew up with. As the world spread open in front of me, I didn't waste time on the place I had left behind. I have no immediate apologies or answers for this, other than perhaps that is the reason I came back.

The next morning I cannot get the Internet to work and the thought of not being able to tap into my New York self is unbearable. "You're going out?" my grandmother asks in disbelief. I'm wearing sweatpants and have barely brushed my hair. I tell her I'm just crossing to my uncle's house. "You're walking?" she asks, continuing to be surprised by my behavior, and in an almost authoritative tone tells me to have her driver, Antonio, take me. "It's half a block," I say. "I like to walk. You should see how much I walk in New York."

"The sun is strong," she insists without looking up from her prayer book and in more of a mumble, she adds, "and it's not completely safe."

"I'll be fine," I say.

I ring the doorbell of my uncle's house and a young maid opens the window next to the door, not knowing if she should let me in or not. "No one is home," she says. The children are at school, and the *patrones,* my uncle and his wife, are working. I explain who I am, and she lets me in. I could have been anyone, but I know how to compel a servant to act using that commanding tone of authority and entitlement that I developed as a child. I pass right in front of her, sitting down at the computer as she returns to her chores. When the phone rings I can tell from the maid's end of the conversation that it is a call from the countryside—her mother, most likely, calling to tell her what is happening over in the hamlet where she had left her children in her mother's care so that she could come to the city and work in this house. I can tell; I remember those phone calls well. They always happen during the day when the servants' families know they are alone, the masters are not around and they are free to talk. Masters don't like maids who receive phone calls.

She hangs up and in a calm voice informs the other maid, the kitchen maid, that her cousin and her cousin's husband have just been killed. The guerrillas, those *hijueputas* (sons of bitches), were to be blamed. This is different from the phone calls that came from the pueblos when I lived here as a child. It used to be that if someone died it was because they had drowned in a river or had been bitten by a snake, or else someone had fallen sick in a hamlet with no hospital. Why would the rebels kill a poor couple? Aren't they fighting for the poor? Isn't it just oligarchs who are their enemies?

I stay for lunch, hoping to see my uncle and ask him about our upcoming secret outing, but when Agustín arrives I don't bring it up. I don't want to say anything in front of his wife. I don't know if he has told her about our plan and she might not want him to go. I could understand her not wanting him to go: Why would he want to give papaya? *Dar papaya* is a popular term meaning making it easy for the guerrilla to snatch you. I'm always taken aback when I hear the term used so lackadaisically. When I lived here *dar papaya* had sexual connotations. If a girl gave papaya it meant she put out.

I ask Agustín if he was going to his office. "Yes," he says. "Come visit."

JOSÉ, MY GRANDMOTHER'S *CHOFER*, IS DRIVING ME TO MY UNCLE'S OFFICE. WE take a right turn on the street that opens up into Villa Country, the development that sprang out of the golf courses that I liked to walk with Allegra after school. The green mantle of our teenage outings has turned into apartment buildings and unimpressive strip malls that are exact replicas of American ones. I feel lost in this new Barranquilla. I would not know how to get to my uncle's office from here. I am comforted when I hear the honking, the strident music, and the shouting from one car to the next, from one street to the other as it has always been.

Barranquilla has always been loud and messy, a melting pot of immigrants who started arriving in the late 1800s from all corners of the world—from villages in Southern Italy, so many crossed over from the port of Palermo, Sicily, and from the small towns of Spanish Galicia, from the shtetls of Russia and Poland, from Aleppo, Turkey, and Damascus, Syria. Located at the convergence of the nation's most navigable river and the Atlantic Ocean, it soon became a prosperous port city. Barranquilla is at the mouth of the Magdalena River, which crosses Colombia from south to north. It has always been the main artery for transportation and communication for the entire country, earning Barranquilla its nickname of Colombia's Golden Gate. The city borrows San Francisco's moniker but Barranquilla's immigration resembles Ellis Island's more than California's and Barranquilla became, like New York City, a place where people stayed and settled, re-creating their past lives. The German community established the German School. The Italians formed the Italian Club. The Jews sent their children to the Hebrew School and socialized at the Hebrew Union Club. The Arabs, known as the Turks, have their own country club. Everyone is apart and together at the same time. During Carnivals, one's country of origin, gender, color, personality, or profession becomes indistinguishable. Rich or poor, all the people throw themselves into the street in celebration.

Barranquilla has been chaotic since its beginnings, and always on the verge of becoming cosmopolitan. I read in the travelogue of Élisée Reclus, a Frenchman who visited in the mid-1800s, that when he first encountered the city, he felt as if he was "about to enter a commercial city similar to the ones in Europe or the United States." He saw people from everywhere working on all types of water vehicles in the small jetties on the banks of the river: Indians and Negroes unloading ships with straw roofs; steamboats anchored at the piers; the sound of hundreds of workers hammering on iron chains. Reclus met English, American, German, and Dutch merchants. At his hotel, people came from "all four corners of the world." Everyone spoke English. He recalled how Madame Hughes, the hotel's owner, ran a colorful outfit that claimed a touch of English etiquette. Lunch was served on the patio under the big trees covered in fragrant flowers and full of singing creatures. The hotel, however, had no private rooms. The beds were lined up under the arched passageways that surrounded the patio and guests would wake up to the first rays of light.

Barranquilla is still as unplanned and as unfinished as Madame Hughes's hotel and as it was when I lived here. Barranquilla's soccer stadium is a source of local pride. It is the largest stadium in the country, with a capacity of 60,000. It was inaugurated in 1986. The old one stands dilapidated, like a UFO, in the center of the city, used sporadically to host concerts and Carnival events. The cathedral, erected before I was born, still has no garden. It took twenty years to finish the stained-glass windows and the front door. My old American school was also moved. The new one is much bigger and prettier, but like the old stadium the old one sat crumbling, as if hit by an earthquake, until a multinational recently renovated it.

Gabriel García Márquez has said that Barranquilla is how he imagined the hamlet of Macondo, from his celebrated novel *One Hundred Years of Solitude*, would look if it grew into a city. While the city might provide vivid material for the creative mills of fiction, the reality is not as "magical," as everyone outside of Colombia refers to the Nobel Laureate's writing about his country, for the two million people who actually live there. Barranquilla has one of the starkest disparities between rich and poor that the history of human society has ever known, as well as a staggering amount of corruption. What happens here is not magical, it is way too real.

The money allocated for public services vanishes every time, leaving Barranquilla without running water, without electricity, and with a drainage system that turns the city into Venice when it rains. When the torrential rains come in May, the streets become swollen with rushing streams that paralyze everything. The flooded thoroughfares swallow people, donkey-driven carts, cars, and the huge buses that roam the city painted like huge tropical parrots. Schools close. As the city has never had a reliable garbage system, everyone, rich and poor, uses the arroyos, rain-created tributaries, as Dumpsters, tossing their trash into the street to be washed away. I've seen car engines, mattresses, old refrigerators, even a few friends float by. When we were in the seventh grade, Antonio, the tallest and craziest of our classmates, wagered that he could swim across the arroyo that formed behind our school. Antonio, who was nicknamed Balín, Spanish for "small bullet" for his love of danger and BB guns, was lost for hours and ended up in the hospital with many broken ribs. My daredevil cousin Jorge, a fantastic water-skier, had a friend drive his jeep as if it were a boat as he "skied" the brown waters barefooted. My grandmother was sure he would die from an infection. Swimming among the dead bodies in the Ganges is a much cleaner bet.

When I get to my uncle's office, Agustín introduces me to the personnel, about a dozen people sitting in an air-conditioned three-room office. "My niece," he says, "the journalist who lives in New York." They smile at me and I smile at them. I feel awkward standing there so I just scurry into the open door of my uncle's office and he follows me. "So when?" I ask. "Patience is the name of the game," he tells me. "Here." He hands me a guest pass for the duration of my stay to Barranquilla's country club. "Use it. Enjoy it. They have a great gym and new sauna. And the old Bar San Juan is still very pleasant. I'll get to work on our plan and will report back."

5

MY BIRTHMARK

I was the firstborn daughter of a very young couple from the Costa Atlantica—my mother was nineteen and my father twenty-two—both blessed with beauty and privilege. They met at an afternoon birthday party and, according to both, they fell in love without even speaking to each other. It happened at her cousin's house, which was the only reason that my mother was allowed to be there. She was standing with her aunt Clemencia in the kitchen in her school's light blue pleated skirt, finishing her slice of cake, when my father walked in. He, with his usual assertiveness, which would win him honors and troubles, turned to Clemencia and told her, within earshot of my mother, that he would marry her niece within a year, and he did.

When my mother first saw my father in late 1959, she was seventeen, a naïve beauty who had grown up sheltered, alternating between the thousands of acres of her father's land and the thick walls of her convent school. She had been born in Asunción, a faraway courtly town in the northeastern Guajira that dated from the 1700s, where her family's house, built by her great-grandfather General Gustavo Montblanc, the region's Conservative chieftain, faced the church in the town's square. "There was no music played anywhere in that town," my mother once told me. Any diversion, consisted of church-related events, and she recalled the huge oil painting depicting purgatory that hung from her grandfather's staircase and welcomed her every day with images of people burning in hell. My mother not only went to a convent boarding school, she lived with the fear of god around her at all times. That was the Conservative way.

I am sure my mother had never met anyone like my father. All the men she had met were cousins or they were her father's workers. The men she knew were country gentlemen, who felt more comfortable giving orders in a stable than in the salons and the cotillions at el Country Club. My father drove a two-toned American car, listened to Bach and to Burt Bacharach, danced the twist, the mambo, and the cha-cha. My mother had never been to a dance in her life. For a few years prior, her parents had sent her to a nun's convent in Barranquilla where she lived with other boarders, girls whose parents lived in the countryside. The rules for the girls were the same as those for the cloistered nuns. They showered with white sheets over their developing bodies and had to speak to the men through a rotating heavy wooden window. At seventeen, she lived a monastic life in a city that had Carnivals as rowdy as those in Rio. She had never participated in one, while my father had danced with every year's Carnival queen.

Because Barranquilla was the cosmopolitan city of the northern coast, many landowning families from nearby, like my mother's, came to live here. My maternal grandparents, Gabriel and Cristina Montblanc, bought a house in the late 1950s and commuted from their *finca*, the Colombian name given to vast holdings of land. El Carmen was named after the Virgen del Carmen, patron of Asunción, the hamlet on the banks of the Cesár River where four Montblanc brothers took over the square at the end of the 1800s and where their descendants have lived since then. Gabriel and Cristina preferred the four-thousand-acre farm my grandfather hacked from the jungles in that region but it was important that their children had access to city life.

My two sets of grandparents lived in the world that they, as members of the coastal elite, had helped create. My father's parents—Antonio, but whom everyone knew as Toño, and Lilia—whom everyone called Lili—were a well-liked couple in Barranquilla. They had moved there as adults and were less interested in the social ways of the Caribbean metropolis. Lili organized afternoons of card playing and eating hors d'oeuvres with her friends. Toño kept a Carnival costume in the trunk of his car, just in case. My mother's parents were their antithesis. Cristina spent her time praying with rosaries, cutting flowers to send to churches, and doing crossword puzzles. Only family was invited over. Gabriel was known for his daring entrepreneurship and for his bad temper.

We were closer to our paternal grandparents. My father had been an overprotected only child and when my parents married, his mother just added us to the list. Lili invited my parents to live with them. My mother was too young to handle the responsibility of running a household and raising a family; my grandmother told her that she would teach her and help her. There was room for all of us in her house in El Alto Prado. My sister, Laura, my brother, Pedro, and I lived with them until my parents built their own house in Riomar, the new neighborhood that would replace El Alto Prado for my parents' generation.

My grandmother spoiled us as she had spoiled her "little bat from New York" (no one knows why she called my father that, not even him). When my father was young, if he was invited to lunch at a friend's house, my grandmother would let him attend only after confirming they weren't serving fish. Her son, her only son, who she would shamelessly describe as prettier than the Niño Jesús de Praga, could choke on a bone, after all. Although an observant Catholic, she did not like Lent. That meant having to serve my sister, my brother, and me fish for lunch on Friday. On those occasions, she had two maids cut the fish into bits and massage them with their fingers to make sure each piece was free from danger before we were allowed to bring the fork to our mouths. They literally stood by on alert and watched our every bite.

My father grew up never having to give up anything for anyone. He was both charming and unbearable, popular with the girls and popular among his friends. He was a man who was hard to negotiate with. Many found him too confident and intransigent, *prepotente,* a word my mother sometimes used when she was mad at him.

When my father proposed marriage to my mother, my grandfather Gabriel was not thrilled. He found my father smug, but more worrisome was the fact that my father was not a *finquero,* a landowner like him. My father was a landless city boy who talked in macroeconomics terms instead of number of hectares. A month after meeting my mother, he left to get a master's degree in economics in the United States. Before leaving, he proposed.

My grandfather would rather have had my mother forget that suitor and marry a cousin with land, in keeping with a tradition that had been ongoing soon after the Frenchman bore the first Montblancs. I never knew the name of my forebear. No one mentioned his name or how he came to Colombia; he was just "the Frenchman who arrived." That's how I had heard everyone refer to him. My aunt named the French commode in her living room the Frenchman's Piece. My mother had the Frenchman's Pocket Watch that got ruined when shampoo fell on the heirloom. The house in Asunción where they all lived is known as the Frenchman's House, by family and by the entire town. Now, after years of hoping to understand why they have become targets of the rebels, I know that "*el francés* who arrived," which has become coded family lore, was actually two Frenchmen. Michel, a sea captain in his fifties, and his twenty-one-year-old son Maurice came to the northern coast of Colombia from Bordeaux. That makes Michel my great-great-great-great-grandfather and makes me a sixth-generation Montblanc, and that, my family tells me, even if I have never used his name, makes it risky to travel in the areas where they had once settled, areas now overrun by armed rebels. I've never lived or worked in the region where the Montblancs "exploit" according to rebel ideology, but for them, I am as much of an enemy. "They'll know you," Agustín had clarified. But don't they know I kept a poster of Che on my college dorm wall?

My father was determined to keep true to his promise. From the U.S. he sent my mother heaps of love letters written on onionskin paper. He also sent his family's priest to talk to my mother's family. The message that Padre Borrero delivered was this: "We get your blessing or we elope." So during his spring break from school, my father and my mother were engaged in a ceremony at his parents' house. My father gave my mother a platinum diamond ring that had belonged to his grandmother, and Padre Borrero blessed their kiss. Everyone, including my reluctant grandfather, toasted *los novios* with champagne. I've studied the photos trying to read into my grandfather's smile, but all I see is the radiance of a young couple ready to begin their life together.

Six months later, during my father's Christmas break, they were married. They spent their honeymoon in a room overlooking Central Park where my mother was mesmerized by everything she had never seen. At first it was New York City lights, then everything from Saint Patrick's to Saks Fifth Avenue to the hotel's revolving door. But in the college town, it was life without family and servants. In a sequence of pictures taken during her first winter, they frolick in the snow. Four months later and keeping in line with the string of new sensations, she became pregnant with me. She discovered morning sickness while living away from every comforting thing she knew. My father fed her Campbell's tomato soup, the only thing he could manage to make on his own as her belly grew and her maternity clothes got bigger and bigger. My mother could not take the foreignness of it all. When it was time for my birth, they did not go to the university hospital that would have delivered me into the world as an American. Those were days with no sonograms, with a mandatory draft, and talk of Vietnam. "What if you were born a boy?" my mother said when I asked why she had packed her bags and returned to give birth in Colombia. That's where she thought we all "belonged."

When I was born, my grandmother Lilia shrieked. Half of my left foot was black and blue. She ran to the obstetrician, a family friend: "What have you done to my granddaughter?" she said showing him my foot. "You held her foot too tight. Look what you've done." No mark of imperfection should stain the birth of her first grandchild. But the mark never disappeared. What my grandmother mistook for a bruise is a dark brown birthmark that still covers half of my foot. Growing up, everyone teased me about it. Other kids loved it when the lifeguard at the club's pool always asked me to clean my foot before I went in. The comments never fazed me. I never hid my *lunar,* as it is called in Spanish, referring to the lunar cycles of the moon. One of our maids told me that I got it when my mother was pregnant and my father had kissed her under a full moon. Another one told me that it was because my mother had eaten a *nispero,* a fruit of the same color of my mark, under the same moon. To me, my *nai* as I called it, was more than something passed on to me by my parents. It was exactly the opposite. To me it has always represented the only thing that was truly mine. My birthmark was the game I played on my birthright, the secret stain on my perfect birth certificate. People thought I should wear shoes to conceal it; instead I've always worn the skimpiest of sandals, parading the black butterfly on my foot. My father would always tell me that I could never get lost. "I will always find you," he would tell me during my moments of panic. "No one has your *nai.*" I wonder if that applies to kidnappings.

LIKE OTHER COUPLES WITH THEIR BACKGROUND, MY PARENTS REPRESENTED the future of Colombia—that is, of conservative Colombia. They both came from families that had strong allegiances to the Conservative party, a party that believed in a state ruled with no separation of church and with a strong military component. On my mother's side it began in 1855 with the birth of Gustavo Montblanc, the firstborn son of the Frenchman. By 1898, my mother's great-great-grandfather commanded the Conservative troops that fought the Liberals, who were a more mercantilist and Masonic bunch in the region around Asunción.

When I was born my father was ready to take on Barranquilla and remake it in his own image. I think it is a blend of Adam Smith's belief in the power of the invisible hand and John Maynard Keynes's interventionism, learned in America, mixed in with his allegiance to the Conservative Party. My mother was prepared to share his ambition and stay by his side, always beautiful, always ready to organize the next birthday party, the next baptism, and the next beach holiday for her children. At twenty-two, my father was among the very few men in Barranquilla to have earned a graduate degree from an American university. As part of the new crop of professionals of his generation, he was soon a very busy man. He taught economics at the first private university where he had a reputation of being very strict. He started his career as a financial analyst for the city's main consultancy firm but soon became a vice president and served on boards of all kinds—except the Carnival one, which was not serious enough for him. After a few years, he was elected Executive of the Year, the first time of many that I remember seeing my father's picture in *El Heraldo,* the city's main daily paper. My grandmother would make sure to buy a handful of copies and kept them in a special drawer.

Once he found the right business partner, another economist like him but bespectacled, my father and he founded the first consulting firm in Barranquilla. As he was always commenting on the state of the public services or of the fluctuation of the peso against the dollar in the newspapers, he decided it was time to offer his services to the private sector. Barranquilla was great in that way: a city where new things could be done, because whatever might exist or be in vogue in the United States would be received with open arms, no matter what it was. But he and his partner had a hard time signing up clients. "They weren't prepared for modernity," I've heard my father say, meaning that at the end of the day the city's economic elite was very narrow-minded. It is a statement that has always seemed more avant-garde than I see him, a staunch and proud *godo,* slang for a member of the Conservative party and derived from Goth, the Germanic tribe that invaded Spain. The term was used during colonial days to refer to South Americans who were loyal to the monarchy.

MY FATHER WAS ALREADY A HUSBAND AND A FATHER, AN ECONOMIST AND A *godo* when the reverberations of Fidel Castro's revolution reached the coast. He was teaching finances at the newly founded private university. He came back from New York ready to spread the gospel that he had learned, committed to teaching modern theories of economics to the younger generation. But to those a bit younger than he, it was the Cuban revolutionaries' promise of takeover through armed struggle that captured their hearts and minds, not my father's capitalist teachings of supply and demand. While my father analyzed financial spreadsheets, Castro's revolution inspired thousands of young university students, priests with a special concern for the poor, men and women who saw a chance to reproduce in Colombia what was happening on the Caribbean island, especially because the Cubans were ready and eager to teach and export what they had just accomplished.

By 1964, as I blew out the candles on my third birthday cake (a gingerbread house, like the one where Hansel and Gretel were kidnapped and caged), Colombia had become a country with guerrillas. The fight between Liberals and Conservatives was one thing, but the infiltration of communism was something else entirely. Both parties agreed: The military had to prevent Colombia from becoming the next Cuba by all means possible. But to those who had always opposed the government, Cuba was a great ally. Those liberal-minded peasants in Tolima, left over from the Violencia years and living in what they called "independent republics," were reenergized by the Communist Spanish-speaking comrades from Havana. The government was aware of the strengthening of armed movements and reacted fast on Manuel Marulanda's republic of Marquetalia. Marulanda promised to retaliate. His independent republic became the Revolutionary Armed Forces of Colombia, today's FARC.

Marulanda's was not the only rebel group operating in Colombia. There was also the National Liberation Army, known as the ELN, the acronym for its Spanish name. A group of seven university students, all in their twenties, trained in Cuba and came back to the forests of Santander, which they chose because the jungles provided cover and the population was used to fighting against the government. Both the FARC and the ELN called for *la toma del poder,* the taking of power.

All of this eluded me in my Conservative household. I have no recollection of ever having listened to anyone—not my paternal grandparents nor my maternal grandparents; not at school; not in the kitchen where the servants socialized—speak about the infamous attack of Operation Marquetalia in April 1964, the event that most Colombians point to as the beginning of Colombia's destruction. If it weren't for the FARC, Colombia would be the paradise it once was. That is what everyone tells me. Why do I doubt that?

In 1969, my father once again tried to do something innovative and modern in the merchant city. He brought the first computer to Barranquilla and offered data processing services to all the city's banks and big corporations. We had just moved to the new house in Riomar and my father convinced his parents to move out of their house. "It's better," he told his mother, "You will be closer to the children. You can come visit every day." The argument worked. In a matter of months, my father turned his parents' old house into the home of a city oddity.

In those days, a computer was literally the size of a house. It took up the kitchen, living room, and garage joined together. Because of the tropical temperatures and intense humidity, the huge machine had to be kept in an air-conditioned building twenty-four hours a day. To keep the strange new piece of technology humming, my father had turned his mother's house into a giant refrigerated vault.

The computer was such a novelty that my seventh-grade class took a field trip just to see it. They separated us into groups of five and took us carefully and solemnly inside the iced house and into a room that was kept at such a cold temperature that twenty-five technicians walked around wearing wool sweaters, which to us was as rare as people in spacesuits. We weren't the only curious visitors. My father tells me that "people would go see it as if he opened with ice in Macondo."

Barranquilla's basic services were (and still are) unreliable at best, electricity was not guaranteed, so my father was constantly awakened in the middle of the night with panicked phone calls when the power sputtered out. The solution: Do not rely on public services; take the matter into your own hands. This is the lesson all Colombians learn at a very early age; today it is called the absence of state instead of corruption and means protect yourself because no one else is going to. The computer soon had its own electric generator.

In time, the first computer, which spouted out cards with punched holes and drew crowds like a circus act, was replaced by a second, equally gargantuan model. I am told that the IBM Burroughs machines of the time that filled up rooms of my grandmother's house had the approximate computing power of a modern wristwatch. As the computers became smaller and more affordable, companies no longer relied on my father's computing services as they could just buy their own machines. When Carlos Lleras Restrepo, the newly elected Liberal president, called him to offer him a job in his cabinet, my father decided it was time to shut down the computer, save on the electric bills, and sell his parents' house. He was proud to accept the president's offer even if it meant going to Bogotá from Monday through Friday, and being as my mother would say, "unable to enjoy his *casa nueva.*"

Ours was one of the first houses to be completed on our block. People were so curious they would drive by slowly to look at the new houses that were springing up in what were, until recently, empty fields. They were called *casas modernas,* and they were filled with extravagant things. Ours had a walk-in closet for my mother, an intercom system with a phone in every room, and big bathtubs made of Italian stone. My mother filled her new closet with miniskirts and evening gowns, her drawers with Mary Quant makeup crayons, and she kept lots of bottles of bubble bath and a red telephone on her tub's wide ledge. The furniture was a blend of old and new. My mother transplanted some heirlooms from the Frenchman's House into ours, like the Thonet chairs, the kerosene lamps, and what she referred to as *el tinajero,* a beautiful wooden stand with two holes that held earthen jars filled with river water. Asunción had had no electricity and no running water so the lamps were actually used and the servants would fetch water and carry it in the vats that would then be placed in the *tinajero.*

In our house they were used as decoration with the help of Matilde, Barranquilla's first interior decorator ever. Matilde, a recent divorcée with an incredible eye for style, had discovered that she could make a living by helping all the new young couples with their newfound modernity. Matilde offered to bring a modern touch to our family's furniture. She painted the kerosene lamps an emerald green and hung them in the kitchen. The Viennese chairs of dark bent wood became pink and yellow and served as desk chairs for my sister and me to use to do the homework assigned to us by the teachers at our American school. The problem was that we were left to our own devices and no one checked our school assignments. The maids were illiterate and my mother didn't speak English, because as she would tell us "her parents weren't modern" like she was and didn't send her to school where she could learn something valuable ("the most valuable thing we could give you": a school that would teach us English). Papi spoke English but was too busy to attend to his daughter's education.

Matilde also transformed the *tinajero* by painting it green and gold. My mother, who was taking a porcelain-painting class, replaced the clay pots with white porcelain vases that she adorned with miniature roses. She placed these against the wall of the pantry—a word actually used in Barranquilla—where my sister, my brother, and I ate dinner every night supervised by the handful of servants who lived in the back of the house.

My parents did not eat with us, which I preferred because that meant I did not have to eat everything on my plate. As much as the maid threatened to tell my mother, I did not have to do what she said—she was the maid. I never wanted my own food but I coveted everyone else's French fries. My brother would get so angry when I reached out my hand to steal his potatoes that he would wrestle me to the ground, pry my mouth open, and yank the food out. The maids were always watching to make sure we didn't bump into the *tinajero*. "Watch it," they would scream. "Your mother will be furious. It came from your great-grandmother's house in Asunción." But that meant nothing to any of us. We had never been there.

EVERYONE TRIED TO BE HOME FOR THE WEEKEND. *PAPI* CAME BACK FROM Bogotá and we saw Ma Cris and Abuelo Gabriel, as I called my mother's parents, on Sundays for lunch. Ma Cris and Abuelo Gabriel spent their week at El Carmen, where we never went. (We did go to Bogotá a few times.) On holidays, my mother preferred taking us to the beach in Santa Marta where her friends with kids our age also went. My mother had no interest in going back to *la finca*. She hadn't lost anything there, she said.

She had turned into a sassy city mother of three with a prominent husband and a packed social agenda. She learned how to drive, discovered fashion, and attended and gave tea parties, which was a misnomer for an afternoon gathering of young women. She and her friends would take out their complete silver sets, received as wedding presents, but they never drank tea. I remember her getting dressed for them: the yellow tin box of Mary Quant crayons with which she lined her almond-shaped eyes and the outfit of the open miniskirt over hot pants that my father thought was too revealing. My sister and I had the miniature version and we would wear them at the same time as evidenced by the photos in my green leather album, the one I confiscated from my parents and keep within reach in my New York life.

As our clothes changed with the pace of the fashion magazines smuggled from abroad, my mother's parents always looked the same to me: Ma Cris wearing her simple dress, her pearl earrings, a tiny round gold watch, and her wedding band, and Abuelo Gabriel with his heavy-framed spectacles, a guayabera, and a linen cap. He had a lit cigarette held firmly between the fingers of his right hand and had to have a *tinto*, a little cup of black coffee that he drank in small swigs. Once he finished one, he asked for another, "Negra, un tinto." Everyone tiptoed around him, careful not to *ponerlo de mal humor*, to irritate him. He had a terrible temper and he was always coming from or going to El Carmen. The *finca* was the only thing on his mind.

On Sundays, Abuelo Gabriel would be sitting on the terrace in his rocking chair, holding a highball, as he called his whisky and soda. And one by one his four daughters and their respective husbands would start arriving. Everyone took to their seats and formed a semicircle around the terrace. His best friend, Guillermo—who I've now learned is his cousin and that they had grown up together, riding their tricycles around Asunción's cobbled square—would always be sitting by his side. Guillermo was the only person there that he could talk to about the *fincas*. His four daughters had married, respectively, a doctor, who didn't last long; a handsome guy with no profession, who lasted despite everyone's disapproval; an architect, the builder of our new house and my father's best friend; and my father, the economist.

All I remember is how long these lunches were. We arrived at eleven and didn't leave till a few minutes to six to catch the six o'clock mass, but that was only if Abuelo Gabriel was okay with it. It seemed like everything required his permission, his approval, or his dismissal. By that time we were seven grandchildren: three girls and four boys. There were three more cousins but they lived in the United States and only came during school vacations. My grandfather was fond of children, but only for a grand total of two minutes, so to keep us away from the adult conversation, he designed a device. Whenever he saw one of us approach the terrace, he would remind us that Pajarito Lindo, Pretty Bird, would be passing by very soon. "Do you know what you're asking Pajarito Lindo for?" he would say, a kind method of shooing us away. We would stampede to the terrace next to their bedroom and call out for Pretty Bird, screaming at the top of our lungs. "Pajarito Lindo, Pajarito Lindo, I want Kraft caramels," I would say. We would then run over to the backyard in time for the storm of chewy squares that fell like ice cubes from the sky and hit our heads. With our tiny hands filled, we would go back to the terrace to repeat the chant. "Pretty Bird, I want chocolate ice cream," my cousin Alicia would ask next. And by the time we went back to the yard a solid block of ice cream was waiting under the guava tree. My sister always wanted to get chocolate-covered almonds and the Bird also granted her wish. The boys were less interested in playing. They preferred finding real birds to aim at with their BB guns. I don't know about them but Alicia, Laura, and I were convinced of Pretty Bird's existence. It was only years later that we found out that Pretty Bird was Alfredo, the handyman who was instructed to climb on the roof of the house with a stash of candy bags, ready to fulfill our demands.

I was too young to understand what the adults discussed. A lot of the time it sounded serious but nothing ever seemed to be worrying them too much. More than politics or danger, what worried everyone was Abuelo Gabriel's bad moods.

6

THE REBEL YEARS

"One day you will vote Conservative too," my grandfather Toño told me as he washed his hands. It was voting day, April 19, 1970, and I was almost nine. I noticed that Toño was washing his hands differently: He wasn't rubbing them strongly as he normally did, an act I tried not to miss every day before sitting down to lunch. He moved his hands in perfect synchronicity like a flamenco dancer. His two hands did a pas de deux, palm to palm, fingers caressing the other hand; a pause and a clap. This time, the sound and the rhythm were off and the sound was fainter. He held one finger straight up. I soon realized that the tip of his right index finger was a deep burgundy, as if he had cut it and he was holding it up to protect it, like people do when they have a cast over a broken finger. He didn't want the soap to wash away his Conservative confirmation. One day I too would proudly show that I had voted.

If Toño only knew that not only don't I vote Conservative, I don't vote. I could go to the Colombian Consulate on Forty-third Street like Emma, Julia, and the Ruiz sisters do on election day. They call me to remind me but I defiantly refuse their invitation. It is how I manifest feeling abandoned, denying my country (or me?) my vote. It is how I parade my anger (and my sadness). When Margarita told me in 1998 that it was my obligation as a Colombian to vote, I could not argue with her. But when she told me that it was my obligation to vote for Andrés Pastrana because he was the solution that Colombia needed, then I argued. Colombia will never find "the" solution, I responded.

That day in April would mark the end of Colombia as Toño knew it. For him, voting Conservative was "the solution" for Colombia. The two candidates were Misael Pastrana Borrero, an up-and-coming Conservative from the interior, and Gustavo Rojas Pinilla, a general who had served as chief of the armed forces. In 1953 Rojas Pinilla had taken power from Laureano Gómez through a military coup, ending the bloodbath between Conservatives and Liberals. He served as dictator, applauded for having restored order but also discredited for his severe rule in having sent in the military to quash a student protest. It was hard to pin down Rojas Pinilla's politics. He was a strange combination of a populist, a modernizer, and a left-of-center religious military man.

But during that first election, Gustavo Rojas Pinilla was breaking tradition in Colombia by running under his party, the Popular National Alliance. Before that Colombians had only two choices: Liberal or Conservative. He outlawed Communists and, with his degree in civil engineering from the United States, built up the country's airport system.

Toño had just voted and it certainly was not for the general. Emma remembers driving around as a nine-year-old, passing out flyers about the dangers of the general's victory. She remembers that the adults were worried he would make everyone go bankrupt. Toño must have been exhilarated when Pastrana won the elections. But many claimed his victory had nothing to do with inked fingers, that the results that made my Conservative grandfather happy had been rigged. After this day, things changed in Colombia.

University students, inspired by the Paris riots of 1968 and by the wave of leftist activity that the Cuban revolution was engendering in most Latin American countries, took to the streets. I read about it at night in the West Village: When the first votes were counted, General Rojas was leading the elections. His sympathizers started celebrating, but not for long. Information on the election process was stopped. When it was reinstated again, Pastrana was announced as the newly elected president. To quell the commotion on the street, the military imposed a state of emergency. It must have been after my bedtime curfew when they announced it because I don't remember that night. My friend David does. He remembers being in the kitchen with the maids listening to the news coming in on the radio. "It was more exciting than scary," he tells me now, in a phone conversation from our homes in New York City.

Up to now I had not realized that as a child I had lived under curfew, a word that I associate with the Dirty War of Argentina and Chile's days of Augusto Pinochet. Unlike the Argentinians and the Chileans, I never saw tanks rolling down our streets. I never heard of people disappearing. I do remember the young Spanish priest visiting one day from the slums where my mother and her friends volunteered getting up abruptly, insisting against my mother's protestations that he had to leave to get back to The Forest, the name of the slum where he headed the Church. The roads were bad due to the rain and he was in danger of not making the curfew imposed by the government. I remember that he mentioned police and streets. I knew that parents told children what time they had to be home; I hadn't known God told priests the same boring things.

When Misael Pastrana became president, many of the student activists splintered off from Marulanda's organization, especially those that sympathized with the FARC. The young students and Manuel Marulanda had different styles. Manuel Marulanda was a simple country man who wore military uniforms and rubber boots, and they were city brats with long hair who wore bell-bottoms and platform shoes. The students believed that a revolution had to include books, music, and fun. And above all, *picardía*, mischief. The students realized that the peasant leader had no sense of humor and was prejudiced against whoever was not a man that toiled the land.

One of the new student groups named itself the Movement April 19, after the date of the fraudulent elections. It soon became known as the M-19; and to its many sympathizers in those days it became more affectionately known as el Eme, Spanish for the letter *M*. Marulanda's group had the mentality of the men of his region: introverted, early-risers, disciplined, untrusting, country men. Marulanda has been a fighter since La Violencia days, a Liberal from the Andes. He was interested in fighting Colombian Conservatives, landowners, and the military. The directorate of the M-19 was the opposite. They were young, urban, and educated. They grew up with Che Guevara, Bob Dylan, and parties. Many were *costeños*. In the words of Jaime Bateman, one of the group's founders: "The revolution is a party. The revolution is not just about having enough to eat; it's about being able to eat what we like to eat."

We had just moved into our house when I first heard of the M-19. And it was not from my schoolmates chanting or at family lunches where the words "Conservative" and "Liberal" were used in all descriptions of events, of people, of moments. I was thirteen years old and was not yet as politicized as Emma, who tells me she made bets during election time. I spent my nights wide-awake, fearful of thieves and shadows, barely getting any rest. Every night I would try to crawl into my sister's bed, then my brother's, my mother's or the maid's, but no one would have me. My sister would kick me to the floor, as if I were an extra pillow in her way. There were nights I just sat on the big chair in my parents' room bundled like a ball. It was a mystery to me how anyone could sleep so soundly knowing what could happen in their sleep.

When it was time to go to school, I was exhausted. I was so tired that I would pretend to shower just to put in a few more minutes of sleep. I would double-lock the brass knob to the bathroom door, turn the shower on, and lie down on the cold marble floor wrapped in a towel. The extra minutes ended with a shout from my brother saying, "I'm leaving you if you don't hurry." Unshowered, without saying a word, I threw on clothes and walked to the car.

Three years had passed since April 19, 1970, the day my grandfather explained that voting Conservative was an obligation for me. Misael Pastrana was still president. On my way to school one morning, I saw red letters scribbled on the yellow walls of the building in front of our house. In big letters, the kind that would be called graffiti now, letters that looked like they had been painted in a hurry, the message read simply "M-19." I looked at it as we drove to school and wondered if the thieves I was expecting every night had done that, but I was too sleepy to say anything. By the time I came back home, the letters were gone. And I don't remember seeing anything like that again.

Now I know that signs like that had appeared in other places. The M-19 acted more like a rock band than a revolutionary group. To introduce themselves to Colombians, they ran ads in newspapers that read: "Parasites? Worms? Lack of Memory? Inactivity? M-19 is coming." Everyone was convinced it was some kind of quack medication. "Wait for the M-19. It's coming soon."

On a regular January afternoon in 1974, they finally arrived. They came in uninvited, slipping into Simón Bolívar's museum and stealing his sword, striking at nothing more and nothing less than Colombia's main symbol of national pride. They were going for undivided attention and they got it. I ask Emma, David, and Allegra if they remember the M-19's coup. None of us does, not even Emma, the most political of the bunch. We remember our parents giving us voting ballots to play with, Misael Pastrana's elections, the announcement of Pinilla's defeat. We all participated, in a way, in our parents' politics, but none of us had any recollection of the young rebels. I am mystified that a momentous occurrence like this, the stealing of Simón Bolívar's sword by cheeky rebels, could escape us. Simón Bolívar was almost as important as Jesus Christ.

The M-19 targeted the Liberator's sword because to the urban revolutionaries, the dagger was sharpened with "the spirit of independence" and its handle was made with "dreams of freedom." Bolívar's sword—be it the one he used in his many battles or the fancy one that was given to him by Peru—was very symbolic. Stealing it had been a way for the M-19 leaders to separate themselves from the autocratic and countryside ways of the FARC.

In the early seventies, Manuel Marulanda ordered Lucho Otero, one of his commanders, to form an urban cell. Otero called on his university pals, mainly middle-class public school kids, although the call reached the boys of the elite, especially those in Bogotá, who were already hooked up to what was going on around the world. A few I've met tell me today that, as a form of rebellion, they abandoned going to school in the United States and enrolled at the National University, known to the establishment as a Communist rathole. The military watched carefully and at every chance they got, they stopped students' protests and shut down left-leaning magazines. The stories that I learned in my political science textbooks about military authoritarianism were to a lesser degree happening in Colombia and neither I nor my professors at the University of

Michigan were too interested. (I have always been surprised about the lack of academics who specialize in Colombia on U.S. campuses.)

At the Nacional, Otero recruited Jaime Bateman, a *costeño,* a typical happy-go-lucky guy who was also a serious thinker. He believed in making history with humor. If Manuel Marulanda's style was rigid and ascetic, in the style of Che Guevara, Bateman was more like Camilo Cienfuegos, the Cuban revolutionary with the Caribbean soul who was always playing jokes on the strident Argentinian. Bateman had read that the Tupamaros, the Uruguayan rebel group, had once stolen the flag of José Gervasio Artigas, their liberator. So why not do something similar? thought Bateman. But when he went to Marulanda with his idea to steal Bolívar's sword, Marulanda scoffed at the notion: What a waste of time, Marulanda replied. He asked how Bateman could think about daggers in museums when Colombia's peasantry needed to revolt? Pranks are for spoiled rich children.

Marulanda reminds me of my grandfather (even if he would roll in his grave at my thought). To these men, who proudly call themselves *hombres del campo,* or men of the country, city life, books, and ideas are for sissies, spoiled boys like my father, who was always quoting economists, or like Bateman. It didn't matter if they believed in the free-market like my father or in a state-controlled economy like the M-19 boys, they were seen with suspicion by the men who'd spent their lives cultivating the land.

Jaime Bateman wanted to follow through with his plan, so much so that he abandoned the FARC. He believed in the importance of urban movements. Taking Bolívar's sword associated the M-19 with a brand of nationalism. Bolívar fought against Spanish rule; he too, like the members of the *Eme,* was a well-bred, well-traveled, and well-read young man who fought to liberate his people. Jaime Bateman identified with Simón Bolívar. The irony is that so did my father the Conservative economist.

Legend has it that the sword was taken from Bolívar's villa in the center of Bogotá to the M-19's favorite brothel and then to the home of their favorite poet. It made a few more rounds before it ended up in Cuba six years later. By 1986, the M-19 had so many sympathizers in Latin America that many wanted to be the custodian of Bolívar's sword. The Order of the Guardians of the Sword was formed. Its members included Omar Torrijos, the Panamanian dictator who negotiated the return of the Panama Canal to the Panamanians from the United States—the same man who granted safe passage to arms, dollars, and whomever believed in fighting American imperialism. And it included the Mothers of the Plaza de Mayo, the Argentinian women who demanded answers from the military, whose children were disappearing because of their parents' left-leaning tendencies. After the M-19 negotiated amnesty and became a political party in 1989, the sword was returned to Bolívar's house.

I HAD NO WAY OF KNOWING REVOLUTION WAS BREWING IN BARRANQUILLA. It was not going to be through my family; and none of the boys who attended my American high school or hung out with us at el Country Club showed any interest in subversive politics. But outside the sheltered enclaves of El Prado and Riomar, there were boys like Horacio Brieva. While I hung posters of David Cassidy on my closet door and Allegra hung Donny Osmond posters in hers, Horacio decorated his wall with images of Ho Chi Minh. I read about this in Horacio's memoir, a book that David gave me a few months after settling in the Village with his family. *Tales of My Generation* is Brieva's account of his days as a member of the M-19. As I read it in my apartment in New York, a whole new Barranquilla opened up, one with professors who sneak Maoist manifestos to their students, who talk to them about Marx while drinking at brothels, and young converts, who like Brieva, throw Molotov cocktails at the police. While Emma, David, Allegra, and I lip-synched "The Star Spangled Banner" on the front lawn of our American school in El Prado, Horacio marched the streets of *el centro,* the downtown where we, the girls of el Parrish, seldom ventured. To go downtown was *corroncho,* a word that defines things from low rent to not cool.

Brieva, who was a member of the Popular Army, modeled after Mao's, writes that he was convinced that their "communist troops would enter the capitals of Colombia." To us, all this would also be considered *corroncho.* It didn't have an American component.

To crack down on the rebelling youth like Brieva, the government fought them with an iron fist. But it seems everyone was pretty radical and intolerant. The rebels were too. The ELN had draconian rules. In the jungles and the hills they had their own judicial system. They held "revolutionary trials." The price for suspicion of treason or dissent was death.

By 1974, the M-19, the FARC, and the ELN were working hard to bring revolution to Colombia. Even if their styles were at odds, the three groups believed in one thing: the overthrow of Colombia's government and the installation of some sort of Communism-inspired power through the armed struggle. There was the recalcitrant FARC, composed of men who had started as Liberal armies in the forties. Then the M-19, popular among young men and women, mostly middle- and upper-class city students, with a certain amount of education and even a touch of brattiness. Among its sympathizers were the children of captains of industry and newspapers. My uncle Agustín has told me he liked them too. The ELN was closer to Fidel Castro's way of fighting mixed in with Christian compassion. It was a favored rebel group for priests. "Liberation theology" as the Marxist-inspired Catholics called their beliefs included priests in long black robes and guns. Many of its leaders were in fact Jesuit priests who had come from Spain. I wonder now if the young and handsome priests that came to visit my mother and liked playing minisoccer with my brother on the beach were what my grandmother disapprovingly calls Red Fathers. One day, the Spanish priests (that my mother liked and my grandmother didn't) vanished. They stopped coming around to visit and I kind of missed their energy. They were always so engaging and they brought my sister and me tiny plastic bags filled with those white circles of bland wafer served at mass as the body of Christ. My sister and I liked to eat them with butter and orange marmalade or we would give them as communion to our dolls. Our communion hosts were unblessed, of course. My grandmother was appalled.

In 1975, armed struggle was the leitmotif for the young generation. My uncle, a law student in Medellín at the time, remembers the concerts with the protest songs inspired by the singer-songwriters coming out of communist Cuba. It was a good year for guerrillas: Saigon had fallen; Fidel had risen. As guerrillas got popular, the government got repressive. If in Cuba the youth was being arrested for listening to the Beatles, in Colombia they were being tortured for calling Cuba the first free territory in the Americas.

But it was one thing for Agustín to sing along to Sylvio Rodriguez, the Cuban troubador of revolutionary hymns, and another to find out that the rebels had arrived at his father's farm in the Perijá Hills. In May 1976 they came up through the state of Bolívar and advanced forward through the plains to the east, settling outside the hills of the farm. Once there, they established the Front Camilo Torres, named after the young Colombian priest who embraced liberation theology and joined the ELN only to be killed three months later during his first ambush as a rebel. The ELN came to the Perijá Hills because they had sympathizers from the states of Bolívar and Santander, who migrated north looking for work as pickers in the cotton fields.

Communist guerrillas might have been lurking but my grandfather was busy planting cotton. Colombia had discovered a golden crop—"white gold" it was called. Landowners turned grazing grounds into cotton fields, more than half a mllion acres of land was converted in this way. More than 100,000 men were needed to pick the cotton, and many of those men who came to work the white gold bonanza came from areas with a fighting past.

From the hills, the rebels observed. They watched how the cowboys grazed cattle all day and how their friends worked the fields. After dusk, they would move around. "They were not exactly soldiers, not even advisors yet, but irregulars, working in remote places under little direct authority, acting out their fantasies with more freedom than most men ever know," writes Joe Broderick, the biographer of the ELN, in *The Invisible Rebel.* It took them a year to really settle down. By 1978, they had no more than forty rebels working with them but they were in no hurry. The conditions had to be right. And they were slowly letting themselves be heard.

"AQUÍ, AQUÍ, EL CARMEN." THE VOICE COMING IN OVER THE RADIO TRANSMITter was fraught with a sense of urgency that made my grandfather jump from his seat and run so fast that my grandmother yelled, "Gabriel, *cuidado,* be careful or you'll fall." I usually liked the sound of the *radio teléfono,* a huge black box that my grandfather kept on the terrace next to his bedroom in Barranquilla. It was always on, its scratchy static providing the background in conversations, chess games, and dinners. We always skirted it when we ran to and fro from the terrace to the garden during our requests to the purveyor of our whims. A distant voice broke in several times each day, sounding like it was coming up from the bottom of the ocean for a quick gasp of air: "El Carmen here? Do you hear me? Roger." If I ran fast enough, I could pick up the microphone and say, "*Sí. Sí.* We hear you. Roger." There were no phone lines in El Carmen, so this was the only way my grandfather could communicate with the overseers when he was in Barranquilla. Conversation was usually short, covering details about the weather and the cattle that ended in a *todo bien, cambio y fuera*—everything is fine, over and out. Abuelo Gabriel came back the night of the urgent call smoking two cigarettes. He held one in his mouth and another one, also lit, tight between his fingers.

"Your turn," my grandmother said motioning toward the chessboard, but he was not listening. He took two drags and put the two cigarettes out, then lit a fresh one before making a phone call. A few minutes later, Guillermo, the cousin-confidant, showed up and the two of them spoke in private. Then my father arrived, followed by my mother. Everyone had worried expressions and I only knew something was wrong when Tía Luisa showed up and paid me no attention whatsoever.

I remember hearing something about "a tiger" and only now do I know that Abuelo Gabriel had heard that the guerrillas had killed a few of his cows and had threatened to kidnap my grandfather unless he agreed to send them meat every month. What he was saying about "the tiger" became his mantra as the guerrillas settled outside the borders of his land, making demand after demand: "If they want the tiger, well, let them come and try to get the tiger."

7

MAKING PLANS AS A JOURNALIST

I've been in Barranquilla a week now, trying to keep busy while Agustín figures out a way for me to get to the farm, but in truth I *am* busy. Every day, I have an invitation to keep. The word is out that I'm in town and everyone wants to do something for me. Family, old friends, cousins, my mother's friends all call to welcome me, to say hello, and to let me know that they would like me to accept *una atención,* in other words, a visit. One day it's my aunt Cecilia, who offers to make the fish and coconut rice she knows I like so much; the next day it's a tea with my mother's friend and after that it's a visit at my cousin Alicia's. And in Barranquilla, as I should remember, *atenciones* are not hurried affairs. No matter how long I've been away, or how much I have decided to give my back to Barranquilla and to the people who saw me grow up, I am still that young girl, and perhaps only that. It is a strange feeling. I say yes to all of the invitations.

During the *atenciones* I try to keep the journalist at bay. There is no room for her here, even when I hear comments that just make me want to run to the bathroom and scribble in my pad so that I don't forget them. I like to sit around these women talking together uncensored and unrestrained. It allows me to take the temperature of cultural politics, important to my idea that more than the fight among armed illegal groups, many of Colombia's ills come from the power structures inside the homes, many of which have masters and servants living as if it were eighteenth-century feudalism. "Vicky is fine," a friend's mother tells me at a tea party when I ask her about her daughter, a schoolmate who is now married and lives in Madrid. "But I'm worried about my granddaughter. You know that to have live-in help is very expensive there and so Vicky doesn't have a maid. And my little granddaughter is growing up like that." These same ladies point and scream, "*Mátenlos.* Kill them," when the television shows images of Manuel Marulanda and his rebel group. My grandmother spews out "atheist, Communists" when they appear on her TV.

To assuage the need to report I tell my cousin Alicia to accompany me to el Country Club where as a teenager I spent every free hour we had. On Saturday mornings I went for a tennis lesson and a swimming lesson; as I grew older I went to sunbathe in a bikini and eat lunch—a grilled cheese sandwich and a lemonade brought to me by the same smiling waiter that we all called Condorito, because he looked like the popular comic book character with that name. Alicia tells me that she doesn't hang out much at the club but she and I drive around the grounds one afternoon. "It's changed now that Barranquilla is so big. You hardly know who anyone is anymore," she says. The clay tennis courts are still here, intact, even López, the same instructor who taught me how to serve, is standing by the water fountain. And so is the new generation, a cluster of teenagers that look and act exactly like my friends and I did when we came to hang out at the club and anything—a new tin of tennis balls or a parfait—was brought to us by waiters, and we just signed our parent's name. I can imagine them lip-synching to the new American pop songs and speaking in English to feel different and special.

A week into my mission to bring war upon Colombians and I am yet to find someone ready to take me on. No one is at war here. Maybe I will ask these kids. I wonder what they think of the war or if they also think there is no war, just a bunch of *hijueputa* guerrillas "shitting" on Colombia. But I am finding out that it hasn't been easy for me to bring up the topic either.

It is perhaps knowing that I have to be patient, as Agustín told me, that prevents me from asking. I don't want to sabotage my mission. When I call him every day for an update, the most I get out of him is "I'm working on it."

Today he has asked me to go to his office, so I am expecting that we are advancing some. As I'm getting ready to head out, I hear my aunt Luisa's voice floating in from the other room. Her block has no electricity and she needs to plug in her computer. Luisa, my mother's oldest sister and my godmother, is one of the people who I hold dearest in my heart. Luisa is my mother with spunk. While my mother is perfectly poised and quiet, my aunt is loud, a bit of a troublemaker, and definitely opinionated.

I don't want to rush out on her; but I also know that if I stay up visiting with her, lunch would turn into dinner and once it's dark I'll have to wait another day to see Uncle Agustín. She intercepts me when José comes in to tell me he is ready to drive me. "Where are you going?" she asks. Reluctantly, I tell her. "I'll come along. I haven't seen Agustín in a while." That's exactly what I was afraid of.

Agustín and Luisa were by far my two favorite adults when I was a child, so I'm in a bit of a bind. I always had a special relationship with Aunt Luisa. To Tía Luisa, unlike my sister and her own daughter, Alicia, I could do no wrong. If my mother criticized me, she defended me. If my hair was too long for my mother's taste, it was perfect for my aunt. On my sporadic visits to Barranquilla, she would bend over backward to make sure I was comfortable and not bored. She would call my friends and tell them I was coming. She would have Estella, her cook, make *marmaón,* the Middle Eastern dish of chicken over handmade wheat balls the size of pearls that I like so much but takes three days to make. "For you, I will tell her to do it."

This time, however, I know I'm asking for much more than a home-cooked meal. Going to El Carmen would pose a huge risk not only to myself, but to Agustín. I also know that Agustín has agreed to take me not because he is floored by the brilliance of my hypothesis, or eager to have me write about the family farm but simply because I asked him to. Like my aunt, he has always indulged me.

I am not looking forward to broaching the topic with Luisa there. Agustín and I had been discussing my trip to El Carmen for months and we both knew it was best if no one knew. When I got the assignment from the *New York Times Magazine,* he never rejected outright my risky request, putting me off gently by claiming "the conditions aren't right," promising, "let me see what I can do." This time things were moving ahead.

When Luisa and I arrive at the bare-bones offices with about fifteen employees, she is treated as "one of the owners" in that Barranquilla way, which is with respect and familiarity. They all smile, especially the coffee lady, a stick-thin middle-aged woman who giggles from being so nervous every time she brings the tray with the tiny coffee cups. "I know how you like it," she says to my aunt. I stand by Luisa's side, but to her I am a stranger. When Luisa says "my niece," as I meet the rest of the crew, they say hello and when she adds, "Francia's daughter" they ooh and aah. I'm not sure if that means "of course" or "oh my."

Agustín emerges from his office. He is slight and about five foot eight but he hugs like a hulk. Flashing a generous, perfect smile, he draws us both into a welcoming embrace. "Come in," he says. "I'm happy. I just received some new photos from the plantation." We stand in front of a group of enlarged photographs. My uncle points out the new reservoir. It took two years to build and it has just been completed this week. He has never seen it in person. He proudly says that it should make the next map of Colombia, that it is so much larger than many of the lakes already on the map. "Don't you want to go see it for yourself?" I ask Luisa. I've been to El Carmen no more than handful of times in my life, but this was where she had grown up. Without missing a beat, she looks at me, "No thank you, I want to enjoy my grandchildren."

"We are going to go," I say almost like a tease but more as a test—a temperature-taking exercise—and wait for her reaction. It is one thing telling an editor in New York City that I will write a story about going to my grandfather's farm and another thing saying it to my opinionated aunt. Luisa is silent, not sure if I'm joking, so I add, "He's coming with me," elbowing my uncle.

"That is his problem," she shoots back.

My aunt's sarcasm belies a serious consideration—if we go to El Carmen we put ourselves out as targets to any of the rebel groups in the area; both the FARC and the ELN, they tell me, would do anything to kidnap a member of the El Carmen family. Both groups have rebel checkpoints on all the roads that lead to the farm. If I drive there myself, if José drives me, or even if I hire a taxi, chances are at one of those checkpoints, they'll ask for my *cédula,* that piece of identification that all Colombians are obligated to carry to tell everyone from the check-accepting cashiers to the police to the rebels who you really are. If I am asked for my *cédula* I am literally screwed. I understand now why they use "giving papaya" as an expression, because if you give yourself up, that's what happens.

If I am stopped, I would most likely be dragged out of the car and taken up to a rebel camp, then held in custody until I am released after a negotiated ransom is paid or kept as a bargaining chip and/or a lesson to landowners like my family or liberated by the army or killed in the attempt. All of which have happened to people I know. "I will gladly leave my *cédula* at home," I tell my aunt, when she reminds me of this likelihood. "I hate the picture of myself in it," I say, offering humor to the situation. It was taken in 1980 when I came of age and it was required by law that I have one. But the black-and-white contrast is so primitive that it looks like a daguerrotype from the 1800s that I recently saw of Monsieur Maurice Montblanc.

"I can pretend I am an American journalist," I say, seriously considering this option. "I can say I am one." After all, I have a New York state driver's license that says my name is S. M. Paternostro and I have an assignment letter from the most respectable *New York Times.*

"The problem is not that you are Colombian," my aunt offers. "The problem is that you are a Montblanc." I might not have personally identified with the ways of my Montblanc grandparents, but their name is still on my Colombian ID. In Colombia no matter whatever else I am, I am Silvana Paternostro Montblanc. I cannot hide from the rebels, my aunt is telling me, because they will know that I am exactly what they are looking for. More than thirty-seven people with that name have been kidnapped.

Montblanc comes with connotations of land and province in a country with a huge Marxist movement. And the ideas that I embraced, even if naively, during my college days in Michigan are now putting me on the danger seat. I'm in a no-win identity crisis. I knew that last name meant something and that it was a good name to have, but I had not grown up as a member of that family.

I knew my grandfather was powerful in some way that I could not define. Birthright in Colombia sets one's destiny in stone. As much as I do not identify myself as a Montblanc, for all practical purposes, here I am one. My passport is Colombian, not American, and it clearly identifies me as Silvana María Paternostro Montblanc.

Today, sitting in my uncle's office, it is clear that my aunt and uncle have not changed. Luisa has never beaten around the bush, and explains why going to El Carmen is "insane" while Agustín prefers to say that it is "not advisable."

"He is coming," I repeat, pointing at my uncle. "With him," she echoes wryly, pointing at him too. "Worse. He can't hide it. For him it's double." His name is Agustín Montblanc Montblanc. It's not only Colombian landowners who are at risk, she tells me, citing the example of the photojournalist who a few weeks ago had taken a picture the FARC didn't like. To teach him a lesson, they had kept him captive for a week. She adds another example for emphasis, describing how the FARC had just kidnapped a German oil executive and threatened a UN official. "Human rights groups and journalists like you say the army does not respect the Geneva convention," she tells me, "but the guerrilla only respects those they find convenient at the time they find convenient."

My uncle is silent. I take it to mean that he agrees with her. Still, I think that he wants to go as much as I do: He wants to see that reservoir. Everyone who had worked on it had been able to see it, to walk on the empty pit when it was being dug, to swim in it now that it is a lake. "How great would it be to be able to go waterskiing?" he had said when he was showing us the picture a few moments ago.

AFTER AN HOUR OF THE THREE OF US BOUNCING THE ALTERNATIVES BACK AND forth, I decide to call Max and put him on speakerphone. What started for both of us as a half-baked idea of running around reporting and romancing had turned for Max too into a real commitment and a professional relationship to report on Colombia. Max had found his Colombian war. It is a country that grabs you, one way or another. Our failed romance had turned into a solid friendship, and when I got the *Times*'s assignment, Max offered to be the photographer for the story.

I ask Max what he thinks about the different possibilities of getting there. I think maybe I can have José, my grandmother's driver, or Juan, my uncle's driver, take me. They often serve as messengers between the estate and Agustín. But that idea is tantamount to inviting trouble. As we know, there are rebel checkpoints on the road every day. I could take the bus, but I had never really traveled by bus in Colombia and I had no idea what to expect if I did. How about my passing as an American journalist. "I mean, I can pass as one," I tell him, with a touch of vanity. "It buys you little these days," he says. He tells me how he had gone to Segovia, a small town in Antioquia with a Colombian journalist because it seemed the paras (paramilitaries) had struck again. They took a winding back road because it was rumored to be beautiful and they also figured it would have fewer checkpoints. The road, part of the path the Spanish opened in colonial times in their search for El Dorado, came to a cross where an entire ELN platoon intercepted them. Max describes them as the skinniest guys he had ever seen. The commander, who informed Max that they were "retaining" him, wore ratty boots with holes instead of soles.

"You can't," Max told him, trying to hide his fear and reminding him that the ELN had a policy not to take journalists, and that taking him could only be called extortion, a highly punished crime. "That's when I realized he was acting on his own. That he was not kidnapping me on any orders but on his own." He told Max he was a commander with a hungry army. When Max handed him his wallet, the rebel commander looked at him and said, "I must make some calls. I know about you Americans who pretend to be journalists and are nothing but CIA. Wait for me over there." Max and the journalist waited for hours. At about five that evening, the commander called Max over to his open-air base. He sat in front of a primitive radio, the antenna wrapped to a skinny tree branch. "I talked to my commander," the revolutionary impersonator informed Max, "and he says you're clean."

But Max was sure it was all an act. "He needed to save face in front of his troop. He would have taken me and traded me." He means he would have sold him to the rebels.

"Were you scared?" I ask, wondering if there is a way to learn how to control fear in the face of hungry and armed men.

"They don't mess around, these guys," he says. "Not the ones that are politically motivated and not the ones that are just plain and simple taking you for their own survival." Max asks me if I can wait for him—he is on his way to do a story in Chiapas and he would be back sometime in mid-September. "I don't know. It all depends on when the conditions are right," I tell him, quoting my uncle.

To pass as a gringa isn't such a great idea after all and I do start to wonder if I'm headed down a path toward self-destruction. I can't deny my need to make things tangible, but I am also finding that before I make grand proclamations as I have been, I must experience life as if I still lived here. Simply jotting down notes from interviews and listening to stories is not enough.

I came to Barranquilla with a mission: to describe the destruction, the violence, the injustice that envelops the place of my childhood. I came absolutely sure of the story I was to tell. At least, that's what I told myself. But I think there is a part of me that is here because I want to stop being alienated from my own people. I want to find out how those I knew and loved as a child survive here today. But I also think I want to reconnect with them. I, the vagrant reporter, inhabitant of small apartments in the West Village, defender of all things labeled American liberal, not Colombian liberal, want to find how the other side of me: the member of a family with land, tap into the girl with the solid home, large family, and tons of friends, wondering what would have happened if I had not left at fifteen.

In the time I've spent away from these streets, Colombia has disintegrated. I remind myself of what has happened. It has become the world's biggest producer and exporter of cocaine. It holds the record for having both the highest murder rate and the highest kidnapping rate of any country in the world. It harbors a guerrilla group that uses kitchen gas tanks as bombs and is incapable of mercy, of liberating a prisoner whose child is on his deathbed and has asked on national television to hug his father before he dies. It also has a paramilitary force that vows to kill every *guerrillero,* even if it means massacring entire towns, children included, with chain saws.

This brutal war between the guerrillas and the paramilitary has intruded on my family's once-happy existence. My grandmother and my uncle live on a seemingly placid street and though they go about their lives without worrying about the state of disintegration around them, they are well aware that the FARC considers them "military objectives," and they cannot take the road trip that had been so much a part of their existence.

I saw my eighty-eight-year-old grandmother this morning, before coming here, rosary in hand, rocking herself in her Viennese chair and I got a kick out of the fact that, to some, she fits such a bellicose label, but I also feel a pang in my stomach, knowing that I had abandoned being part of this life, that I would never feel things as she does. I ask her what it's like not to be able to go back to Asunción, the town where her family has lived for the last one hundred years, now off-limits to them because of kidnapping threats. All they have to see is the last name on your *cédula,* she says, surprising me by how hip she is to the ways of the rebels. She tells me more: She has heard that to fool the rebels, some people have *cédulas* with fake names. My grandmother misses going to visit with family and friends but what hurts her is not being able to go to the wakes and funerals. Still, I tell her in a bout of schizophrenia that she is luckier than the millions of peasants who bear the brunt of the fight and who don't have second homes to run to when the guerrillas or the paramilitary enters their town.

Before we leave, while Luisa is having a conversation with the coffee lady, Agustín pulls me aside to tell me that he has an idea that he needs to check on but he will let me know what he finds out. I feel a rush of excitement—will we finally be able to go?

A few hours later Agustín calls and asks me to come see him again.

"This is the plan," he tells me, leaning on his desk. For seven hundred dollars we can rent a small plane, a six-seater, that can take us there and wait for us. We won't land on El Carmen's airstrip," he tells me, "but I'll ask Sergio if we can use his. It's at the *finca* next to ours—*¿te acuerdas, no?* We'll stay for four hours. The plane will wait for us." Agustín not only misses El Carmen, I can tell from his determination that he wants to defy the people who have sent him on an imposed exile.

We both agree that this will be the chance we take. Agustín mentions needing to make a few phone calls and "arrange for security." I tell him I am not in a hurry—now that I know we have a plan, I'm much more willing to be patient.

I leave my uncle hunkered down in his office. His walls are covered with photographs of the plantation, and a blueprint of the farm rests under the glass of the round conference table; a television runs the latest videotape that he has managed to receive from the farm. Armed with a cellular phone in one hand, he tries to make decisions with Fernando Preciado, the agronomist he has hired as his replacement at the *finca*. Preciado, not being a Montblanc, can live there.

He walks me to the door. A computer specialist is waiting to meet with him. They are installing a WebCam system so that they don't have to rely on tapes—which can be confiscated at checkpoints. "It is the new modern agriculture," he tells me. "It is called precision agriculture."

8

RESEARCHING MY STORY

While I wait for Agustín to set up the trip, I spend my days riding around Barranquilla in José's car, observing, keeping in mind W. H. Auden's words that before there is history there must be observation, something I read in a *New Yorker* piece or in *Harper's* but right now I cannot remember which one of those two magazines it was, those magazines that I read religiously and keep in my bag, waiting for a moment when I can stop and pick them up again in New York. Here, they are as out of place as the clothes I bring. José, the chauffeur, enjoys our outings. I purposely sit in the co-pilot seat, which is not where I should be. Women always sit in the back of chauffeured cars here.

The war killed thirty thousand people last year, and I still have not heard the word mentioned, not once. War is like sex—spoken in secret and filled with innuendoes and euphemisms. It's called the "situation," "the internal conflict," or at most the "armed conflict." People talk about peace instead. Driving around with José, I saw a huge billboard outside the city's main hardware store. Their construction materials, they claim, are building *la paz en Colombia,* Colombia's peace.

One of the places I tell José to take me to is the Nacional Bookstore, Barranquilla's premier bookstore, a chain brand like Barnes & Noble but with the size and service of a mom-and-pop operation. Edgar, the manager, is a personable man, formal because he is a *cachaco,* but who engages me in conversation every time I come in. The store is full of customers asking about the new self-help book. The average adult in Colombia reads less than two books per year. But regardless of reading rates and little interest in high-brow literature, La Nacional is always buzzing, alive with people of all ages. The men buy *El Heraldo,* the local paper, the younger ones get the soccer magazines and leaf through the imported issues of *Popular Mechanics.* The women, without hesitation, grab a few more magazines than the men do. Their selection always includes *Vanidades,* the Latin American woman's bible, no edge to it but reliable in fashion, cooking, and lifestyle pieces. *Hola* is an all-time favorite, a necessity more than a luxury. (If in the United States women follow Hollywood celebrities, in Barranquilla they fixate on European royalty.) The hit of the moment is *Who Moved My Cheese?* Three women, all with drivers waiting for them while they shop like José does for me, come in asking for it and say hello to Edgar, who asks one of his clerks to go fetch a book for the lady, who then takes out her wallet and pays for it. The entire transaction takes less than five minutes. I go at a slower pace, spending hours catching up with some celebrity news in the magazine racks, looking at the books in English that Spanish-speaking publishing houses chose to translate. I ask if there's any James Baldwin—there is not. But I see Dave Eggers and Jonathan Franzen in Spanish, and Barranquilla feels less foreign and less lonely when I can hold a book that is part of my American self.

I ask Edgar to show me what he has on contemporary Colombia, my own euphemism for war. He directs me to a long aisle. There are more titles than I could have imagined. I am the lone customer in this aisle. The saying that books speak volumes is an understatement here. These are a few of the titles I found; they are all in Spanish, so this is my translation: *The Pain of Uncertainty: The Experience of a Kidnap; Fraud in the Election of Pastrana Borrero; Anthology of Corruption in Colombia; The Narco Treasurer; The New Jockeys of Cocaine; Cocaine & Co.; The Economy of War in Colombia; Eight Violentologists Tell Their Stories as Victims of Violence;* and *A Country of Barbarians.* I decide not to purchase any of these damning books about the state of this country. Even if most Colombians do not read them, even if most Colombians want to deny this, the books are there. If any of them is any good is beside the point. Edgar recommends that I take *The Coast's History,* a three-volume account of how *la costa atlántica* developed, by a Marxist anthropologist. I walk over to pay for the books.

I notice *El Heraldo*'s front page in the pile next to the cashiers. There is a half-page photograph of next year's Carnival queen. It is the last week in August and Carnival is in February, six months away, but the blond twenty-one-year-old, the daughter of prominent people, adorns the front page. By her two last names I make out that she is the daughter of Guido and Ilva, two people I vaguely knew when I lived here. That's how easy it is to decipher people's genealogy with this two-last-name system. If I can do it with the Carnival queen, a pretty girl I've never met, the same rule applies to me. The idea of taking the road to El Carmen is feeling less appealing, especially when below her picture, in a small box, I find another reminder: seven people were kidnapped yesterday at checkpoints. This brings the number of kidnappings in the last six weeks to seventy, making Cesár, the state where El Carmen is located, the place where one may likely get snatched. I am glad Agustín came up with the plane option.

Everyone who passes in front of the paper has something to add about *la reina*'s dress; no one and I mean no one comments on the news of the kidnappings. But the reality is that I am looking for the war and they are, rightly or wrongly, putting it out of their minds. They are forgetting that they live in a place that breeds the violence and corruption that results in the sensational titles I found on the books about contemporary Colombia. I want to breathe it all in and they want to breathe it all out, like Virginia Woolf once remarked that one has to do when writing.

On August 8, 2001, the *New York Times* ran a big story about how ranchers in "a swath of northern Colombia that is one of the few rural areas not under the guerrillas' sway" have created an eight-thousand-man militia, known as the United Self-Defense Forces, or the AUC, and it "has wiped three rebel groups from the area in a fierce campaign characterized by massacres of peasants and assassinations." I had still been in New York preparing for this trip when I read the story. I ran to my kitchen map and found the state of Córdoba under the right armpit to the north. I called Mario, another Colombian in New York. His grandfather's farm is in Córdoba. Mario and I have had long phone conversations about the paras, and how popular they are among the population, even if the *Times* reports that in the last eight months they have killed nearly 1,300 people. I had circled the seventh paragraph, which reads: "But perhaps more troubling to Colombia's democracy is how outwardly respectable citizens, fed up with the government's failure to control the guerrillas, have willingly financed the paramilitary group." The story went on to quote an established rancher: "How do you defend yourself against a well-armed, well-trained and numerous guerrilla force? With an equally well-armed, well-trained and numerous organization." Another source, a former member knowledgeable about the organization's fund-raising told the *Times*'s reporter that if the government legitimized the United Self-Defense Forces, "many people would confess that they are giving money."

I cannot help but notice that in the two weeks I've been in Colombia I have yet to read about the paramilitary. They are completely absent from the local news.

WHEN ANDRÉS PASTRANA, SON OF MISAEL PASTRANA, WAS ELECTED PRESIDENT in May 1998, he promised to bring an end to the conflict through a peace negotiation with the FARC. He ordered a large swath of land in the south to be emptied out of all military presence and handed it to the FARC leadership.

From there, he said, the government and the rebels would negotiate a cease-fire. They would exchange kidnapped soldiers, industrialists, politicians—there were three thousand men and women held in captivity—for political prisoners. It was called a humanitarian exchange. They would exchange notes about how to make Colombia a better society, discussing agrarian reforms, health care, and education. Ten countries, the Catholic Church, and a United Nations negotiator would serve as witnesses and facilitators of this historical and conciliatory gesture from both sides. There were two thorny subjects: For the government, the rebels demand that the paramilitary be dismantled; for the rebels, the government's insistence that they stop kidnapping.

Even President Clinton was surprised by President Pastrana's largesse. Pastrana later recalls in his memoir that when he first met Clinton at the White House, a meeting arranged at the last minute by a friend of both presidents, the U.S. president had a map of Colombia spread out in the Oval Office. When Pastrana walked in, the American president's welcoming remark was "So Andrés, what is this?" circling with his finger the demilitarized zone, an area as big as Switzerland. If Colombians, like Clinton, had been surprised in 1998 by the boldness of such a move, three years later they are fed up with his antics.

I notice how different the FARC is treated now. The guerrillas were previously treated like drug dealers. They always existed, but no one really paid much attention to them. Unless you absolutely had to, unless they came into your *finca*'s living room, life was about Carnivals and not about the group of men who once in a while kidnapped someone you knew. The FARC were *guerrilleros,* which is synonymous with "bandit," and undeserving of being recognized as an army. War, they said, was a respectable thing, fought only by armies, like the English fought the Germans during World War II. The FARC was not worthy of being seen as fighters of wars. The FARC, the government said, could not fight a war because they were not an army or important political actors.

Now, with the demobilized zone they are known worldwide. They've been interviewed by CNN. They've traveled to the European parliament. FARClandia, as it is now called, has become the latest hot spot for political tourism. U.S. congressmen have visited, so has the founder of AOL and the head of the New York Stock Exchange. Colombians are baffled by the popularity of the place. Every freelance journalist I bump into or have a beer with at bars in New York is pitching a story. Many journalists I know tell me the FARC has a press office in the jungle and that they will gladly put me in touch with the rebel who handles foreign reporters.

In three years, Pastrana has gotten himself in a tough spot. Those who voted for him are now disappointed at how much he has conceded to "those murderers," which is how everyone I've met this past week thinks of them. "For God's sake, one Colombian is kidnapped by these gorillas, I mean, guerrillas, every three hours and he insists on talking to them," one of his most staunch support-ers spewed on television while we watched an evening newscast. "They are monkeys; that's what they are."

THIS SUNDAY, *EL HERALDO* COMES WITH A SPECIAL CARNIVAL SUPPLEMENT. There is the queen again, this time making the rounds, visiting the poor neigh-borhoods, explaining to all her subjects that this Carnival will be the Carnival of Peace; that on February 2002, the country should forget about "the demilita-rized zone" in El Caguán and come to Barranquilla because for three days it will become the "demilitarized zone" of Happy Colombia. "Come on down to this zone," she says, inviting everyone, this one promises to be much more fun.

Lost among the splendor of the queen's costume and the smiles of the peo-ple celebrating is a black-and-white photograph of six men, looking very seri-ous, sitting around a table. Three of them are in camouflage, their rifles resting on their knees. I recognize Manuel Marulanda, the Liberal of the Violencia days, now a man in his seventies, perhaps the oldest living guerrilla the world has ever seen, still fighting for social justice. But according to most people I speak to about him, he is the symbol of the devil. I have yet to hear anyone refer to him as anything more than a murderer and a drug trafficker. He sits with a handful of his commanders and I wonder if any of these is Simón Trinidad. Born Ricardo Palmera, Trinidad is the son of the *costa*'s upper class. I have fam-ily links of sorts to this FARC commander who refers to his upbringing and his class background as the only shameful thing in his life. He calls it his *lunar*, an imperfection in his birth, like the birthmark I sport on my left foot.

I am fascinated by the story of this man. Palmera has a similar trajectory as my father: He studied abroad, he worked as a banker, he taught economics, he was wed at the country club and was raising a family. However, one day he left it all behind and joined the FARC. I had heard that he not only had joined the rebels but that he had personally made a list of everyone in the region who should be kidnapped. As a banker to *finca* owners for twenty years, he knew what everyone was worth. I had heard that he handled El Carmen's lines of credit. But I have no way of identifying him in the picture. The caption does not name the rebels.

On the other side of the table there are men with softer faces and wrinkled city clothes. The young members of the president's cabinet face the rebels. I notice the round baby face of the peace commissioner in his preppy clothes. They also go unnamed.

The government and the FARC have been sitting at this table under a thatched roof in the middle of the jungle talking about peace and all that has happened is that violence has increased. Thousands of displaced families sleep outside of Barranquilla's cathedral and I have not heard anyone connect the new faces of people who walk the neighborhoods of Riomar looking for work and settling for anything, a piece of bread, a banana, or a peso bill to feed their families, with the war that is being fought in the countryside. When people read the paper in the morning they skip the news about the *desplazados* and about the DMZ, and go straight to *Sociales* to see what kind of dress the Carnival queen wore.

ON MONDAY, AS I WAIT FOR AGUSTÍN TO CALL, I CONTINUE TO EXPLORE THE city of my past. I ask José to take me to El Prado where most of the mansions built by my friend's grandparents have been turned into banks, supermarkets, clinics, and kindergartens. I also want to visit the mansion that has been turned into the museum of Barranquilla's history and that has the wonderful anachronistic name of the Romantic Museum. Two-storied with a light yellow colonnade entrance, it was built by a German immigrant couple during the heyday of the 1930s. Their two daughters, who never married, spent their time collecting historical memorabilia and when the last of the two died, she bequeathed the house and their collection to the city. I am looking for memories— and explanations for the war—wherever I can find them. I figured the city's museum, el Museo Romántico, might hold some clues.

I invite José in but he declines. The part of his job that he enjoys the most seems to be waiting. He parks the car with a smile, waving to the fruit vendor and the lottery seller; it is obvious by their response that they are friends. He walks to the *mataratón* tree that serves as a mammoth umbrella for the street vendors and those waiting for a bus, a taxi, or a lover to arrive. He joins a group of men leaning against the solid trunk, other *choferes* waiting too. I try to make sense of this. Does the fact that José does not want to know the history of his city, the fact that he is happy just waiting, especially under the shade of a tree, is that related to why there is chaos in this country? They sure seem indifferent to the way traffic swirls and tangles and horns blow and people scream around them.

Walking into the museum is like walking into my friend Pablo's mansion down the boulevard where I spent many afternoons. As a teenager I loved going to Pablo's parties. He called them friends' gatherings and they always consisted of six guests, always the same ones. We would arrive at six sharp, and talk and dance to American music. We loved "Band on the Run" and "Bennie and the Jets." We drank Coca-Cola or pineapple juice served in tall glasses of fine-cut crystal. At about eight we were served dinner, usually lasagna and salad, and we all knew to put the starched linen napkins on our laps. By ten-thirty, Alfonso, the house butler and driver, would knock on the door announcing he was ready. We would all squeeze into the back of a 1950s Cadillac, the kind with fins, as Alfonso deposited each one of us at our respective homes, never leaving until he made sure we were safely inside the house.

The Romantic Museum has the same musty smell that comes from the blend of tropical humidity and cold air coming from air-conditioning units in every room. Like at Pablo's house, the windows here are kept closed, the curtains drawn and the crystal chandeliers illuminated in the middle of the day. Room after room of memorabilia only tells me that Barranquilla's history— which I did not know, for it was not taught in my American school—is extraordinarily ordinary. Forget the conquistadors, the city was founded in 1611 by a lost and thirsty cow. A shepherd found her drinking from the river's bank and as it was so close to the water, he stayed; others followed suit. The newcomers would soon start referring to their new settlement as Barranquilla, which means the small bank in the river.

The glass cases of the museum do not have Magna Cartas; they have Carnival gowns and scepters. There were no independence heroes born here; we have no founding fathers in our city's annals. Our history began when foreigners started arriving in the mid-1800s with the founding of the port of Sabanilla. Boats arrived from everywhere filled with men, women, families escaping poverty or persecution; Barranquilla claimed itself as the cosmopolitan, bustling port city of South America. I see photographs of steamboats that seem to tell the stories of Joseph Conrad and Mark Twain. My father's family owned three: the Barranquilla, the Atlántico, and the Paternostro; they went up and down the Magdalena River. I now have seen them in Nereo's photos.

A row of mildewed black-and-white photographs shows the captains of industry that turned Barranquilla into the Golden Gate. Among the portraits is General Vengoechea dressed in formal military galore and brandishing a mustache of the turn of the century. The rest of the celebrated men have foreign-sounding names. The boat captains were called William Bradford, Alfred Wessel, and Julian Hoeenisberg. Alfred Steffens was the chemist. The merchants who bought and sold the boat merchandise were called, among many others, Ferhrmans, Stubs, Steggman, Shuttman, Freund, Chapman, Bickman, McCausland, O'Byrne, and Hannabergh. The first photographer, Emmanuel Certain, came from France in 1867 and the first filmmaker, Allegra's great-grandfather, came from Italy. So that's what Karl C. Parrish looked like, lanky with a receding headline. And that is what El Prado's boulevard looked like with its houses of cream-colored columns and verandas, each mansion sporting a Ford parked outside.

And now the women of Barranquilla, all wearing crowns. There is Julia, the Carnival queen of 1899 and Makú, who was elected Miss Colombia the year I left. The crown jewel of the museum is a Hercules typewriter. It has its own glass case. According to the explanation, the machine was used by Gabriel García Márquez when he started his poorly paid journalism career at *El Heraldo*, living in a rented room he shared with prostitutes in a low-rent pension on Bolívar's Boulevard, close to the newspaper's installation.

In those days, García Márquez wrote a column under the peculiar pseudonym of Septimus, after Septimus Warren Smith, the shell-shocked and very quirky war hero who commits suicide in Virginia Woolf's *Mrs. Dalloway*. Woolf describes him as "aged about thirty, pale-faced, beak-nosed, wearing brown shoes and a shabby overcoat, with hazel eyes, which had that look of apprehension in them, which makes complete strangers apprehensive too." García Márquez, a Caribbean through and through, must have felt he identified with this poor Englishman.

Barranquilla's moment of glory happened on December 5, 1919, and it is commemorated here with great fanfare. On that day the first plane to touch South America landed at the mouth of the Magdalena River. They've dedicated an entire room to the seaplane. At last, I think something grand happened here that is pretty historical. Everyone in the world knows about the feats of Charles Lindbergh, Amelia Earhart, and Santos Dumont. But the fact that the pioneers of Latin American aviation came from a Colombian port city is unknown to world history. Like the Panama Canal had done in 1903, making the world closer by boat, the arrival of planes to Barranquilla fifteen years later would be a catalyst for the country's progress. I understand why Barranquilla was known as the Golden Gate and also as the City of Progress, yet it is hard to see how those monikers apply today for something prevented the city from taking that next step. Just like the French traveler had noticed about Barranquilla in 1800 when he described the bourgeoning city as almost First World but not quite. What prevents Barranquilla from making the jump? As I think that to myself, as if on cue, the lights go off and the air conditioner stops humming at the Romantic Museum.

"What happened?" I ask the young man of twenty dressed in olive green who had escorted me around the rooms. He was serving his military requirement, obligatory by law for all men in Colombia, and easy to avoid if you have the right connections. He was in between the two. He didn't have enough pull to get him out of it completely but he had some that kept him away from where the fighting was going on. It was so much better to be a guard at a museum even if the electricity went off almost every afternoon, leaving everyone sweating in the dark.

9

TRICKY, TRICKY

I must shelve my obsession with my road trip—Agustín has warned me: "I hope the *New York Times* doesn't need this right away." I decide to focus on my grandmother, who cannot make sense of why I have descended upon her. I ask Ma Cris one morning to tell me what the road from Barranquilla to El Carmen was like when she and my grandfather took it every week for more than twenty years. I ask with double intentions: as a way to get to know her better and to give her the pleasure of reminiscing. I know she loved taking that road trip. But I am also doing it on the record. I take good mental notes. "What was the road like?" I ask her. "All Fords," she says in her own laconic way, and it takes me a second to understand that by Fords she means the make of the cars. That what she means to say is that because Fords were the cars of choice of *finqueros* in northern Colombia, a road full of Fords to her means the golden days when she and my grandfather and all the other landowners in the region could enjoy the trip back and forth from the city to their farms. She and my grandfather surely did. The road must have been packed with Ford cars that had a driver in the front and a landowner and his wife in the back. Just like they had day laborers to work the land and women, usually their employees' wives, to raise their children, they had men to drive their cars. I'm not even sure my grandfather knew how to drive. Ma Cris, for sure, doesn't.

My grandparents had it all worked out, taking their time, balancing work with pleasure, and going from city to country life. She tells me how, on the same road where her cousin Guillermo was kidnapped, she counted rabbits and deer to entertain her children and keep them from screaming on their way to visit Abuela Eva at the Frenchman's House. She tells me that they left El Carmen at dawn so that they could drive by the river for a swim and be in time for lunch with friends, and then continue on to Santa Marta for a visit at a relative's house, all perfectly timed to arrive in Barranquilla in the early evening so that the driver could rest from the trip after unloading the fruit, meat, and cheese that had been accumulated on the way. Juana, the cook, would transform all that fresh produce into Sunday's lunch, for which we—meaning their children and their children—would all be summoned and expected to attend. Everyone did. I don't know how the adults felt about being on the terrace for hours, captive to my grandfather's whims. But I loved those times, not because I talked to my grandparents or they to me, but because Pretty Bird lived with them.

My grandmother has a set of framed pictures in her bedroom, all of her and Abuelo Gabriel together, which I've started to study whenever she goes to mass, which she does twice a day. It tells the story of them as a couple, with every indication that they were in love for more than fifty years, and they tell the story of a lifestyle that vanished. I see my grandfather on a horse, looking like a darker Clark Gable. In the backdrop, I see a sea of green and white, and I realize they are the cotton fields that afforded my grandparents and their children and grandchildren a comfortable lifestyle. It was a very strange and obsolete one if compared to modern life in America, yet not very different from the life of plantation owners in the antebellum South, comfortable for the masters and full of complications. In the early seventies, Colombia had developed, especially in Medellín, an important textile industry and the government decided to compete with international cotton prices. Instead of the local textile factories having to import cotton, Colombia would produce its own. Many landowners, especially in the north, adhered to the government's plan. My grandfather turned El Carmen's cattle fields into a fluffy white blanket and it paid off. He did not make a fortune that would show up on any list, not even close, but we surely had a lifestyle of luxuries in a city that has a huge disparity between the rich and the poor. But what made my childhood more peculiar was not pecuniary; it was the fact that having land in the countryside afforded us a feudal life of masters and servants in a burgeoning merchant city. I grew up with things that money cannot buy: serfdom. I treated other human beings in ways that could not be bought in a developed society with all the money a fortune might afford.

Before Pretty Bird, I had Imelda to fulfill each one of my whims. Imelda was the eight-year-old who was given to me—yes, given—when I was two and who one day disappeared. But she was only to be replaced by another one. Servants seemed like toys that could talk, dolls that actually responded. When I realized that many of them did not know how to read and write, I asked for a blackboard for Christmas. I became their teacher and I took my job seriously. Using chalks of many colors, I stood in front of the handful of live-in servants giving them lessons and grading their homework. I also decided to teach them English, but when I realized that they didn't know how to pronounce it like I did, when I offered to share my Mother Goose rhymes neither did they know what they were repeating, I could not help myself from making fun of them. It gave me some strange perverse pleasure and so I made the English lessons much longer than the math ones. With other kids from the block we organized talent shows and beauty pageants. As we couldn't round up our busy parents for an audience, we turned to the servants. We would go from house to house summoning them for the show. Sometimes we would even pass out written invitations to the mostly illiterate men and women who worked in our households. I wonder now if they thought of it as an obligation, as part of their chores, or if they actually saw it as fun. The only rule we gave them was that they had to clap very hard after every performance. It got a bit dicier during the beauty competitions because they were put in a bind: they were expected to vote for the girl whose home they worked in, almost like during presidential elections when they were taken to vote Liberal or Conservative depending on the party of their *patrones*.

THE REASON I BELIEVE I FEEL SO DISCONNECTED FROM MY GRANDMOTHER AND think of myself as more of a gringa today stems from the day I entered nursery school, and my own particular fractured destiny was set in motion. My parents abandoned their own parents' traditional notion of education for girls—to sequester them in convents—refusing to send me to La Enseñanza, the all-girl Catholic convent that my mother had attended before she dropped out to marry my father. As long as they were doing things differently than their parents, they might as well go all out and send us to Karl C. Parrish School, a secular—sin number one—and co-ed—sin number two—American school named after a real-estate developer from Boston who made his fortune by selling suburban dreams to Barranquilla's newly enriched merchants, bankers, and professionals in the 1930s. He turned what till then were cow pastures into an enclave of good living for the newly enriched and called it El Prado, The Lawn, where the Romantic Museum and Pablo's house sit. The package included a boulevard lined with these mansions modeled after the ones in Beverly Hills; a majestic hotel, El Prado, more appropriate for a place with a riviera and a film festival than for an industrial port city; a country club with a pool and a golf course. It was inside Mr. Parrish's brainchild that I spent the first fifteen years of my life. And thanks to a worried American father I became the *gringa-barranquillera* that spins out tales from this place.

The Karl C. Parrish School was added to the American-inspired barrio because Nancy Agarino, a young American girl, the daughter of an expat who needed to be schooled the right way, not by nuns, but in English and with an education that would allow her to go to college in the United States. Nancy was the daughter of a high-level executive at the United Fruit Company, the American multinational, the company responsible for the globalization of banana eating (bananas are still, hands down, the number-one fruit consumed around the world) that has had so many historical episodes in Latin America's history, the same one depicted in *One Hundred Years of Solitude* in which the American expatriates lived in such splendor as if they were in William Faulkner's South, with imported honey-glazed hams from Virginia and grass tennis courts while the day laborers picked fruit for miserable pay and lived in subhuman conditions, who, when they went on strike, were massacred by the military and dumped in the ocean. The rest of the American expatriates, a handful of executives for other large corporations with operations in the country, names of equal resonance like Standard Oil and Chase Manhattan Bank, were thrilled. The school started with the lower grades, but soon continued through the eighth. The courses were modeled on those of New York State and the students took the New York State Regents exams, far from the place they were supposed to be given. By the time my parents enrolled us in the midsixties, it was a full-fledged high school with student teachers flown in from Huntsville, Alabama. Our textbooks were leftovers from the U.S. Army schools overseas. Karl C. Parrish was a miniature version of say, Ridgemont High, locker walls included. We had a cheerleading squad (I was on it) and pep rallies. We had a student newspaper, student council elections (I ran for vice president and won). I felt our books looked modern compared to those from the Colombian schools (as we referred to every other school in the city), only because they were in English. Every week we had a flag ceremony on the front lawn. We raised both the Colombian and American flags, and while we sang both the Colombian and the American anthems, we also were asked to lay our right hands on our hearts and say the Pledge of Allegiance to the red, white, and blue. No one regarded this as strange, much less imperialistic, a word I would only hear when I got to college in the United States.

We took American holidays as seriously as any high school in the USA. On July Fourth, we wore flag colors to school. I even had a special pair of red, white, and blue suede shoes for the occasion. On St. Patrick's Day, the entire student body wore something green. The year we were in ninth grade, Allegra glued clovers to her cheeks. For Thanksgiving, my mother would tell the cook to roast a turkey. It wasn't that we sat around and ate all day with the entire family but Allegra came over. Instead of steak, fish, or chicken, we got turkey served with white rice and sweet plantains.

When I was about to start tenth grade, I was crowned most popular girl but I abdicated. My mother asked me if I wanted to go to school with Susana, her best friend's daughter, who attended Sacred Heart in Michigan. It was not an easy decision to make and I remember crying one day when I thought that I would not have a senior picture in the KCP yearbook, which was one of the big reasons to go to that school in the first place. Driving with José one day by the

old building, now turned into the headquarters for a multinational coal corporation, I try hard to look for the teenager who felt so confident and happy
growing up in a world that believed in America and in servants at the same
time.

We were the only ones to celebrate Halloween, by far our favorite American
holiday. We wore elaborate costumes to school. In first grade I was a witch.
Naturally I wanted to be a princess but my mother, not understanding that in
America children dress up as whatever they want, told me that was not appropriate for Halloween—only ghoulish outfits were—and so I have a picture in
my green album in which I'm wearing a long black tunic, a pointy hat, an oversized plastic nose strapped around my head, a broom between my legs, and a
very sad face. Another year she dressed me up as a bat. That was much better. I
liked the black-hooded cat suit that, when I stretched my arms, had winged
sleeves with points and bells. It made me feel like my father when Lili would
call him a "bat from New York." And of course, we went trick-or-treating,
except we called it "tricky tricky."

The year we moved to our house in Riomar, a few classmates came over to
go trick-or-treating in the new part of town. Halloween happened only on the
other side of Washington Park, where everything was just a bit less Colombian,
even the names of the public spaces. I was Mary Poppins—my mother was
getting the hang of American things—and my sister was Carmen Miranda. My
brother was the scarecrow, a colorful version of the one she saw in *The Wizard
of Oz.* My friend Alexandra came dressed as a Russian ballerina. Ana Rita always
had the best costume. She was always a princess in a gold-threaded gown. We
hit the streets early, while the sun was still out, knocking on doors for candy,
handed out by uniformed maids who stared at us in silence.

After a few hours, careful not to miss the houses where American treats
were handed out, our friends would leave and my sister and I would return
home for our Halloween, Part II. Sitting open-legged on the kitchen floor, we
spilled out our booty between our knees. That's when the counting, the separating, and a bit of the cheating began. Our mother made us, or told the maid
to make us, put half of what we had into a yellow plastic bowl. This was to be
set aside for "the little angels" who would start ringing our doorbell early the
next morning. After Halloween came All Saints Day. The *angelitos* were the
poor children, mostly boys, from the poor parts of town. They would show up
the morning after our trick-or-treating with painted faces.

My sister and I devised a complicated system to obey my mother but also to
satisfy our disappointed greed. We set aside the American brands. The two-
inch-long Milky Ways and Three Musketeers, the little packets of SweetTarts
and pink rectangles of Bazooka bubble gum were treasures. There was no way
that they were ending up in the bowl. Then we counted the lollipops that,

though not from Miami, our preferred source for candy, we nonetheless liked. If we had more than one of the same colors it went in the bowl. The rest was easier to give up—I kept a few of the Super Cocos, bite-sized morsels of toasted sugar and coconut flakes, but dropped most all of the assorted hard candies that said *hecho en Colombia* in the charity bowl.

Some of the neighborhood children would go out again that morning to get more candy, but we stayed home. "You've had your day," my mother would say, "now it's their turn." I was always curious to see the *angelitos* who didn't say "tricky tricky"; I had heard from my grandmother Lili that the *angelitos* sang beautiful rhymed verses. When the door opened, they smiled wide and stretched out their hands reciting in unison:

We are angels	*Angeles somos*
from the sky we come	*del cielo venimos*
asking for your alms	*pidiendo limosna*
to feed ourselves	*para nosotros mismos*

Usually it was our maids who met them at the threshold. But one year I wore my favorite pink and white gingham nightgown and waited for them. I stood behind the long window next to the front door waiting for the *angelitos* to ring the bell. I wanted to give them the candy myself, to see them face-to-face, but mostly I wanted them to sing to me. I had heard that the boys would say pretty things to those who gave them gifts. Lili had told me they said:

This house is made of roses	*Esta casa es de rosas*
It is the home of a beauty	*donde viven las hermosas*

Through the lace curtain, I watched the first group approaching, walking up the brick path to our carved oak door. I lifted the bowl from the floor. There were three lollipops in the bowl and they were a group of three. I knew that I was not supposed to open the door, only the long rectangular window. I could have opened it before they rang but I hid instead. I didn't want them to know that I, the girl who lived in the house, who had servants, a pink room, and a pretty nightgown, was waiting for a little band of *niños pobres* from the unknown parts of town.

They rang a second time. I opened the window and saw the three boys, smiling and standing there as straight as choirboys, their skin the color of the Super Cocos in the bowl. "Angels we are . . ." they began. My heart was racing. An eternity passed as they recited their rhyme, and the lollipops slipped out of my sweaty fingers every time I tried to take them out to hand to them. Once I had all three in my hand, I cautiously reached through the bars, making sure not to touch the cold black iron between us. I proudly handed a lollipop to each angel.

They looked at each other, another eternity passed, and they began to sing:

This house is made of thorns	*Esta casa es de espinas*

What were they saying to me? Lili told me they said pretty things.

This is the home of the stingy	*donde viven las mezquinas*

I slammed the window and ran to the kitchen. What *malagredicidos,* I thought, how ungrateful. This was what my grandmother called Imelda when she ran away. I wished that I would never see them again. But why didn't they come back? Why didn't they call me a beauty and my house a rose garden? What had I done wrong? I felt angry and hurt but I was mostly enchanted by their freedom—they said exactly what they felt. The maid touched my forehead gently, calming me. She told me she had told my mother that *angelitos* want coins, not candy.

WHEN I TURNED FOURTEEN I BEGAN TO NOTICE THE TENSION AT SCHOOL THAT ran like a raw electric wire from the boys a bit older than I, but it didn't compare with what I felt for Remberto, who also came from the farm to work as a live-in servant. I knew he got on the roof whenever I took a shower. The marble tub in my bathroom was open and I stood under the shower knowing that he was watching me as I lathered my hair with Herbal Essence, the green shampoo from Miami that made all that white foam and it all went smoothly down, caressing my body.

Tacitly Remberto and I had devised a system, allowed to us thanks to the city's badly run public services. The water would be out so often, or the pressure would be so low, that the house had its own water well and pumping system.

"Remberto, please turn on the water," I would say even when I didn't need him to.

"*Ya voy,*" he responded. "Be right there."

Remberto slept in the sewing room on a thin mattress, armed with a machete. Part of his job was to guard the house from the *ladrones,* the thieves that lurked outside and could come in any night, the potentiality of which kept me up most of the time. When our parents were out, which was many evenings, the maids would get us ready for bed so that by nine sharp they could retire to their quarters and listen to the new chapter of the *radio novelas* that our parents had told them they could not let us hear, that alone would be reason for dismissal. *Zandocan* or *Kaliban* I knew were scary but I think some were romances like the ones that were shown on television. The reason for the prohibition was that the radio was not considered to be good enough for the children of the house. In their free time, the maids listened to the radio in their musty rooms while we went up to our air-conditioned bedrooms well stocked with music, books, and televisions. I don't know about my friends but I was always drawn to how the servants lived in the back of our houses. So I would sneak in and lay on their beds with the thin mattresses and listen to their stories, most of which did scare me.

One night, I told my sister that we should go scare Remberto. I think it was more that I wanted to see how he slept. It was so different than how I did. Every evening at six p.m. one of the uniformed women came to turn on our AC, close our pink curtains, and remove the crocheted bedcovers with the pink flowers from our twin beds. Our nightgowns were put on our pillows.

My sister was not sure of why I wanted to do this, but she played along. I told her that we needed to see if we went into his dark room whether he would scream because we had actually scared him or whether he would be brave and wield his machete as he was supposed to do. He did neither. I think the real reason was that I wanted to see what his pajamas looked like, or maybe I wanted him to see me wearing the pink and white checkered gown, the same one I had worn for the ungrateful *angelitos*. I liked the way I looked in it. The moment the door creaked he calmly told us, "Girls, go back upstairs." I was angry, and blaming my bad luck with boys twice on the nightgown, I told the maid the next morning to put it in the bag of old clothes for the *niños pobres* of The Forest.

To get back at Remberto the next day I told him that my mother had left specific instructions for him. "You have to do a general cleaning,"I ordered him.

"What does that mean?" he asked and by his tone I realized he both didn't know what I meant and that he would do whatever I asked. "That means you have to sweep and mop wearing this." I handed him my father's old *kepi,* an olive green military cap that was kept around the house for my brother to play with. My mother found him cleaning away. When she asked what he was doing, he told her that I had told him to do it. The next day, he was sent back to the farm. This time I did miss the servant who had left. I missed him telling me how he knew how to ride a horse, and he knew how to milk a cow, and he knew how to cross a river, and he would know what to do if a snake bit me. Was I missing his stories or was I missing him because he was a boy who made me blush when he looked straight into my eyes?

Is Remberto a rebel now, a para, or is he still working at a farm or for our family, a seed picker in the plantation or a supervisor in the air-conditioned office? Will I see him if I make it to El Carmen? I contemplate asking my uncle if he might track him down for me but decide against it.

10

ASKING THE TOUGH QUESTIONS

When I decided to open up the Pandora's box of my Colombian past, I knew that coming back to find Imelda was an important part of the journey. But I had no way of starting to look. I don't know how she arrived but she came to live with us after my sister Laura was born. The adults thought that I needed to be distracted; I could become jealous having lost my parents' (and Lili's) complete attention. I knew Imelda for ten years but I never even knew her last name. I thought that I needed to start that search after my trip to the farm because it was going to be like finding a needle in a haystack. I mean, how many nannies and maids and cooks and gardeners have passed through our house in my lifetime! Agustín had implied that things weren't moving any faster for our trip, so I decided to start my inquiry to see where I could track down Imelda, who was probably, I realize, my first friend. Imelda was a girl who lived with us but I never knew where she came from, nor where she eventually disappeared to. I was waiting for the right moment and today, feeling settled in, more comfortable around my grandmother, I decided this was the time to ask.

She is sitting in her usual two-in-the-afternoon spot, on the Viennese rocking chair of her bedroom. I stand on the threshold of the door, which has become my comfort zone when talking with her and I wait for her to look at me. It takes her a bit to realize I'm there. "Ma Cris," I say, "Do you remember that girl who lived with me when—?

I didn't have to finish. "*Imeldita, sí. ¿Por qué?*" she says, completely unfazed by my bringing up her name out of thin air. "She came to see me about six months ago. But she hasn't come around since. Why? You want José to go get her for you?"

I nod my head. "How was it," I ask instead, "that Imelda came to our house?"

My grandmother does not have to think to answer this question either. She explains to me matter-of-factly that Imelda is the daughter of a *trabajador* from the interior. Tulio and his wife showed up in El Carmen one afternoon, "about ten little children behind them," looking for work. The boys were stark naked; the girls wore only underpants. After walking for days, Tulio had brought his family to the coast. "They were escaping the violence," Ma Cris tells me. This happened at least fifty years ago and yet the story of Imelda's father is a replica of the one that I heard on the street the day I arrived. But here everyone says it's different; that in La Violencia of those yesteryears, it was a political war because it was between the two traditional parties. During that time, Conservatives killed Liberals and Liberals killed Conservatives, and it is explained as if it just were so rational, just like the Israelis kill Palestinians and the Palestinians kill Israelis, just like the Sunnis kill Shiites and vice versa or the hatred between Serbs and Croats, a hatred that has existed for so long that to explain it is deemed unnecessary.

My grandmother tells me she was there when they arrived; that she and my grandfather were playing chess on the veranda when they saw them come inside the property. My grandfather asked Tulio if he was willing to work, "really" work. Tulio immediately said he was, with a *sí, señor*. "So Gabriel told the foreman who was there with us," Ma Cris continues, "to hand him a machete and sent him off with Tulio's children to the town of La Fortuna to clothe them. He told him to charge it to El Carmen."

Gabriel stopped the game to walk Tulio to a piece of land and told him that would be his. He could build a house there and he could farm the land. Tulio built his large family a one-room hut with adobe walls, dirt floors, and a zinc roof. In the plot, he grew yucca and rice and raised hens and pigs to feed his family that grew every nine months. "Every year," says Ma Cris, "they had one more. He couldn't feed them all." During harvest time in El Carmen, he worked as a day laborer.

Tulio was so grateful to my grandfather that he often sent an extra piglet or a chicken or a sack of yucca. When he found out that my mother had given birth to a second child, he sent her Imelda. "Take her," he said to my grandfather, "she can be of use to your daughter in the city."

My grandmother sees nothing wrong with Tulio giving up his child, or with our family accepting her. The exchange worked for everyone. Imelda could help out by entertaining me. To her family, Imelda's move was a relief, a kind of charity on our part: "One less mouth for Tulio to feed," my grandmother says. These are familiar explanations, words that I grew up hearing and accepting without question, until the day I started college, or maybe until the day I became an adult, with thoughts of my own.

I have no recollection of ever being introduced to her, but Imelda was so much a part of my life as a child that every one of my friends today remember her. "She always wore that yellow dress," Emma tells me when I ask her if she does. "And she always came with you to my birthday parties." Imelda would do whatever I asked her to do. Though we grew up together, I knew but was never able to articulate how she was different from me.

Imelda lived in my house but, unlike my friends during sleepovers, she did not sleep in my room. She slept in the maid's room, where I was told not to venture. She didn't attend the same school as I did, the large modern yellow building with teachers from the United States who taught us that Jack and Jill went up the hill. Imelda went to what my grandmother called *la escuelita de los niños pobres,* a concrete one-room house adjacent to Marymount School that the nuns ran for servant girls. Colombia has few public schools and even those are unreachable for girls like her unless a household like ours takes them in. Their own families cannot afford the school uniforms, the books, and the supplies, I was always told.

My favorite game to play with Imelda was called Bathing with the Hose. When I came back home from my school, Imelda and I ran to the backyard where I would take off my shoes and then my clothes, always leaving on my white cotton underwear. Imelda would fetch the long, green hose while I waited holding a golden tin cup, anticipating the moment when she would turn the hose on me under the playful pretext of trying to fill the cup in my hand. I would get wonderfully, giddily, hysterically soaked. Imelda had a streak of mischief that made the game more exciting. She would increase the pressure of the water spouting from the hose and run after me. I loved feeling the *chorro,* on my back and over my head. "Stronger," I ordered. Whenever Lili saw what was happening, she would yell at Imelda, telling her that she was going to make me get a cold. That she would be punished if I did. This did not deter either of us. Our game went on for hours every day, though the roles we played were set in stone. Imelda never got to take off her clothes and hold the cup. But sometimes she would turn off the hose, making me beg her to please not stop. At times, she would make me cry, holding on to the hose spouting only drops. "Open the faucet again," I would instruct her. "I will tell your grandmother," she would reply, not letting me get away with everything I wanted all the time—only most of the time.

I never thought of Imelda as my friend because my friends were the children of my parents' friends, those with whom I swam in the pool at the country club while Imelda sat in a chair and watched us. Imelda came with me pretty much everywhere. At birthday parties she helped us with the blindfold and to break the piñata, but she was not allowed to gather the candy on the floor and she knew to eat her slice of cake and her Coca-Cola in the kitchen with the maids, not on the patio with us and only after the children were served. Imelda never put up a fight. The rules were unspoken but somehow she and I both knew what they were.

As we grew older, Imelda often got in trouble. The nature of this "trouble" was never explained to me, but it sounded very serious. I only knew that she became absent from my life for short periods of time. My grandmother would feel sorry for her after a few days and would bring Imelda back home. I once went to retrieve Imelda with her. We went inside a building that had the thickest wooden doors and more nuns in habits than I had ever seen. I knew from my mother's stories about her nun school that living in convents is not much fun, but something told me this was much less nice and much more strict than my mother's boarding school. My grandmother had such say over Imelda's life that she felt authorized to take her to be locked up inside an institution to pay for her bad behavior in our house. "She was treated like another grandchild," my grandmother says. But punishment for her real grandchildren never included a stay with the nuns away from home.

Then one day when I was nine Imelda disappeared. I came home from school and she was gone; just like she had come, she went away. I never asked what happened. No one told me what happened. It was just *ya no está,* she is no longer here. I cannot remember if I ever missed her.

I WAKE TO A CARESS THAT TRAVELS FROM MY LEFT SHOULDER TO MY WRIST, up again and down, again and again, slowly and softly. I open my eyes and immediately recognize her. Imelda sits on the edge of my bed. She has the same delicate features of the past. Her dark curls are set right against her face and it still has that happy impishness of my memory. Her dark, oval eyes and thin lips that conceal a wide smile are unchanged. Imelda's smile is so beautiful that you could think her life has been as perfect as her teeth.

As my sleepy myopic eyes focus, I start to feel her presence. When I was in college, I indulged in the fantasy imagining Imelda in camouflage, with a Kalashnikov on her shoulder and bandoliers strung across her chest—not like Tania, Che Guevara's comrade in the mountains of Bolivia, that was me; more like the pretty girls with mestizo faces and wearing berets pictured on the postcards that celebrated the revolutions of Cuba and Nicaragua that I defended with an emotional fervor that transcended political or intellectual concerns. I always thought Imelda would be the perfect candidate to have joined a revolutionary movement. I would have if I were her I always said. Sitting on my bed, taking as little room as possible, she says "Nani"—only very close family members and servants who knew me as a child call me that—and I knew instantly that it had never occurred to Imelda to pick up a rifle. The habit of subservience had never left her.

"Your grandmother sent for me," she says.

I stay in bed, under the covers, so I can hide my anxiety. Imelda, effortlessly resuming the ritual of so many years ago, turns off the air conditioner, asking me if what I was wearing needed ironing, and then goes to the bathroom and turns on the shower. "I know how hot you like it." In the hour she stays in my room, I learn that she has a grown son, that, in fact, she is a grandmother. The man with whom she had her son had been well-to-do, but he was married. All he had given Imelda was a small piece of land outside Soledad, a town outside of Barranquilla whose name translates to Solitude.

She has worked, on and off, as a maid and slowly was able to build a house on her little plot of land. First came the cement walls, then a cement floor, a kitchen and an outhouse. But the house needs a new roof, she says, and sitting next to me, she asks me if I could help her out. With sixty thousand pesos, she says, she could keep out the rain—and the robbers, who had twice climbed into her house and stolen what few valuable things she owned. She still has not been able to replace the electric Sanyo fan.

I sort through the mess in my purse, looking for my wallet and as I take it out I am relieved to see my airline ticket back to New York and my passport with the U.S. resident card inside it. I hand Imelda a few worn red and brown bills, which, because they are Colombian pesos, feel to me like we're playing Monopoly. Pesos have stopped carrying the value of money to me. I cannot tell the one-thousand-peso bill from the two thousand or the ten thousand one, each escalation of zero adding to my alienation to the currency. I stare at one trying to figure out its denomination and notice the image of a beautiful dark-haired woman. It is Policarpa Salavarrieta, the only woman patriot as far as I know, accused of treason by the Spanish Crown and executed for collaborating with the independence movement. I give Imelda six 10,000 peso bills, the equivalent of thirty dollars. The amount that buys me a mediocre plate of pasta and a cheap glass of red wine when I return to the West Village will put a roof on Imelda's house. My grandmother's voice comes through the door as Imelda tightly rolls the bills I had given her, wraps them in a square of toilet paper, and slides them between her breasts before my grandmother comes into the room. Neither one of us wants to be caught.

NOW THAT I'VE SETTLED AT MY GRANDMOTHER'S, IMELDA CANNOT STAY AWAY. "Nani, close your eyes," she says on her second visit a few days later. Her hands are behind her back. "I have a gift for you."

My grandmother lifts her eyes from the prayer book she is reading.

I close my eyes and extend my arms in front of her, palms facing up. I can't imagine what she can give me. She opens her palms on mine and I feel a tiny object in each hand.

I open my eyes and see two pink plastic figurines of two girls sitting on each of my palms. The two miniature girls face each other. The one in my right hand wears pigtails and a red sundress and holds a big silver pail that reminds me of the one I used to make sand castles with in El Rodadero, and Imelda would help me. Her job was to fill the pail with sand while I molded the sand into architecture. The girl on my left palm is holding a beach ball. It feels as if the two are actually talking to each other, playing on my hands.

"She thinks she's still coming to play with you," Ma Cris whispers under her breath, talking to no one in particular and returning to her prayers.

I make fists around the gifts and tell Imelda that I am not feeling well, that I need to go and lie down, that she can come to my room when she finishes talking to my grandmother.

As I turn my back to them, Imelda sits on the rocking chair and I remember that no other servant, former or current, does that. I also know that she calls my grandmother Ma Cris just as I do. Others who worked for longer still call her Doña Cristina, or Doña Cris.

Ten minutes later, Imelda comes into my room to ask if I want her to get me an aspirin. I nod yes. She comes back with a glass of water on a tray and sits by my side on the bed, again taking as little space as possible. I want to tell her to take off her shoes and sit fully on the bed like any of my friends do. But I don't. Right away she bombards me with questions: Are you still scared at night, Nani? Do you still hate the dark? Do you still cry when you read books?

But aren't I the one who has questions? Yet her questions and mine are so different because mine have an ulterior motive and hers are innocent; she just wants to know about me. I have not even started and she is already telling me what I want to know: When her sister was born my mother took her back to El Carmen, to her parents' house so that she could see her new sibling. My mother had gone with a basket of diapers. "Not just regular diapers," she tells me, "but the embroidered ones, just like the ones Laura had." She tells me that the same doctor diagnosed both of us with myopia, and that Lili had ordered contact lenses for me and had bought her pink cat-eyed frames. And that Abuelo Gabriel paid her to comb his hair for hours and she would get extra pay for every white hair she found. There is not a trace of resentment in her voice.

Imelda cannot go see her parents because she doesn't have the money for the bus trip. They moved from the parcel of land inside El Carmen and now live in the town of La Fortuna, the closest urban center to the farm, about half an hour away, which means a good eight-hour road trip from Barranquilla. Her siblings are all there too, doing odd jobs mostly, making ends meet. "Hard," she says, "but at least none has joined the guerrilla.

"I have seen those rebels, Nani," she continues. "They look tough. The girls, they look like something I don't. I see them sometimes at the river; they are crossing to go up the mountain and they bathe next to us. I think they have fun." Imelda notices how they look pretty in their uniforms and they always have fancy hair and eye makeup. *"Son unas berracas,"* she says, using a word to describe people that are both tough and cool. And as if she were catching herself from saying the wrong thing, she repeats that her parents raised good children because "not one is a *guerrillero.*"

My inability to feel comfortable being a journalist when I'm living as one of the masters begins to weigh on me, making me feel like a fraud. Why do I blame it on everyone but myself that I cannot live here?

"Nani, you were such a *llorona* and a *miedosa,* a crybaby and always scared. She tells me that I cried every time I saw the kids at the ferry on our way to El Rodadero, asking why they were poor. And I cried every time I was read a story. "Your mother had to send the book about the Match Girl to The Forest," says Imelda, remembering the poor neighborhood where my mother volunteered and the story about the orphan girl who on Christmas Day had nowhere to go: The little match girl supported herself by selling matches but it was so cold she used them to keep warm and watched through the window how a family of parents and children celebrated inside keeping warm, eating, and opening presents. "I could not read you that story without you breaking down."

I want to know more about what she remembers and about how she feels about what she remembers. I want to ask her questions but I can't. My words get stuck in my throat every time I try. I don't even know what it is I want to ask. Can I just ask: "Do you think you were better off growing up with us?" Whatever it is I cannot ask it. Is it because I'm getting all the answers without having to conduct an interview? Do I tell her it's one? Or do I schedule one?

Perhaps if I met her somewhere else, not with my grandmother around, not with the surroundings that gave us the dynamic that she was there to serve me, we might be able to talk more openly. I ask her if I can come see her in her house. She tells me that if I go, she will cook a *sancocho,* the local stew, for me. I feel like I am using her, like I just want to see her house and talk to her because I need to answer some questions for myself. I want to be left alone, so I tell her I'm not feeling any better, that I need to rest, and like the obedient servant, she walks out, closing the door gently behind her.

11

KIDNAPPING, INC.

The rebel's game of stopping cars at gunpoint has a name. Called The Miraculous Catch, it involved going out hoping to catch a big fish, not with rods but with rifles. They were scoring big-time these days. I still can't get used to the word *secuestro* thrown out in conversation daily; it is strange living an existence where being kidnapped is more likely than being mugged on the New York subway. One Colombian is kidnapped every three hours. Between 1996 and 2000, 12,834 people were kidnapped in Colombia. In 2000 alone, 3,706 people were victims. Twenty percent of those kidnapped were women, and almost nine percent children. That is why I am not surprised when I see a young boy at a pre-Carnival parade holding a sign that reads "Better to die drunk than kidnapped." There must be a backstory to why the FARC has decided to institutionalize this method that they call retentions and their opponents call extortion. The conditions are still not right for our trip, according to Agustín—"more *secuestros* every day"—so I decide to investigate the history of kidnapping among those I know.

El Carmen is located in what is known as a *zona roja*, a red zone, meaning it is infested by heavily armed rebels who are incredibly successful at running a pretty slick kidnapping operation. The rebels have already made it known that any family with land will be kidnapped if encountered in the area. I might think I don't fit in with my family's landowning ways and my family might think that I am a strange rootless bird, but to a conscript of the rebel army, I am the enemy, and perhaps capturing me might get a rebel a promotion or at least a new pair of boots. Everyone assures me that in their hands I am nothing but another hit.

Secuestros started in the sixties but it skyrocketed when the FARC's Central Committee passed Law 002 in 1999, creating a "revolutionary tax" for the New Colombia. It turned into an industry, something like Kidnapping Inc.

According to the law, every Colombian worth more than one million dollars was to pay the group or be "retained" (read kidnapped), until the fiscal debt was canceled. To find tax evaders, the rebels would set up checkpoints along the main roads, especially on long weekends when the traffic gets heavy. The FARC figured that this practice could raise them the same billion dollars that Washington had promised President Pastrana. Kidnappings, I learn, are no longer simply a revolutionary statement. It is a profitable business that has created ancillary markets. There are now kidnapping consultants, kidnapping insurance salesmen, kidnapping negotiators, all working for a fee. Common criminals kidnap the big names and sell the coveted targets to the rebels. There is a market for buying kidnapping futures and for negotiators who buy and sell kidnappings at a discount. Kidnapping has become a commodity as legal as financial advising and as criminal as the cocaine trade. I even heard rebels are kidnapping people's dogs. Classified ads have been used for the negotiation between the owners of a French poodle, the number-one targeted breed, and the captors.

So now cars are inspected, and when stopped, the rebels or the fake rebels demand to see each occupant's *cédula*. In Barranquilla, I am Silvana María Paternostro Montblanc. The only time that I have used that name was as a child. When I was invited to a birthday party, my mother would wrap a gift and next to the bow she would insert a tiny engraved card with my four names on it. That way the mother that threw the party knew that the present came from the daughter of Pedro Paternostro and Francia Montblanc. Today, I am trying to figure out how I can hide who I am.

This naming system fits nicely into such a class-conscious society. The first question people ask when they hear my name for the first time is "Silvana Paternostro, *qué*?" That's where the second name comes in. By giving my mother's name, my entire family genealogy is revealed. Everyone is basically asking, are you from a good family? From a Christian union? From Barranquilla or the provinces? Are you a Conservative or a Liberal? It's like walking around with a laminated copy of your family's social registry in your wallet. It straightens facts out. The two names give the entire story. The irony is that not long ago, it was a way for parents to know who everyone was and cast a vote of acceptance or not, of entry or not. Today the tables have turned. The social registry is in the hands of rebels, of young men and women with guns who are told that our society is divided into two: you are *el pueblo*, the people, or you are the enemy. Just like the society ladies have been able to tell the respectable members of society from the riffraff, the rebels also know what are the "good" names to have; everyone does. In the name of New Colombia, "*su cédula, por favor.*"

Law 002 has changed the way people with "good names" live. During the week, it is about getting to your place of work safely. During the weekend, it's about getting to the beach or the country home. Last year for the Miss Colombia pageant, Emma's mother was furious. The FARC announced a huge fishing fest for kidnapping victims. The military intelligence found out who was on the list and informed them. Like many families my friend's family have been driving to Cartagena, a pleasant ninety-minute journey south, for the festivities for more than twenty years. "This year, my sons had to watch it on TV. As you know, it's not the same thing," she says. But I also hear there are ways around it. I hear that those with coveted names are now getting *cédulas* with common last names.

THERE ARE ALL KINDS OF KIDNAPPING STORIES: TRAGIC ONES THAT END WITH death; long ones where families wait for year after year for their relatives' release. Kidnappings had become as common as birthdays for certain families and like birthdays sometimes there are reasons for celebrations. Back in 1990, I was in town for a short visit and my uncle invited me to one of the strangest parties I've ever attended. "Get dressed," he said on the phone. "I'm coming to get you. I'm taking you to a party."

"Whose party?" I ask.

"A surprise," he says.

I notice the amount of four-by-fours outside the Club ABC and I realize that I am being taken to a party of people with *fincas,* and that I not only don't know them well but I don't fit in like Agustín does. I barely know the lyrics to "House in the Air," the popular *vallenato* song that everyone knows and loves.

"Lots of cars," I say, and as a way to fit in, I add, "Will there be a *vallenato* trio."

"I am sure," he says. "It's a big celebration."

"What?" I insist.

Francisco, a distant cousin, held by the FARC or the ELN, my uncle wasn't sure—"both the same thing"—for eight months, had just been released. His friends and family are throwing him a Liberation Surprise Party. I was stunned by how normal he looked. Wearing a button-down shirt and smelling of cologne, he was smiling and dancing and chatting as if he had woken up today just like yesterday. I, a bit shy to say anything, feeling I didn't know the appropriate release salutation, kept to the sides. What do you say to someone who has been kept at gunpoint for eight months? It was he who came to say hello when he saw me, kissed my cheek, and asked me if I was still living in New York.

There are also the "funny" kidnapping stories that people tell, like Manuel's tale. Manuel was the classmate that everyone bullied, the one who was always pointed at because he was slower than the rest in a country of people pulling fast ones. There is a name for people like Manuel: *el bobo,* Small Bullet. The "He-Master Bully of The Bobo Universe" nicknamed him that and it spread like a prairie on fire among all bullies, who lived by the rules that there was nothing worse than to be the last and earn the title of being *el bobo*. All races begin with "One, two, three, go, *bobo el último*," fool if you're last, be it a sack race at the school's fund-raiser or in later life.

Manuel, the story goes, was driving to his family's farm where he had been working since he finished college (which is in the same general area as El Carmen). Manuel's family, like my mother's, are descendants of Frenchmen who arrived in the early days of the republic and who are now established landowners. His great-great-great-great-grandfather Monsieur Parfait is a legendary figure in the region's folk music. Manuel, the so-called bobo, escaped kidnapping by outsmarting his captors. "Can you believe it?" asks a former classmate, who tells me the story when we run into each other at a local restaurant.

A few years later, I ran into Manuel. Even if I had sometimes bullied him too by asking him to carry my books, I had a sweet spot for him. I found out he was divorced, had a son, and was running the family's new African palm plantation. I asked him to tell me about what had happened. He knew exactly what I was referring to. "Were you scared?" I asked, which seems to be my first and recurrent question to people who tell me stories about living and traveling in Colombia. I wanted to know the answer before he told me his story. He said that he wasn't, that regardless of the AK-47s pointed at him, it was "easy to be strong."

He had been driving to the farm and ran into a rebel checkpoint, didn't really know if it was FARC or ELN; they both operate outside of our families' *fincas*. He was asked for his *cédula*. The moment the rebels—he describes them as *pelaos*,with the nonthreatening slang for "kids"—saw that they had one with a name they wanted (no, with two names they wanted), they kept saying on the radio, "We have one. We have one." What followed next happened so fast that Manuel doesn't remember it well, but he does remember that the rebels were waiting for orders from command to come in when they saw a police car approaching. The rebels ran and so did he, hiding for hours under his car.

I asked him why he wasn't scared. He must have known they had no qualms when it came to using their guns. "I could tell they weren't sure what to do with me." He might not have been the most assertive boy at school, allowing himself to be taunted by classmates, but talking to poor children with authority came easily to him. He had been doing that all his life, and it apparently saved his life the day the rebel kids were reversing roles by force.

It was time for them to play the game of *bobo el último* with the boys they grew up with who owned the land, the ones with the names that came with *fincas* attached to them. Manuel's story I think is like a double-bill parable of poetic justice. Manuel *el bobo* had become *el chacho*, the strong and cool one, who pulled a fast one on the scum of the earth, those who are ruining Colombia.

12

RUNNING IN RIOMAR

I wake up with a desire to go running. I throw on the clothes I usually wear to run down the Hudson River Parkway, a few blocks from my apartment in New York City. I feel self-conscious and a bit ridiculous when my grandmother asks me where I am going and I tell her *a trotar*. I am really going for a trip down memory lane. My plan is to do what I used to do every day after school when Allegra and I walked home from school and for hours on weekends. I want to see the blocks that we walked together. I want to feel the Barranquilla of the days when we went back and forth from each other's house endlessly.

Allegra and I lived around the block from each other, so instead of calling each other on the phone we would meet to walk together. Anything that needed to be discussed—"What are you wearing to the party?" "He told me I looked pretty in my blue skirt." "I saw him talking to her."—was better done in person. We perfected the teenage "best friend forever" tell-all method. Today, we are still better in person than on the phone.

I feel pretty stupid in my black tights and the torn T-shirt that says Häagen-Dazs in the front and Coffee on the back, which I've had since college. My sister gave it to me when Häagen-Dazs was a new brand, coffee was my favorite flavor, and I ate a pint every night. As acceptable as a frayed T-shirt of senti-mental value is in New York, it is simply poor people's clothing in Riomar. Also, running on the streets at one in the afternoon in the tropical heat is not what the female residents of this neighborhood do. They jog early in the morning in a cement park called La Electrificadora, which takes its name from the elec-tricity plant that stands in front of it. The ladies who frequent the park wear brand-new matching athletic outfits bought in Miami and they run at six in the morning. I admire how they get up so early but have never understood the attraction of going around a track with a view of industrial coils.

Today I turn left, not right as I usually do to go to Agustin's house to check on the status of our journey. I am walking toward my old house, and Allegra's house, and David's house, the houses that I walked to, the houses where I could name who lived where, one by one. I could even tell which of the servants worked where. People who lived in these houses didn't walk—except for Allegra and me. Only servants walked. Allegra and I walked these streets in complete comfort. Now as I walk slowly with my head down, I realize that back then we didn't walk on the sidewalks. The sidewalks were where the servants socialized. We walked in the middle of the streets, side by side, as if together we made up for a whole car. I don't know if it was because the sidewalks were full of potholes, which I see today though I had never noticed them before. Or because when Allegra and I walked, strolling languidly down the middle of the road, we had an ulterior motive.

We wanted to be seen, noticed by the two boys who were in turn navigating the streets in their cars looking for us. When we actually intersected, they screeched, we stopped, and a second later we would be inside their cars, which was where we wanted to be. Today I don't want to be recognized, and I take cover on the badly kept sidewalks of my teenage walks. The sidewalks are filled with shadows, some come from the foliage that is constantly being watered by the ever-present gardener in each household. I am interested in the moving shadows. These sidewalks, I realize, are full of interaction, lives that cannot be lived inside the households where the servants work. It is on the sidewalks where their relatives visit, where the maids and the gardeners, the nannies and the drivers conduct their romances and family affairs. The owners of the houses don't walk; the sidewalks are reserved for people who offer their services. They are used by people looking for work or offering food, fruit, or lottery tickets. I see a group of servants standing in the front doors—a maid or two, a chauffeur, a gardener interacting with the seller of fruit, of lottery tickets, of fresh bread or visiting with their family who've come from the countryside to see their city-dwelling relatives and, most likely, to ask them for money.

I am walking slowly, consciously taking in every detail I can. With every step I look left, right, up, down. I notice the holes and the garbage piling up. I smile at the man selling the slushes that we call *raspaos,* from a bicycle cart. I liked the cherry-cola cones topped with condensed milk but I had them only when my mother was not around. "Dirty," she would tell us every time my sister and I asked for one, or for anything sold on the street, even a cut mango or *alegría,* balls of sugared popcorn with pieces of fried brown coconut inside. Their taste gave me pure joy, which is what *alegría* means in Spanish.

When I begged for an *alegría,* I was stopped with the same reasoning: "How clean can the kitchen of that *negrita* be?" The mangoes we ate were cut in our own kitchen with the clean knives. But the *alegrías* were very difficult to make and I liked them so much. Only the women who sold them really knew how to make them. The *palenqueras*, black and tall, with sturdy legs and sturdy arms left bare under their sleeveless floral dresses walked the entire city from dawn to dusk, erect like ballerinas. On top of their short rounded Afros they placed a big metal bowl stacked with *alegrías*, announcing to everyone in a singsong voice that they were carrying "joy made of coconut and anisette."

"*Mami*, please," I would ask every time I heard them pass by our sidewalk. She never relented. But my grandmother Lili, always there to indulge us, figured out the perfect solution. She paid the *palenqueras* to come to her kitchen to make the candy with her ingredients. She would then bring over a big bowl of antiseptic balls of joy for me to taste.

THERE ARE NEW HIGH-RISES ON THESE STREETS. I REMEMBER HOW, WHEN MY parents and their friends built their houses, they were considered so modern. They had left behind the old 1930s mansions of El Prado and the hard lines of the houses built in the fifties in the Alto Prado to build what they wanted, in the style that was now *de moda*. On our block all houses have the Spanish look with the red tile roof and the white stucco walls that was my uncle's signature. He built all except one of the houses, so they were perfectly synchronized, as if it were one long Spanish-style ranch.

Riomar today reminds me of *The Donny and Marie Show* I liked to watch when I first arrived in the United States. It's a little bit country and it's a little bit rock and roll: a hybrid between Albuquerque and Miami. There are fifteen-story buildings made of marble and glass the color of a chlorinated pool, crowned with the satellite dishes that bring American entertainment to these families, most of which I know and they know me. Their garages are filled with BMWs and Ford SUVs. They travel to Europe, they shop in Miami, and they love Carnivals and Vallenato Festival, a three-day music festival held in Valledupar.

As I go up Fifty-sixth Avenue and cross Eighty-fourth Avenue, I mentally note the name of the family whose house it is, or used to be. This was my grandparents' and Allegra's street. I pass the Guzmáns' extremely white house on the corner. As imposing in its size as I remember it and as equally strange, with white structures that resemble the bleached dentures of a snow monster. I wonder who keeps it so white now that they are in Miami?

My heart, like my legs, feels heavy at the thought of time past, and of people who once were a part of my daily life. But what was once so familiar now feels as remote as the peculiar architecture of their abodes. Some of the houses, like my grandparents' house, are abandoned and run down, none as much as my grandparents', which has a young sentinel living inside to guard it. I ring the doorbell and he gives me a tour of the dilapidation. Marta's house, which once had an Olympic-sized pool and a crystal staircase, had been torn down, leaving an empty lot of overgrown weeds. The entrance of the Solanoses' house has so many clay pots with plants in full bloom that it is hard to see the front door. This is quite a change from Paco's mother, who liked to keep the clean lines of her house free from the exhorbitant colors of the tropics. There were no fuchsia hyacinths and purple hydrangeas at the Solanoses' during my youth. They were more sober—they were *cachacos*—and preferred to refrain from the color-coordinated *costeño* gardens. But the new owner is certainly making up for any lost time.

Other houses I simply cannot find, as if they were lifted from where they were and new ones implanted instead. I had never seen Corinthian columns on Fifty-sixth, I say to myself as I search for Allegra's house. Her mother had an iron bench in the center of her front lawn, a sculpture more than a functional piece—she would not let anyone sit there. Sometimes we found beggars resting on it and Allegra's mom fiercely shooed them away. I reach the part of the block where I could always see the peculiarly placed object and think how her mother and mine were so different—hers was so much more outrageous. She had a vintage bronze bed and drove a turquoise-colored Thunderbird convertible. Allegra told me recently she found a copy of Virginia Woolf's *Three Guineas* that belonged to her mother when she was unmarried. My mother was not that "emancipated." But then again Allegra's mother did not come from a Conservative, landed family. Her grandmother had even married twice and her second husband was a professor. I am assuming that reading was encouraged.

For God's sake, could it be possible that I have gotten the street wrong? I knew exactly where Allegra's house was. I went there every day. It was unmistakable. The most daring of all of the other houses, it offered the neighborhood's sole avant-garde design. My grandparents had a 1950 California ranch-style house, very long and low, and my parents chose the Spanish-style with red tiles, white walls, and terra-cotta floors. Allegra's house was geometrical, a little like the Guzmán's except hers was the color of the bronze powder we put on our cheeks to look prettier when going on our walks. Many people called it the Orange House. Allegra was always proud of it, a precursor I think to the nontraditional turn her life has taken. Allegra studied urban design and spent many years designing objects and furniture that was as different for Barranquilla as her parents' house.

I stand in front of where I know her house has to be; and instead of her house of modern lines, the house in front of me boasts a facade of enormous columns. For a second I hesitate. Have I been making things up in my mind? I knew they had sold the house but I never thought anyone would buy a house, especially that house, to change it. But as I look around I catch on. Our neighborhood has changed hands, a trend that started around the time I left for Michigan. Colombia was beginning to introduce marijuana to the United States, a well-renumerated endeavor in those days. Some of its new inhabitants have different tastes and obviously much more money.

I keep walking, turning right at the corner to arrive at my parents' old house. It is midmorning and the sun mixed with the humidity is at full blast. Sweat drops roll from my hip to my knees, making the black lycra running pants wrap my body tightly. I welcome the hug. "You and I don't belong here," I tell my sweaty clothes as I walk past my house, head down. When they left for Panama, my parents sold it to a *marimbero,* as the men in the marijuana business were called, who bought it as a wedding gift for his wife, Eugenia, a recent divorcée of great beauty and my mother's classmate. My mother's only consolation was that she was leaving her perfect rosewood floors to a woman whom she knew would take good care of them, not to the newly enriched *corroncha* who had come to see it and had wanted to put shag carpet over them.

But Eugenia and her new husband did not get along. When the marriage broke up, the house sat empty for more than ten years. Rumor had it that Eugenia's husband buried his riches in the garden and the watchmen guarding the empty house spent their time digging to find them. The rosewood floors were left to rot. A year ago, a Montblanc bought it. My grandmother told me that when they had first moved in they found bullet holes in the wood.

The house is in perfect condition now. I think to ask my grandmother to tell the new owners I would like to see what they have done to *mi casa.* But I pick up the pace and realize that instead I am running away from my past.

I RUN FAST. I PASS A GROUP OF MEN WAITING FOR THE BUS, SITTING ON THE ledge of David's old house. I don't want to look at it. I can't do it, I say, feeling sad and alienated. "Psst, *Mami,* why are you running so hard?" the man in the short-sleeved shirt and the pencil mustache whispers as I rush by. "What's the hurry? No need to get so agitated. Want me to get you a cab?" I laugh and with that comment I walk back to my grandmother's house feeling the *alegría* of the *costeños,* the warmth of this Caribbean city that sometimes feels as un-Colombian as I do.

13

THE BEST IN ALL THE LAND

When Richard Nixon declared the War on Drugs in 1972, as a measure to bring hippiedom to its end, he ordered the military to fumigate the entire U.S.-Mexican border with poisonous DDT. Ninety percent of all marijuana smoked in Haight-Ashbury in San Francisco, in New York's Washington Square, in the Diag in Ann Arbor, and wherever else hippies congregated came from Mexico. Nixon vowed to bring America back by putting an end to the youth's consumption of marijuana, the drug that American parents—and Elvis Presley—felt was responsible for turning their children into peace-loving, barefooted, long-haired revolutionaries. Presley was so impressed with Nixon's decision that when he sat next to a cabinet member on a flight to D.C., he sent the president a handwritten note on American Airlines stationery offering his services to combat drug consumption. The King met with Nixon at the White House wearing a purple, white, and gold embroidered cape to discuss his involvement. But the Peace Movement wanted drugs and the drug trade simply moved south (because moving elsewhere is what it always does), arriving in Barranquilla less than two years later.

In 1974, two guys from Queens, New York, flew into the city's Ernesto Cortissoz International Airport, a big name for a one-tarmac, one-gate affair, but it was the only airport on the entire north coast that received planes from the United States. They must have arrived in the daily flight from Miami. The two friends rented a car and drove north to Santa Marta and up the Sierra Nevada de Santa Marta, that beautiful snow-peaked mountain near the Caribbean Sea that has always attracted foreigners. Even Baron Alexander von Humboldt stopped by during his botanical expeditions in the nineteenth century. The New Yorkers too were on some sort of botanical voyage, except they wanted to find only one plant, not do an inventory of all species like the German botanist did in Latin

America. They had been told that marijuana grew wild in the sierra. The two travelers soon found out that it was true and that it was of great quality, even better than the Mexican stuff. It shortly became known as Santa Marta Gold.

The story as told by local journalist José Cervantes Ángulo in his book *The Night of the Fireflies* has the pair of Americans persuading every local farmer that they could find along the entire Caribbean coast of Colombia—from the tip of the Guajira all the way south to Santa Marta—to grow marijuana for them. To their advantage, these were unhappy farmers thanks to the feudal arrangement that landowners like my forebears had established. Day laborers rarely achieved independence from large landowners, who employed them for little pay and no benefits. Small landowners were also trapped in the system. Bank loans were reserved for the very few that used their selective last names as collateral. The faceless farmers were barely even allowed inside the buildings.

The men, hippies like the ones Nixon abhorred, with long hair, tie-dyed tunics, and sandals, were modern-day Jesus Christs to the locals. They had rarely seen men dressed like that or employers who offered good deals. What the agrarian bank didn't lend the peasants the gringos gave to them. "They came in with sacks of dollars and they would say, 'Here's some money to get you started,'" Luis Peña, an employee of El Carmen during those days, tells me one afternoon sitting outside Agustín's office. Luis has worked for my family for fifty years, helping out at the farm in various jobs. "Then they would show you another sack and say, 'Here is another one to pay you for half of the harvest in advance. I'll come back in six months,' which is how long it took for marijuana to grow. Six months from seed to bud. When they came back, they brought more sacks." He can explain to me how it worked because he was a recipient of the gringos' largesse. Many in his situation said, "Yes, mister, we will plant for you." Who was going to refuse being paid in dollars and in advance? My grandfather was surely not going to top that.

Luis tells me that while he worked for my grandfather during the week, he spent his weekends tending his own plot for the gringos. "I would work from Monday to Friday in El Carmen helping out in the cotton and rice plantations, and do extra stuff like send messages to the girls around town that your uncle Carlos liked, in secret because you're grandparents usually didn't approve of his choices. On Fridays I'd go take care of my marijuana field. I would hire the day laborers from your grandfather to come help me in my farm and I would pay them more than he did." He doesn't remember how much that was. "That was a long time ago," he says. In *The Night of the Fireflies*, Cervantes Ángulo claims it could have been as much as five to ten dollars a day, which was what they would make picking cotton for an entire week. People from all over the country came north in pursuit of the dream.

Americans also came in hordes—pilots, economists, farmers, adventurers, and hippies, of course. They brought in manuals, fertilizers, tractors, and Cessna planes. Today I often bump into Americans who, when they find out I'm from Barranquilla, tell me that they've been there, a town of absolutely no tourist interest. At first I would ask, truly surprised, "Really and what took you there?" The answers were usually "Just traveling" or "On my way to Santa Marta" or "To the Guajira." Now I know enough of them to just smile and say, "Oh sure, in the seventies." The marijuana from Colombia grew to international fame. Ringo Starr immortalized it when he wrote: "A lady that I know just came from Colombia, she smiled because I did not understand, then she held out some marijuana. She said it was the best in the land."

FROM THEN ON COLOMBIA WOULD BECOME THE GOLD STANDARD OF DRUGS, great for producers and consumers, not so great for Colombians, like me, who were starting to travel the world with a green passport with a gold seal that read República de Colombia on its front flap. Or for my friends from Bloomfield Hills who came to stay for a month after we graduated in the summer of 1977. When Sarah arrived at the Miami Airport from Barranquilla, they made her take off her new Nikes, the kind with rubber cleats. In front of everyone, the customs official took out a pair of scissors and cut the top of each one with no explanation, no restitution, not even an apology. The searches became indiscriminate. I remember the adults talking about their friend's daughter, Claudia, a stellar student in her class, who was strip-searched in Miami. The event had been so traumatic that everyone in Barranquilla was saying that she was being treated by a psychiatrist. In those days going to the shrink was reserved for the clinically insane.

The map I have in my kitchen does not show it but the Guajira, that feisty head, and Florida appear close enough to the Florida Keys. No doubt the geographical convenience wasn't lost on the Americans who plied the drug trade. Kicked out of Mexico, they went to the coast of Colombia, selling dream of riches to anyone willing to grow pot instead of cotton. A salesman never had it so good: It was easy for the Americans to recruit the locals. The Americans were not only offering work to the poor, they were also doing business with many other *guajiros*, the people who came from the Guajira Peninsula, the extension of land jutting out like a long nose from Colombia's north coast into the Caribbean, a word loaded with all kinds of stereotypes following the Colombian tradition of branding regions with generalized traits. *Guajiros* are known to be Colombia's pirates, the pioneering smugglers. Families in the Guajira have been bringing in untaxed goods since the republic was created. I remember their houses in Barranquilla filled with refrigerators, cigarettes, and whisky for sale. Smuggling had long been a way of life. What was the difference between smuggling clothes into Barranquilla, cattle into Venezuela, or whisky from the Caribbean and smuggling marijuana into the United States?

The difference was money, mountains of money. Toting Samsonite brief-cases stuffed with cash, entire families from La Guajira and the men who entered the trade began to settle in Barranquilla and soon the word "*guajiro*" became synonymous with "drug trafficker," the ones who came in wanting to buy everything. They wanted to buy the houses, the big ones, the ones in the nicest parts of town like ours. Legend had it that they drove around town and when they saw a house they liked they would simply pull into the driveway and knock on the door. If they were invited in, they would politely remove a gun from the waistband, set it on the coffee table, and make an offer, a very attractive, hard-to-say-no-to amount, in dollars. Adults whispered about whom among them had been approached, speculating about what they would do when their own turn came. Many succumbed; even if they snubbed the *guajiros* socially, selling them real estate, cars, jewelry, and furniture was different.

Members of good Barranquilla families, especially wayward sons who preferred cars and women to university degrees and traditional office hours, joined the marijuana bonanza as well. I was too young to know them but I would hear bits and pieces about a friend's cousin who was making millions "in the business" and was scandalizing the city. He imported Barranquilla's first Ferrari. The city's high society called him a degenerate who consumed drugs and had orgies, but when he flew Olga Guillot, the Cuban queen of ballads, from Miami to sing at a party, everyone wanted an invite. Rumor had it that even the mayor attended, that maids passed around platters of rolled joints, and that instead of decorating the house with flowers they decorated the vases in the salons with marijuana leaves.

THE TRANSSHIPMENT OF THE DRUGS WAS SO PERFECTLY ORCHESTRATED, according to the chronicles of the bonanza, that if it all went as planned, the entire operation from beginning to end, of moving the marijuana sacks from the northern tip of Colombia to the southern tip of the United States, would take no more than twenty hours. This is how it worked: An American pilot would wake up at dawn, say in Miami, or in any of the Florida Keys, and land in less than three hours in one of the hundreds of clandestine strips that had sprung up all over the area. From the air, the pilots and the Colombians were in constant radio communication. They spoke in codes, just as people do when talking on the phone with their pushers. For example, when the pilot asked "How healthy is the bambino?" he was referring to the quality of the grass. And when the Colombians asked if "the food" was coming, "food" was code for dollars.

When those guarding the marijuana field heard the planes, they ordered the loaded trucks to take to the road and meet them at the hidden airstrip. The trucks were guarded by so-called flies, men carrying guns and bags of five- and ten-dollar bills to hand out in case of emergency, say a run-in with cops or with soldiers. Occasionally, disagreements over the amount of the bribe would end up in shootouts. But once the planes were airborne, it was time to celebrate, usually right there on the airstrip with a case of contraband whisky and a *trío vallenato,* a singing group. These trios began taking shape in the fifties when a troubador lady-killer took to the road with an accordion. Today, there is no celebration in Colombia without a *vallenato* group. They sing macho lyrics about their lives, loves, and hates, as well as about politics. During the cotton bonanza of the sixties they sang about the landowners with the fluffy fields; in the days of the marijuana bonanza they celebrated every new pack of dollars. They also sing to presidents, ministers, brides and grooms. When the rebels took to the sierra, their songs were heard up in the hills. Lately, they've been singing to those men macho enough to take up arms to fight the rebels.

I too went to the Sierra Nevada at around the same time that Americans trekked to the snow-capped mountain in search of Santa Marta gold. Pablo's parents and a handful of their friends had built cabins way up in the sierra and sometimes *el grupito,* our clique of teenage friends, would get invited to go with them for the weekend. The trips to the sierra were special mostly because "the group" would spend all this time without curfews under one roof. Emma, Allegra, and I could stay up talking in our room with the bunk beds and wondering what the boys—Pablo, Miguel, and Alberto—were doing in the next room. Emma and Pablo were boyfriend and girlfriend but it never crossed their minds that they would be sharing a bed.

No one told us about the history of this mountain, so unusual for being so tall that it had a snow-covered top and at the same time was so close to the Caribbean. It had fascinated adventurers, botanists, and scientists from the day that it was discovered by Spanish conquistadors. Élisee Reclus came from France to study the plants, the animals, and the Arawaks who lived near the top. To them the mountain was their sacred mother. He had plans to exploit its land and its people in the name of anarchic progress. He left, unable to do so, but with a wonderful travelogue and a few verses to his muse:

> *the excelsior Nevada*
> *that plants her foot on the back of the Atlantic*
> *And its limpid front stand-up straight to the sky.*

The Sierra Nevada is a freezing wayward snowman with a Caribbean personality; a massive isosceles triangle that walked off and went its own way; an independent island of the Andes gone cool; and oddball, like a *cachaco,* on the Caribbean coast.

The road we took to go feel the cold air of the mountain was opened by Don Manuel de Mier y Terán, who came from Spain with titles to the land. He founded a coffee plantation two thousand feet above sea level. As the jeep went up the steep cobbled road, we opened the windows to let the clouds come in.

Part of the fun of going to the sierra was how difficult it was to get there. Because it took so long and we had to factor in the delays due to weather and road problems, we usually left on Friday before school let out. Pablo's father, Ernesto, would coordinate the time of departure with the other jeeps heading out so that we could all meet at the foot of the Sierra in a little town called Minca. To get there we drove north, crossing the Pumarejo Bridge over the Magdalena River, passing through Ciénaga, the place of the legendary banana massacre (which no one ever mentioned to us), and then along the sea to Santa Marta until we got to Minca. It was essential that before we embarked on the uphill road to the Sierra we all met there so that the rest of the trip would be done as a convoy, especially during the rainy season. The narrow road would turn into deep mud pools and when this happened, the jeeps ran the risk of getting stuck. Only another jeep could pull one out. Each car was equipped with a siren like police cars have that were used when the road got too foggy or the turns too sharp. We had heavy rope in case the jeep needed to be pulled and chains to put on the tires in case we ran into slippery stones. The boys did all the work, but when local kids came to help, the boys would let them take over. We girls stayed with Beatriz, Pablo's mother, by the side of the road.

Before Ernesto would put the jeep on the double transition, Beatriz would take out her rosary and we all, including David, who was Jewish, repeated the prayer reserved for road trips. Whenever it became treacherous, we repeated the words she would instruct us to say. When the road was clear, Ernesto would break into poems and songs. We all giggled when he sang about the "perfumes" of a woman, which was a euphemism for breast. Beatriz would blush and tell him to stop it but he just sang louder and we laughed some more.

Unbeknown to me then, on the other side of the Sierra Nevada lay my grandfather's world; I now see it on my kitchen map. According to Reclus's diary there are two entrances to the Sierra: one from Santa Marta, the one we took, and another one, a cobblestone path, opened during Colonial days, for the conquistadors to step on, from Valledupar, the biggest city close to Asunción. On that side, the sierra was equally difficult to penetrate but the colonizers of land and the coffee planters came up anyway. In those days, the first

Montblancs, rode up on their mules using the Spanish stone covered with moss just like we did in jeeps.

We went there to pick blackberries and orchids, and catch butterflies. We found streams to cross and liana to hang from. At night we sat around and played parlor games. We listened to "Benny and the Jets" till the batteries in the boom box gave out. Sitting down in the evening to play the game that Beatriz taught us was less exciting. It was called What's in Grandma's Chest and we played in a circle. We repeated the list of things that were in the imaginary chest and added our own item. It was not as much fun and little by little all the boys would stop playing but the girls never did because it was the game Beatriz wanted us to play. It would have been rude to tell her we were bored. Especially because many times, Doña Susana, Pablo's grandmother, a Queen Mum of sorts, was sitting right there with us. And she was having the time of her life.

Pablo's brother Fernando was older than us, old enough to drive his own jeep up the Sierra, and he would come with his friends too. One afternoon the older boys invited us girls only to go for a ride in their jeep. They told us they were on their way to see the Indians who lived at the top of the mountain. Fernando's friend Frankie, the boy with the blue eyes, was in the jeep with him. He wore a *mochila,* a woven bag across his chest and a pointy woolen hat like the Arawaks make and wear. It was the first time I saw a hippie, I guess the Barranquilla version of one. I thought he looked both funny and cute in his strange getup. The visit was not as exciting as they had made it out to be. But crossing the rickety bridge was fun; the planks of wood shifted dangerously as we rolled by and we all held onto the roof as we jumped and bumped along the way. On the curves, Frankie's and my rib cages would touch, which I thought was the whole point of the trip.

We got into trouble for doing that. The boys our age wouldn't talk to us for abandoning them for the older boys. Beatriz told us young ladies shouldn't be riding in jeeps with older boys, especially without asking for permission. That night while we sat around naming slips and slippers, coats and cameos, books and whatever feminine bric-a-brac we could think of to appease the female adults, I could not stop thinking about the rock music coming out of the older boys' cabanas till late. Everyone was in a bad mood. The boys were so mad at us that they threatened to find tarantulas and we slipped into our bunk beds under woolen blankets not knowing if they had.

The reason the older boys liked going to the mountaintop was not so much to see the Indians or that they got us to sit tight next to them during the ride but because marijuana grew at those altitudes. I later heard that they got in trouble and were not allowed to return when Beatriz found that her Bible was missing the entire Genesis. The boys had ripped off its onionskin pages and used them to roll their marijuana cigarettes. I remember Frankie had pointed out a plant, the one with leaves with five fingers like a hand. I took one back home and planted it in my mother's garden. I instructed the gardener to water it daily and told him if it died, I would bring back a tartantula the next time.

Black spiders were about the scariest thing the Sierra had then. Today that is certainly not the case. The Sierra has now become one of the most dangerous places in Colombia. Our ancestors had been colonizers; and we were the children of the first white men to plant coffee and graze cattle in the shadows of these mountains. Neither they at the turn of the twentieth century nor we in the 1970s would ever think that the paths they carved would put us in danger one day. The rebels, as they like mountains, took the Sierra Nevada and the cabanas, as we called them, with their built-in antennas and ham radios, were perfectly equipped for the rebels to want them. The cluster of cottages for a group of friends to enjoy nature became a training center for and the headquarters to one of the FARC's fronts. "*Esos hijueputos* probably peed on my mother's orchids," Margarita's son, who had a cabana next to Pablo's, wrote to me in an e-mail from France a few years ago. Now the Sierra belongs to the paras, those in the know, like Max, the American photojournalist, tells me. And I am starting to understand the game played out in Colombia's war: it is primarily a fight for land. If the rebels had the Sierra and the paras now want it, then Ringo Starr was absolutely right: this area must be the best in the land.

14

HIGH TIMES IN BARRANQUILLA

Four years after Nixon's plan, more than 80 percent of all small farmers and large landowners in the states of Guajira and Magdalena were growing marijuana. More than fifteen planes flew across the Atlantic and came to the region every day. By the end of 1976, more than one thousand clandestine strips had been built to accommodate them. Rumor has it that after midnight Santa Marta's airport was available to rent by the hour.

Barranquilla, being the most cosmopolitan city of the region, became the beneficiary of the new money. Heavy-hitter *marimberos* started settling there, and the city changed overnight. It was always dusty, cheerful, disorganized, glitzy, and loud—the marijuana money only magnified these traits. Blazers, the SUVs of choice in those days, started rolling into town. New arrivals window-shopped from behind the tinted glass of their air-conditioned cars, bringing enough cash to buy up whatever they wanted—priests, policemen, women, and homes.

But soon, the happy discovery of a cash crop that paid in dollars making everyone rich overnight mutated into an enterprise that claimed danger and absurd accidents as its trademark. A DC-3 plane on its way to the United States was so heavy with marijuana that it fell from the sky and into the Atlantic Ocean. In the Guajira desert, a peculiar cemetery was discovered where both the crew and the Cessna that crashed had been given a proper Catholic burial. On the way to the beach in Barranquilla one Sunday, a group of my friends and I ran into an abandoned plane on the road. The local kids had turned it into a street-fair attraction and were charging admission to those curious to walk inside.

The *marimberos* from the Guajira arrived in Barranquilla with their dollars but they also brought their laws. The up and coming city of merchants and landowners, the City of Progress, as the *barranquilleros* liked to call it, turned, by 1978, into a tropical Wild West. People, some of whom I knew, were being shot—in discotheques, at parties, at art openings, in confrontations over women or over profits. When the city's chief of police ordered house searches, he was transferred out the next day. "The police roll with our punches or they go," they told him. It seems as if no generation in Colombia will be spared living with violence. My grandparents lived the years of La Violencia. Their children, my uncle in particular, have lives caught between the fight of the so-called Communist rebel forces and those who oppose them. By the time I turned fifteen, I too saw some violence. I saw the arrival of drug feuds.

For us teenagers, there was an undeniable element of excitement. Who were those men behind the dark windowed cars that started showing up? We heard that when their daughters turned fifteen, they handed out insanely expensive gifts. At one quinceañero party they gave out eighteen-karat-gold long-stemmed roses to their guests. We wanted to go to their houses, be invited to their festivities, but our parents preferred we didn't. Not only were they considered *corronchos,* sometimes they had surprises that were not as pleasant as the party favors. They shot their guns at a whim, even at teenagers. Luis, the seventeen-year-old who was my steady boyfriend, was attacked a few months before I left for Michigan. On the eve of Mother's Day, five of his friends were riding around, squeezed in his car going from house to house serenading their mothers. As they disembarked in front of one of their stops, exactly at midnight, a car without its lights on flew by. One of the boys yelled, "Hey man, the lights." The car screeched to a halt and from inside someone began shooting, striking one of the boys in his shoulder. What could have become a tragedy became simply a *guajiro* story.

Soon, like with kidnappings now, everyone had a *guajiro* story to tell. It became the name used for everything that was drug-related in Barranquilla. One of the neighborhoods they bought into was dubbed the Upper Guajira. The word "*guajiro*" became an adjective: There were *guajiro* stories, *guajiro* sons, *guajiro* parties, *guajiro* cars, and *guajiro* taste. The unthinkable started to become routine, a tragic theme that seemed to repeat itself in Colombia's history. My mother's friend, the wife of an important politician, was driving back from the beauty parlor one day soon after the *guajiros* moved to town. When she blew her horn at the driver of a Bronco who had stopped at a green light to chat with friends, the man behind the wheel, a seemingly pleasant man she would later say, stepped out, slowly walked over to her car, and knocked gently at her window. When she rolled it down, he put a gun to her head and politely instructed her to repeat after him: "I shall not blow my horn at a *guajiro,*" one hundred times over. My friends would keep me entertained with their own *guajiro* stories, telling me about all the fun they were having while I was away cold in Michigan. Sandra, the daredevil of the posse, invented a game called

Let's Go Look for *Guajiros*. The game consisted of a handful of girls walking the streets of Riomar to see if a *guajiro* car would stop. The girls were not only pretty but also well bred and that made them more attractive to the newcomers; who were not only armed and nouveau riche but also macho womanizers. The idea was to go for a ride in their big cars with the electronic windows, the air-conditioning and the stereo system at full blast. It was titillating to hang out with them; I imagine that seeing the guns and the houses with the gaudy decoration was part of the fun. The element of danger that made it all more fascinating: Everyone knew about the *guajiro* temper that could flare up without warning. With all those guns around and the macho posturing, things could turn scary in seconds. That was part of the excitement.

Over the years I would get word of people I once knew, or knew of, who had been shot: A cousin's boyfriend was gunned down as he was leaving the gym and another acquaintance as he exited Dulcerna where Allegra and I would go for an afternoon brownie.

Before leaving Barranquilla for Michigan, I had a few of my own *guajiro* experiences. My friend Emma fell in love with a *guajiro* son. Tony was never scary even if he had a gun in the glove compartment of his Cadillac, the longest car I had ever seen in my life, longer than Pablo's grandfather's Cadillac. He was soft spoken and wore silk shirts but her parents told her that she was not to socialize with him. The problem was Emma was already going out with him. And we loved riding in his white car with a burgundy leather top that had a sun roof and an eight-track player, two things we had never seen. Our parents' cars did not have such extravagances. We would all get in Tony's car so we could drive around listening to "Ain't No Way to Treat a Lady." Tony was also very generous. His wallet, unlike our friends', seemed to be replenished automatically. He would stop at Dulcerna and buy brownies for all of us and one day he showed up with tapes of the car songs for all of us. As soon as Emma's parents found out that it was going to be impossible to keep them apart, they sent her to live with aunts in Bogotá first and then to boarding school in Massachusetts. "It was like Romeo and Juliet between us," she tells me as we chat from Miami where she is waiting for the rain to stop.

When the *guajiros* arrived and Emma met Tony, *el grupito*, with our childhood pals, was breaking up. We were meeting the girls who lived on our blocks but didn't go to our American school. Barranquilla was becoming more than our tight-knit handful of friends. Walking around one day, Allegra and I met Paula, Ana María, the three Fernández sisters down the block, and the two Perez sisters who lived in the yellow building where I had seen the M-19 sign. We became friends, tentatively at first. They were Marymount girls, and there was rivalry between the Parrish girls and the Marymount girls.

Allegra and I would speak in English when we saw them coming. It was known that Parrish girls had better accents, so we would purposely stop them on the street, asking "Do you know what time it is?" to prove our accent was better than theirs. Also, they had to wear baby blue jumpers with white blouses to school while we were free to wear our Miami-bought miniskirts and platform sandals to our school. Despite these differences, we soon became friends, good friends. We formed a unit so tight that we came to be known as the English Girls, named for our love of the language.

When a boy liked you in Barranquilla, he would manifest it by driving in front of your house. It was called "the pass." The idea was for you to see him doing this. Allegra liked Pedro, who drove a beat-up Land Rover. Paula liked Mario, who was driven by Sam, who liked me, in his red little Renault. And Ana María liked Roberto, who drove a black VW bug. By keeping an eye out for each other, we would know which of the guys had passed, even if you missed the one intended for you, someone else saw it and that counted. To wait for "the pass" and to exchange pass information we would meet on Fridays after school in front of my house. Soon, my front lawn became more popular for teenage rendezvous than the parking lot of any suburban 7-Eleven. On weekdays, my mother would not allow us to receive on the front lawn but starting Friday it was open season. One by one the cars started arriving.

The neighbors complained but my parents were supportive of our meeting place. Barranquilla had become dangerous and they preferred having us around. Some women from the block tried everything to prevent us from using the sidewalk. They planted cacti on the side of the ditch to stop us from sitting there. They started rumors that involved drugs and sex. It didn't work. The popularity of The Hole, as it became to be known, was too great. We stopped going to the club and to each other's houses. Love stories began and ended here, even unacceptable ones like Emma and Tony's. Some even ended in pregnancies. It was also easier for David or Sam to hang out with us here. At The Hole we didn't have the hassle of sneaking them into el Country Club, where Jews were not members. When I recently asked if it was in the club's statutes, a friend's father who served on the board said, "No, that would not have been nice. But it was understood. And they had their school, their club, and their synagogues that were lovely."

IT WAS NEW YEAR'S EVE, ON THE CUSP OF 1977. MY PARENTS TOLD ME THAT my grandparents, aunts, and uncles were coming over and we were to be "all together" that night, but if I wanted I could have friends come by after dinner.

My parents always preferred this arrangement. They didn't care how many friends came over—ten, twenty, fifty—as long as we stayed home.

At around midnight, the cars started rolling in. The boys honked their horns to welcome the New Year and some of us got on the hoods of the cars. No one noticed the red car that joined our party until my cousin Alicia jumped on its hood. A man pointing a gun at her from the other side of the windshield startled her. So scared that she couldn't even scream, she ran inside. "A *guajiro*, a *guajiro*," she yelled as soon as she got to where the adults were gathered. "I saw him."

My father went outside to see if he could figure out what she was talking about. She went with him. "There, there," she shouted. "It's that one." As girls waiting for the pass, we kept good track of which boy drove what car and we were wondering who the newcomer was. I was under a tree talking to the blue-eyed boy who made my palms sweat when I saw him. When my father walked out, we all froze. Parental presence in a bunch of partying teenagers was pretty intimidating. All fifty of us stopped what we were doing.

My father told Alicia to stay behind, very calmly walked to the car, and tapped on the window of the passenger's side. "Good evening," my father said to the face that appeared as the glass rolled down. He proceeded to tell the stranger that this was a private party and that he would appreciate it if they were kind enough not to come by again. Alicia was right. The man had a gun. It was pointed at my father. Next came a screeching of the tires and the first round of gunfire I'd heard in my life. My father fell to the ground. He was fine. They'd had the decency to shoot at the stars.

As scared as we all were, someone had taken down the license plate number and my father went back inside to make a call to the police. The car never drove by again and the boy with the blue eyes and I never got to have our Happy New Year kiss under the *matarratón* tree.

A few weeks after our party, Allegra and I saw the red car again during one of our walks. It was parked at her grandfather's house, which had been sold after he had died. "Allegra, look at the car," I said. We commented that it was *guajiro* children who would be using the pool now and playing with the shiny wooden balustrade as they went down the marble staircase that we had used so many times. We said it in a discriminatory way. *Guajiros* were definitely *corronchos,* which for our purposes meant they weren't Americanized, like us.

EVERYONE GOT SPRINKLED WITH SANTA MARTA GOLD DUST. IT WAS SO IN YOUR face it was hard to resist and everyone wanted some. The desire for it brought rivalries of course. My favorite story is that of the feud between interior decorators fighting for clients. To hear the story from the source, in 2003 I visited

Matilde, the dame of the city's interior decorators, in Miami where I prompted her to reminisce about the marijuana days over a long lunch and a bottle of red wine. We had met a few times when I was a teenager and she came over to my house in Riomar to help my mother decorate it. I remembered her as a handsome and portly woman with amazing style and a contagious laugh. I also remembered that in those days Matilde and Rubén were the Harold and Maude of Barranquilla's marijuana bonanza, even if their age difference was not as dramatic. She was a recent widow in her late thirties with four children, a respectable last name, and a big mortgage. He was in his early twenties, penniless, and very rambunctious. They met when he walked into her former husband's appliance store to inquire about the pair of chairs displayed in the window. The store normally sold refrigerators, not fabulous pieces of furniture.

Matilde had decided that to help with the store's dire financial situation she would sell used furniture brought in from Bogotá, the sophisticated capital where the *cachacas,* the ladies from the capital, had long ago established antique and vintage shops. She had an eye for interesting objects and a knack for arranging interiors so she decided to bring the art of recycling heirlooms to the coast. Rubén was a high school dropout, a precocious and charming young man who hung with a small artsy crowd. Together they made a great decorating duo.

Matilde and Rubén also fell in love, and moved to the biggest house in Puerto Colombia, next door to the party-throwing smugglers, where they could be together, free of judgmental looks. But regardless of how much everyone talked about their relationship and their decadent lifestyle, everyone—from senators and industrialists to newly married couples starting their first home— wanted a piece of Matilde and Rubén. They wanted their adventure, irreverence, and style. Matilde and Rubén brought interior decorating, a previously unknown profession, to this Caribbean port city. Barranquilla is one of the most fad-oriented places on the planet, and the trend took off. Everyone had to have a *casa hecha por Matilde y Rubén,* even if it was just a matter of having the couple rearrange the heirlooms in order to get the coveted signature look, as my mother did.

They opened an antiques shop, they made furniture, and with a purse filled with pesos they traveled the entire coast of Colombia in search of ornamental treasures. By jeep they scoured nearby villages; by dugout canoe they went up and down the Magdalena River, visiting the ghost towns left behind by the banana bonanza. The United Fruit Company had long gone and taken its dollars with it, but the Thonet rocking chairs, the Elizabethan double beds and dressers, and the silver candelabra were still there. "It was so much fun," Matilde recalled. To save on transportation, for example, she would rely on friends like Rosita, the wife of a local politician who ran a charity that gave prescription glasses to the poor people who lived in the hamlets along the Rio. Everyone in Barranquilla knew to drop off their old frames at Rosita's house. When she had enough sacks filled with old frames to go hand them out, they took a *piragua*, a wooden dugout canoe, down the river. "The entire population was waiting for us," Matilde said with a chuckle. While Rosita and her assistants opened the bags and tried to find a match between the prescription of the lenses and the strength of the problematic eyes, Matilde had a few hours to scour the town. She even told me about the trip she made with my aunt once where they found five spinster sisters living together in a house filled with decaying treasures. They offered to buy a bronze double bed but when they were negotiating the price, they heard a woman's voice outside screaming obscenities. "Our crazy sister," the seller said. "Don't mind her. She is tied to the tree and she hates it." They ran out empty handed. "They were fun, those trips, but not exactly profitable."

Traveling back in time looking for the days of banana splendor—when it is said men lit their candles with burning dollar bills—sounds fun. Things turned in the late '70s, and soon the days of decorating with stringent local budgets, with requests driven by nostalgia, were over. When the marijuana bonanza arrived Matilde and Rubén were there and their business boomed. *Marimberos,* those from distinguished families as well as those from the less sophisticated country class of the Guajira, all were fast spenders and equally ostentatious.

"They all came," Matilde told me as she cut a piece of her steak. She was still as charismatic and full of life as I remembered her. If she was a bit reluctant to meet me at first, talking about the good old days has made her more comfortable. I feel her nostalgia and her naughty glee as she tells me how she became the most popular decorator on Colombia's Caribbean coast, through word of mouth, through what they read in the society pages, through family—"one smuggler cousin brought the other," she says. A house in Barranquilla would lead to a three-story house in Riohacha or to a summer home on a deserted island. The road was unpaved. Matilde and Rubén helped pave it. High-rises, houses of a size never known before, went up along the coast. Matilde and Rubén were busier than ever. The *marimberos* wanted what the sociey couples had: decorated homes. Matilde and Rubén could do as they pleased.

The only thing the *marimberos* required was a discotheque, complete with black walls, strobe lights, and mirrored balls. After that it was carte blanche for the decorators. Matilde and Rubén were no longer going out on riverboats to buy their wares. They were going to the design districts in Miami and New York, the Via Condotti in Rome and the islands near Venice, the auction houses of London and Paris. To be in New York in May for the auctions of Latin American art at Sotheby's and Christie's was a must. "We brought back spectacular things," says Matilde, her eyes rising skyward almost in ecstasy as she remembers the spending sprees: the gold faucets and doorknobs, the pair of stone lions, the Saporiti pigskin and sealskin couches.

It was mostly all paid for in cash. Even the $30,000 for the sealskin sofa. In New York early one morning in 1979, Matilde woke up to a rain of money, literally. Rubén was pouring out the $150,000 in cash that had been left in a duffel bag outside their hotel room. "He was screaming, 'Bathe in it; let it touch you.'" "'Maybe it will stick.'" A very satisfied customer once gave them a beautiful stallion so they threw a party that lasted days. Rubén, like Bianca Jagger had done at Studio 54, came into the living room riding the horse.

Matilde remembers the morning she was awakened in her house by the sound of motorbikes and trucks rolling down her cobbled driveway. She opened the curtain and saw half a dozen motorboats along the small pier outside her house. She could see men loading sack after sack of Santa Marta Gold into a small motorboat. Once the motorboat was full it disappeared into the horizon where she could detect another bigger boat. She grabbed her robe and went to the terrace. When her neighbor saw her, he waved at her and with a huge smile invited her over for breakfast. "Come see. Come see a loading. How we load the boats. We have some Americans here who came to watch it," he screamed as if he were inviting her to go watch something as natural as a sunrise.

BONANZAS BRING COMPETITION. MATILDE AND RUBÉN'S WAS NAMED ROCCO, A spitfire talker of four languages and a lot of pretense. The gay son in a very conservative family that wanted nothing to do with homosexuality, Rocco was sent away from Barranquilla and ended up in New York City, arranging flowers in the basement of the Waldorf-Astoria Hotel. To make extra money he would buy crystal knickknacks and send them back to his sister, who would sell them out of their mother's garage. Eventually, he was allowed to come home, and slowly he turned his family's garage into the most prestigious flower shop in the city. Rocco was more of a businessman than the happy-go-lucky decorating couple of Matilde and Rubén. The flower shop expanded into an art gallery. Rocco sold gigantic flower arrangements, expensive baubles, and artwork from Latin America's most important masters from Galeria Rocco.

It is hard to tell if Rocco's timing was due to fortune or to his business wiles, but he opened his exclusive gallery—a three-story extravaganza of cut crystal doors and smoked mirrors—exactly at the peak of the *marimba* bonanza. The *marimberos* wanted what every other emerging group in history has wanted: recognition, gentrification, and the grand life. They would read about an art opening at Rocco's shop in the paper and the next day they were there. "The old money elite took forever to pay, but these people arrived with the full price in cash," recalls Manuel, Rocco's favorite protégé. "Rocco's eyes were opened wide."

He hatched a plan that would cause Matilde and Rubén's outfit to pale. He would offer more than decorating services. He would be their party planner, and their personal shopper. He became Pygmalion to the *marimberos*. He would transcend the local clientele. Cali, Medellín, Bogotá—the whole country was catching up to the business of trafficking in drugs. The client list was endless and he was ambitious. I hear he brought Pablo Escobar to New York once and they stayed at the Waldorf Astoria. And that money became more important than style, soon winning him the nickname of "La Rocco-co."

His break came when he learned that a narco-couple from Medellín was getting married and the bride came to Barranquilla to have her dress made by one of the local designers. He convinced the groom, who was paying for it all, to hire him and hold the wedding, not where the bride and groom were from, but where he, the party planner, said it should be. The couple was married in Barranquilla. For the wedding, Rocco ordered a plane-load of flowers from New York. The lobster tails came from Maine and from the Caribbean. The champagne and the cheeses were from France via Aruba, as was the fancy garters that the bride threw to the many out-of-towners.

Rocco not only planned the wedding but he went on the honeymoon. "No matter how much money they had, they would never have dared to go to the Ritz in Paris of their own accord," Manuel, who also lives in Miami now, tells me. My friend Juliana met Rocco a few times in Miami as he passed by with clients. She met a couple and Rocco for dinner at the Forge, then the best and most expensive restaurant in Miami Beach. She remembers Rocco telling his clients to watch him before picking up their forks, and ladies, please use napkins to wipe your mouths, not the sleeves of your brand-new Valentino gowns. The wine was Chateau Lafitte, $1,400 a bottle, and the bill was paid in cash. "Rocco and I would wait in the car while the clients settled the check," she says. "He was a brilliant businessman," Manuel told me. "He would take whatever he saw on his trips and would sell them as his own original ideas." One year, he sold seven-foot lacquered double doors; the next season it was round Oggetti lamps. Matilde said she couldn't believe it when she went into a client's house three months after having finished decorating it and saw the beautiful Saporiti sofa reupholstered in satin chintz and the exquisite antique silver fruit bowl from Rome replaced by "a huge horror" that was made with fourteen porcelain horses pulling a carriage. "He'd leave their houses saying 'now it's divine.'"

The truth is that no matter what he sold or how he sold it, people bought into Rocco's lifestyle. "He would set a price by closing his eyes," Manuel told me, "and say 'This job will cost this much.'" It was steep and perhaps three times what it was really worth, but he had his reasons. "There were risks in working with these people. The client might be caught or killed, and then Rocco would be stuck with a bunch of couches and crystal lamps." But there was a limit to how much you can get away with overcharging. Once they started educating themselves, his clients realized it was all too much. They got suspicious. "At first everyone is excited and agrees to anything the master indicates," Manuel continued, "but once they begin understanding how things work and the party is over and then they get his exorbitant invoice, everything changes."

Eventually, after using Rocco's services, everyone would feel cheated. For a first communion party he bought hundreds of gold-filled rosaries to hand out as favors and charged for them as if they were made of eighteen-karat gold. One client issued a death threat. Soon, Rocco spent his time escaping from one unsatisfied customer after another, from one brawl after another. When a powerful *marimbero* realized that he had been sold a replica of a Colombian master as an original, Rocco's car was set on fire. He knew it was time to move to Miami.

The end was near. Not only had he been diagnosed with AIDS, but Colombia had signed an extradition treaty with the United States and the days of the *marimberos* were dwindling. The United States was now growing its own pot. Like the bonanza and many of his clients, Rocco died.

As for Matilde and Rubén, they never ceased being their wonderfully outlandish selves. When a favorite client was extradited and imprisoned in Miami, they flew over to visit, only to be denied permission. Refusing to leave, they parked their rented car, headlights pointing toward the cell, and stood in vigil, armed with cheap disposable lighters. For hours Rubén called out the prisoner's name.

"It's cursed money," Matilde has concluded. "I don't know one of these guys who made it rich and is also alive. Today, they are either poor or dead."

The decorators are no longer a couple but they are still a family—they have two children together—and are growing old in the house they built on the beach outside of Barranquilla. Nearby, the smuggler's house sits abandoned. He was gunned down many years ago around Christmastime. The pine tree with Christmas balls still on it and all the fantastical things Matilde and Rubén bought for him are caressed now only by the Caribbean breeze.

HIGH SCHOOL LIFE IN BLOOMFIELD HILLS, MICHIGAN, WAS VERY DIFFERENT than life in Barranquilla. I had to get used to not walking with Allegra. No one walked here, and what's more, no one had drivers. Girls my age had their own cars, which gave them an independence unheard of in Barranquilla. For all the things that I missed, there were many aspects of life in the United States that, to me, were wondrous. My friends lived in huge houses where the doors were left unlocked. No one worried about the dangers of living face-to-face with poor people. Downtown Detroit and the state of Michigan might have one of the worst unemployment and poverty rates in this country, but I never saw it in the suburbs of Bloomfield Hills with its houses with pine trees, circular driveways, and more than one Cadillac. The fascination was mutual. To my classmates I was somewhat of a novelty for one reason only. I came from a foreign country. It didn't matter which one. To them, Colombia was just the country of Juan Valdez and his coffee beans.

My contact with my friends back home became sporadic, in the form of letters written on colored paper. A year later, Allegra moved to Baltimore to live with her aunt and we talked on the phone at least once a week. We would catch up with what information we had gotten in the mail from the girls who stayed behind. That December Allegra went back and I stayed to experience my first white Christmas. It was definitely not as much fun as the previous year when the *guajiros* had caused such a panic, which, truth be told, had been more exciting than scary, especially as time went by. And I missed the outdoor quality of life in Barranquilla. When Allegra returned from her break, she came with news about a new boyfriend. "You're not going to believe it," she began. "I'm dating Román Delgado."

Of course I recognized the name. Román was a few years older than us and ran with a faster crowd than ours. He was also known to be a total mango, the word we used to describe handsome boys. And so much cooler than the boys we had liked before. I remembered him as a taller and lankier Johnny Depp, who wore faded bell-bottoms and a Jim Morrison T-shirt and walked the streets with a swagger. He was not only gorgeous but had style, someone who is immediately liked by everyone. Very simply put—Román was cool. He was so cool that girls wanted to go out with him, even though he didn't have a car.

Román came from a reputable family but they were less comfortable financially than the families of the boys we knew. His father had died in a car accident and his mother was left a young widow with five small children to bring up. Román was sent to live with an uncle in California. There he grew up like most American kids, going to a public school and working at restaurants for pocket money. When he would show up in Barranquilla for the summer, girls couldn't believe someone so cool existed. We would hear about whom he had asked out because everyone kept track of who was the lucky one. Usually they were girls older than us, girls who went to Marymount, or girls who were racier than us. We were part of such a different crowd. We were so overprotected, maybe even prissy. What had started with driving around with Tony for ice cream became much more complicated after I left. Barranquilla had changed and so had the rules for socializing. Allegra tells me stories of going out with a new type of guy. They were not exactly *guajiros* but were more "mysterious" than our school pals. They drove fancy American cars, especially Ford Broncos with antennas and tinted windows. They wore designer everything: Versace sunglasses, Versace jeans, even Versace perfume. When they asked girls out they took them to discotheques, places the boys of our circles would not frequent, and bought champagne. Allegra told me she ventured inside the Clockwork Orange. When I lived there it was seen as a place where easy girls went. It was also where many husbands and fathers would meet their mistresses, another reason our parents didn't want us to go.

But I also knew that these places Allegra was gushing about were also dangerous. I had heard that the high-rolling, high-spending *marimberos* were taking over Barranquilla's nightlife. Every weekend there would be a new story of how there had been gunshots at the Clockwork Orange or at the Worm: If you looked at their women you got shot; if they looked at your women and you complained, you got shot too. Would I too have played the game of going out with *marimberos,* if I had stayed?

"Where did you even meet him?" I asked her.

"You are not going to believe it," she said, clearly excited. "On the plane from Barranquilla to Miami." He was flying first class and he even sent over the chocolates. Two days later, he paid her a visit. "I couldn't believe it. Román Delgado. In my house. My father was a bit surprised."

A year later Román and Allegra were married. She moved to her father's apartment in Miami, had a son, and took on the vagaries of a life with a man in the business. Over the next twenty years, our lives took very different turns but I saw her occasionally. I would make a point to stay a few days in Miami on my way back and forth from college. I even went to visit her on a long weekend from school when it got really cold in Michigan. I decided to fly down with two friends. Román and Allegra came to pick us up in a red convertible Alfa Romeo and took us dancing at the Mutiny Club, my first club with a velvet rope and a no jeans dress code for men. My friend Tom was not going to be allowed in because he was wearing Levi's. But as we were being told that, another man dressed in jeans was whisked in. "What about him?" he asked the bouncer as he opened the cord. "That is different," he replied with derision. "Those are designer jeans." When the bouncer realized we came with Román, he apologized profusely. That night, Román bought all the drinks. Every time my friends would make an effort to pay, Román would take out a wad of dollars from his pocket. "Absolutely not," he would say as he talked to them about his worldview. "Look around you," Román would begin, "You see a bottle of alcohol and a pack of Marlboros at every table, don't you? Well, soon you will see another package. Soon you will be able to buy a package of joints like you buy tobacco. Marijuana will become so common that it's going to be like buying beer at the supermarket. Remember Prohibition? And how many fortunes turned legal overnight when it ended? It's going to be the same for me. Tobacco companies will be buying marijuana from my fields." My two college friends exchanged glances, half scared, half titillated by the entire situation. Faces I knew from Barranquilla started showing up at our table to say hello. I saw Albert, who told me he was living in a mansion next door to the Bee Gees. When Andy Gibb's song "You Are My Everything" came on, everyone got up to dance under the disco balls.

On the plane back, I tried to catch up with the required reading but was distracted thinking how things felt different between Allegra and me. Over the years we saw each other less and less. We met in New York during a Thanksgiving break. Román wore a star-shaped diamond in his left ear, and a beautiful Giorgio Armani tuxedo. As we walked into Studio 54, Allegra turned to me. "He is so much more handsome than Richard Gere in *American Gigolo,* don't you think?"

15

NEED HELP FROM ALLEGRA

The morning after my running in Riomar, I ask José to take me to see Allegra. I need her as my guide. I was not Silvana when I lived here: I was Silvana and Allegra. We were inseparable from the day she flunked seventh grade. But we like to say that it was all predestined. Our parents were friends. I have a picture of the four of them toasting, wearing Happy New Year hats at el Country Club's San Silvestre Ball. Plus our sisters were born on exactly the same day in May of 1963, in the same hospital, on the same floor.

When Allegra turned thirteen, she invited me to her birthday party. She doesn't remember but I do. It was the most peculiar birthday invitation I had ever received. First because we weren't friends. I knew who she was—everyone did. She was like Pippi Longstocking because she was very tall and long and when she cried, which she did often, she stomped her feet and grabbed her hair, which was always messy. Sometimes she had knots that were so big her hair had to be cut short. That particular day, it had to be mid-March—she is an Aries, as she likes to say—when she stopped me halfway and without saying much more than "my birthday," she handed me a piece of paper. She handed it to me during one of the three-minute class breaks we had, to get from one classroom to the other. I was in an advanced reading class, which meant that I would leave my homeroom and go down the dark staircase next to the principal's office to get to the classroom in time. Allegra took math with the fifth graders and so we passed each other sometimes on the staircase, the one with the oil portrait of John F. Kennedy, the father of the Alliance for Progress, the U.S. response to guerrilla warfare in Latin America and the reason we children of the elite were so Americanized. With textbooks and talent shows they would make *gringitas* not Soviet supporters of us, as was happening in so many of the non-American schools.

I was also taken aback because her birthday invitation sure didn't look like one. Everyone's birthday invitations were the kind that came in boxes and were all the same. Because they came from Miami, they had the date, time, and place written in English, and they had colored envelopes. Allegra's card didn't have an envelope. It was a folded piece of paper so in a sense it was a card because it was something you opened. The paper she gave me had a drawing on the front cover, something she had done. I opened it when I reached the bottom of the stairs and all I saw was a blank sheet of paper. I shoved it inside my book, a bit surprised and maybe disappointed. Was she mocking me for being the fifth grader who went to sixth grade to read? But again, it was Allegra and everyone knew she did things differently.

I did not go to her party. I was too proud to tell her that I did not get the information to attend. We didn't speak again until the year I got to seventh grade and Allegra was in my classroom. After that day, we did everything together; from the moment we woke up we were in touch.

No one understood our friendship. She was tall. I was not. They called her A Liter of Coca-Cola. They called me Silvanita, little Silvana. She was extremely loud. I was only a little loud. She was straightforward. I was coy. When it came to food she was a glutton. I, everyone told me, ate like a bird. But I also would say I didn't want anything and pick from Allegra's plate. She hated that. Her younger sister Doris would look at us and say, "You guys don't match, why are you friends?" and my younger brother would have a fit every morning when it was time to go—I always insisted on a detour to pick up Allegra at her house because we loved arriving to school together.

Allegra always asked what was for dinner at my house and if she liked the menu she simply stayed, especially when she heard it was the sweet and sour chicken with the curry rice and the clusters of super thin and crispy French fries. She also liked staying over during weekends even though my bed was so much smaller than hers and sometimes her feet dangled out. When my mother got pregnant and she and my father called us into the library den to tell us something that sounded very important and serious because of my dad's tone, my mother's outfit, and the closed door, Allegra was there and received the news about the new addition as if it were a sibling for her too. Her scream of surprise and excitement was definitely louder than mine. I tell Allegra now that the blank paper she gave me on that dark stairwell was not a birthday invitation to her thirteenth birthday party but an invitation for life. That's why it was the only one that was left blank.

ALLEGRA, WEARING A PAREO, LEANS ON THE DOORWAY TO HER HOUSE. "IS THAT you, Silvana?" she says and I immediately think how easily she breaks with tradition. No matter that the beauty expectations of this city are fashioned after

Entertainment Tonight and plastic surgery, she does not give a damn. As a big woman she is expected to wear nun's habits, not the bikini top and wrap-around cloth she is now wearing.

"Come in," she says. "I was just reading that Román died of a heart attack. It's the first time I have been able to look at Román Delgado's death certificate." We had not seen each other in at least a year, when she was last in New York but Allegra's never been one to bother with pleasantries. That was what was on her mind when I arrived in her driveway and that was the hello I got. Román had been shot nine months previously.

"I remember his face when I went up to the coffin," Allegra tells me. "I saw him wearing a blue turtleneck and it made me so mad. They had to bury him in this heat of Barranquilla wearing a turtleneck as if he were in New York because of the bullet holes. It made me so mad. I wanted to kill him."

Allegra was angry at him not for dying—they had been separated at the time—but for dying that way. Allegra has never spoken to me about how it felt being married to a man who was in *el negocio,* the business, as it is called here, but today she is struggling with their shared history.

Today, at forty-two, Allegra is a widow living in a borrowed house on the beach. But her story of marrying, as a young girl, one of the first *marimberos* in our city, albeit a small fish, is the story of Colombia's love affair with the easy money that came with drug deals. For twenty years she enjoyed the luxuries of that lifestyle. She has only told me bits and pieces beyond what I saw during my visits to Miami, and the one time in New York when she carried Louis Vuitton duffel bags filled with one-hundred-dollar bills. I have wondered what it was like—the daily life, how it actually works—but now is not the moment to inquire.

We sit down to talk in her studio facing the Caribbean Sea, surrounded by the huge canvases she now paints. She seems happier than I've ever seen her. She barters her artwork for dresses, haircuts, medical appointments, and massages. I ask her what happened to the Cartier tank watch and pearl-and-diamond set of earrings and necklace that her husband had bought for her. "I have nothing left from those days," Allegra says, "and I don't miss any of it."

She asks me why I've come to Colombia and I tell her I want to write a piece about my grandfather's farm as a way to explain the war. She doesn't even pretend to be mildly interested. As we sip our coffee, Allegra repeats over and over that she is not interested in the country's political situation, adding with pride that she does not read newspapers, does not have an opinion on the War on Drugs, much less on the war I've come to find: the FARC, the paras, the politicians—all mean nothing to her. She is more interested in healing the wounds that life has inflicted on her. Allegra's paintings are as vibrant as she is with strong strokes of blues, reds, purples, and greens. Leaning on the wall are a few of her latest paintings. One is a collage that includes a picture of her as a young girl with a bruise on her knee. In another she borrows a bull's-eye from Jasper Johns, converting it into the yellow, blue, and red of the Colombian flag.

ALLEGRA STRIPPED HERSELF OF ALL HER PAST, NOT ONLY THE ONE SHE HAD when she was married to Román but even the one before that. The one we had; the one that meant we socialized only with a certain type of people, drove in the cars of a certain type of boy, and walked only certain kinds of street.

Allegra is not as interested in going down memory lane with me as she is in showing me the Barranquilla that we had made invisible. For the next few weeks, we establish a routine similar to the one we had as teenagers, but this time we need phones, so at the start of each day she calls me or I call her and we organize how we will spend the day together. This time, we don't walk. We have her car; even though it's old and in bad shape, it's one of the few luxuries that survived.

As soon as I get in her car I immediately leave behind my grandmother's oasis of feudalism and now that I'm settled at my grandmother's, I need to breathe some. My grandmother operates in a vacuum of virgins and servants. Allegra's life is on the streets, screaming at the other cars, at times because they get in her way, at times to say hello to a friend driving by, or to offer her new painting. "It's beautiful," she always says; Allegra is not modest about her art. During the day I accompany her on her errands. In the mid-afternoon, we drive to Sabanilla, Barranquilla's beach, the place where as teenagers we would while away our Sundays. During weekdays, Sabanilla is pretty deserted and Allegra loves knowing that while everyone else is at work, she can come here and have the Caribbean to herself. She looks out at the horizon, looks around, and sighs, "Paradise." I tell her it is not—she rolls her eyes. At night we cruise the streets of her Barranquilla. It all feels new; I could be anywhere I have never been before, like a place I need a visa to travel to. I am just not sure if I'm on vacation or hunting down a story.

Allegra, a woman of obsessions, is hooked these days on an audio book of T. S. Eliot reading the *Four Quartets*. She is listening to the tape every time she comes to get me. Something feels incongruous about hearing Eliot's British accent, articulating thoughts of beauty in a place that for me holds so little aesthetic pleasure and so many stories of violence. Allegra finds solace and complicity in his words. "Listen," she orders me. *The river is within us, the sea is all about us.* The poet's English cadences caress her; she holds onto the steering wheel and closes her eyes. Eliot is surely talking to her about her Barranquilla. To me the river within her is a muddy Magdalena; and the Caribbean Sea that envelops her with calmness fills me with judgments as I see how the rich go to the ocean in their cars and the poor run up to serve them.

T. S. Eliot continues. Allegra repeats with him:

Or when, under ether, the mind is conscious but conscious of nothing—
I said to my soul, be still, and wait without hope
For hope would be hope for the wrong thing; wait without love,
For love would be love of the wrong thing; there is yet faith
But the faith and the love and the hope are all in the waiting.
Wait without thought, for you are not ready for thought:
So the darkness shall be the light, and the stillness the dancing.

"I want Radio Trauma," I say, popping out the tape and searching for the radio station with the twenty-four-hour string of saccharine ballads that I've given that mocking nickname. I can only deal with cheap sentimentality, with hysterical cries of love gone wrong right now. I slip off my sandals and put my feet on the dashboard, belting out the lyrics to these soap-opera symphonies because if I didn't I would just scream.

"Hold on," she says. "Listen to this part." She pops the tape back in.

In order to arrive there,
To arrive where you are, to get from where you are not,
*   You must go by a way wherein there is no ecstasy.*
In order to arrive at what you do not know
*   You must go by a way which is the way of ignorance.*
In order to possess what you do not possess
*   You must go by the way of dispossession.*
In order to arrive at what you are not
*   You must go through the way in which you are not.*
And what you do not know is the only thing you know
And what you own is what you do not own
And where you are is where you are not.

I let her have her poetry as we drive into an unknown part of town. Allegra has offered to take me on a tour of what she calls 'the real Barranquilla.' In Barrio Abajo, which means the "Low Barrio" neighborhood, she shows me the gingerbread houses, one glued next to the other, lining the streets. "This is where the real people live," she tells me. Doors and windows are left wide open and we take in vignettes of family life as if we were in a moving drive-in movie: in this neighborhood a family sits down to dinner; a couple slow dances in a tiny room where their furniture is covered in plastic; men play dominoes on their front porches and hold bottles of beer. Strident music—some Shakira and some *vallenato*—wafts out of many of the scenes. Christmas lights are lit in September, casting shadows on altars devoted to patron saints. I can sense Allegra is attracted to what's inside these homes.

"It is all so orderly," she tells me. "These people are happy, Silvana. I know them. They have so little and I know they are happy." She knows them because they are the carpenters and the painters that she hires to make her furniture pieces and her sculptures. When her car is in the shop, which it often is, she rides the bus with them. "I love the bus. They play great music. Life is perfect for these people."

It is not my concept of happiness, I tell her. And I give her my reasons: Not when the children of these households cannot go to school because it's unaffordable; not when everyone tricks one another in business deals; when politics is relegated to a machine that buys their vote and offers favors. I argue that the fact that she likes to participate in their lives now as they dance and eat dinner, that she finds their plastic flowers perfect does not mean that "life is perfect," the expression she likes to use when she has found solace in an artistic epiphany. To some, Allegra is the real deal, a true artist. To others, she is a Pollyanna, admirably getting on, doing what she believes and always with a love of life that is contagious. To me she is both, but she knows that her "I'm not interested in politics because I'm an artist" position bothers me, just as it bothers her that I am becoming more estranged in her city, our city. As she drives by the old stadium where the opening ceremony of the Carnivals takes place, she tells me about the beauty of Carnivals. I respond that Carnivals is an experience that does not attract me in the least, that three days more of this loudness and this chaos sounds like pure hell to me. She asks me if I've heard the Carnival song for the president when he comes to sit in his high box to see the floats go by at the flower battle on the first day. I, of course, have no idea what she is talking about.

"Come to Carnivals in February and hear it," she tells me defiantly. Allegra sings the song for me, and as I listen to the lyrics I think of the little angels on the morning after Halloween.

I am very much from Barranquilla	*Yo say barranquillero*
And I will not permit	*y no puedo permitir*
That a stranger comes in here	*que aqui venga un forestero*
And throws their mud at me.	*a echarme vainas a mi.*

Disagreeing with each other has always brought us closer.

——————

ALLEGRA COMES TO GET ME AT MY GRANDMOTHER'S WITH HER NEW FRIENDS: a good family boy with a drug problem, a poet who carries his work-in-progress in a *mochila*, the bags woven and worn by the *indios* of the Sierra and the Guajira. He reads it as we drive around. I like the painter who called the *trupillo*, a tree that grows everywhere in Barranquilla, our only democracy. One afternoon, he tells me that I have "slow eyes and low blood pressure." And I hope that my cover has not been blown. My secret for tolerating my existence here has been revealed. I was trying a new way of coping by going around without my contact lenses; that way I cannot see too much. I think otherwise I would not be able to smile, to talk, to sleep, to stay here much longer. I wish I could be less uptight, less critical, that I could just let go. This life doesn't work for me so I should just let it be. Leave and let them be happy here; they all claim they are.

I decide to try a different way to manage being here, to find distance by thinking I'm a character in a Paul Bowles novel, enjoying "the other" as if a ride through the city of my childhood could be turned into an exotic camel ride through the desert as it does for a young American woman. I tell Allegra that I have a theory that we should prove, that we can spend an entire day in Barranquilla and she can run all her errands without ever leaving her car. She laughs with gusto and takes on the mission. She tells me we will do it with the accompaniment of my music selections.

The first stop is at the fruit stand where we order juices and cheese with the local version of cornbread. I get *níspero* and she gets tangerine. Although I refuse to accept Barranquilla, the sandy taste of a *jugo de níspero* in my mouth is the most comforting moment I can have. It's brought to us on a platter and we eat it as if we were at a drive-in soda fountain in the fifties. Up the street, at the intersection, we buy two single Marlboros from an old man who sits on a stool holding a pack of cigarettes all day long. People here are always so short of cash that buying an entire pack can throw their budget off so vendors like this one adjust to the market. He prefers to open up a pack and sell them one by one rather than lose the opportunity to make the pennies that a single Marlboro brings.

We then stop at a client's house where Allegra has to pick up a check for a desk she designed for the owner. She honks. The maid comes to the window. Allegra signals her to come to the car, which she does, but she tells us that her *patrona* is not home and that no, she did not leave the payment. "Typical," Allegra says.

Next we go to *el centro*, Barranquilla's downtown, now taken over by a maze of small tin huts where anything is sold, a local bazaar where everything is so cheap and so cheaply made that Allegra and I go on a shopping spree for flip-flops. They have more than one hundred different models and they cost a dollar a pair. We have still not left the car. The vendors bend to our every request—"Show me this one. Can I try this other one?" We are obviously breaking the rules. This is a pedestrians-only street. No cars are allowed but no one is surprised when we drive through and no one asks us not to. Breaking the law here is done as often as crossing the street or honking your horn.

The guy brings what we order him to bring, calling her *doñita* and *patrona* regardless of her paint-stained pareo and her cheap flip-flops, bought in this very market. Allegra thinks she has broken class barriers but she must know she is treated differently.

On our way back, we pass Bolívar's Boulevard, with the big statue of the Liberator on a horse. We pass the Paternostro Building owned by my father's family, an Art-Deco five-story structure that was once beautiful, when *el centro* was Barranquilla's bustling business center, where our grandparents and parents came to work. Now, it looks dirty, dilapidated, and abandoned. "No one comes here anymore," Allegra says, explaining that all offices have been transferred to the mansions of El Prado, "but I love it." I recognize the building where my father managed a network of banks across the Atlantic coast after he returned from Bogotá and before we left for Panama, never going back to work in Barranquilla again. I see the iron gates with the geometrical figures and remember how the guard would open them and I would walk inside a big marble vault, with a row of tellers and people would stand in front of them waiting their turn. It reminded me of what happened at mass when people lined up for confession to receive the Holy Ghost. I remember the echo of my footsteps as I went up the white staircase looking for my father. And how I always felt relieved when I saw him. He had assured me that I would never get lost. "I will always be able to find you," he would tell me. "I will know it's you when I see the black mark on your foot." It seems like I was that girl a million years ago.

Our last stop that afternoon is at the Olímpica, the local drugstore and supermarket. As soon as the car is parked, we are attacked by a swarm of street boys, the kind I have seen all over Latin America but had never seen as an adult in Barranquilla. They shower us with offerings, pictures of baby Jesus, compliments, tiny packets of Chiclets with such intensity and desperation in their voices. "Please, please buy something. Here, here, a pack of gum." It is the tone of begging that is so ingrained that it comes out the same whether they are selling two-cent gum or pleading to be admitted to the public hospital where every day children die outside the gates, their plight ignored.

"*Patrona*," they repeat as if it is a mantra that will hypnotize us and compel us to hand them all the things that their skinny dirty arms are already grabbing from inside the car. One goes for an old plastic whistle; the other for half a bottle of warm Coca-Cola. The word *patrona* means "master," with the same insinuation of superiority and subjugation as it had in the American South during the Jim Crow days. Allegra tells me that this is really a modern city, cosmopolitan like no other in Colombia, the place that brought the airplane and is known as the City of Progress, but it is hard for me to understand her perspective with a desperate boy standing in front of me, calling me his master.

Allegra turns to them. *"Fuchi,"* she says. *Fuchi* is slang for "go away," accompanied by a furious wave of the hand. No matter how many times she rides the bus that we didn't take as youngsters, in her car she is still the lady that they come to for a coin and who, out of habit, shoos them away. I don't say anything about how this is what I mean when I disagree that life is perfect. I am happy to be with my old friend, back in a comfortable routine.

IN BARRANQUILLA, INSTEAD OF GOING TO BARS FOR BEER, PEOPLE GO TO A *tienda,* a neighborhood bodega with tables, usually set outside on the sidewalk. The more popular the neighborhood, the more *tiendas* it has; there is one for every one hundred Colombians, even the most faraway *cacerio* has its *tienda,* many operated from the garage of a family house. *Tiendas* are open late into the night and sell everything needed at a moment's notice: lightbulbs or candles and batteries for flashlights for when the electricity goes out; all kinds of basic cooking necessities like oil, salt, sugar, and rice; cigarettes (also sold separately), sodas, snacks, and sweets. You can buy two fingers of butter or half a cup of cooking oil, a cup of sugar, like going to a neighbor for it except it costs money. Tienda owners also give credit, keeping tabs of the number of cups of sugar, the number of beers and lightbulbs marked in a notebook until the client is able to settle the debt.

There is a specific way of drinking beer in Barranquilla and although I've seen it, I've never partaken in the activity, until today. The men like to keep the empty bottles on the table. They can both keep tabs of how many beers they've had and compete with one another. When Allegra comes with a friend to pick me up, I tell them I want to sit at a *tienda.* They name a few but settle on La Esperanza, Hope, in the neighborhood called The Paradise. Next to us the four men who have been clearly sitting at their table for a while place their bottles down with a thump when they're empty and call out for more. The night is pleasant, less humid than usual and I feel lost. My vintage Ungaro silk skirt makes no sense. Vintage in Barranquilla is simply old. I look around me and where Allegra sees life, I see a broken cement sidewalk, macho men with menacing demeanors, and annoying music. I notice that the *tienda's* neon sign has iron bars around it. "Because people steal them," Allegra's friend offers and I am not sure if he's being defiant because he senses my being judgmental. "Or sometimes they just shoot at them."

On our way home, we drive by Washington Park, where Allegra and I would glide on the smooth granite area on our rollers skates for hours, round and round the statue of the American president. We liked skating here because this was the busiest intersection of our Barranquilla so we were guaranteed to spot those cars that were driven by the boys we wanted to see. The park is not a meeting point for teenagers anymore. It is now a commercial roundabout with a taxi stand. They've added a statue of the Virgin Mary and she too is surrounded with protective bars. I don't say what I think about the imprisoned saint when Allegra points at it, laughing, making a mental note to take a picture of it. "It would be great in a collage."

THE NEXT MORNING, I WAKE UP TO A STORY ABOUT THE MURDERS OF TWO *tienda* owners. Both were drive-by shootings, motorcycle shoot-bys, a Colombian specialty. While one drove, the one on the back shot and it was impossible to identify them thanks to the helmets they wore. It seems that the style of killing in Medellín in the late eighties has arrived in Barranquilla. I wonder if they'll reinstate the absurd law that prohibits wearing a helmet so the authorities would be able to identify the criminals.

The article calls this "another one of the many mysterious drive-by shootings of *tienda* owners in the past few months." The shooting occurred at the same time that we were having our beers. When I call Allegra to tell her, she laughs and she tells me she hadn't heard of that, as if I am making it up. But Allegra, like most people in Barranquilla, does not read the stories of shootings and kidnapping, the makings of a war, because not knowing all that means theirs is a normal life. More than that, theirs is a happy life. In case I forgot about the English study that named Colombians to be the happiest in the world. I am told that in the fifties, a Conservative would shoot a Liberal and vice versa, and that there was disagreement among parties. In the seventies and eighties, a *guajiro* would shoot on a whim and that was the *guajiro* temper. Today, the shooting continues. And yet this is Happy Colombia.

Am I not happy like they are because I went to the University of Michigan, where American professors explained Latin America to me? Professor Marks described it as an unjust society divided into two: the haves and the have-nots. From the description in the required reading list, I gathered I was a have. The haves are the enemies, and they are the friends and the accomplices of the imperialist United States. Confused after class one day, I told Professor Marks that the haves were not evil, that my mother volunteered at The Forest and that my grandmother sent Imelda to school. He shrugged his shoulders, disinterested in my story.

The University of Michigan was keeping me up at night. It was not a fear of *ladrones.* It was a fear of what I was learning, what I was encountering. Soon after I saw *Hearts and Minds,* I witnessed my first political rally. Crossing the Diag, the center square of the campus, I saw young men and women, some whose faces I recognized from Professor Marks's class, walking around in circles, screaming through bullhorns and holding signs. I stood in the margins of the circle in awe of their intensity as I read the words of what it was they wanted to convey: US HAND OUT OF EL SALVADOR. Someone gave me some literature. In the back of the pamphlet I found the name of an organization, a university address, and a phone number. "I am Latin American," I said when the voice answered at the offices of the Latin American Solidarity Committee. "I want to be involved."

I went to a few meetings but felt as uncomfortable as I had felt the time I heard "Fuck U.S. policy" from the professor's mouth that first semester. This time, the strong words against the United States came from young men and women like me. They felt so sure about what they were saying. When it was time for the newcomers to introduce themselves, I said I was from Colombia. But they were uninterested in that, as if being from Latin America was actually a drawback at the Latin American Solidarity Committee. There were mostly Americans at the meetings.

I was still drawn to the organization and the Americans who were so committed to the place where I came from. Although, frankly, until that moment I had never thought of myself as Latin American. I came from Barranquilla, not even there—I came from el Parrish and Riomar and el Country. I was the girl who lived in the house that held the best gatherings. El Hueco had closed but my friends and Luis still wrote to ask when I was coming back, saying "we miss you; come home," but I had already read the literature in the pamphlets passed out at the rallies. Somewhere in the back of my mind I knew going home would never be simple again.

The committee used to set up a table in the Fish Bowl, the building where I had class every morning and I noticed that Alex, who was also in Professor Marks's class, was there almost every day, standing behind the table covered with piles of flyers, always asking for a signature, organizing a rally, a sit-in, a march, or a symposium. He would sometimes wave at me and I would walk to the table. Handing me a pamphlet from each pile, he would shove the list of signatures under my nose; he would smile for a second, then turn to the next person who would hear him out. I stuffed everything inside my book bag, not the nylon backpack that most students carried but a big cream-colored leather bag that my mother had given me. I read each one of those flyers attentively once I got home. The papers that a blond boy who had never been to my country gave me were filled with the saddest statistics and the most outrageous accusations about the place I was from. They all said in different ways the same thing: Everyone in Latin America is poor except for a few; those few ones were bad people, exploiters, puppets of the United States. I knew that Imelda, the servant child-maid that lived in my house when I was little, was poor and that I wasn't but it was tough, all of a sudden, to be told that my grandmother who carried a rosary in her hands and my grandfather who was always putting his hands in his pocket and handing bills to those in need were as evil as could be.

By the time of the first snowfall, I had only gone so far as to buy a muffin and a poster from the Latin American Solidarity Committee. From that day on, the face of Che Guevara adorned the wall of my student apartment. Underneath the iconic photograph of the revolutionary in his starred beret, every morning I read: "A revolutionary is only guided by true feelings of love."

After that semester, whenever I went home, my mother called me a *nadaista,* alluding to the poet movement, the Colombian beatniks who rejected traditional ideas and believed in *nada,* nothing. It is not that I believe in nothing; it is that from the time I was torn away from Barranquilla I have not been able to come back the same.

As I hang up the phone with Allegra, who does not want to hear about the shootings, I recall the man I met on my first day back in Barranquilla. He had asked me for work and I told him I had none to give him because I didn't live here. I remember how his eyes had turned as bright as the stars that were lighting the broken sidewalk. "You don't live here," he said. "Lucky you, *doñita. Qué bueno!* What's it like outside. It's not like here, right?" A plane flew over our heads. He looked at the sky and pointing at the plane, said, "You have been on one of those. My Lord, you are going aboard one of those breasts. Lucky you. How does it feel, to ride in one of them? They are so beautiful; they resemble a tin breast. Go *doñita,* go. Don't stay here. Take the flying breast and go far away from here." That's exactly what I want to do today. But I am not ready yet.

BOOK TWO

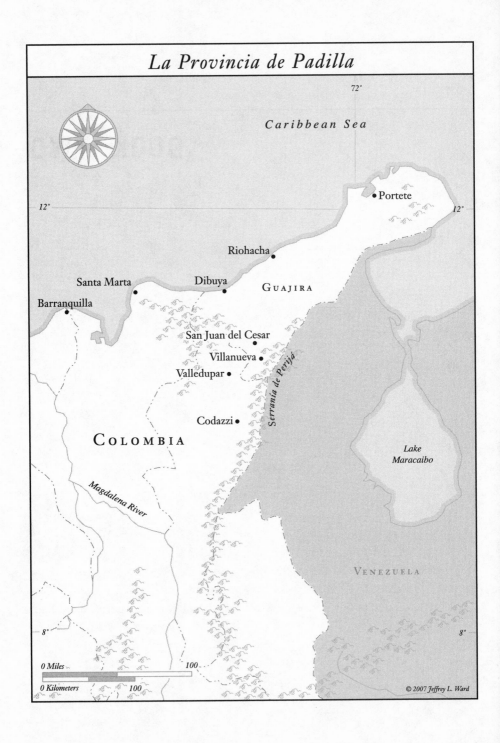

La Provincia de Padilla

Caribbean Sea

72°

12°   12°

• Portete

Riohacha
•

Santa Marta   Dibuya   GUAJIRA
•   •

Barranquilla
•

San Juan del Cesar
•
Villanueva
•
Valledupar
•

Codazzi
•

COLOMBIA   Lake
Maracaibo

Serranía de Perijá

Magdalena River

VENEZUELA

8°   8°

0 Miles   100
0 Kilometers   100

© 2007 Jeffrey L. Ward

16

WHO IS SHE?

Three weeks have passed and the room I've taken at my grandmother's feels like it's finally mine. While waiting for the trip to El Carmen to happen, I've managed to make it so messy that she and I both make sure the door is always shut. My grandmother has never lived with beds left unmade, worn clothes thrown over chairs, strewn shoes, and piled newspapers.

I could have stayed at my aunt's or at my cousin's but I want to spend time with my grandmother for the first time. During my childhood in Barranquilla, our disinterest in each other was mutual. When I kissed my grandmother hello, I would feel the rub of her cheek on mine and the absent sound of her kiss. She couldn't care less about the Mother Goose nursery rhymes I was learning at the American school and I was not in the slightest interested in what she did: She was busy with picking the anthuriums she grew in rows of clay pots on the patio that needed to be taken to the Virgin's altar in the Torcoroma Church, along with packages of fruit, fresh milk, and cheese made at the farm for the various priests she liked. Or she was playing chess with my grandfather in the dim light of the pantry or they were away at the farm. Going to see her always felt like an obligation, like church, which her house had a resemblance to with all the framed letters of the Pope's blessings and the statues of saints.

When I landed at her house a few weeks ago, she was a bit perplexed. I had never stayed with her before during my visits to Barranquilla. After Imelda's visit and Allegra's coming over we've established a more comfortable rapport. Now when I go up to kiss her good morning, she actually makes the sound of a kiss, not just the sign of the cross. I make a point of sitting down to lunch with her every day, and I think she is a bit mystified by my sudden interest. I've been quizzing her about our family history, asking her daily to pull from her supply of stories about life in the countryside. Ma Cris is not a forthcoming person so it has not been easy.

When I arrived I told my grandmother I would soon be going to El Carmen, thinking this would make me more interesting in her eyes; it would bring us together, just as it had divided us before.

"You shouldn't," she had said to me, with a calm tone of advice. "It's not good to go anymore."

My grandparents are from what is known as La Provincia de Padilla, named after an admiral who fought the Spaniards next to Simón Bolívar, remote from hustling and bustling Barranquilla. They come from the small town of Asunción and from the open prairies close to the Venezuelan border in the north where the cattle roamed free, leaving behind trails of steps in the shape of hearts, as the popular cowboy song goes. I had never paid much attention to these songs known as *vallenato,* and I continue to find the accordian-based sound quite unmusical even if I have started to show interest in its lyrics. That's because I'm looking for clues about the war I've come to explain anywhere I can find them and for me song lyrics have always been a great place to find insight into a culture and its people's stories.

Local historians refer to La Provincia de Padilla as *tierra de nadie,* no-man's-land. My relatives refer to it as the birthplace of "brave men of progress" who "conquered mountains and opened the roads." Or in the words of Pepe Castro, one of the region's patriarchs, la provincia was forged by them, men who "sent in the bulldozers, macheted the mountains, and then went back to ask if the land had an owner." It is also known as *la tierra del olvido,* the forgotten land, referring to how isolated it was from Bogotá and government. My grandparents come from a place that is so disconnected with the country's capital that people have made their living making deals, selling anything from cattle to crops of all kinds, including marijuana, on the foreign market. It was easier for my grandfather to sell his cattle in Venezuela than it was to sell it inside his own country. It would take my grandfather a few nights to walk it over to Venezuela, at least ten to try to find buyers in Bogotá.

"Why, is it so dangerous?" I ask her.

"*La Provincia* is nothing but a *zona roja,*" she says, referring to the place she loves as a red zone. "Red" stands for dangerous, for Communist, for being a place riddled with armed men who don't like the Montblancs.

"They"—they being the way everyone refers to the rebels—"say that they won't stop until they have each one and every one of us," she explains. I tell her that I don't think I am at risk, repeating the argument I made to my aunt that "They" don't know me; I have not lived here in so long. They will have no way of knowing who I am. "They sure will," she snaps back. "What if you ran into one of the Fishings and they ask for your *cédula,*" she explains. She sounds like a police agent on a television show explaining a dangerous zone to a newcomer.

"You are clearly and simply in trouble. They will ask for your *cédula*. And there they will read your name."

When I told her that I was going with Agustín, I was unprepared for her reaction. I thought mentioning Agustín was a way of overriding her authority. "He knows he can't go. I have told him he is absolutely not allowed to go." For the first time, I hear maternal authority and concern in my grandmother's voice.

This all increases my desire to go to the place that my grandfather "colonized, when colonizing was a good thing," as I am told. To them he turned nothingness to produce. I have not been there since 1982: Straight out of college, I spent a weekend there. I sashayed around the cotton and rice fields with my newly acquired gringa attitude, and dressed in my newly discovered style of a white T-shirt, Levi's, cowboy boots, and a bright yellow Walkman playing the Rolling Stones. I was as odd to everyone there—the workers, my grandparents, and the cute distant relative who caught my eye—as they were to me. But I realize and wonder why—already versed in political science theories and infatuated with the revolutionary movements of El Salvador and Nicaragua that were so popular on my college campus—it never occurred to me that El Carmen was being prepared for a rebel takeover. I spent two days with my headphones on and didn't ask a single question about the history and workings of the farm. Now I am convinced that El Carmen holds a secret key to explain Colombia's war. Listening to Ma Cris's concern about concealing my name opens an entire new set of questions: Why are the Montblancs such a target?

A FEW YEARS AGO, BEFORE MY GRANDMOTHER MOVED TO HER APARTMENT, I found a bag of pictures stashed away in the closet where she kept a pile of silver bowls and platters under lock and key. I took them to New York with me, thinking they would be nice heirlooms to have. But once in New York I lost all interest in them. They were mostly blurry. I could recognize my grandmother and grandfather in some of them, on the day of their wedding, for example, but the rest of the people were as foreign as those in the boxes of daguerreotypes and old photographs at a thrift shop.

I've brought them back, hoping that they would unlock some mysteries of why and how it became so dangerous to be part of this family. After God and priests, my grandmother's primary concern is family—so these photos are the perfect conversation starter. I've only assembled bits and pieces of family history since I started being interested in my own family. All I know is that the Montblancs took over the square in Asunción, the hamlet in the southern part of Guajira, where General Montblanc commanded the Conservative troops during the War of One Thousand Days. In the bag, I had found two portraits of the general but they didn't convey much. I hoped my grandmother could bring the photos to life. I'm only hoping she is a good storyteller. I've never been around her long enough to know if she is. But I have an ulterior motive in her stories about the Montblancs. I also want to ask her to tell me what she remembers of that period known as La Violencia. I want to ask her if she was afraid during it, what it's like to live around such hatred. Ma Cris was in her twenties and the mother of five when 300,000 people were killed, many in a most brutal way—remember the T-shirt and the Monkey Cut. I want to know if that Violencia feels different than today's violence, which is not yet called anything. I want to know about her life to better understand the war, but I'm afraid to be discovered so I don't ask.

As she rocks gently in her Viennese chair I wonder what she thinks about when she is not reading her prayer books or the pile of newspapers she keeps on the side table. I feel like a spy, monitoring her days and her phone calls, but every time I think I'm ready to walk into her bedroom with the bag of photos, I stop myself from doing so. I'm finding it hard to ask her to go back in time, to a time when she thought everything was perfect. She had the farm and she had her Gabriel, her husband of more than fifty years now, a boy she had known since the day they were born. "It was normal for us to fall in love," she had just told me when out of the blue I garnered up courage and asked her about their courtship. "We grew up like brother and sister." My grandmother's answers are as succint as they are absurd to me.

AFTER MY GRANDFATHER DIED IN 1996, MY UNCLE CONVINCED MY GRANDMOTHER to leave behind her big house in Riomar. The upkeep required at least a handful of maids plus José, a gardener, and Alfredo, our Pretty Bird and the watchman with his machete, who dozed at his guard post but no one had the heart to fire him. Safety in the increasingly urban Barranquilla was also a concern. Agustín suggested she move into one of the new high-rises on his block. "*Mami*, houses are obsolete, too hard for you to handle now that you are alone. Buildings are the new way." But my grandmother was reluctant. She didn't like so-called modern things like elevators, neighbors, and smaller rooms. Agustín tells me with a smile that she finally agreed to move because the building was called Virgen del Carmen. She was sold on it when she saw the tiled mural of the Virgin in the lobby.

Every bit of the house was transplanted here at the Edificio Virgen del Carmen. The bentwood rocking chairs that were on the terrace are now near the balcony. The Louis XIV chairs and the same glass table with the legs carved with roses still supports the same porcelains; I recognize the statue of a man with holes in his pants holding a red, a yellow, and a green balloon. The alabaster vase rests nearby, empty. I don't remember ever seeing flowers on the table.

Agustín sent Alfredo back to El Carmen, where he had come from, and reduced the domestic help. Currently there's Fanny, who cooks, cleans, answers the phone, and serves meals, and her twelve-year-old daughter, Lucero, who goes to school in the mornings and then helps her mother with some of the household chores. When mother and daughter are done with their work, usually in time for the evening soap opera, they sit on the floor and watch television in the sewing room. At night, they sleep in a room in the back of the kitchen, next to the laundry area.

María, a registered nurse, administers my grandmother's medicines, but more importantly she keeps her company. She is a lady-in-waiting in a white uniform who walks her down the street twice a day for mass, at seven in the morning and six at night; who accompanies her to the doctor's office or to the house of the *modista,* the lady tailor that makes the unadorned chemise dress that my grandmother owns in every subdued color, and that are all the same exact style she has been wearing since I've known her. When a cousin or a niece has a birthday party she sometimes asks María to go with her. Other times she asks her to comb her hair. María, a wife and mother in her midthirties who sees her family only on Sundays, her one day off, complies with her every whim, always smiling and saying "*Sí, Doña Cris.*" Cris is short for Cristina. Her cousins and sisters call her Cris; her nieces and nephews call her Tía Cris; and I, like the rest of her grandchildren, call her Ma Cris.

Then there is José, my grandmother's driver, also in his midthirties and with skin the same color as María's and Fanny's, a few shades darker than mine. He comes over at six every morning and stays till about seven. He is referred to as the driver but he is asked to do and does much more beyond obvious chauffeur duties. He runs around Barranquilla picking up every cousin and niece who needs a ride; he collects prescriptions at the pharmacy; he changes the lightbulbs; he fixes the lamps. José acts more like an on-call handyman. He does the food shopping and now that I'm here, he drives me around. I take advantage of our outings to interview him as well.

My grandfather hired José in 1989 to drive them back and forth from Barranquilla to El Carmen. He knew the road well, he explains, because he had worked with Don Guillermo, my grandfather's best friend, driving him back and forth from his farm and Barranquilla for more than ten years. He soon became my grandfather's trusted companion. When my grandfather had his aneurysm, it was José who shaved him every few days. When my grandfather insisted on going to El Carmen when it was no longer possible thanks to the guerrillas, José would distract him by driving him around Barranquilla until he fell asleep in the back of the car. My brother and I jokingly call him José Montblanc and he just smiles and says *ajá*.

When Ma Cris goes out, José holds her left arm as she goes down the four steps in front of the driveway and helps her get into the backseat of the car, waiting until she is completely comfortable before closing the door. He usually calls her Doña Cris but I've also heard him call her Ma Cris, indicating a familiarity that violates the rigid hierarchy I've built up in my mind. Over the past few weeks, I have found José sitting on her bed, like a grandson would, when they are making a grocery list, and have felt exposed when I'm in my nightgown and have found him sauntering around a room as my cousins and I do. José has told me that my grandmother lets him have the supermarket points and that he is saving up for a refrigerator. I have heard my uncle Gustavo, Luisa's husband, ask, "So José, how much more of Doña Cris's groceries are left to buy for that new ice box?" José responds, "Oh, about two more months, Don Tavo." Is this paternalism? Feudalism? Is it this type of dynamic that makes Colombia ill and that I have come to expose? I stand at the doorway to my room and watch José leaning on the threshold of Ma Cris's room. "Doña Cris," he says, "I just drove by the fruit stand and the sugar mangoes look delicious today. Should I bring some home?"

I WAKE UP TO A HOUSE FILLED WITH WHITE ROSES. FOR A SECOND I THINK ITS my grandmother's way of welcoming me. Fanny tells me there's going to be a party but I'm skeptical. My grandmother does not entertain; when my grandfather was alive he complained that the only time she brought out the silver platters was when priests came over for lunch.

The party is for the Virgin, Fanny tells me, pointing at a large statue next to the porcelain man holding the balloons. One more virgin at my grandmother's house is not surprising but the size and the dress of this one is impressive. This virgin looks so saintly that she belongs in a church, not next to figurines and flowered couches.

As Fanny explains the presence of the statue, I notice how thin she is, and how disheveled she looks. She wears a pale green cotton uniform that is too big for her. She is barefoot and her hair is uncombed and I cannot tell if she is forty or if she is sixty years old. Every time my mother comes to stay with my grandmother they fight about Fanny. "Make her wear shoes and have her pull her hair back," my mother insists. My mother makes her maids wear clean, ironed uniforms, sometimes aprons too. My grandmother's servants have always been left to dress how they please. I wonder if maids prefer to work in houses with strict dress rules. Or why my grandmother doesn't say anything. She doesn't like to see me disheveled. "You need to comb your hair," she says every time she can.

Fanny's attitude throws me off. Like José, she seems content, even happy. They smile, they laugh, as if they enjoyed life at my grandmother's. I cannot detect a trace of resentment in their words or behavior, just like I didn't with Imelda.

Fanny explains to me that they are welcoming the Virgin back to Barranquilla. "She has been living in Miami," she informs me, telling me that "knights" had taken her there a few years ago when things got too dangerous here. She's back for a short visit, Fanny continues, and her bodyguards, who are devoted gentlemen, members of the Virgin's society, are taking her around. "She needs to say hello to those she really wants to see. But it's not everyone who gets to host her for a night." Fanny is honored that the Society of Virgin holders have chosen to leave her in the household where she works. "Like you, she came back," Fanny says. "We have such important guests in the house."

Living in my grandmother's apartment is like taking up residence in a convent spa. My grandmother mixes rosary whispers and Bible readings with rest, meditation, and cures. A manicurist, a masseuse, and a physical therapist come once a week and I take full advantage. In the midafternoon Fanny cuts up cold papaya or mango into little pieces and serves them in white china bowls. We have them on the terrace and as I watch Ma Cris I wonder how someone can live like this, so disconnected from the reality outside her walls. I try and tell her about my life in New York but stop when she doesn't ask me any questions. The only two foreign places that interest her are the Vatican and Madrid; the former for obvious reasons and the latter because her favorite priest, Padre Mariano, now lives there. She concentrates more intently on the cubes of cold mango than on our conversation, as if the world is fine and contained in that delicious piece of fruit.

Two papers are delivered every morning and Fanny is instructed to leave them on the pile on Ma Cris's reading table. But I rarely see her reading the newspaper and when I do it is never that day's. "I am behind," she tells me as she reads a two-week-old *El Heraldo*.

A few days after I arrived my mother called from Bogotá to check in on me. I am sure she was curious to know how my grandmother and I were dealing with our obviously different lifestyles. I told my mother about the absurdity of the Virgin's party and that I couldn't get over how much my grandmother prayed. Later when she told my grandmother what I had said, she reported to me that Ma Cris had replied without missing a beat that she couldn't get over how much I slept. My grandmother and I inspect each other and amuse each other. We are so unfamiliar with each other's routine. She gets up at four in the morning; I am still up at four in the morning.

It is at night when everyone goes to sleep that I start doing my work as a reporter. But even after I finish working for the night, I remain awake, my thoughts running ceaselessly through my head. I am in some state of journalistic limbo, waiting for my sources (meaning my uncle) to come through. I am a bit antsy and it is getting in the way of sleep. The interesting trip down memory lane in Barranquilla is over, the rides with Allegra are becoming repetitive and the other part of me, the New Yorker is pounding harder and harder to come out. I don't know how long I can keep her in restraints.

I have been so unable to sleep that I'm sometimes still awake to hear my grandmother getting ready to attend her first mass of the day. She and María walk down the street a little before six o'clock. When she comes back, she reads until lunchtime. Fanny is ordered to serve at twelve thirty but tries to wait a bit. However, if I'm not ready by one—a big wait for a person who has never waited for anyone—she will go ahead without me. But she tries to wait for me and I try to be not just awake but also showered and changed. There are days when it is impossible. She sees me emerge in a state of sleepiness and undress simply unacceptable to her. She says nothing for a while, trying to accept, but then she suggests in a soft and poised voice that I get ready for lunch, that I am wasting the day, and that Fanny has to remove the lunch plates from the table. "*Nani, ves bañate,*" she says. "Darling, go bathe." If she only knew that in New York I often go without taking a bath for an entire day.

EVERY NIGHT AFTER MY GRANDMOTHER GOES TO SLEEP, I GET TO WORK. I GRAB the day's papers, untouched still, from the pile in her room. She doesn't like it but doesn't say anything. I close the door to my room and spend hours trying to make sense of what goes on here. I turn into a curious teenager to find out more about my country. I start my research with the first newscast of the evening, sitting on the bed, with the television on. I stare at the faces of everyone on the TV screen, searching for answers to the mystery of this life: the peace inside this house; the affection that exists between my grandmother and her servants, like I questioned the mysteries of the church as a child. My grandmother has never questioned—not the church, not my grandfather, and not the situation outside the doors of this house. I rejected the church and I rejected my country because to me neither of them made any sense.

I look in *El Tiempo* for the national stories; to take the temperature of the situation, I read the columns but I'm easily turned off by the amount of allusions to democracy in ancient Greece and the lack of stories about people living in Colombia today. I then turn to *El Heraldo,* the Barranquilla daily, only to find the news revolves around beauty queens, current and future ones, in bikinis; Carnival queens, current and future ones, dancing and smiling; soccer scores and society pages. The little there is on what is happening in the city frustrates me even more. If the amount of cleavage in Colombia's journalism makes me want to scream, the amount of violence in the one-paragraph stories about what is happening makes me want to run away: A man was shot dead for urinating outside of a bar, not a pleasant act but not one that merits death as punishment. More than a dozen women have been killed by death squads, identifying themselves as the Squadron Against Unfaithful Wives. All that happens not so far from here. But my grandmother, like Allegra, doesn't seem to know or to care about these murders. Tomorrow, I will find her placidly rocking on the Viennese chair and checking her watch as I emerge from my room, definitely after noon.

After the papers and the newscasts on TV, I turn on the radio; I'll keep it on all night both for company and as research. Radio is really the only way Colombia, the fractured doll, converses with each one of its parts. One night, I hear a story filed from a town in the south that has been without electricity for 408 days. The town is so isolated that it took the reporter three boats and a helicopter ride to arrive. The residents had spent more than a year trying to reach the proper authorities to report their situation. But in Colombia media conglomerates are more effective in reaching hamlets than the government.

And then making sure it's late enough for Ma Cris and María to be safely sound asleep in their twin beds, I pop open my laptop computer and type in NuevaColombia.com. No matter how many times I do it, I always feel like a teenager surfing for pornography. The FARC's Web site is interactive and it is updated daily with versions in English, Italian, French, and German. I read articles by Noam Chomsky and the same statistics, and the same explanations about the haves and the have-nots that I was shown at the Latin American Solidarity Committee in college. After that I type in Colombialibre.com and find the other side of the FARC's story on the Web site for the paramilitary. But what keeps me perplexed and awake are the messages that I find in the chat groups. They are filled of a vitriol and a hate so raw and so vicious that it is impossible to stop reading; it is impossible to see how these two sides can ever be at peace. And this is perhaps what makes it so hard to sleep these days.

ONE MORNING (WELL, AFTERNOON) I WAKE UP TO THE SOUND OF MA CRIS'S voice, louder than ever. She is quite deaf and wears a hearing aid, especially when using the phone. I wonder who's on the line making her shout at the top of her lungs, her voice so loud it breaks through the closed door and the roar of the air-conditioning unit. It is louder but it is also different: She is excited. My grandmother is not one to show emotion, always very matter-of-fact, calm and poised, supportive to those in need and always invoking God and the Virgin. Sometimes her voice can turn authoritarian if she is asking Fanny about food missing from the refrigerator or speaking to a grandchild who has taken José to run an errand without asking her. But this voice is new, the conversation peppered with questions and giggles from her end. I hear her ask if he is visiting soon, and offers to send an airplane ticket. I realize that she must be talking to the priest from Madrid. My grandmother is convinced that priests are superior beings, that they surely are closer to God. I have never heard her talk that way to anyone. Not to my grandfather whom she adored, not to her firstborn son; and definitely not to another woman, be it a daughter, a sister, or a friend.

But her vivaciousness soon turns into a tone of torment. She confesses to the priest that life here is "agonizing." I can't really understand what she is saying but I make out some of the words. I hear her mention "violence"—*mucha violencia*—and I am surprised at the way she can be more expressive than I've ever heard her. When she talks about *la situación en que se vive,* "the situation in which we live" worries her more than she cares to let out. Like everyone else in Colombia she calls what I see as war as "the situation." Maybe it's too hard to live with the word "war." Who hasn't called things by other names? Who has not said "we are taking a break" knowing damn well a relationship is over? In Colombia a rose is not a rose is not a rose. Colombians are wonderful at creating euphemisms to avoid calling things by their proper names. The war is the situation; being in danger is waiting for the rain to stop; Colombia, the most violent country in the world, is Colombia, the happiest country in the world; a rebel checkpoint where one can be killed has the name of a children's game, the one where you throw a rod into a tank filled with baubles and hope to hook the big treasure. And still, I want to play the game of Miraculous Catch that rebel men and women play with guns; I want to see what happens if I run into a checkpoint, which is like playing an On-the-Road-type of Russian roulette. I want to see what "they" will do if they stop me but who am I taunting here, the rebels, my family, or myself?

I lean on the door, my ear on the cold lacquered wood, and I hear my grandmother say, "What do these people think will happen to them on Judgment Day?"

That to her is a straightforward question and I wonder who is crazier: she for thinking there will be one or me for wanting to make this trip.

17

MY GRANDMOTHER EXPLAINS KIDNAPPINGS

The moment I come in from an outing with Allegra, I realize something unusual is happening. The TV is not turned to the program my grandmother watches in the afternoon. María calls me aside and tells me that she received a call "with bad news" from her niece Rose. I know they are close. Rose's husband, María explains, a salesman traveling on a bus, was taken, the word that has replaced "kidnapped." "They got him," she says, "in a Miracle Catch." "They say they will not stop until they get the last Montblanc," my grandmother bursts out, looking at the floor. "And it seems they will do it. Those who have and those who don't."

I ask Ma Cris to tell me what happened and she answers with what was on her mind. "They are going to think that he has," she says and I notice how she never says the word "money." She always stops at "has." "Because he has the name, they are going to ask for a lot but I know how little they have." I stand in the threshold to her bedroom door unclear of what to do next. Should I leave her alone or should I offer to help? I immediately think about my own trip. Of course, it makes me rethink my own plan. My desire to go ahead with it seems offensive as I face my grandmother's anguish. She surprises me by telling me that the guerrilla has already made contact. "They say they want radios, rubber boots, and batteries." All afternoon long I watch my grandmother on the phone with her sisters, nieces, and cousins. I hear her talk to Cecilia, widowed when she was thirty-three more than fifty years ago, and she wears black. They exchange information on how and where they can get the demanded ransom. José stands by and explains to her what hardware stores sell the supplies the rebels need. They were all pitching in to buy what the rebels want. "It is so easy for a kidnap to turn into tragedy these days," my grandmother says softly. How absurd, how heartbreaking to see a handful of widows, praying dames in their eighties, looking for things needed to fight a war in order to save the life of a relative. I stand and watch, unable to know what to feel, and it is at times like this, caught between my family's life and how foreign it seems to me, that I am from nowhere, forever fractured, unable to control which one of the many sides of me will spring out.

I ask her if she has any idea why this kidnapping happened. I know I'm guilty of bad timing if not of being insensitive, using my grandmother's situation as research. She shakes her head no, a no so lost, so full of obscurity that I understand that she really has no idea why this is happening to them. She sits in her chair and starts talking as she's never talked to me before. She tells me a story about the kidnap of a Montblanc, prefacing it by saying he is a Montblanc whom she doesn't know. By this she means that he is part of the out-of-marriage Montblancs, *hijos naturales,* natural children, which is how illegitimate children in Colombia are referred to (and there are hundreds, perhaps thousands of those, many more than the legitimate Montblancs). One of the things I am learning about the family is how big it is. I now understand the joke about them not being a family but a plague. The family historian has counted more than 3,500 members of the clan that he calls "a noble and distinguished breed" and that the rebels call "enemies of the people." My grandmother only keeps in touch with those who grew up with her in Asunción's square.

I never could remember their names when I saw them at her house and I always had to be reminded. It was hard to tell them apart. "Your grandmother's sister," my mother would say, but they seemed as distant and as uninterested in us children-who-didn't-go-to-the-farm. I had no idea that apart from El Carmen, there were towns and hamlets where my grandparents had been born and where my mother too had lived. I guess I never thought of either of them as children, and no one had ever taken me there. I have no sense of what they possibly look like. In fact, I have never been to a small Colombian town, one of the pueblos with the adjacent so-called *veredas* and *cacerios* that today are flashed on my TV screen at night: *"Ataque de las FARC"; "Masacre paramilitar"; "Explosión del ELN."*

Ma Cris tells me how difficult these negotiations can get by relating the case of an *hijo natural.* After months and months of negotiations, his children paid ransom but the father was not released. "For some reason, they killed him instead," she says, "and they had the audacity," she continues, "to call the children and tell them that if they wanted their father's body back they had to pay for it. They did; they paid again." My grandmother is looking straight at me like she hasn't before, as if she knew I kept that poster of Che on my wall. "*La guerrilla,* you know what they did. They put his body in a burlap sack and dropped it outside their front door." How can I ever bring these two sides of my life together, I wonder. How can I feel that these things are part of the daily life of people as close to me as my grandmother? I don't know how I could survive the negotiation of a loved one. "If it was me," my grandmother scoffs, " I would have never paid for bones."

My grandmother is starting to confuse me as much as Colombia. The woman with the saintly pose surprises me more and more. She says she wouldn't pay for a dead body. She fund-raises to buy war equipment for rebels. A few days ago I saw her turn to the TV and scream "atheist" at the image of Manuel Marulanda. And just last week she and Cecilia had wondered jokingly about who was going to be next. "I think it's your turn," Cecilia answered. "You're the only one whose children have been spared. If I were you, I would tell Agustín to be careful this weekend. There is a *runrún*, a rumour, that this weekend the fishermen will be out in full regalia." She says this in the tone of confidential information, *cositas* she hears because her son is well connected, important enough so that the *militares* call with an update on the condition of the roads. "Not a good weekend to go out," as if they were talking about a weather report.

IN 1994, WHEN I WAS NOT INTERESTED IN COLOMBIA, MUCH LESS IN THE MONT-blancs, my mother had sent me a newspaper clipping. In the margins she had written, "One of those good Montblancs from the province." I had not paid much attention to the story but I saved it. I read it now, eight years later, and for the first time in my life I see a picture of Asunción, the town that looms so large in their minds and now in mine. The church looks lovely with its white walls and the three bell towers. Finally I get to see it even if in a yellowed newspaper clip. It is the church where Padre Martínez married my grandparents in 1926, the church that my grandfather helped rebuild in 1947 when the monsignor preferred a modern altar and whose saints were kept in the Frenchman's House during renovations; the church where Padre Martínez wore the fancy vestments that my grandmother had commissioned for him in Spain and were made of gold thread, the ones my mother remember as being the first beautiful thing she ever saw. It is the church where the children of Conservatives like all the Montblanc boys were allowed to go to the bell tower to announce the time for the mass and the time for the movies. The children of Liberals were never chosen to do so by Father Martínez, who lunched with my grandmother a few times a week.

And there's the square—the one where all the Montblancs, and only the "good" Montblancs lived, the direct descendants of Maurice Montblanc and Carmen Ariza, not the ones the Frenchman had outside of wedlock. The caption under the photo reads: "Mario thought that nothing would happen to him in Asunción." When the story was published in 1994 Mario had already been in captivity for two years. "His family needs to know where he is," the tagline reads "at least so they can take him flowers." I look at Mario's picture. I recognize the same blue-gray eyes of my grandmother and of Dr. Francisco Montblanc, my cousin's mother, and my pediatrician. Under his picture my mother wrote, "This is another case of one of the *hijos naturales* of the Montblancs, hard-working men who today like so many others are being kidnapped."

El Tiempo ran an entire page with the story: "Don Mario was stolen one evening, dragged out of a friend's house by seven armed men. He had never thought this would happen to him. He believed that his people, *el pueblo de Asunción*, would never allow this to happen to him. After all they had protected him for four years already." The tone, the story, the image of the square takes me back to the opening line of García Márquez's *Chronicle of a Death Foretold*.

The rebels had announced that they were coming for him, but unlike Santiago Nasar, the protagonist of the novella, Don Mario stopped going out. He hired four bodyguards and didn't return to his farm. Every night when the clock marked six, he locked the front doors and the windows and turned off the lights of his house. To remember the smell of soil, he lay down, for hours, nose to the ground in his backyard. García Márquez was right when he said to us at the workshop that to write magical realism, to move between the magical and the real, one had to become a journalist in Colombia. I continue reading.

Life had taught Don Mario to be austere, the story explained. His mother had died when he was still a child and because "he was an *hijo natural* and as per the tradition, natural children were not heirs," Mario had known hard work all his life. I wonder if Mario's father was the Conservative general of the war and if the young boy ever knew his father. He grew plantains and sold them, traveling by mule from town to town. By the time he was nineteen he had five cows. That was the first real step toward his dream of becoming a cattle breeder "like the respectable and rich men of the region." He married well, meaning up, the story said, had cattle, and acquired land but he always remained a simple man. Later I learn that he married a "true" Montblanc. When one of his daughters suggested he should buy himself a Cartier watch, Don Mario snapped at her, "How can you suggest that I wear such a costly thing when so many people here are starving."

After four years of being taunted by the threat of rebels, he felt safe again and decided to resume an outside life. Two weeks later, he was kidnapped. The family received a letter soon after he had been taken saying that he was alive. But two months passed before the rebels made a request. They wanted pretty much the same thing they wanted for Rose's husband: rubber boots, uniforms, thirty radios, and a small electric generator. The family complied immediately. But Don Mario was not liberated. In fact, it took two months before Don Mario's children heard from their father's captor again. This time they requested that one of the sons, the one who worked as a manager—"a bureaucrat," the rebels called him and as such an enemy of the people—resign from his job. They asked that the family run a campaign in the local press calling for peace negotiations between the government and the rebels. The family paid for the ads.

Another two months of silence went by. Then, a tape arrived. In it, Don Mario said he was happy and proud of the way they were handling the negotiations with the rebels and that soon he would be there with them. But then another tape arrived. This time, Mario's voice was different. He begged his children to do as the captors say. "Give them whatever amount of money they want," he said, his voice breaking, adding that he was being tortured. "His voice was drowned by the laughter of his captors and a *vallenato* song blared from a radio," the daughter told the reporter.

This time, his captors demanded two million dollars. I have no idea what provincial landowners like Mario or like my grandfather are worth but I know that having land is one thing and being able to stuff a duffle bag with two million dollars in cash in a small hamlet like Asunción is another. For all the talk of being "a have," and a "landowner," and my family fitting the description of "oligarchs" and of "enemy of the people," I have never felt I come from a family with loads of cash. Land and money are two different things, you can have one without the other and vice versa. The newspaper story says that the family paid, not the full amount but a lot of it. Six months later Don Mario was still not home.

The rebels now accused them of not caring for their father enough and that the children had offended them by sending such a humiliating amount of money, enough to pay for "some" not a lot of medicines. By now all seven of Mario's children had left their jobs to deal with the negotiations.

Plus, they had to do everything on their own, the paper reports. The authorities were hopeless. At one point, when some of their cattle was stolen they went to the army but the captain told them the army knew where the cattle were but couldn't help them. The police station had no gas for cars.

Once in a while the army came to their house but it was not to give them an update, but only to ask what they knew about their father. "I couldn't believe it," says one of Mario's daughters, "I told them, 'I thought you had come to give us information, not to ask for it.' They just lowered their heads."

Not being able to rely on the government, they relied on religion. The children made wooden rosaries modeled after the one Don Mario wore. His wife relied also on accounting. She wrote everything in notebooks, "keeping an inventory so I can tell him what happened when he comes back."

But when Mario returned, he was just a sack of bones as my grandmother has just informed me.

Don Mario's story is sad, shocking, sensational, emotional, dramatic, horrible, chilling. But something is missing; there is no context; there is nothing other than a family tragedy. Why him? Is he linked to paramilitary groups? To drug trafficking? Why doesn't the journalist put it in perspective? Where is her nut graph? Where are the interviews with the other side? What does the rebel spokesperson (they have them) say about the case? Where are the interviews with the local authorities? With the federal government? The historians? The experts? Why is it that in Colombia people do not ask all the questions. It is always about one side of the story. Is it the fault of the journalism schools, of newspaper editors, or of the sobering fact that in Colombia "the wrong question can be a bullet in your head," as a young journalist who had been forced into exile had explained to me in New York.

I thought I had it all figured out. As someone who has been fascinated with revolutionary movements since the day I first heard about Che and the Sandinistas in the late seventies, I felt I understood what was happening in Colombia. But I am willing to think for a second that perhaps I should stop trying to accuse and start to listen. Why hasn't Imelda taken up arms as I had wrongly predicted or fantasized? Why does José tell me that rebels claim they are fighting for the poor but when they blow up the electricity tower in his hamlet it is the poor, not the rich, who have their own generators, who suffer? It is their electric bill that goes up. All my plans to take the road seem superfluous, self-indulgent, a perverse death wish, or a simple need for family attention.

My grandmother lives in her own feudal universe without much analysis. *Barranquilleros* are happy to be from here, especially during Carnivals. I have not met anyone who feels this is wrong. El Carmen has been transposed to Barranquilla, and Barranquilla is fine with the feudalism that the people of the province bring in; that is just the way it is. Who am I to come here and tell them how things should be different, arriving from New York, fists raised, and then just like they do, I too ask Lucero, the eleven-year-old daughter of the maid, to fetch me a glass of water.

I came here saying that Colombia will not be fixed with Washington's billion-dollar blessing; that peace will not come by praying to the Divine Child for *la paz de Colombia* as millions faithfully do. I still believe this to be true. But the premise that I came here to prove had a flaw. It did not take into consideration the relationships between people. There are complexities here that the activists from Michigan have never seen. I made up my mind about what the ills of El Carmen were before knowing anything substantial about it. I let go, for the moment, my trip to El Carmen because going now is not only reckless, it is also dishonest. I want to hear the other side of the story, the perspective of those that I have considered guilty for so long.

AFTER THE KIDNAPPING OF ROSE'S HUSBAND, MAKING AN EFFORT TO KEEP HER company, every afternoon I bring the bag of aging photographs into my grand-mother's bedroom. My abrupt inquiry had broken the ice between us, and I'm no longer reluctant to ask her about a past that I now realize she considers daily, and not just through a rose-colored perspective. She rocks gently on her chair and little by little she tells me the story of our family, six generations of Montblancs, but her recollections are not always full of all the details I wish they were. I show her photo after photo but sometimes all I get is a name and the blood relation. Sometimes I am sure she is enjoying it and at other times I think she wants me to stop and won't tell me.

I have tried to organize the pictures chronologically. The first one I have dates to 1905 and it is of a man with a handlebar mustache. To her it's Papa Alberto, her grandfather. To me, he is General Don Alberto Montblanc Ariza, the bigwig of the Conservative party in the region, the man who won his title fighting on the government side in the War of One Thousand Days. I've heard two things about him. One is a family story, more a myth than perhaps truth. The general, family lore has it, left a letter saying that if he were wounded in battle, the only blood he was to receive was French blood. "Make sure," he said, "that my pure French blood is not mixed." The other thing I knew is what I read in his obituary written in 1926. First it calls him a man of "tormented impatience" but at the same time "no one was more ready to serve." The writer calls him "the prince of generosity" who made "his public spirit shine over the dark anguish and the pain of his birth land in order to make her grow and become richer." He helped establish "the Church, the city hall, the school and all of the many municipal buildings" and his name will "eloquently and perma-nently tell the story of Asunción." But then he goes on to say that "it is to be expected that time, the best cure for all human conditions to heal, will dab with the perfume of forgetfulness the boiling passions that this man agitated with his virility and his bravado." I ask my grandmother if she has any idea that Alberto was so controversial and she nods. I try a follow-up question, knowing that she will not budge from her monosyllabic response.

I move to the next picture, of a man who looks like a replica of Agustín and wears a pocketwatch, which I recognize is the one my mother ruined with shampoo—Ma Cris's father, René. All she tells me is that he died young, at forty-two. Then comes the picture of a handsome man with a close beard dressed in a white suit and sitting on a horse. Her eyes shine some as she tells me that is her uncle Javier, who is also my grandfather's father. "Let me see it," she says taking it from my hand but she returns it without offering anything more than "he is your great-great-grandfather." I write Javier Montblanc Ariza on the back, the grandson of the Frenchman who arrived when Colombia was ten years old and was called Nueva Granada: the son of the general who fought in the war, the father of my grandfather, who colonized land when "colonizing was a good thing," my mother's grandfather whom she had never mentioned until I asked after him, and my great-great-great-great-grandfather.

I also have pictures of her at three, a beautiful face; at fifteen, more beautiful, smiling coquettishly at the camera; group photos of her and her cousins wearing school uniforms. About that she tells me it was a convent called San Façon, run by French nuns in Bogotá. Knowing that traveling to Bogotá was so difficult then, I ask her about it. She tells me it took ten days: She was driven from Asunción by a car service to Riohacha, where she would take a boat ride along the Caribbean coast down to Santa Marta, drive inland to Cienaga, on the banks of the Magdalena River, to get on a steamboat that would take her to La Dorada, the last navigable stop. From there, she would take a train to Bogotá. The journey sounds so complicated and it surprises me that she did all that traveling. I only seem to see her as the grandmother with the rosary.

The pictures of her on the banks of the Cesar River, sitting on the fallen branch of a sturdy tree with her cousins Cecilia, Rosa, Clara, and Leonor surrounded by rocks the size of prehistoric eggs, as García Márquez once described them, make her smile and it only gets wider when I show her the one of my grandfather, handsome and wearing a tie, being part of the Virgin's procession. "That's when he was courting me," she says. "He knew it would make me happy to see him be chosen to be one of the Virgin's escorts." I hand her the one of them sitting together on the back of a Ford car. "We were *novios*, engaged in that one." I close with the one of their wedding day. I have more in the bag but I feel I need to be careful not to push my luck. Stories take time to tell.

18

MEMORY THREADS OF EL CARMEN

At my parents' house in Bogotá in December 2000, where I spent an entire month, I found a black-and-white photograph, the kind that has scalloped edges, the kind that I immediately thought of framing as I had framed a sequence of photographs I had found of El Carmen's fields taken in 1973 when my grandfather decided on a whim to try growing pepper and peanuts, two crops that had never been planted in the area before. (One of the things I seem to do lately during my family visits is scavenge. I go through attics, closets, and drawers looking for objects, photos, and letters as if in them I will find answers, clues to what happened then that can explain today. I always come back with something new for my New York walls.) I look at the picture, a girl, aged seven or eight and looking very uncomfortable, is sitting on a bull. The girl could be me but I have no recollection of ever riding a bull. "Is that me, *Papi*?" I ask my father. "What the hell am I doing sitting on a bull? Who put me there?"

"A Holstein," he says as a way of answering. I find the word in my memory file; my grandfather owned bulls of that breed. I stare closer, hoping that I could indeed remember that trip to the farm. There are lots of people around me, including a young man standing next to me and another one holding a rope that is tied to the animal's mouth. I ask my father if he knows who the other people are. "*Trabajadores*," he answers, offering no names. The word is Spanish for "workers." After a pause, *papi* adds, "Those were the days when one could go to El Carmen and stay overnight." And turning to my mother, he tells her that there are people in Córdoba who can now go back to their farms. I have heard that too: people say that the reason is that Córdoba has been "cleaned" of rebels. It's been cleaned by a man who goes by the name of Carlos Castaño who has vowed to kill every motherfucking guerrilla (like Charlie wants to kill every motherfucking drug dealer), after the FARC killed his father. It is true that there are no rebel fishing expeditions on the roads of Córdoba, that the people can go back to their farms, and even spend the night there. Mario has told me about it; his grandfather's farm is in Córdoba. But I also have heard of the methods they use to clean. Thirty-five-year-old Castaño runs the Autodefensas Unidas de Colombia, the paramilitary group that is known to go into hamlets and towns and kill anyone who could have been remotely related to a rebel in any way. I've heard that their preferred method of killing is to use *motosierras*, chain saws, the modern version of the Tie Cut, the Flower Cut, and the Monkey Cut.

Castaño has explained it to the *Washington Post:* "We do not pretend to be charity nuns. I do not permit the destruction of towns or the kidnappings of honest people under the excuse that it is a just cause. We are growing exponentially and don't have time to train correctly. The only ones responsible are the guerrillas and the Colombian government, which has made the people feel there is an undignified state defending their national interests." In this explanation, Castaño captures the contradiction of Colombia. Otherwise decent people are turning a blind eye to the reality of Colombia's countryside. When I pointed this out to a friend, his answer was immediate, "If the people of Sweden had to put up with guerillas like ours, they too would support Carlos Castaño." No one around me seems to think that Castaño should be stopped. In fact I hear he should be Colombia's next president.

When Carlos Castaño gave his first televised interview in August 2000 from an undisclosed location in the Nudo de Paramillo he talked about his faith in God and the sacrifices he had made to save Colombia. He had given up his family life—his children lived in London and he communicated with them via videotape. Looking straight at the camera, Castaño spoke about his army's way.

"Yes," he said. "I am also an extortionist. It's very similar to what the guerrilla does but I do it more tenderly, with more affection. Because they are my friends, they can bargain with me. To some I even give them IOUs. With some, our friendly ties help. But they all have to pay something. That we use drastic measures is true but Colombians must understand that when you have to exercise authority it is too difficult to limit yourself to moral norms. If the narcos offer help, I take it. If the army offers help, I take it—although they haven't. If they want to stoop down to the level of the devil with me then we stoop down to that but I swear I will finish these guerrillas. If the army did what we did, they would all be in jail. This produces excellent results because we can attack our enemy using their same methods. It is inevitable that in an irregular war, human rights get violated."

The interview was a sensation, though not for the reasons one would expect. Tapes were being passed around so that those who had missed it could breathe a little easier. Carlos Castaño could save Colombia; it was a hope that millions of Colombians seriously pondered.

Soon after the interview, Castaño wrote a book going deeper into the history of his vigilante group. It was an overnight sensation, a huge bestseller among everyone from the señoras who took it to the beauty parlor to their chauffeurs who waited for them outside, reading their own copies. Carlos Castaño became cocktail and family conversation. Most everyone was delighted that he had finally spoken. Whatever he did, however he did it, he was getting rid of the guerrillas. The people of Córdoba were boasting. In an interview with *Semana,* a landowner from the region said that if they hadn't formed these groups, "they would be an endangered species." With three kidnappings a month in the area, he said, he was just waiting for the day it would be his turn. In an area where eight out of ten people made a living from cattle, the situation affected everyone. Before Castaño came to "save" them, there were already more than forty thousand abandoned hectares, ready to be sold at any price. Now thanks to Carlos Castaño, they were sleeping at their *fincas.* In Montería, Córdoba's capital, they removed the statue of Laureano Gómez, the favorite of all Conservative presidents, and replaced it with Fidel Castaño's, Carlos's father.

While the people of Montería celebrated their good fortune, the people of Padilla's province were suffering at the hands of the guerrillas. The hippies and the gringos had stopped coming with their dollars and gone were the days of the cotton bonanza when the fields resembled white blankets and there was work in the region for more than seventy thousand pickers. But when a nasty larvae and long spells of rain got in the way of delivering to the textile factories in Medellín, imports of cheaper, higher-quality cotton obliterated the business, and things changed. There were no more three-day parties with whisky, *vallenato* music, and goat stew. The fields no longer resembled white blankets. Instead, seventy thousand hands were laid off and searched for new work. Abandoned equipment rusted under the sun. The situation was so dramatic that more than a dozen cotton growers and cattle breeders committed suicide. The seventies and eighties had been tragic. As if the debacle of the cotton bonanza were not enough, the guerillas were now killing the cattle. Then hope arrived in the form of a new crop that everyone hoped would rescue them from deprivation. African palm, called such even though it was planted more widely in Malaysia than in Africa, germinated seeds that could be pressed for oil production. Many *fincas* were transformed into fields of *palma africana.* This was the solution that workers and *finca* owners alike had been searching for.

Why not call in the paras? It seems as if the paras have been called. In the papers that I read in my grandmother's house at night, it was reported that in Pelaya, a hamlet in the same state as El Carmen, a woman told the paramilitary that her husband was abusing her so they forced him to clean the weeds of idle lands, later taking him to the town's square, tying him to a tree, and whipping him in public. There were towns where the paras set a seven o'clock curfew. "We can't visit our girlfriends anymore," a young man complained to a journalist. They made sure murals of Che Guevara were removed and that the Bible be fervently read in schools. Teachers who did not comply would be killed, sentenced to death for being Communist. In another city, thieves had stolen the crown of the Virgin of Fátima. The paras found it and the city thanked them by celebrating mass in their honor. But it wasn't as clean as Córdoba or I would not have had to wait this long to just spend a few hours in El Carmen.

I DON'T REMEMBER THE RIDE ON THE HOLSTEIN BUT I DO REMEMBER RIDING a horse, which I liked, and riding in the car between my grandfather and the overseer. I would hear them talk about the milking, the grazing, the rain, and the rivers as we drove through the plantations. Abuelo Gabriel would tell the driver to stop the car in front of people who had machetes in their hands. I remember the way they answered his questions about the weather, about the water level in the rivers. I was a young girl but I sensed the respect with which they spoke to him. I could also sense that, as with Imelda, there was something different when I played with the sons and daughters of the *trabajadores*. But I didn't play with them or ride around with my grandfather as much as the boys did.

El Carmen had not been a significant part of my childhood. To me, *la finca* was the place where my grandparents went in their jeep or in their small bimotor plane and came back loaded with crates of mangoes and guavas, gallons of fresh milk, blocks of cheese, and gobbles of cream. I've been there maybe a handful of times at most.

In my grandfather's mentality, *fincas* were for boys, not for girls, and so he was not so forthcoming with inviting his granddaughters. My cousins and my brother would be invited constantly. In the pictures I've seen them holding iguanas and driving tractors—things I surely didn't do. I was to stay in the house with my grandmother and her solitaire games.

They hunted for ducks; they squeezed on udders and tasted the milk of hundreds and hundreds of "their" cows; they swam in the river that lined the corrals: they loved going.

There was nothing there for me. I preferred staying in Barranquilla where I could go out with my friends wearing bell-bottoms and platforms, listen to pop tunes from Miami, exchange secrets about boys, and chew Bazooka gum rather than having to sit and listen to my grandfather and his best friend, Pedro, talk about crops, politics, and the currents of the wind, the amount of rain, and the level of the river while having whisky and soda on the rocks. To guess their choice of whisky was one of my few distractions. At seven I knew the brands: Chivas Regal, Buchanan, and Old Parr. Chivas was my favorite because I could have the ocher velvet bag that the bottle came in. If it was Old Parr I had to wait until the bottle was finished so I could remove the little clear ball inside the beak that made it pour smoothly. I would see their wives next to them silently and always wondered how they could sit still for hours and not be bored.

Visiting El Carmen felt as if I had traveled to a place as remote as Tahiti, the islands in the Pacific that we studied in the social studies textbook of my American school. It all felt foreign and I wasn't particularly having the time of my life but I don't remember ever feeling scared or that having land was associated with exploitation. It was exactly the opposite. Being a Montblanc made me special. It did even in Barranquilla. I knew that there was a world of people who had *fincas* and that my grandparents were always on their *finca* but I preferred playing tennis to solitaire and swimming in the pool rather than in the river. I preferred my pink bed and air-conditioned room and my house that had no mosquitoes and many phones, including a red princess one next to my mother's marble bathtub. In El Carmen I was always spraying insect repellent on my legs and the electricity only came on if my grandfather asked one of the workers to turn on the generator. There was not even a phone for me to call Allegra, just the big black box with its constant static. If I wanted something, all I had to do was ask for it. Never did I feel that the woman who made my favorite juice, that the young man who had saddled my favorite horse could hurt me. It felt exactly the opposite. All they wanted was to do anything and everything to make me happy: I was Don Gabriel's granddaughter.

I remember the door was kept open and people walked in and out all day asking for Don Gabriel. Some came to ask for favors, many came to sell or to offer wild game. I saw the delivery of goats, pigs, ducks, and hens but also animals that looked like big rats called *guartinajas* and even an armadillo. I was petrified that they would serve the rodents for dinner but my grandmother told me that she didn't. She just didn't like to turn down the peasants' gifts or not to buy what they offered. I remember how the word *serranía,* so linked now with rebels—that's where they hide, where they live, where they take you—was so evocative of an adventure that no trip to Disney World could match. The sierra was where the Motilones Indians lived.

Being taken to visit the Motilones is one of the best memories I have of El Carmen. My grandfather had a message to send to the chief, so he sent Julio, one of the overseers, loaded with gasoline, salt, and Kent cigarettes to offer as gifts. Gabriel told Julio to take me along. He came over with another worker and a saddled horse for me early the next morning. The Motilones live very deep inside the hills and I remember first crossing the fields of El Carmen, toward the end of the horizon, to where I could see a faint line of the spine of the hills. "From here to the sierra," Julio had told me proudly. "It is all El Carmen." When we got to the foot of the mountain, the road thinned and turned into a dirt path. Julio asked me to let him go first, that I should always be in the middle. The other worker, whose name I never got, was always to be behind me. We started going up the mountain, on roads like the ones I imagine the Spanish explored looking for El Dorado. As we went up and up, the track got steeper, leaving us sometimes with deep precipices on both sides.

I was sandwiched between two of my grandfather's most trusted workers, who held the ropes attached to my horse that protected me from the crevices. It was these deep holes that scared me, not the men. I knew that if something untoward were to happen, they would do anything to make sure I was protected. To distract myself from my fear of the crevices, I would ask if we would soon get to cross a stream. I preferred crossing them, letting my horse get some water, drink some myself. It was the coldest and the clearest water I have ever seen in my life.

Those were all my memories of El Carmen. Not many. Not very significant. For my grandfather El Carmen was the world. El Carmen was not just his pride and joy. It was his life. But I never knew the history behind the thousands of acres of *la finca*. I know now that he almost single-handedly had turned a swath of no-man's-land into his fiefdom. "When he got there it was mountains, snakes, rain, tigers, hogs," Agustín had said to me as I waited once again in his office for the call from the military commander to come in with the latest on our journey.

It makes sense to me now to know that it was he who had built El Carmen, because I can now see he had done it just the way he liked it. El Carmen was temperamental and quirky like he was. It followed no rules or design: the huge thatched patio in the back of the house; the air strip a few steps from the main house; the pool, not near the house but close to the warehouse where the cotton was stored. My grandfather liked to take a *chapuzón,* a dip in the pool, to refresh him from the heat. He wandered around his land, which he had turned into an important cattle ranch, a producing agribusiness with its own irrigation system, and he harvested cotton, rice, and soybeans in his pajamas and a tweed cap. He explored, risked, commanded, produced, and as my grandmother told me this morning, "did good." If there is an idea of a feudal hacienda, this was it. My grandfather was one of the *latifundistas*—a word I first encountered in a political science class and in Communist manifestos at the University of Michigan. Abuelo Gabriel is a character out of *Eva Luna* and *House of Spirits,* the Isabel Allende novels that made me want to write, and the Mexican *telenovelas* I hated to watch—a hero to some, a villain to others.

El Carmen was the world and he was the king. If it was up to him, he would have preferred his daughters to marry men of the land like him. He mistrusted anyone who could not look up at the sky and foresee the weather, who could not tell a stallion from a mare or a Holstein from a *cebú*. My grandfather died in 1995, wondering every day what was happening on the farm, in the country-side, what would happen with the relationship between his land and his work-ers, the ideas that were being put in their heads. Every evening my uncle would stop by and give him a report, a report he had received secondhand himself. Sometimes he would stop by with a videotape. Way before the FARCs's Law 002 was passed, Agustín had decided that it was too risky to keep going to El Carmen. There were no fishing expeditions yet but with a few of the kidnap-pings around them, it was best to play it safe. Last time I saw Abuelo Gabriel, we sat on the front porch in Barranquilla while he fed bread crumbs to birds and tried to tell me how much he missed watching the cattle return to the corrals.

19

MA CRIS AND HER COUSIN DESCRIBE
A WORLD OF PEACE

"It's time, Doña Cris, for your medication," María says as I'm sitting with my grandmother one afternoon. Ma Cris is on her rocking chair and I am on her bed wondering what is the best way to start a conversation today. Talking to my grandmother still makes me nervous. I have no more pictures to show her. After administering her pills, María takes out the blood pressure cuff. "After you're done," I ask, "will you take mine?" As María wraps my arm with the cuff and tightens it with the air pump, I ask my grandmother to tell me what it was like before, when she and my grandfather were able to travel back and forth between Barranquilla and El Carmen safely. She tells me that things were "perfect" then, that everyone lived "in peace and brotherhood," and that "they were all very good people." This time the "they" are not the rebels that cause *la situación,* the "they" she means are the ones who sit on the side chairs, not on the rocking chairs, when they visit. The "they" are the servants, day laborers, the peasants, *los pobres,* the men and women who worked El Carmen's fields, who worked for her, the *trabajadores* that surround me in the picture with the bull, the ones who took me up the sierra, the ones who give up their children so they can be better fed in the house of their master. She explains how in those days my grandfather would leave *el ganado,* the cattle, unattended to graze alone on the plains. If one got lost, "they" would bring it back; "they" wouldn't steal anything.

"It was healthy—*sano,*" she says. But then, *la inseguridad,* insecurity, arrived. She means the guerrillas and by "arrived" she means they came from elsewhere and with ideas from elsewhere. Her people are not like that; here they are "people of peace," she says. It is those who come from other places, from the interior that made them and everything change. At first, the cattle started to disappear, she says, as I get comfortable on her bed. María stays for the storytelling, holding onto the pressure valve. I feel as if she is telling me a spooky children's story, a tale of terror like those that kept me up all night, the ones that made me beg for company before bed, making me scream and see shadows wherever I looked. "They would kill it," she says, meaning the Holsteins and the *cebús,* "with bullets. Everyone knows slaughtering cattle is not done with guns," she tells me, and she wonders out loud who would do something so wrong. It didn't stop there, she assures me, it got worse: The carcasses of the cattle were left to rot. "What a waste," she says, "with so many people needing to eat." And "they" call themselves the fighters for social justice. These "they" are the guerrillas. No one has a name: not the rebels and not the workers. "Not only that. Whoever got close to the dead meat would be shot. I don't know what gets into these people's hearts. Because they would also tell them that it was okay to kill their mothers and their fathers for the cause."

Che Guevara's fierce call for revolution never made it to my grandmother's night table as it made it to mine in a snow-covered ivory tower, where nothing close to what my grandmother saw ever happened. She still keeps the same missal with a mother-of-pearl cover that her mother, Isabel, gave her when she made her first communion, with the date inscribed on the first page, September 15, 1908. For all her Christian compassion for the poor, she has never foreseen a world that would make a *trabajador* turn against her. An armed rebel is as incomprehensible to her as servility might be to me now. "What goodness can exist in the heart of someone who accepts that?" my grandmother asks, overwhelmed at the thought of rebellion. "But then again," she says, trying to make sense of it all, "if they don't accept it, they themselves are killed."

My grandmother had lived this. I had not. My mother would keep me up-to-date with phone calls that began sometime in the late eighties. In 1986, she faxed me a story from *El Heraldo.* More than twenty rebels had stormed into El Carmen. Of course, no family members were there. The story reported that the rebels walked in "like Peter inside his house," meaning as comfortable as if it was theirs. The rebels were looking for a place to have a party and chose my grandfather's farm that holiday weekend. They arrived prepared, with women, whisky, and the ominous *vallenato* trio, used in every Colombian party as macho ego-elevators. The musicians' job is to ad-lib about male prowess and *vallenatos* are the favorites of landowners, rebels, and paramilitary. The musicians sing to all sides—it's all about who pays. After the *parranda,* the rebels slept off their hangovers comfortably and took off the next day, with two of the guard's pistols, leaving behind an inscription on the wall instead of a thank-you note: GRACIAS. MANUEL MARTÍNEZ QUÍROZ FRONT.

There was a part of me that enjoyed listening to my mother's stories. Those days in Michigan had marked me deeply. I had followed the story of Gioconda Belli, the brown-haired Nicaraguan princess-rebel-poetess-turned-Sandinista comandante in Nicaragua. When I read *The Inhabited Woman,* her fictionalized

account of her transformation from *niña de sociedad* to *revolucionaria*, I
underlined almost every page. I even traveled to Managua to see her up close.
But I never considered going to Colombia to do what she had done in
Nicaragua. Why were Che's writings and the Sandinistas' victory more romantic than the FARC's fight? My family's life was disintegrating in front of them
and I thought I could see why better than they could. I had come to tell them
that theirs was a fight between the landowners and the laborers, a feudal fight
between those who have and those who don't, as I had been taught by my U.S.
professors.

The Montblancs are hiding in Barranquilla and the rebels are looking for
them on the roads but inside my grandmother's house, I have entered the time
warp of peace: entering the door is like entering the Colombia of my childhood
even if the pretension of peace couldn't fool me. José sits on Ma Cris's bed again,
going over the grocery list; Fanny bakes the plantains to my grandmother's
favorite browning point and her daughter Lucero cleans the bathrooms before
going to school.

No matter how much I try to disconnect this life from the fight between the
rebels and the paras as they do, I can't. When I hear that two silver-spoon-fed
sons of the province, men who grew up in households not very different than
this one, decided to leave it all behind to take up arms, even if on opposing
sides, it is a sign that the belief in the law of the rifle lurked everywhere. Simón
Trinidad helped bring the law of the FARC in; Jorge 40 did the same with the
AUC. Both men are very close to this feudal lifestyle, and yet I seem to be the
only one who sees the connection to the way things work in the countryside.

THE BALCONY DOOR IS OPEN AND A SOFT BREEZE ENTERS THE ROOM WHERE
Gustavo, Ma Cris, and I sit in rocking chairs. The sun is setting on the horizon,
and I look for the river that I have now learned how to locate. My grandmother's seventy-two-year-old cousin, Gustavo, is considered the family historian and my grandmother has invited him over to field the questions I've
started to ask her. All I know about him is that he moved to Barranquilla from
Asunción about six months ago to live with his daughters, also fleeing from the
town where he had lived all his life and planned to live for the rest of it. But
after he spent seventy-seven days in captivity, his daughters decided it was best
for him to come here.

Ma Cris looks at the floor and I look straight at him when I ask him how "it"
happened. He settles in to tell me the story of the day when he came face-to-
face with the rebel threat. He got up that morning at five, as he has always done,
ready to start the day's routine. As he slipped into the backseat of the Ford
Bronco, waiting for the driver to go open the door of the garage, two armed

men appeared from inside and got in the car with him, one at the wheel, the other in the back with Gustavo. They left the driver behind and took off, straight toward the sierra. When they got to a certain altitude, a vehicle was waiting for them. They transferred him to that one and drove "up the mountain until the car couldn't go any further." The rest of the trekking was done on mules. After hours and hours, they reached a rebel camp, where they held him for seventy-seven days. "As we were going up, people came out of their homes to see who was being taken this time," he says to Ma Cris more than to me. "They all know me but they couldn't do or say anything."

Ma Cris interjects, "He was unable to bathe or change clothes," and I know that to her that is the cruelest punishment possible. Gustavo turns to her and in a whisper tells her that he was able to escape thanks to one of the boys who was assigned to guard him. The rebel boy happened to be the son of a woman who had worked as a cook in Gustavo's cousin's house for more than twenty years, like a male Imelda. He sketched on the sand a safe route out of the sierra and left the gate to the camp open. (I was definitely not the only Colombian child to have a live-in servant.)

GUSTAVO AND MY GRANDMOTHER JUMP FROM BEWILDERMENT TO GIDDINESS when I ask them about their childhood and they recall lovely Asunción, peaceful Asunción, and the Asunción when it had *gente sana,* which means "healthy people," meaning servants and workers who don't kidnap people or kill cattle with bullets. It also had Father Martínez, and thanks to him, they say there were no *gente pobre,* nor prostitutes—and not many Liberals, the Conservative cousins joke—in Asunción.

They talk about the good times at the church like Emma and I talk about how much fun it was in Barranquilla, when we see each other in New York, and friends at parties ask us how we know each other. Asunción's church was a mix of tree house for the boys and salon for the girls. Padre Martínez was the town's mayor, fun coordinator, moral cop, and country club president. As the children of Conservatives, descendants of General Montblanc, they got to do pretty special things, things that the children of Liberals didn't do. Gustavo remembers how Padre Martínez taught him to toll the bells to announce movie ratings. If it was appropriate for children, Gustavo rang the bell once. If it was only for adults, he pulled on the chord twice. He loved going up the tower. It made for a perfect place to throw rocks at Liberal children, though there weren't many, he concedes. Ma Cris remembers how her tío didn't mind offering his trucks to the Liberals during elections. "It didn't really matter. There was no way it was going to hurt the Conservatives. There were no Liberals to haul to the voting polls all around Asunción."

Mixed in with the photographs of the Montblancs, I had found one of the priest wearing a monocle, a Panama hat, and a long white robe. I also found the letters he wrote in calligraphy and with a greeting that invoked Our Lord Jesus Christ. In the early 1950s, when he decided to demolish the colonial church, he reached out to my grandfather. He asked my grandfather to contribute to the renovation. My grandfather paid for the new altar and for the priest's new clothes, the ones my mother says were made in Spain with threads of gold. "It was the most beautiful thing I had seen in my life," she tells me. "More beautiful than your grandmother's emerald ring."

During the renovation, the church's saints were kept at my grandparents' house. Tía Luisa has told me that she would find strangers in her house kneeling in front of the saints. She would offer tea made with tree leaves and cakes made with sand to the pious visitors who left them untouched at the feet of the religious statues.

What I really want to find out from Gustavo is what no one has been able to. Who is this Frenchman who arrived? I figured that as the self-appointed family historian who has been working on a book about the family history for the last twenty-five years, he must know more than Ma Cris or my mother. My grandmother has told me about her life and has explained the names of the people in the photos but she doesn't know anything or has any curiosity to know how she came to be seen as better because she has *sangre francesa,* due to the travels of a young man from Bordeaux who decided to settle in 1848 in a place so faraway from the France of those days. After all, the Frenchman arrived in the time of revolutions and counterrevolution. No matter the reason, 1848 is a marked year in France.

"So who came here from France?" I ask and he is delighted and surprised to know that he has found an audience for his story. No one in the family, he tells me, especially this generation, is interested in history. He jumps right into it, just in case I might change my mind. "No one knows why Michel and his twenty-three-year-old son, Maurice, came to Colombia. Michel stayed a few years and went back to his family. Maurice stayed, and never once returned to France." Gustavo thinks that father and son might have spent time in the French colonies of Martinique and Guadeloupe "exercising commerce" before coming here. My grandmother thinks wishfully that they were missionaries. They both make sure they tell me that what is not true is that they arrived to the shores of Dibuya, "holding on to a plank of wood." The "bad tongues" of the region say they escaped from Devil's Island and were convicts on the run. "But that is pure invention," Gustavo says to dispel the rumor, because in 1848, the penal colony from where Papillon escaped was not open yet.

When Maurice arrived, the Caribbean had been a land of contraband and Colombia's northern tip was the "land of pirates and smugglers of cigarettes, silk, whisky, and gin coming from the islands of Aruba and Curaçao." It was also the land of tribes with chiefs and princesses. There were the Wayuus and the Goajiros. My grandmother insists that our ancestors came to help spread religion, but the anthropologist Reclus describes most Frenchmen as adventurers and charlatans. Riohacha was a favorite port for pirates and drunken Frenchmen with fake professions who sang "La Marsellaise" at every opportunity. It was also famous for its pearl divers, young children who would go fetch them underwater for a small price. The coast off Riohacha was as rich in pearls as the inside of the Andes were in emeralds. But the Frenchmen from Bordeaux preferred settling in boring Valledupar than in the raucous Riohacha. According to the family historian, they made a toast with champagne and set off on the Spanish trail by mule, passing through thirteen towns on their way to their final destination.

They chose to live away from the port, going instead to courtly Valledupar, a sleepy town on the foothills of the Sierra Nevada, where Michel bought a house in the fancy part of town that he paid for with gold coins, Gustavo's way of telling me they were not starving immigrants. The two started working "in commerce," which in those days meant trekking by mule from Valledupar to the port cities Riohacha or Santa Marta to buy and sell merchandise. With a few hired local hands and a convoy of mules, they went from Valledupar to various ports loading up along the way with whatever fruit, tobacco, and cattle they could get their hands on to sell to the anchored boats that came from all over. From there, they would bring back objects the province had never seen, like mirrors, soaps, silk stockings, and salt for the women, cologne, handkerchiefs, wrenches, and whisky for the men. The Frenchmen with their mules brought the outside to the forgotten province. The journey took six days and it was mostly traversed at night to avoid the heat of the day. I read that the wheels of the oxcarts were heard all over the cobbled streets of Valledupar. As they made their entrance, women knew they could have new dresses and men could count on new tools.

"IT WAS A PASTORAL LIFE OF GREEN FERTILE VALLEYS AND HILLS," WROTE ÉLISÉE Reclus, the Frenchman who traveled the province taking notes at the same time that Maurice decided to colonize the land and start a Colombian family. No one really knows how Maurice Montblanc felt about this land—he left no trace behind, other than eight legitimate children and at least three *hijos naturales*. Reclus wrote to his father that the place had caught his attention because "it looked prosperous and it was beautiful. The houses were painted yellow and shaded by trees of rare corpulence." Abandoned by the central government, he said, a group of Frenchmen had turned the region into an important cattle and agricultural zone. He even mentions his encounter with Manuel's great-great-great-grandfather.

These lands had never mattered to the people in the capital who considered all of this too remote, too rural, and too primitive. Not to be bothered, they handed all political power to local politicos who were given no resources but were given absolute control.

For two hundred years, a handful of families, many of French descent, have developed the region. It was they who built the roads they can't travel on and the bridges they can't cross, Gustavo tells me. *El Tiempo* ran an editorial that my mother sent to me. On Bastille Day 1999, it said, "We are so close to the United States and the rest of the American countries that we tend to forget Europe and specially France, a country whose ties with Colombia is rarely known, but to those fellow citizens over half a century old they constitute a permanent reminder of an entire generation that was educated *a la francesa* and whose intellectual, literary and political values had deep roots in the way of thinking and of the life of the French. . . . In Colombia, many are the families whose ancestors come from the villages and the beautiful cities of France—the Parfaits and the Montblancs, to name just two, and who are now *colombianísimas*."

It is Reclus, not my family's historian, who guides me through the "young land" of "isolated hamlets surrounded by solitude." In his *Voyage to the Sierra Nevada of Santa Marta*, half travel book, half geography textbook, with a touch of Bentham's anarchic views, I learn about the marshes, jungles, and mountains that the Frenchmen encountered. It is a kind of magical realism: The locals, he writes, live in an "imperfect state"; the republic is "poor" and "weak" but they will undoubtedly form the "most powerful empires of the world." As a true anarchist Reclus relied on the importance of nature. This place was Arcadia: "What can we expect of this country where the oceans meet, where all the climates of the world live one on top of the other, where all the products grow, where five chains of mountains open into a fan of varied possibilities?" That I imagine is what Maurice Montblanc also saw. If not, why stay? Reclus also noted: "They are eager to build their own country" and "France is the golden example." So to be French is to be revered, a good reason for a young Frenchman to stay.

Colonization was encouraged in the fertile valley between the two sierras. The government allowed every family—national and not—forty hectares of idle land. I transfer it into a measurement I can understand; this is the size of twenty New York City blocks, a walk, say, from Times Square up to the entrance of Central Park. All they had to do was agree to developing it within two years. Frequently, colonizers settled wherever they wanted to live and without asking for the concession and without committing to anything, they became the owners by virtue of being there first.

Reclus tried it but failed. He was unable to realize his dream of an agricultural cooperative. To him, the locals lived lackadaisically, not worrying about the future, spending their lives in a lazy daze. He also makes note of landowners that are too "capitalistic." People, he perceived, who don't even know how much they have, like Manuel de Mier y Terán in the Sierra Nevada, where coffee was already being grown. Coffee beans were already popular and lucrative. It was a sureshot crop with little risk. The bushes gave fruit twice a year yielding as much as twelve kilos of beans per foot. Maurice became a coffee grower, owning his first land at the foot of the Sierra Nevada.

There are other lands that are more accessible to the new immigrants, says Reclus. These areas are only reachable through roads or through the tiny towns along the Río Cesár. To make the trip he hired the required three guides, locals that the administration assigned and who were paid a flat fee. One carried the mail, the second the provisions, and the third the guns and the bags. But soon, he noted, the luggage got lighter. The termites had eaten half of his books, entire volumes of philosophy books. Reclus saw altars adorned with images of the heroes of the French Revolution. It must have been alluring for men like Maurice to find a place where the prairies could be theirs, where their ways brought them privileges, and where women tended to them like gods. They found a place where a monkey is taught to hug; a parrot knows the name of the neighborhood children; a parakeet throws kisses to those who feed him, and where, at night, the streets come alive with fairs and dances. Being French gave you an upper hand. In Riohacha, Reclus met Monsieur Jules, who kept a jaguar and a monkey as pets, and who boasted he was related to the famous courtesan Ninon de Lenclos, known for her aristocratic lovers and her literary salons, attended by Molière, in pre-revolutionary France. Monsieur Jules also said he was a medical doctor. And although he had no proof of either claim, he would take to the Perijá Hills where locals paid for his medical advice, allowing him to draw their blood, and they took his drugs, "unclear of what they were or how he got them," because he was French. Jules was paid with hammocks, with rugs, and with stirrups and then he would set up shop and resell them.

Even Reclus fell for the charm of the women. He tells the story of when he fell from a canoe, feverish and almost delirious from the trip, and slipped into a mangrove. A guide arranged to have him tended to. He remembers waking up to the soft caress of a feminine hand, offering him a drink from a bowl. Her black eyes twinkled with "tender piety," her bright face surrounded by her long flowing hair felt like "she was full of light." For a second Reclus "wondered if it would be a good idea to end my trip and build a cabin on the banks of a stream right here. Should a man travel the world senselessly when he can find happiness inside a straw thatched hut or under the shadow of a palm tree?" Is that what Maurice felt? Reclus resisted "with everything" he had to "the voice inside that spoke those words." Was it a call that captivated the young Montblanc?

When father and son arrived, Colombia had been independent from the Spanish Crown for only twenty-eight years. It had gone from Viceroyalty of the New Granada to Republic of the New Granada to becoming the Republic of Colombia. But the transition from colony to republic was proving to be more difficult than anyone had expected. Simón Bolívar and the rest of the army generals might have gotten rid of the laws of Spain. But that was the only thing the *criollos* had in common when they agreed to revolt. The *criollos* of Santa Fé de Bogotá were immersed in political debate. There were two opposing views on how to run the new republic. The Conservatives wanted things to remain the way they were during the viceroyalty. They wanted a Colombia guided by a government that believed, followed, and lived the ideas of the Catholic Church. They fought to have a government that would give power only to landowners. It is the idea that certain men are chosen by God to rule, and others are chosen by God to follow. The Liberals embraced the ideas and the writings of the French Revolution. They believed in a secular government, in education, in masonry, in science, and in free trade. The Liberals and the Conservatives fought so doggedly that by 1843 each party ran neighborhood associations to recruit members. "These societies only promoted intolerance and fanaticism by indoctrinating and becoming ideological," writes Rafael Pardo in *History of the Wars,* confirming my belief that the exclusionary and violent mentality seen in Colombia's recent history has existed since the days of the new republic. Liberals, wearing red towels hanging from their waists, went around inciting violence against the Jesus-loving Conservatives; and the Conservatives, wearing blue-ribboned hats, went around hating freethinking Liberals. Everyone knew that both sides carried sharp knives under their ponchos. I am going back this far in history for a reason. Not much has changed: Today, if you don't defend the paras, you are a FARC and deserve to die; and if you are not a *guerrillero* you must then contribute to the AUC and turn a blind eye to their brutal methods of exterminating rebels.

After twenty-two years of fighting, the Conservative government was in ruins. Things were so bad that the government considered selling the best emerald mines to pay its public debt. Realizing that this back and forth could not go on, the Liberals and the Conservatives sat down to talk. They made a pact like the one they made almost one hundred years later with the National Front. Colombians prefer pacts to shared power—pacts instead of reconciliation. "They like [a] pact in a way that legitimizes absolute power [for] one party at a time." And it is this type of arrangement, according to Pardo, that dominates Colombian politics for the rest of the century. Is this the curse of Colombia?

The fighting that was mostly confined to the south, reached Valledupar during Holy Week in 1854. Seven years after Maurice Montblanc settled there, the sons of the artisans attacked the sons of the landed merchants during a procession. As the Conservatives paraded the Virgin around town, the Liberals went for the kill. Only Conservatives were allowed to carry the Virgin in 1854, but Gustavo and Ma Cris tell me it was still the case when they were growing up. "It was an honor to be asked," Ma Cris told me with pride. Later that night in the bag of photos I find one of my grandfather wearing a tie and holding the Virgin at the procession. The thought of that day still makes my grandmother beam with joy. She tells me that Gabriel did it so that she would notice him and like him more. "It worked," she says smiling. And I wonder if the Virgin that slept in this house last week was brought here because she prefers households with Conservative pasts.

I ask Gustavo to tell me more about Maurice. I am trying to nail down the Frenchman's politics. "It seems that he was very good-looking and popular with the ladies," he explains and I can tell my grandmother is hearing this for the first time. The young Frenchman captivated Tomasa Puche—"of the Puches," he says turning to my grandmother and I take that to mean that's a good family—and her family had accepted his visits. But when the virginal dame got pregnant, she was disowned, expelled, sent out. The two settled in a nearby hamlet where Maurice continued making a living taking the long trips to the ports. But he never returned from one of them. Stopping at a coffee plantation on the outskirts of the Sierra Nevada, to buy the beans he would sell to the European boats, he met Carmen Ariza, the daughter of the plantation owner, and a woman "of a great beauty." (There are no pictures of Carmen in my bag, and Gustavo tells me that the Montblancs have not paid enough attention to the importance of women. "We only care about the men," he says, "and that they're French.") Maurice stayed. He married Carmen, whose family was happy to add French blood to theirs, and took to raising cattle in his in-laws' extensive landholdings. So, the Frenchman was just a smoocher?

Carmen proved to be as fertile as her father's land, giving birth to nine children of French blood, which helped them enormously. Four of the sons married women from the nearby town of Asunción and by 1898, at the time the War of the One Thousand Days broke out, the Montblanc Ariza brothers had all moved to the town's square. From there, twenty-year-old Alberto de los Angeles Montblanc Ariza, the firstborn son of the Frenchman, commanded the Conservative forces sent out to fight the Liberals. "Asunción has always been Conservative," Gustavo explains. "So Conservative that during the wars of independence, it was on the side of Spain not of Simón Bolívar."

The Montblancs took their Conservatism so seriously that Alberto, now made general, painted his house in the party color and it came to be known in the region as The Blue House. The general, who also loved cockfights, always made sure his animal fought with a blue ribbon wrapped around his neck.

"What did it mean to be a Conservative then?" I ask.

"It meant that you believed in tradition and the laws of the Church," Gustavo explains. But later I find out that the Conservative general, who should have believed in the sanctity of marriage as imposed by the religion he so furiously defended, had thirty-five children out of wedlock.

THE PHONE, LESS THAN A FOOT AWAY FROM WHERE WE ARE SITTING, RINGS. It interrupts the conversation, but neither my grandmother nor I moves to answer it. Fanny has to come from the kitchen to pick it up. "It is José," she says to Ma Cris. "He says that there is no more raspberry sorbet left. He wants to know what he should get." Gustavo and Ma Cris agree on mango and tangerine.

"Tell him to hurry up," Ma Cris tells Fanny. "It's late." When Fanny brings the tray with the ice cream, José walks in to hand my grandmother the change from the errand. Ma Cris tells him to leave it on her night table and to hurry up. "I was worried about José's bus," she says in the tone of a mother concerned that her son might get stranded. "He has to take three buses to get to where he lives. We've kept him too late," she says, taking a spoonful to her mouth.

I feel so lost in this tableau, there are so many things tugging at my heart and at my mind that I can only ask, "Why do they kidnap us?"

"They kidnap us because, because we have a reputation of being hard workers and we have something," Gustavo responds. "They have kidnapped thirty-seven people with our last name. We in La Provincia are the hardest-hit family." Ma Cris finishes the thought with the now-familiar refrain "And they say they won't stop until they have kidnapped us all."

I let them speak; I'm working slowly but I am in no hurry. The trip to El Carmen does not seem to be materializing any time soon. Plus, I have fallen into something I had not planned to do. I have started to live like an insider in their reality and with their thoughts. I am being allowed in to see how it feels, for them, to be the victims. With the Magdalena River visible on the horizon, I am letting go of my black-and-white long-held perceptions and I listen for the first time to the Montblancs.

20

GUILLERMO'S TERRACE

Guillermo is surprised that I've asked if I could see him. I can tell because when I arrive at his house accompanied by Agustín, he is waiting outside. We exchange awkward hellos. With his kiss on my cheek and the smell of his cologne, I feel the familiarity of family but also the strangeness of strangers. He is my grandfather's best friend, a landowner from Asunción and by the nature of these provincial relationships, they are also cousins, many ways over. My father likes to joke that one day, the Montblancs, like the fictional Buendías and their inbreeding, will one day bear a baby with a pig's tail. The last time I saw Guillermo I was fifteen years old. Every Sunday, on afternoons very much like this one, I'd find him sitting with my grandfather on the terrace, during those long weekly gatherings. But I had never exchanged a word with him beyond a few quick greetings. *"Hola linda,"* he says softly, placing his hand between my shoulder blades, guiding me to the terrace. I wonder if I am still seen as family, after such a long absence.

My grandfather died more than ten years ago but the way Guillermo says his name, it feels like he is sitting next to him as Gabriel used to, with a whisky in hand dressed in a cotton guayabera, his legs crossed, holding a Parliament cigarette tightly between his fingers, the index one bent noticeably to the right where a horse had once stepped on it.

I sit in a white garden chair directly in front of him. I tell him I am interested in knowing how my grandfather acquired El Carmen. He crosses one leg over the other, visibly relieved. I am known as the granddaughter who wrote a book about how men treat women badly in Latin America. I think that the last thing he was expecting was for me to ask about El Carmen. The women in my grandfather's family have never been interested in *la finca*. I have my notepad in my bag but I decide to leave it there. I am going to go with what my father calls my elephant memory, meaning that it's good, and that my years as a reporter have honed my power of recall.

"No one was interested in land in those days," he starts by saying. "Gabriel was one of the first ones." He explains that when he left Asunción in the late 1940s and moved to Valledupar, he bought a piece of land that today everyone refers to as one of the best pieces of land in the region. He sold Esperanza because he was obsessed with the foothills of the Serranía de Perijá, virgin land that he wanted to colonize. "But your grandfather was a man of obsessions," he tells me and I wonder if obsession is my genetic inheritance. "When he wants to do something, he just has to," he says and for the first time I identify myself with my grandfather. Guillermo also describes him as a risk taker, one who went against the current, one who had always scoffed at convention, one who challenged everything, even the earth. We remember the time he was obsessed with growing pepper in El Carmen. He found a Japanese expert who indulged him, moved with his wife and daughter to the farm, and for years tried and tried. All there is from the pepper experiment is a pearl necklace that the agronomist gave my grandmother as a gift and that I sometimes wear in New York.

Abuelo Gabriel had an uncle, the general's brother, who had a big cattle ranch outside of Asunción. Abuelo Gabriel, who preferred making a buck than being in his boarding school in Santa Marta, dropped out and started working for his uncle. He would walk his uncle's cattle to Santa Marta, where the Americans who worked at the United Fruit Company would pay for the meat in dollars. Or he would transport it down the Magdalena River to sell it in Medellín or Bogotá, a trip that took more than fifty days. He also crossed it over to neighboring Venezuela. "Selling cattle was the way to make money in those days," Guillermo explains. He would walk up to one hundred heads at a time. The best route was to Santa Marta. The trip took only ten days and the Americans paid generously for good meat. He would leave Asunción with two or three cowboys and they would walk all night and rest during the day. "It's better to walk with no sun. The animals don't get as tired with the light of the moon."

It is easy to sit here and listen to these stories. It is easy to romanticize about my grandfather crossing mountains and plains with a herd of cattle. I have a lovely photo of him on his horse looking like a character from a Cormac McCarthy novel about the Texas-Mexico border, with his hair combed as if he were on his way to a ball, not to transport cattle. Agustín and Guillermo regale me with their memories of the trips on the steamboats with the cattle and the cases of Buchanan to celebrate the sales but it is Guillermo who snaps out of the good old days.

Guillermo tells me that it is a blessing that my grandfather had his aneurysm in 1989, which left him disabled and with a failing mind "before this tragedy began." He is referring to the incipient trend of kidnappings. In those days Guillermo and Agustín kept what was happening on the *fincas* as classified information, on the orders of his doctor, the son of cousins, of course, with roots in Asunción. The doctor whose brother had already been kidnapped (and later his father) preferred that all of this news was better kept from a man recovering from a stroke, with diabetes and a bad temper. For eight months Guillermo had to pretend when he went to visit him, that everything was all right when his youngest son was being held hostage.

Guillermo tells me how it happened. He was locking the front door of the *finca*'s house early on a Sunday evening when "they" arrived, "bringing the doors down, screaming and yelling the most horrible insults and obscenities." Guillermo is so well mannered and so perfectly groomed that out of respect I don't ask him what it is "they" were yelling. The racket woke up his son at the moment the rebels were taking Guillermo away. "My father is sick. He needs medicine and he is seventy years old," the son explained. "Instead of taking him, why don't you take me?" They did. "I was ready to go," Guillermo tells me, "but Gabriel would have never accepted." I perceive that it is almost harder for Guillermo to talk about my grandfather than it is about his ordeal. Guillermo misses his friend. "He would always say that no one would take him from his land, that first they would have to kill him." He had slept all his life with his front gate unlocked and always carried a pistol. But that's what he must have meant when I heard him say that they would have to come and get the tiger. He was the tiger.

I ask again about El Carmen.

He sold Esperanza, which was a perfect prairie, because he had his eye set on a new piece of land, Guillermo says, glad to continue his narrative. This time it was a piece of wilderness, land that was inaccessible; there were no paved roads. It was in the foothills of the Serranía de Perijá. To get there from Valledupar took hours. "Gabriel starts exploring it, cleaning it, cultivating it," he tells me, "until he was able to put it to use. That's when those things could be done." I take that to mean that something has changed, that what he is describing sounds like a land grab.

My uncle crosses his legs the other way and offers his explanation. "Land had no value then," he says. "At first, the land belongs to no one. It had no price. No value. That's all there was: land. What was lacking was who would work it. There was land out to infinity; it seemed that it would never end. And the land would be of the one who had the capability to buy the chicken wire and hire labor to knock down the mountain and level off the land. Your grandfather did. He was making good money selling cattle. He starts to think as a capitalist, and puts others to work. The land starts to have value because it starts to have an owner."

"That's how it was done then," Guillermo adds. "That's how everyone did it. I did it. Your grandfather did it. By fencing in uncultivated land. It was virgin land, mountain, pure mountain."

I am getting a history lesson about Colombia, about her forgotten provinces, about my grandfather and the men of his generation, men who opened the roads because the state didn't build them; men who hired with no labor code because there was no one to enforce it; men who paid for their workers' doctor bills because there was no social security. I do not tell Guillermo that the reason I want to know all these stories is because I think that what is happening today is a result of practices and politics that started way before the rebels began kidnapping landowners but I sense that I've brought him some happiness by asking him to tell me about those days and I don't want to take it away, so I leave it there. Is the important thing to tell Guillermo that what they did was wrong or for the landowners of today to understand those imperfections and to work on changing them?

Guillermo asks me if I want something to drink, so I know he is not ready to stop answering my questions. "A *jugo*," he offers and I nod my head, reminded of when my grandfather would ask me if I wanted a juice made with the fresh fruit of the day and would then tell me to go ask for it in the kitchen. Guillermo calls for the maids but no one responds. "They must be outside talking to their friends," he says. "It's a holiday." He walks to the front door and calls out their names again, almost like a father telling his daughters to come in on a school night to finish their homework. He asks them to please bring three juices to the terrace.

When he comes back, I ask him to tell me about life when he, my grandmother, and my grandfather were all children in Asunción. He explains their blood relation but my ignorance about my family's genealogy makes it hard for me to follow the intricate web of marriages that took place between the few "good" families of the region. It reminds me of the same confusion I had when keeping track of all the Buendias in *One Hundred Years of Solitude*. I've gotten to the point where I have stopped trying. It doesn't matter if you don't get all the family ties and who married whom. I have learned to assume that if someone sits on the terrace of a Montblanc, he or she is a relative.

When I ask Guillermo why, he tells me that there was no one else to marry—even though it was a town of a few thousand souls as recorded by Father Martinez's baptismal books. It takes only one description to understand the importance of European heritage, like my grandmother, for the people of Padilla's province. I read in the description of a family wedding between a Parfait and a Montblanc that the bride is "a pretty girl of smooth skin and languid eyes whose features revealed her elevated origins."

Two uniformed women come to the terrace. One holds two glasses, handing one to Guillermo and the other to Agustín. The younger one, a step behind, holds the third glass and hands it to me. I notice the sparkling silver paint on her nails, and the contrast it makes with the cranberry-colored juice she hands me. Our maids never wore nail polish. I take a sip of the *corozo* juice, and the bittersweet taste of it is better than I remember it. It must be because it has my past mixed in it, like for the Montblancs when they talk about Asunción, nostalgia makes everything tastier, prettier, better.

"It was the best town, no exaggeration," says Guillermo describing it almost exactly like my grandmother and Gustavo's recollections. "It was a town that stimulated people to work. People were entrepreneurial. They wanted to bring progress." The picture I am making of Asunción is that it's a town run by a few families, all married to each other, who lived around the square, and by the rules of Father Martínez in the church across from them. Family members today recall the hamlet as a town of "good, hard-working people," a prosperous town thanks to the conservative ways of Father Martínez. And yet it was a town where the men who lived around the square bore children who weren't allowed to live as they did.

They could partake in some of the celebrations in the square, like when the first car came to Asunción brought in by a son of the general, Guillermo says with pride. It came in parts and was assembled in the square in front of The Blue House. A line of donkeys brought it from Santa Marta. In one came the motor. In another came the frame, then the tires. Once it was assembled it went around the square. People were looking out the windows; others stood in the square. It became known as *el torito,* the little bull.

Not just the car arrived by mule, everything did—ice, rice, clothes, furniture, gas, whatever had added value. The country was so fragmented and the provinces so isolated and so unimportant to the capital that the government never had a real plan to build the necessary infrastructure to connect the capital to the provinces. My grandparents traveled for days, again by mule, to get to school. My grandfather went to the only private school in the area, a Jesuit school in Santa Marta; it took three days of travel to get there. My grandmother went to the school run by Franciscan nuns in Riohacha until she was eight. That trip took two days. My grandfather's older brothers were sent away to Belgium for schooling. It was almost easier to cross the Atlantic than to go to the Andes.

Eliseo Parfait, named after Élisée Reclus who immortalized the first French colonizers in his writing, says that he decided to become an engineer when, in 1923, he saw his grandfather's car arrive in parts too. The governor of Magdalena had to send a crew to help the car get there. The roads between Santa Marta and his town were so primitive that a handful of men went ahead wielding machetes, freeing the road from weeds. Another group of men walked behind, ready to carry the unassembled car on their shoulders to cross the many rivers and streams along the way. Young Eliseo was a twelve-year-old when he witnessed the first Ford's journey. His life, and that of the entire province of Padilla, changed that day. Eliseo promised himself he would learn how to build bridges and he fulfilled his promise. He studied engineering at the Sorbonne and came back to open roads and build bridges along the route that had previously taken a car twenty days to travel. By 1957, thanks to him, that twenty-day trip could be driven in half a day. "While Eliseo learned how to build bridges and speak perfect French, Leoncio came back with a billiard table and French learned in bed," Guillermo tells Agustín with a naughty nudge. Leoncio was my grandfather's youngest brother.

I have opened up an entire box of memories. I wish I had my bag of photos with me. Guillermo is turning out to be a wonderful raconteur, filled with facts that finally clarify my grandparents' trajectory from Asunción to Barranquilla. When Gabriel bought Esperanza and his cattle business started growing, he decided Asunción was too small of a town and told my grandmother that they were moving to Valledupar. It was where his business partners lived, a much bigger city, a place he liked. But my grandmother didn't like the idea of leaving the Frenchman's House on the square, or the proximity to the church of Father Martinez.

Cristina was unhappy in Valledupar, Guillermo explains. My grandfather was always on the road and she missed the perfect life of the plaza she left behind. To compensate for or because of what Guillermo calls "that mysterious love for the church she has," Ma Cris grew more involved in her religious life, so much so that when Valledupar's monsignor asked her if he could borrow the garage of her house and turn it into a chapel for a few hours every morning, she was thrilled.

"Cris is difficult," Guillermo offers. In Barranquilla, my grandfather had to move around with a little bell to call for a servant to take care of him, because "Cris wouldn't." She only had time for the church. He tells me that's why they had all those fights. And that Gabriel would take off for El Carmen and leave her in Barranquilla, "in the big house all alone." A few days later, she would have the driver take her there. "But they were really in love." If one can measure love by the way two people hold hands, rest their hands on each other's knees, then Guillermo's statement is true. I was always amazed to see the way he rubbed her knee.

It is hard to resist these stories even if they do not shed light on why Colombia is at war. My grandparents are coming alive, and so is Colombia. My grandparents' love story is much more complicated than I had ever cared to imagine. And I find myself more open to listening to their side of the story than I have ever been. I came to write about war and for the past week I have only heard about love, love for land, love for God, the love between my grandparents, the love among friends, and the strange accepted conjugal love of relatives. Whenever a Montblanc wanted to marry, Father Martínez made it possible by asking for a dispensation from the Vatican, as he did when my grandparents married in 1936. I once asked my mother if there had been opposition to their marriage, but she answered by quoting her grandmother, "If strangers can love each other, cousins will love each other more." My grandmother tells me that they fell in love because they lived in the same house "like brother and sister" and that to her was the most matter-of-fact statement in the world, and the antithesis of *To a Passerby,* the Charles Baudelaire poem I've framed, which is about the possibility of finding love among strangers on the street, not among your own family.

I leave Guillermo's terrace tickled by the image of my grandparents' fights. There is something romantic about their tormented relationship that I would have never guessed. I wondered what their reconciliations were like. But if the stories of love and the perfect life of the Montblancs in Asunción drew me during the day, when I return to my reporter's den at night, the confusion soon takes over. I now know that places like El Carmen were hacked out from the wild somewhere in the midforties to the midfifties and the timing of this coincides in my timeline with the years of La Violencia. I had asked my grandmother if she remembered the day that Gaitán was killed. Do they relate?

If you listen to the FARC they do. Back in my room, away from Guillermo's terrace, I sit cross-legged on the bed. I take the pillow with my grandmother's embroidered initials, and I place my laptop on it. Instead of going to the chat groups of the FARC or the paras, I open to the timeline I've been making.

When I started my fight with Colombia, I started going through all the books my father had sent throughout the years and that I had piled in a corner, leaving them unread. I've spent the time since taking notes, underlining, and making a timeline that I divided into three categories: Colombia's history, the one that I had missed with my American schooling; my family history, the one I was gathering from anecdotes and memories; and my own history, the one where I am born Silvana María Paternostro Montblanc, with a set-in-stone birth certificate (and a strange stain on my left foot) and where I mark the chronology of my split, of my tugs, of the transformation of the spoiled *niña del Parrish* to the hard-core believer of progressive causes, the liberal American-educated reporter of Latin American ills in English.

I open the folder so I can incorporate Guillermo's stories into my timeline, in the category of family history, the pages with the yellow borders to differentiate them from Colombia's, which have a purple border, and mine, which have green borders. According to my yellow-bordered timeline, the years when my grandfather invested in livestock to fence in El Carmen were the years of La Violencia, a period of fighting between the Conservative government and the Liberal rebels that left 300,000 people dead and two million people displaced. This is the first case where something is called by its name, where euphemisms are avoided in Colombian names; the first time that Colombians had used honest and naked words to describe a situation; where violence is violence is violence. No one can pinpoint a specific date to the beginning of this period—it is usually the death of Jorge Eliécer Gaitán, but now I know it includes the time when my grandparents were fighting over priests; when my grandfather was traveling selling cattle and busy fencing land.

The assassination of Gaitán marked an entire generation of Colombians, like the assassination of John F. Kennedy marked an entire generation of Americans. It happened in Bogotá on April 9, 1948. From then on, everyone short-cuts the history and the events by calling it *el Gaitanzo* or *el Bogotazo* and it's the benchmark used to mark the beginning of La Violencia. I have always heard the catcalling between Liberals and Conservatives, even as a child—my grandmother's pretty friend who, after she divorced, turned her Land Rover into a school bus service of sorts. The children of Liberals chanted the *Vivas* that they had heard from their parents and grandparents, and I knew from listening to family conversations that we were Conservatives. I don't remember any Conservative chants but I do remember the Christmas card that arrived every year from the leader of the party, thanking my father for all of his help. My father was proud to call himself a *godo*, the moniker of a true Conservative, and a word brought in from colonial days and that goes as far back as when the Goths invaded Spain; then it mutated to describe the Spanish-born who lived in the colonies. It was that hispanocentric ideology of the Conservatives that earned them the name from the early days of the Republic up to today. Everyone could identify the Carbonells as the prime Conservative family and the Pumarejos as the prime Liberals. As I started to make sense of politics, neither seemed too captivating. They represented labels more than ideas. They felt they were tools for identification more than anything, ways to be members of one club that would have personal benefits. I knew both the Carbonells and the Pumarejos and there were no immediately recognizable signs of great difference between them. In fact a Pumarejo and a Carbonell were both at a tea party I attended during my visit to Barranquilla. So why had the line between the two parties become so charged during La Violencia?

Ma Cris was in her early thirties on the fated day in 1948 "when they killed Gaitán." No one really knows who killed the leader who had encouraged workers in Colombia to unionize. (Recent documents reveal that the CIA kept tabs on him, citing dangerous Communist tendencies.)

JORGE ELIÉCER GAITÁN, A MAN OF HUMBLE ORIGINS, COPPER-COLORED SKIN, and a knack for oratory had been leading the way for an inclusive society in the late 1940s. People, especially the mestizos like him, and the workers, listened to Gaitán like the blacks and the believers in civil rights would listen to Malcolm X and to Martin Luther King in Harlem two decades later. His constituency was the Liberal gut of Colombia and many were the mistreated workers in the coffee fields and the small farmers who were losing their lands to the boom of international coffee drinking. The landed coffee growers wanted more land and Gaitán was telling them that enough was enough.

The Conservatives won the election in 1946 and President Mariano Ospina Perez wanted to make sure Gaitán and his cohorts stopped in their efforts to promote workers' rights. In Tolima, a Liberal stronghold, the Conservatives had to worry about losing ground. The Liberals of Tolima were fierce and they were as organized as any rebel army. They gained courage and denounced their employers' mistreatment of workers in the fields. They even stopped accepting the opportunity to parade the Virgin around town during the processions. They attended union meetings and were ready to vote for Jorge Eliécer Gaitán. When drunk they shouted "Long Live the Liberal Party" in the plazas. But then on April 9, 1948, Gaitán was killed. There would be so many more presidential candidates shot in the years to come. And my generation of Colombians would have to become used to the word *magnicido*, the assassination of a very important person.

Ma Cris had been living in Valledupar with her five children and was six months' pregnant with her last. When I bring up the *gaitanazo*, Ma Cris remembers being alone that night; my grandfather was away and she could hear the noise on the streets outside in the square, a lot of yelling and screaming. "We were the only Conservatives on the street—Valledupar is a Liberal town—and I remember the scratching of machetes on our sidewalk. Men standing in front of the house, walking up and down, dragging their machetes behind. The noise was unbearable. I had to close the windows." These stories confuse me. She doesn't sound as scared as I would be if I heard a hissing machete and threatening name-calling outside my window. My father remembers that when he was eleven, the adults talked about the possibility of a civil war that night. The men asked one another if they had arms; the women asked around about what food they had. "In that moment," my father tells me, "there was no differentiation between parties in our socioeconomic class. Everyone saw the bigger threat where everyone would lose." My mother was six and she remembers the men listening to the radio and the panic inside the homes; the adults repeating the word "assassination" over and over and how grave that sounded. She tells me that when she went to El Carmen that weekend she was very careful while going to see some newborn chicks. "I picked them up so carefully, afraid that they would die in my hands and it would turn into an assassination."

My understanding of La Violencia came from a picture Nereo showed me in New York of two couples on their wedding day, posing right after the ceremony. Once a movie projectionist from Cartagena, Nereo became a pioneer photojournalist during the years of La Violencia, when he traveled through the entire country. In the wedding image, the women wear wedding dresses and the men wear suits. They are not fancy nor do they have the look of bliss that one expects from wedding portraits. The men hold to their newlywed brides' waists awkwardly, and the women look scared, and perhaps too young to be marrying the two men. They are standing on dirt, and that's when I notice the womens' shoes. They are too big for them.

"I took this picture in a coffee field outside of Bogotá," Nereo explains. "I walked from six in the morning to four in the afternoon to get there at the time of the wedding. Two brothers were marrying two sisters. The two men were displaced from their town and they came back to find out that their wives and children had disappeared, not sure if they had been run out of town or killed. The men needed new wives. So the new brides used the wedding dresses of the men's first wives. "This is the story of the Colombian countryside," Nereo tells me. "This is what happened to regular people, during La Violencia. These two men had to be Liberals because it was they who were being displaced. The killers were on the side of the Conservatives who had a squadron called the Black Birds, just like today's paramilitary." Many years later, I read a story about Pedro Marco, who, when he was a young boy, lived in a hamlet in Córdoba, so remote from anywhere that the news of Gaitán's death arrived three months later, delivered by a man who rode a donkey into town. Soon after that, bands of Conservatives showed up looking for Liberals. When the Conservative men were close, Pedro's father, a Liberal, would take his wife, his six children, and some provisions and flee to *el monte*, Colombia's name for "jungle," and stay there for several days. "I never saw dead bodies," Pedro Marco, now sixty-two, tells the reporter. "They say they floated down the river."

What went on during La Violencia was not very different than what I had encountered on my first evening in Barranquilla when I ran into the young man who had walked for days after his two sisters had been killed in front of him. And it is very similar to the story that my grandmother had told me about Imelda's father. Does she know if Tulio was a Liberal? She did tell me he came to El Carmen to escape The Violence. Nereo explains more. "The whole purpose of this persecution was not so much political but it was to grab land from the peasants. Those who have land, the *feudales,* want more land. So now the paramilitary come in and with the pretext that they are getting rid of guerrillas they harass and displace entire towns and keep the land. Before they were displaced for being Liberals and today for being guerrillas. Today's violence is the same as La Violencia's."

To blame the Conservatives exclusively for La Violencia would be too narrow-minded, simplistic, and unproductive. The men in southern Tolima, the members of Vengeance and Black Blood, who called themselves Liberal guerrillas, were conducting "big massacres and big assaults on the towns and especially on the police force," General José Joaquín Matallana, the colonel who directed Operation Marquetalia, said to *Semana* in 2003. He explained how Manuel Marulanda had learned to use explosives when he worked for the Ministry of Public Works and that he had been a significant force in the fight between the Liberals and the Conservatives.

JUST A FEW HOURS HAVE PASSED SINCE GUILLERMO REGALED ME WITH STORIES of their paradise lost and kissed my cheek good-bye. He told me that 1936 marked the first time that Asunción was visited by a president of Colombia. He visited the Frenchman's House. It was the only house around "fit for a president" who had arrived in the tropical heat of the coast wearing tails and a top hat. "He needed a good *jugo* and a rest and Papa Alberto offered his house." From Guillermo I now know that my Conservative forebear entertained the most Liberal of all presidents in his home. I learned from my grandmother that her uncle would lend trucks to the Liberals and from Gustavo that as kids they provoked and bullied the children of Liberals. From my mother I know that because theirs was the only house in town with a radio, both Liberals and Conservatives came over to listen to it. "In those days to say Conservative and Liberal is like today saying Israelis and Palestinians," my mother wrote to me when I asked her to tell me about her childhood, "but there was another rule for marriages. We were told that our boyfriend had to be from a good family, yes, but he had to be from a Christian and a Conservative family. This was not a joke. It was a rule to be obeyed." No one in my family tells me a story like Nereo does or like the ones I find elsewhere when I punch in the FARC's Web address on my laptop that rests on the pillow with the white pillowcase that has two beautiful *M*'s monogrammed on it. I caress my grandmother's initials, thinking she was not once but twice a Conservative, as I view the timeline that the FARC has for La Violencia. It is very different from the one I had just heard from my relatives but closer to Nereo's. This is their version: The Conservatives created private armies to increase their landholdings, these were the so-called Chulavitas, named after a black bird. The purpose of the Birds was twofold: One, it would instill fear in those peasants who would be in favor of voting for the Liberal party. Two, with threats first and then with horrible forms of violence, the Chulavitas would get the peasants to leave their lands so that a Conservative could appropriate them or they would kill the peasants. The purpose was the same: One less Liberal meant more land for a Conservative. "They came in and mutilated, decapitated, conducted massive killings, killed children so that they wouldn't grow up to be the enemy." La Violencia, the FARC insists, is the fight between the Liberal guerrilla and the Conservative paramilitary.

I continue reading. "The Forties were one of the most horrible moments of our history. The massacres of Liberals and Communists in the countryside could come to one or two hundred victims a day. The Church put all of its doctrine in the conflict and many of us, the survivors, would hear the crazed priests: 'We must kill the bad Liberals and the good ones as well because they will turn out to be bad.'"

The rebels' history lesson reads like a gory film: "Pregnant stomachs were opened with knives"; "men skinned alive and tied to ant colonies"; "others with their genitals inside their mouths"; "or with their tongues hanging from their chest." I can't read anymore. I do not know where to file this information, in my brain or in my heart.

The Birds were a "strategy organized directly between the Conservative Party and the State to appropriate land that was taken from peasants, initiating a wave of violence against liberal peasants." The FARC explains that the fight between Liberals and Conservatives was simply "an excuse for the expansion of the *latifundio.*" They argue that protected by the violence, the political authorities, the local bigwigs had the most to reap. This, they say, is what contributed to their generation of wealth and regional political power.

I read all night. I sweat all night. I go back and forth from my conversations of the past few hours with Guillermo, of the past few days with Gustavo and Ma Cris to the absolutist words of the rebels on my computer. I know I am getting as extreme positions as I can find on the history of this conflict, but by juxtaposing Ma Cris and her cousins and Manuel Marulanda and his supporters I have come to understand something about Colombia's war: Neither side sees a middle ground. To Ma Cris and her cousins it is okay to have relationships between masters and serfs and to Manuel Marulanda, landowners like them are displacing and killing peasants to take their land.

Reading about the Birds all night and about their alleged connection to the Conservative party, the party that my mother's ancestors so proudly defended and she was told was a prerequisite for marriage, and about the Conservatives' methods of acquiring land has made me queasy and sleepless. After all, the Colombian me is the granddaughter of a Conservative landowner. My tongue tastes like metal and fear lurks under my arms. My hair is tied loosely, falling around my face. My breasts are too exposed in my unadjusted nightgown. When I look at the clock on the computer, it is past lunchtime and Ma Cris stands at the door.

My grandmother is truly irritated by my ways that next morning. "Go clean up," she says, wondering what has gone wrong in my life that I have forgotten how to groom myself. "Lunch is served." I smile absently but I am not listening. I close the door behind her but she returns a half hour later. She finds me in bed, the covers pulled tightly across my chest like a strapless dress. This is what

I do when I am lost, when I am sad, when I am confused—as the rush of adrenaline leaves my brain, my body often starts to convulse. I have to let it happen. It has to be released. What is she doing here? I need to be alone. Can I tell her that? But she is walking closer, so close that she is standing next to the headboard, and she sits beside me. She has never sat this close to me before. "I can tell you this," she whispers down to me, "because I am your *abuelita*. I want you to listen to me and not take it badly."

She takes my hand, wet and cold and clammy as a dead corpse left on the road by a killer Bird. "Nani, my dear, this smell of yours, you have to do something about this. You do not smell of *señorita*." I want to tell her that I know that and that it's the smell of fear, and of being confused. It is the smell of realizing that I don't see how the rebels will stop kidnapping her relatives in the name of social justice and taking their land and I don't see how the paramilitary groups are going to stop massacring in the name of revenge, and appropriating more land. "Nani," she says, "not even the *negritas* smell like you anymore." *Abuelita*, I would like to tell her, I'm sorry but this is the smell of being here.

She means that the *palenqueras* who were too dirty for me to eat their *alegrías* are now cleaner than they were a few decades back. My mind kicks into overdrive, and in that second I wonder if my grandmother's statement is stupid or sage, if it indicates that things are better today for average Colombians. Is it because *negritas* are better off in Colombia? Or is it that now, thanks to globalization, the *negritas* can buy deodorant? Thanks to large conglomerates, anyone can afford a bar of soap and fashionable if cheap clothes. I have noticed how the people that work for her are dressed differently than when I lived here and servants only wore our hand-me-downs. José wears good jeans and good sneakers and T-shirts of good quality with made-up logos that pretend to be American words. Lucero has cute color-coordinated outfits that are no different from those of a girl her age in middle America, and the clothes were bought brand-new.

Still, the way people kill one another is the same as when General Montblanc commanded the Conservative troops in the War of One Thousand Days and the same way Liberals like Black Blood avenged the massacre that the Birds inflicted in the hamlets of Tolima. Outside her house I had met a man whose father and two sisters were hacked to pieces and he had to use their bodies as shields to save his mother, wife, and three children. This, grandmother, is what you smell: the knowledge that this happens and that the smell of deodorant is not what makes things clean.

"Juana is here," she says. "She came to say hello to you. Get dressed and come out."

21

JUANA'S SMELL

Juana is so put together, she is the pulchritude of poverty, dressed in clean, ironed clothes. My grandmother had mentioned, when Juana called on the telephone, that I was visiting, and she said she wanted to come and say hello, so my grandmother invited her for lunch. I get out of bed and decide to forgo the shower. I'll try to cover up the smell with sprays. I throw cold water on my face, put in my contacts, a choice I make; I want to see Juana. I comb my hair to please my grandmother and I even throw on a pretty dress. When I kiss Juana she smells of baby powder and I can see how the moistness of the air has marked her cleavage with deep lines of sparkling white dust. She has probably been on the bus, sweating since very early to make it here on time. Her blouse is the color of moss and it is the exact same color of her skirt and of the plastic headband that keeps her *pasitas,* her tight curls, in place. She smiles big, happy to see me, and I wonder if my grandmother paid for her dentures.

That Juana worked for my grandparents for twenty-five years is a miracle; she was as badly tempered as my grandfather and the two fought like cats and dogs. But neither wanted to let go, for Juana cooked the goat stew just the way my grandfather liked it and brewed his tiny cups of black, sugared coffee perfectly. So he made her a deal: If she agreed to work in his household for twenty-five years, he would buy her a house, an opportunity too good to pass up in a land where her prospects of owning a house were closer to impossible than to slim. She knew it would be her only chance to have such a retirement plan. No maid could be so lucky in a country where neither labor nor pension plan existed. It is now starting to change. Servants are not called *sirvientas* any more. An education campaign has been under way and they are now called *empleadas domesticas,* domestic employees. But habits die hard, and there are still those who slip back to the feudal language they know so well. And of course the domestic help still calls the employer *mi patrón*. She had never paid a penny in taxes and no bank would ever provide her with a mortgage.

During one of our car excursions exploring Barranquilla, José told me about the deal Juana made with my grandfather, confiding that he still had about twelve years to go before he gets his house. I had asked him where he lived, curious to know who he was outside of this job. I wondered if José lives in the *tugurios,* which are the slums, houses with stolen public services and improvised architecture, or in one of the new housing projects for the poor. I had seen a sign as I was coming from the airport that had caught my attention. It indicated an intricate labyrinth that resembled a sprouting neighborhood. What had caught my attention was its name, Por Fin, which means "finally" as in "our family finally has a home." I had scoffed at the name, finding it almost cruel. But now I am wondering if there is an irony in the names that I am missing. It seems that I have misunderstood Barranquilla humor: Allegra tells me about others: No Me Quejo, which translates as I'm not complaining, or El Silencio, The Silence. There is a new, more upscale urban development called Los Simpsons.

To get home, José takes three buses; a trip that would be twenty minutes in a car takes him more than two hours every morning and two hours every evening. I had asked him if he owned his house and that's when he told me the story of Juana's house. "You should see that house," he says. "It even has a tiled floor."

"Yours will also have a refrigerator," I say alluding to the one he was planning on getting thanks to my grandmother's supermarket points.

THE PHONE RINGS THE MOMENT FANNY ANNOUNCES LUNCH. MY COUSIN Patricia, who is finishing architecture school, may call to say she needs to be driven immediately to school for an exam or she'll flunk. My aunt may call saying she needs José to run to Carulla to get flour or her dessert will be ruined. But José's lunch hour is sacred—he is not available between noon and one, no exceptions, by Doña Cris's order. After eating alone in the kitchen with a different plate and with a different fork and knife than my grandmother and I use, he goes into the living room to watch the news. He grabs the remote control with complete ease, just like he would in his own house, and turns on the television. There are four bentwood chairs that he can choose from but José sits cross-legged on the floor.

My grandmother and I sit at the table, while Juana keeps us company, sitting in one of the dining room chairs against the wall. Juana doesn't eat with us. She will take her lunch in the kitchen once the visit with us is over. Servants don't sit at the *patrón*'s dinner table; neither do former servants, even when they are beautifully groomed. My grandmother, who loves her food, savors every bite. Juana tells her to watch what she eats. "Go slow with the cheese, Doña Cris," reminding her that she has to watch her cholesterol. "It's not good for you."

From the dinner table, I can hear the news that José is watching but cannot see the images on the screen. The leading story the anchorwoman announces comes from Asunción. Five policemen who had been held captive by rebels have been liberated. I jump from my chair and run over to the television, excited to see the storied town, the famous square, the Frenchman's House, the balcony, the church with the three spires that my grandfather helped build. But all I see is an ordinary street that looks like every other street in every town in Colombia that has a war-related story in the day's newscast. I see the same cars, the same donkey carts, the same gray cement light posts, the same tangled wires, the same types of small shops along the street: a video store, a hardware store, a bakery, and a shoe repair. "Come take a look," I prompt my grandmother, but she doesn't move. "Don't you want to see Asunción?" I insist. "What for? It's not the same," she says without lifting her eyes from her plate. "That was such a good town. Everyone was good. Not one petty thief."

"And now?" I ask, knowing the answer. "Aaaauuu," she howls, an expression from her town, essentially meaning "oh boy." Her eyes roll toward the heavens asking for salvation. "Maybe they'll show your house on the square," I say. "Don't you want to see it?"

"I hear it's in ruins," she tells me. "La guerrilla took it a few years ago and moved in. But last I heard the paras had it." So she has heard of them too. Juana nods her head, agreeing with my grandmother, and I go into my bedroom to get ready to leave with José as soon as he starts his afternoon rounds of errands. I want to stop at Agustín's office to check on our plans, to see if perhaps the tide has turned and I can make it to El Carmen anytime soon. I am getting antsy.

When I come out of my room, Juana is leaning on the doorway to my grandmother's room, the same place I've stood for the last few weeks. I can hear my grandmother opening the closet in her bathroom. Juana smiles, a bit embarrassed. As I walk by she says, "That's a pretty dress, Nani," and extends her hand to me, turning it into an iron. She pulls the linen skirt down to make sure it sits perfectly on my hips and flattens the wrinkles out with the palm of her hand. She tells me she remembers my birthday every year and I am surprised that she does—we are more than a dozen grandchildren—and at the same time I am not surprised at all. I bet she knows the birthdays of the six great-grandchildren even though she stopped working for Ma Cris before they were born.

Ma Cris is back from the bathroom but I can tell she is waiting for me to keep walking. She has something for Juana and I know exactly what it is: that roll of bills that is given secretly to those who once served. "*Que Dios le pague, Doña Cris,*" I hear Juana say. I can see this as an act of generosity but in it I see a frozen hierarchy of those who give and those who are given to that makes things better for a moment but no longer. I know that this is what my grandmother means when she says that the Montblancs did good and in Juana she sees the people that she once trusted where everyone lived in "peace and brotherhood." Is this enough to be good? Does it even count as doing good?

When my grandfather fell in love with my grandmother, could it have been because he saw her compassion toward those less fortunate, or did he also see the tenderness and the strength in her eyes that I am starting to see in them? Or maybe it is because they are deep blue, almost gray, considered an especially good color in La Provincia's eyes. In the photos I have in my plastic bag I see them sitting together as boyfriend and girlfriend, a handsome couple, both happy to be next to each other. In her bedroom she has a row of pictures of him, of them together and sometimes the mention of his name brings tears to her eyes. Would she have loved him if he was not a cousin, if they had not grown up together "like brother and sister"? Would he have loved her if she did not have the traits that made her stand out as being "a fine lady"? In their world, Baudelaire's infatuation with a passerby would have been unthinkable.

I kiss my grandmother and she kisses me back. "What do you want to have for dinner, Nani?" she asks. "Tell Fanny on your way out. Where is José taking you?" I wish I could tell her that I was still planning on seeing El Carmen. But I flee without responding just like the woman slipped away from the possibility of love in the streets of Paris. I tell her that I would be home to have dinner with her, something I have not done since I arrived. "Tell José," she says as I close the door, "to stop at the Olímpica and get you a bar of Jabón Neko. It's very strong soap."

22

AGUSTÍN EXPLAINS THE RULES

On the way to the office, José tells me that he will drop me off, but that it will take a while to come back and get me. "I have to go pay for the masses."

I wonder who has died that my grandmother is having a mass said in their name. I ask José if he knows and he just laughs. "No, Niña Silvana, no one has died. I have to do this every week. Your grandmother has masses said every day. Three a day. Two for Don Gabriel and one for her father, so I have to pay for them. It will take time with the traffic."

This is so absurd I better just enjoy it. My grandmother has masses said for the souls of her father and of her husband every day. Two for my grandfather, her cousin-husband of fifty-five years. He gets the fancy churches. The other one is for her father, who died of a liver infection at age forty-two, leaving behind seven children, of which she is number five. I wonder why my grandmother thinks that after all this time she has to continue paying for masses to save her father's soul from flames. What could my grandfather have done that makes her so convinced he might still be in purgatory? "I hope she gets a deal paying for them in bulk," I joke with him. "So how much are they?"

"It depends," says José. They are more expensive at the Immaculate than at the Charity. Of course, the Immaculate is a church in a Six neighborhood, but the other one is far away from El Prado and Riomar. Also, she has some said at the Torcoroma because she likes the priest there.

"Who gets what?" I ask.

"She changes them every week. You never know who gets what."

I tell José that all those masses for the afterlife could buy a lot of milk for children in this life. He smiles at my comment but I am not sure if he thinks I am crazy or if he agrees with me. "Come back to get me," I tell him as I close the door.

"I also have to stop at the drugstore for that soap," he tells me. My grandmother is very efficient when she wants to get something done. It seems that cleaning me up is at the top of her list, just like her getting Rose's husband's ransom was a few weeks ago, and he was released.

THE EMPLOYEES OF EL CARMEN DON'T REALLY KNOW WHAT TO MAKE OF ME OR how to treat me but I also think they are getting used to me. Margarita, the coffee lady, asks me if I want a *tintico,* Colombia's word for espresso, which is really an *espressito.* Diego, the computer engineer, agrees affably when I ask him if I can use the Internet on his computer. Nancy, Juana's daughter, is the firm's accountant. She is the most uptight with me. I say hello, self-conscious perhaps, thinking that she is different than the rest of the employees. I ask her a personal question, which I do not do with the rest. I can tell she feels that I am singling her out for exactly that reason and I sense she does not like it. Or maybe she is simply shy. Like her mother, she is always perfectly put together. Her tight curls are pulled back and her earrings are small pearls. Today, she is wearing a brown shirt, a shade lighter than her skin, and she smells of soft cologne.

My mother has told me that Grandfather sent Nancy to school and then on to technical school. She was always the best in her class, the example my mother gives whenever I bring up the subject of domestic help. When I have tried to explain that I think the story of Imelda is awful, my mother makes her case. She thinks it's giving these girls opportunities that they would never have if they stayed in their hamlets. "Look at *la hija de Juana,*" she always tells me. Imelda, she says, is an example of how "some don't know how to take advantage of the opportunities presented to them." I have no memory of having met Nancy as a child. Had she seen me? What goes through her mind as I stand in front of her? As with Imelda, I want to ask her a thousand questions and I don't know how to do so without unintentionally insulting her. Maybe next time, I say to myself.

Gladys, my uncle's secretary, tells me he is off the phone and that I can go in. He knows why I'm there so he starts talking as soon as he sees me walk in: "I will make a few phone calls while you're here."

"Okay," I say sitting in one of the two chairs in front of his desk.

"A few days ago the conditions were good. Perhaps we can plan it for Saturday. I think we should forgo the road idea. Let's take the small plane that we can hire. We'll stay five or six hours, maximum. The plane will wait for us. I've already spoken to the pilot. In fact, I have a surprise for you; it's going to be *el capi* Lara. remember him? He was your grandfather's first pilot when he got the Cessna."

I don't really remember the captain. It was the boys who had fun with the plane, not the girls. A first cousin was nicknamed *el capi,* as in cappie, short for captain, because the pilot sat him on his lap and told him that if he steered all the way to the farm he would be made captain. In one of my many scavenging hunts, I found a picture of him, a tiny thing with red sneakers and white trousers, standing on the wing of the plane.

"I've told Lara he is to wait for us. I don't want the plane leaving us there in case we make a rapid exit," he explains. "Better not to give papaya," he says, reminding me again of what in macho terms used to mean "to put out" now means to put your life on the line. "I've also arranged for security." I wonder what arranging for security means and as I am about to ask, a call interrupts us and Agustín picks up. He talks for twenty minutes as I wait on tenterhooks, trying to read his face and the doodles on the paper, hoping to decode their communication. I can tell he is speaking to someone in the military and that it is they who will provide us with what he calls security.

I can make out that the person on the other line apologizes for not having called before, telling Agustín that he was busy. The copy of today's *El Heraldo* on my uncle's desk confirms what I am hearing. On the front page are a photo of tanks rolling into a village that I know is very close to the farm and a story about 1,500 new soldiers that had arrived to patrol the area.

My uncle relays the details of the conversation. The army will provide us with all the soldiers necessary *con mucho gusto.* But that we have to do two things: We have to provide for the soldiers' transportation from the barracks to the farm and back. And we have to give them lunch. They agree on two truckloads, somewhere between thirty to forty conscripts to be deployed in the surrounding areas where we will be. Given the recent kidnapping that had scared me off from my El Carmen idea in the past few weeks, I welcome the news. Still, I am surprised by the number of soldiers we need. That sounds like a minibattalion and wonder if I'm pushing the envelope to satisfy my indulgence. In time, the journalist in me stops the thought.

As if reading my mind, Agustín tells me that it is the government's duty to give us this protection, as there are no institutions for Colombians to feel protected and he is a contributor to this country's progress. He has a business to run, an employer contributing to the economy of the country. Thanks to him, more than two hundred families eat well every week. This is part of what it means to live and work in Colombia, he tells me, making sure I understand that to him this is not ideal, that he knows how outrageous it is to have to call the army in order for him to be safe in his workplace, as he refers to El Carmen.

"My generation has been wasted," he tells me and I sense not only frustration but anger in his voice. "We have not had the opportunity to go after our dreams. We have had to give up so much to deal with things like this. Look at what your grandfather was able to do. I just spend my days putting out fires."

He doesn't want to say more. "Back to work. I have to find out where I can rent the two vehicles and that is not going to be easy. And I have to organize the food and that can also be a problem. I have to see who wants to sell me a cow." We no longer have them at the farm.

He dials Fernando Preciado, who is El Carmen's administrator, an agricultural engineer, hired by Agustín to run the day-to-day operations. As he is not a Montblanc, he can work there in relative safety. Both on cell phones, they coordinate our trip. Agustín tells him to "send" for Luis Peña. I ask if I can also meet Pablo Gomez and Imelda's parents but Agustín tells me that Pablo died more than ten years ago, but that he will send for his wife, América, adding that he still provides for her. "I'll have them brought to El Carmen. I won't say that I'm coming and you'll identify yourself once there."

Preciado calls a few hours later to tell him that the cow to be slaughtered has already been bought but that no one wants to take the transportation job. "Why?" I ask. "Why would anyone refuse a job?"

"Too risky," he tells me, getting somewhat fed up with my questioning. But he explains nonetheless. He still has a hard time saying no to his favorite niece even if he just wishes I stopped nagging him. "Of course there are a handful of these small transportation services around but La Fortuna is a small town. Everyone knows everyone. The owners are afraid of retaliations. If the guerrillas see a truck full of soldiers, they will accuse them of being government sympathizers or more likely paramilitary. The consequences," he tells me, "can be terrible." The rebels kill those who help the army. I had witnessed it firsthand on my first day here, when the maid was told that her cousin had been killed by the guerrillas because they owned a *tienda* that sold to men and women in the armed forces, or men and women in the paramilitary. Gladys comes in to announce that José is waiting for me. Agustín is relieved. He gets up, grabs my shoulders, plants a strong kiss on my cheek, and sends me on my way. "Be at my house by six-thirty. Don't be late or I'll leave without you." My uncle has taken me to Bogotá, to Cartagena, to the restaurant of my choice and now to make me happy, he's taking me inside Colombia's war.

I GET HOME IN TIME FOR DINNER. WE ARE BOTH MAKING A TURNAROUND. MY grandmother would like to see me living a life with sit-down meals and appreciates my being there, and so I comply. She too has changed, instead of rattling off dates and bloodlines, she now tells me stories with details, even suspense. I want to know more about her marriage, wondering if the love found in anonymous crowds, as happens in New York, is different than the love found in the safety of those you know, as happens here. I want to ask her how she and my grandfather turned from being "brother and sister" to being in love. The only way I can find to ask her that is by asking something that involves the Church so I ask how he proposed marriage to her. She loves the question.

The girls that made up the Church committee (my grandmother names about eight of them, all Montblancs in one degree or another) approached my grandfather to sell him a raffle ticket. They were raising money for the pews for Father Martínez's renovation project. The prize consisted of a brick of homemade candied grapefruit. "That is my favorite thing in the whole world," she says, "and he knew it." She is recounting a story that happened more than seventy years ago, but my grandmother is blushing. "So," she tells me, "Gabriel bought all the tickets and had the girls give me the prize as the first sign of his courtship. He sent me the *dulce.*"

I am in such a good mood that I am ready to sit and watch *Sor Angélica* with her, a talk show like *Oprah* if Oprah were a nun and wore a habit. As I sit with her I think that perhaps I will ask her for the envelope of cash she is keeping for me. I want to take out the amount I need to pay for the plane that is taking us to El Carmen. On the first day I arrived, she pulled me aside and whispered that I should give her the money I brought for the trip so that she could keep it hidden away, secure. But tonight she, who never lets go of her keys, gives me the cluster she always carries with her, all kinds of keys that open all kinds of doors. She has eleven closets under lock and key. She usually gets up to open them when Fanny asks her for something, but she is letting go of them. With the tangle of keys the size of a baseball dangling from my hand, I walk toward the bathroom closet, the one where she had gone to fetch a roll of money for Juana. I find my envelope in the first drawer next to the envelopes of cash my uncle brings her every two weeks, money that covers the costs of the fresh papaya, guavas, first mangoes that José buys from the fruit ladies, the sugary kind that she prefers. It's also where Fanny's monthly salary comes from and the bills she slips into Juana's hands every time she comes to visit. Last week, some of it went to buy rubber boots and batteries to pay for her nephew's release. It is also the mass money. The green invoices from the churches pile up high in her boudoir.

Like the family snoop I am, I gaze up and down her closet. I see more than half a dozen bottles of scented talc that her cousins gave her for her birthday and that she will never use; a pile of pieces of cotton cloth all in neutral colors that will slowly become the same simple dresses that her lady tailor has been making for her for the last fifty years; more green invoices from the church masses; more novenas, those tiny booklets with prayers to unknown saints that concede favors; a plastic bottle in the form of the Virgin that holds holy water. I undo the blue cap, only because it is the Virgin's crown. Not knowing what to do with holy water I smell it. I raise my eyebrow, disconcerted not at her faith in water in bottles in the shape of virgins but because I feel so foreign, disconnected from her world and because at the same time I feel so safe. A covered plate rests on the bottom shelf, the kind with the green rim that Fanny uses to serve lunch. Strange, I think and I kneel down and remove the top plate. My grandmother, I discover, keeps a brick of candied grapefruit and a knife in her closet. They are so hard to get these days, these *dulces,* that they cannot be left out in the open for everyone to take; who knows when someone will be able to go to Asunción to bring her another, the sweet candy that tastes of young love and hometowns. My grandmother keeps not only her silver platters and the paper napkins but also her heart and her pleasures, under lock and key. I wonder when during the day she yearns for a bite of sugared grapefruit.

23

SEEING YOU AGAIN
SEPTEMBER 10, 2001

I tiptoe out at six a.m., scaring Fanny on my way out. She has never seen me up and about this early. My grandmother has already gone to hear her first mass, so I ask Fanny to tell her I should be back shortly. She asks me if I would be back by lunchtime. She was making *arroz con pollo*, Barranquilla's version of paella that she knows I like. I don't answer as I close the door behind me and walk the half a block to my uncle's house. I've left my iPod and my note-pad behind, not really sure why but in my bag I have my passport and my *cédula* in one pocket; my New York driver's license and the envelope with the *New York Times* embossed on it in the other pocket. I decide to wear, not jeans like I had done last time I was there, but something my grandmother would like better. I choose a blue cotton T-shirt with a scoop neck and a cream-colored skirt with hand-painted flowers that look like forget-me-nots in pink and white. The hem twirls with my steps and I like the swoosh and the feel of the silk dancing softly under my knees, and for a moment I feel I'm that passerby in Viktor's version of Baudelaire's poem, crossing the street into the unknown.

I am going. Will this furtive encounter bring me back to life? Am I the lovely fugitive or the trembling fool?

At the airport, my uncle takes charge. He finds the *capi*, he signs the flight papers, he pays, getting interrupted here and there by people he runs into who are getting ready to board the day's first flight to Miami. I am the fly on the wall that I have wanted to be but I don't like it. I stand next to my uncle looking for recognition through proximity, but I get a nod of acknowledgment, not a kiss on the cheek like he does. I have succeeded; I have become the person disassociated with this place that I strived to be. The rejection is now mutual and like any rejection it doesn't feel good.

Okay then, I think to myself. I will be the journalist again. I will put on my special-observation eyes, the scrutinizing ones, the ones that can also be so judgmental. I will go and get myself a notepad to replace the one that just a while ago I had decided to leave behind. Surveying the options available at a nearby newsstand, I see a notebook with a sunset and a couple holding hands and another tiny one meant for a child, with pale blue pages and twinkling yellow stars on the border. "Excuse me," I ask. "Do you have a plain notebook?"

"No, *mi amor*. Only what you see," the woman says. "Why? You don't like these? Take this one," she tells me, handing me the one that is meant for a young girl. "Okay," I say, giving her a two-thousand-peso bill. "I'll take that one and a copy of *El Heraldo*." I throw it in my bag wondering why she had chosen that one over the one meant for romance. I'm distracted from these thoughts by the paper's front-page story: Secretary of State Colin Powell, I read, will be in Bogotá tomorrow to meet with President Pastrana. I'm encouraged by this; if Colombia's on Washington's radar, so too will it be a priority for the editors when I hand in my story. I make a simple calculation: Today is September 10. I will transcribe my notes tomorrow, September 11. I will probably have a first draft in two or three weeks. I tell myself that if I hurry, I can have a story by early October. Reading about Powell has just given me an extra boost.

"IT'S A CLEAR DAY," SAYS LARA AS HE TELLS ME TO TAKE THE COPILOT CHAIR. Agustín and I boarded the biplane, here just for our use. "We will get to see the Sierra Nevada. It will come up on your left."

The tropical sun's rays turn the peak of the Sierra Nevada into the biggest diamond in the entire Caribbean. It looks sharp and clean and pure because of the white snow. When the sun hits the crystalline transparency of ice, it sparkles like bits of tourmaline. This is the snow I never saw on that outing that got us into so much trouble as girls and that is now disputed territory between the rebels and the paramilitary.

From the air, Colombia looks serene. A wide prairie stretches out to a distant blue backbone of hills. I think of what my sources, the relatives that I have interviewed in the past few weeks, tell me about how these prairies were made, how the mountain was slashed to make it produce. The only signs of human presence on the vast property are a huge reservoir, a few head of grazing cattle, and some glinting rooftops made of zinc. For the most part, though, the forest canopy stretches like a great, green shroud, quietly concealing the vicious civil war that has raged here for the past fifteen years and that has us so scared, so excited and weary to finally be here.

The pilot circles a few times, not to provide a panoramic view but to check out a small plane flying close to us. "How strange," he says under his breath. "I wonder if it's authorized. These days you never know." As the other plane heads off into the distance, the pilot relaxes and I sigh with relief as he settles into his approach to an airstrip that is nothing more than a narrow dirt path surrounded by high grass. We are landing on a neighbor's runway. "It's safer," my uncle told me before we left, and I can see that the "security" has been arranged. Two jeeps, four motorcycles, and a dozen men, some wearing camouflage, await our landing.

The pilot opens the door a moment too early, just before the tires touch the ground. A gush of air rushes inside the cabin, blowing dust in my eyes. But each second counts. I have only hours here. That's it. Still, I have been told, "Each minute is a risk." Precision is the name of this game; anticipation is one of its rules. Any delays will undermine the precautions we've taken, the secrecy, and the subterfuge. Just coming here is risky, and perhaps just plain stupid.

I pass four young men in military uniform holding Galils and carrying grenades in their vest pockets. I am introduced to the men in civilian clothes. We shake hands. The one with the mustache, the cell phone, and the walkie-talkie is Fernando Preciado, who has been managing the property since 1989. He directs me to a red four-by-four and gets behind the wheel. Agustín wants to drive one of the jeeps, so he takes the keys from another one of El Carmen's supervisors who is there to receive us. I am glad that I insisted my uncle bring me here. He is beaming. I can't wait to see his reaction to the reservoir that he built from afar but had yet to see in person. Right after my grandfather had an aneurysm, Agustín and Fernando started transforming the land, despite the impending threat of rebels in the area, from feudal farm into an agro-industry. To prevent a *mala hora,* a bad moment, Agustín decided to mastermind this transformation from Barranquilla.

We move ahead behind Agustín's jeep with Preciado at the wheel and Captain Lara in the backseat talking about how it was when he came here in the sixties as my grandfather's pilot and would get bored, stuck in this "middle of nowhere" from Monday till Thursday. "I'm a *barranquillero* who likes Carnivals," he says, "not a man of the land. All there was to do here was play dominoes and drink scotch. There wasn't even a phone to call my family except that big old *radio teléfono.* Even the television was bad—you could only get Venezuelan stations." Captain Lara hated coming here but he still keeps a framed copy of the first paycheck my grandfather gave him. "He was the first one who trusted me as a pilot."

It feels like this is illegal when in fact there is nothing illegal about any of it. This feels like the marijuana trips that Román would tell me about, always promising he would let me report on one. The farm could be the backdrop to the images I see on the evening news of government officials when they go visit the FARC at El Caguán to see if there is a way that they can broker a truce. But it is neither. It is a contained trip. For Captain Lara, it's the way he makes his living. For my uncle, it is like going from Miami to Barranquilla is for me, with all the implications of angels and demons that that implies, not knowing which is home, El Carmen where he grew up or Barranquilla where he lives. Being in El Carmen gives him a chance to feel he is in control of his land and a chance to see the reservoir he spent two years building and has never seen. As for me, well, it is unclear. I am bringing a small Cessna-load of memories, not a big-plane size, for I don't have too many, and don't need to take bags, lots of bags, extra bags filled with questions to a place that I am not sure I like or understand or is special in any way but a place that looms large in my life nonetheless.

I think of the last time I visited, in 1982. I remember rising at dawn to accompany my grandfather on his errands. I went to see the milking of the cows and the weighing of the cattle. I can recall how I felt so sleepy, so dizzy, but I never felt unsafe. I wasn't exactly at ease either, especially after my afternoon with the handsome son of my grandfather's other best friend (and cousin). Carlos, a medical student in Bogotá, was spending his summer here, both working on the farm and vaccinating the children of the region. His father's *finca* was not far from El Carmen. My grandmother watched that afternoon as I got into Carlos's jeep with him. We met the morning I arrived and he promised to show me around. As he drove he kept his window down and went slowly as he observed the fields and explained to me what everything was, stopping to say hello whenever we crossed paths with a worker. He would ask about crops and rain like I had seen my grandfather do and he would also remind each one of the men not to forget to bring their children to the health post. I wanted to kiss him everytime I heard him do that so I put my earphones on his ears and made him listen to my Rolling Stones tape. Carlos looked at me and told me he didn't like that kind of music. Still, he asked me what the lyrics meant; he didn't understand English. I didn't answer, first because I did not know where to begin to translate "Let's Spend the Night Together," and second, because those weren't words for his Uncle Gabriel's granddaughter. I contemplated crossing the line but realized that to him I was as strange and different to this world as I was to my grandparents. "Why did they send you away to school in America?" he asked me. "That is so not like Uncle Gabriel." After a few hours he brought me back to the house, kissed my cheek, saying he had to go vaccinate. I spent the rest of my days there reading *Out of Africa* and waiting for Carlos to come back, just like Dinesen did for Denys Fitch-Hatten.

TODAY, EL CARMEN HAS NO CATTLE AND NO GUARANTEE OF SAFETY. WHAT IT does have are acres and acres of palm trees, which produce a fruit that yields a vegetable oil. And it has a surplus of insecurity—*inseguridad,* as my grandmother refers to it, the byproduct of a war that has forced her and her entire family off the farm and into the relative safety of the city.

At about the time the world saw the Berlin Wall crumble, my family saw Marxist rebels settle on the foothills of the Perijá Hills, outside their land. When things became unbearable for landowners, counterrevolutionary groups, so-called self-defense units, arrived. The paras, as they are known, promised to wipe the rebels away. Since then, El Carmen has been isolated between the war trenches, with leftist rebels on one side and right-wing paramilitaries on the other. Outside its gates, and sometimes inside, Colombia's war is fought. This war, still unnamed, has killed forty thousand people, displaced two million people, and triggered three thousand kidnappings. Amidst the three-year-old peace talks between the government of President Andrés Pastrana and the FARC, the FARC and the ELN continue to kidnap and kill when things go awry and the AUC massacres in plain view. The army, now reinforced with Plan Colombia, provides us with soldiers to protect us from the guerrillas who have declared Agustín Montblanc a "military objective." In strict and predictable guerrilla language, all landowners are enemies of the people, and I have been told that to them I am not a journalist from New York but a Montblanc with all the stains that birth name brings to the table here. Gustavo told me that the Montblancs have suffered more kidnappings than any others in the region. But I also know that at least once the rebels have been rational and have shown some compassion. I heard about the "poor Montblanc." While they kept him in captivity, his wife had showed the rebels her husband's accounting books and proved that, despite his last name, he had no money. For some reason, I think of this retention and not of the many others that have ended so badly as we ride through El Carmen. To be able to enjoy the next hours, I convince myself that I too can prove my case of poverty to the rebels.

I am here because the stories that I distilled into two categories— revolutionaries fighting for social and economic justice versus an elite that refuses to allow it—weren't holding up under the close scrutiny that my trip back into the fray, back into daily life in Colombia, finally allowed. Back in the eighties, when I heard that the guerrillas had stolen hundreds of head of cattle from El Carmen, I thought it was part of the ideals to redistribute the wealth. I smiled at their irreverence when I heard how they had arrived fully equipped with booze, music, and women, partied overnight, and left scribbled revolutionary slogans behind. But I could not come up with a valid explanation when they set fire to a piece of the property. One thing is for sure. The more I followed the stories of my uncle's commitment to bring El Carmen into what he called modernity, despite the war, the more complex the stories got, reflecting the situation of the entire country. I watch him in the jeep in front of us, his arm out playing with the wind, ecstatic to be here.

I understand that Colombia is not another Cuba, Nicaragua, or El Salvador. The relationship with the United States is different. The size of the country and of its economy is of another scale.

El Carmen is, indeed, like a miniature Colombia. Both are struggling to be modern, progressive, and inclusive while their basic structures remain feudal, inefficient, and exclusive. Both are caught between the rule of law and the rule of the rifle; between what the owners want and what the poor need. So many Colombians today talk about globalization and civil society but they are trapped in a country that has operated since its inception around a weak state—a central government presiding unsteadily over local political systems based on paternalism, nepotism, clientelism, and corruption, big words that mean the same thing: they are synonymous with undemocratic, intransigent, obsolete, even fundamentalist. They get in the way of freedom and definitely of happiness. The incapacity of the political and economic elite to develop and share the country's immense natural wealth and, by the same token, the rebels' unwillingness to listen to the voice of a civil society that is rejecting their methods, has 44 million Colombians caught in the cross-fire.

This is, of course, if one thinks of Colombia as another black-and-white case of an oligarchic Latin American country ripe for revolution. Twenty-six of 40 million Colombians live in poverty, 9 million in absolute misery; 97 percent of the arable land is in the hands of 3 percent of the people—that is if we also keep drugs out of the Marxist equation. Salomón Kalmanovitz, a Colombian economist whose writings have helped me educate myself and prepare myself to fight my war with Colombia, questions my reasoning on the side of revolutionaries. "How do you explain that the rise of the guerrillas in this area," he once asked rhetorically, "comes only after the death of Communism? The guerrilla does not develop because of a feudal system. It doesn't fully explain what's happening. Why didn't they emerge before? All the conditions were there."

The rebels, Salomón explained, are businessmen more than revolutionaries. They not only tax per head of cattle, acre of land, or pound of tobacco. They also charge per gram of cocaine, or to guard poppy fields, processing labs, and airstrips. The paramilitary, in their struggle to defend the concept of private property and punish and take revenge on the rebels who have kidnapped and killed their family members, does the same. They are neither guerrillas nor paramilitary—they are warlords.

It is unclear whether the motivation of the warlords—those on the side of the FARC and those on the side of the AUC—is ideology or territory, or a mixture of the two, but it is painfully clear that violence and human rights violations toward the civilian population increase by the second. All of the actors claim they want to end the war. Peace is everyone's sound bite. Still, the FARC uses home gas tanks as bombs, refuse to liberate the more than three thousand men that they hold hostage, and are full of a rigidity that makes them unpopular. (At less than 1 percent approval by the population, they are perhaps the least-liked revolutionaries in history.) The AUC, accused of having military ties, is known to assassinate teachers, human rights defenders, and union organizers because they are considered subversives. They massacre entire hamlets and are known to do so by using chain saws. Both use children as soldiers. Neither is respectful of journalists—last year twenty-two journalists were killed in Colombia.

Being that I am a journalist and a member of the landed, this trip is a double-whammy of danger. What the hell am I doing here?

I KNEW THAT THE ARMY HAD ALLOCATED US MORE THAN THE FIVE SOLDIERS that I had seen when we landed. I had noted their young faces and the Pokémon stickers on their guns. Not feeling very safe, I ask where the rest of them are. "They are already stationed in the areas that we will be visiting," says Preciado in an effort to emit confidence. "It is better this way. You should feel more comfortable not seeing them. Strategically they should be stationed away from the people they are guarding. It is best just knowing that they are out there."

The sense of imminent danger implied by the presence of the soldiers disappears as soon as I smell burned sugar in the air. I know it is coming from the mill nearby where as I child I would pilfer long, sweet stalks of cane to bring back home and freeze. ("It brings out the flavor," my grandfather had taught me). We pass a peasant woman and her young daughter washing clothes on the stream that borders the entrance to the farm. They smile and wave the same way I remember they waved to my grandfather.

The jeep stops in front of a yellow gate.

"Welcome to the new El Carmen," says Preciado, replacing my grandfather as my guide.

We drive through infinite and perfect rows of palm trees. It feels like a thousand green umbrellas open up and cover the sky as we roll by. Preciado shouts: "Los Mangos; Nuevo Mundo; Las Cristinas." They are the names my grandfather gave to his grazing grounds that turned bright green when the rains arrived and the rivers flooded. The prairies he and Pablo Gómez hacked out of a wilderness of "ocelots, snakes, hogs, and rain," has been turned once again into a jungle, an orderly jungle with numbered rows of beautiful palm oil trees.

My grandfather had fifty sharecroppers and their families—overseers, cowboys, grazers, and cooks—living permanently on the farm in small wooden houses with dirt floors and zinc roofs. Another couple hundred came during harvest time from all around the region. They were mostly single men who lived in open wooden barracks. None received benefits or were even paid as the labor code required. The law demanded double pay on Sunday or the obligation to provide work clothes. Under my grandfather, they received neither. "This was not uncommon," Agustín had said as a preamble to explaining how this was more complicated than what I was ready to label as the inhumane practices of the landed elite. He explains: Just as there was no state to reinforce the labor laws, there was no state to attend and provide for the basic needs of its people. "Yes, they did not pay as they were supposed to," he says, "but when Pablo Gómez died we became his widow's social security." And the school he had for the workers' children guaranteed them a government-approved high school diploma. "There was complete absence of the state," Agustín explains using an expression I have heard so many times before: by rebels to explain their control of all the towns in Caquetá, of the paramilitary to explain their taking into their own hands the extermination of the rebel threat in Córdoba.

But that was the past, Agustín has insisted repeatedly. That was his reason for showing me El Carmen. While I am fixated on the past, he is in the future. He wants me to see how in the new El Carmen workers are being treated differently. When I asked after the overseer who had taken me to see the Motilones, he corrected me. "El Carmen no longer has overseers," he says. "It has managers." El Carmen is no longer *la finca,* the farm. Agustín and Preciado call it *la empresa,* the company.

I surrender to the beauty of this land and turn my complete attention to Preciado's explanation about the plantations of African palm. Preciado is amiable, but above all he is an impressive professional, an engineer with a specialty in forestry, well spoken and informed about politics, ecology, and geography. By his accent I can tell he is not from the area. I ask him how he got here. "I applied for the job," he tells me. He had worked on another plantation so when he heard that El Carmen was looking for a manager, he sent in his resume, perhaps the first one ever to arrive at the office.

The difference between Preciado and the *trabajadores* I knew as a girl is immediate and palpable. My grandfather commanded. "He only had yes-men," my uncle had told me. "We immediately got rid of them all." To Preciado, my grandfather is not Don Gabriel, *el patrón.* His ties with this land are linked to his professional standing as an engineer and a manager, not to his loyalty to a family. He works here because he is qualified and because he loves his job.

"Landowners like your grandfather hired without any guarantees or benefits," he says. "Before, if a worker had a problem they went to your grandfather— 'Don Gabriel, my tooth aches; Don Gabriel, my tenth child is sick.' Don Gabriel would put his hand in his pocket and hand him some cash. We had to explain to the worker that there is a better way for him and his family," he continues as we drive to the reservoir. He too is excited that Agustín will finally see it. It was started in 1995 and hacked out of 150 acres of land. Preciado often sent videos and pictures but he had never walked around its beach or touched the water filled from a pump and rainwater. I think of how much larger, seven times so, this private pond that I am somehow connected with is than the one in Central Park, where late one night I took a gondola ride with two close New York pals. White herons fly by as if to welcome Agustín; they stop, land, and walk with him.

Agustín stands in front of it, takes pictures, asks questions about the water level. It looks too shallow, he says, and Preciado agrees. "We are praying for rain," he responds and it always strikes me how they talk more about the worries of weather and plagues than they do about "the situation." My uncle looks at me and then out at the lake. "Wouldn't it be nice," he says, "if you could come once in a while from New York and we could stay here and go swimming." My grandfather once stuck a ladder inside a huge water tank used for irrigation and I had swam with him in that. Agustín cannot enjoy El Carmen the way he would like to, the way he thinks his father did. Even when he concentrates on agricultural matters, there is a continual state of fear that lurks like the clouds and one never knows when the rain will come, or when the rain will stop.

With the help of a consulting firm, El Carmen began to change from a paternalistic management and hiring process to a more corporate mentality where merit and laws are important. It was difficult to get the workers to understand that what they thought of as complicated, such as social security deductions, were beneficial to them. "We teach them that they do not have to be *macheteros* and dirt diggers for twenty years," says Preciado. "That they are not working for a family but that they are working for themselves. That if El Carmen does well, then they and their children will also do well. That this land does not belong to one family." Preciado points out that one of the most difficult hurdles to get over has been to convince the male workers to register the number of children they have so that they could all receive benefits. They all have them, out of wedlock and unregistered. When we run into Alirio, a seed picker who is bused in from La Fortuna, Preciado reminds him that his wife is pregnant with his seventh child and that he should come around the next time the family-planning doctor is here for the classes on sex education, he should remember they offer free contraception and vasectomies. But Alirio makes a comment about how he doesn't want anything to get in the way of his virility. "Not easy," Preciado says, turning to me.

It all sounds so good, so modern, just like the courses on sustainable development that were offered in my master's program in international affairs at Columbia University. Preciado is sounding more progressive than the FARC. All of a sudden he stops talking. His face tenses up. I see a brown Trooper approaching.

I look at the captain in the backseat and his face has turned livid. "They will take you," he says, not jokingly. "Not me. This is yours. Not mine. I'm just the pilot." Preciado picks up the walkie-talkie and asks the men in the other jeep if anyone recognizes the car intercepting them. In a second, everything can and does change. The smooth ride, the sense of comfort from the sweet smell of sugar, the beauty of the terrain, the intelligence of Preciado all stop right there. Apart from fear, I feel stupid, childish, and irresponsible. Nothing in the world should have made me come here. As I wait for the incoming Trooper and the men ahead of us to exchange words, I feel a rush of fear, and then the pain of confusion. I am ready to admit that it is pain more than reporting that has made me come here, the pain that comes from watching destruction and feeling paralyzed in front of it; the pain that comes from knowing that the only recourse Colombians have in dealing with pain is to mix it with anger and fear and go get revenge. If pain is as uncontrollable as a wild animal then what they do is what a wild animal would do: bite and attack, bite and kill.

As much as I have tried to turn away from Colombia, there was a force that drove me here. I came to face them but I am really only facing myself. I came to contradict, to confront, but the tables are turning. I remember riding here in 1982 with the cowboy boots that I had worn through Michigan winters. After my first semester, I switched the Calvin Klein jeans and high heels for a pair of Levi's and cowboy boots that took me through every winter and spring, summer and fall I was there. I loved the feeling of control I got from the Tony Lamas I had bought on the Upper East Side in New York because cowboy boots were trendy. The fashion moment passed and I kept them on.

I wore them here in 1982 thinking that my grandparents' farm was the perfect place for cowboy boots. Isn't that what they are ultimately made for? That had been the wrong outfit: women wear dresses and sit quietly, and alone, or next to their husbands. Twenty years ago, I wore the wrong clothes to come here; I brought the wrong music and the wrong books and I felt the abyss between my past and the turn my life was taking. I caught a plane back to school knowing that I had been divided and that the division was to live with me forever. In coming here today, I had thought that they would come together. I wore a skirt and left the music behind as peace offerings: I will listen to you, if you listen to me. I will open to you, if you open to me. But right this second when all I feel around me is concern, I understand that there is not a middle ground, that boots or skirts are irrelevant, that English or Spanish do not matter because in a situation like this I am not sure—no one is sure—of the outcome.

I see the car drive away and the relief on the faces of everyone around me. It was a state truck, they tell me, engineers measuring the electricity lines. But I will never know who they really were. When I stop feeling nauseated from the rush of adrenaline, I gather my voice again and ask Preciado how he deals with these scares. "With all the different groups in the zone," he says, never letting go of the cell or the walkie-talkie, "you never know what can happen." When he first arrived in 1995, he lived in the ranch house. "So nice," he says, "the breeze, the space for the children to run and play, to be outside." But one night when a group of rebels stormed into the warehouse and tied up the guards and partied for a night, he decided it was best to live outside the *finca*. He now drives ninety miles each way, each day.

"What about the roadblocks?" I ask.

"I have to work," he says matter-of-factly, directing me to the jeep. "One must go on living."

WE ARRIVE AT THE MAIN OFFICE IN TIME FOR LUNCH, SERVED IN AN OPEN-AIR dining room where more than a dozen people wait for Agustín. Five supervisors arrive on brand-new motorbikes—"No more mules," Preciado remarks. Everyone is excited to see Agustín—"el doctor," they call him, not "don."

I see an elderly woman supported by her son who is as strong as she is fragile, who is as distant as she is emotional, who wants to run away as she wants to come close and touch my uncle.

América is tiny and dressed in black.

She taps me on the shoulder and proudly says, "I am one of the founders of El Carmen. I held your mother in my arms." She is in mourning because her thirty-three-year-old son was recently murdered. When I ask her by whom, she shrugs her shoulders and says, "How am I to know? By one of the many armed groups that have taken over the region." She looks at the open fields in front of us, the ones in which her husband toiled. "This was not like this before. This area was *sana*," she says using the Spanish word for "healthy" that Ma Cris also uses. "In the old days, when your grandfather lived, people here were good and decent, not like now." But the old days also meant that landowners like my grandfather paid less than required by law and gave little or no medical and social benefits. El Carmen had a health post and an itinerant dentistry van would visit once a month. That is what she and my grandmother refer to as healthy.

She is here with her eldest son, now a doctor, I am told, educated at the one-room schoolhouse that my grandfather built for the workers' children. I know that our family helped her son get through medical school, paying his tuition and his room and board. I look at her son and I see a difference in the way América kisses my uncle, but her son shakes his hand. I sense tension between them. She has only known and understood a world of paternalism. I can tell that he is not comfortable with his mother's servility. He represents the possibility (or the impossibility) that average Colombians from the rural provinces have for upward mobility. What happens to the dark-skinned son of day laborers who wants a professional life? And if, one day, he is a prosperous doctor, would he hire servants to take care of his children? How do we get from here to modernity?

Preciado has prepared a long table for everyone to sit together for lunch, but I maneuver my way to a separate table alone with América. We have never met but by being part of this family I am immediately a confidante: she has just told me that they've just killed her son; that they also tried to steal his animals. When I ask who "they" are she says, "You don't know anymore who kills. Too many die to know who kills whom." I ask if this was different before and she says that when she "founded" El Carmen, "those were very good years." Her husband and about thirty other men built a bamboo hut, hung hammocks, and for months hacked the jungle that became El Carmen. She cooked their meals. She tells me that my grandfather would stay overnight with them too and that the only difference was that he had a bigger hammock. "It was all good until the armed groups started coming." She holds my hand as if she had raised me; an instant affection and familiarity passes on to me just because I am Doña Cris's granddaughter.

After we all serve ourselves grilled meat and stewed cassava, Preciado calls for the soldiers to come for their lunch. There are many more here than just the handful I saw when we landed. They poke fun at one another about how hungry they are and how much food they are stacking on their plates as they walk to a terrace under a thatched roof. They sit on the floor and eat with their hands, ripping apart the meat with their teeth. Some take a nap. Others watch television. Many come back for seconds. "This is definitely a treat for them," Preciado tells me. "I don't think the army feeds them this kind of meat."

In Nicaragua, a young Sandinista soldier once asked me what was the yellow box I carried with me. When I explained my Walkman, he asked if I would let him listen to a song. I gave him the earphones and turned the music on to a tape of Led Zeppelin. War sounds more important when it is not in your face, when you are not a part of it. Mundane activities make up the bulk of a war, soldiers watching a soap opera on television while they're doing their jobs or listening to a song while they guard what is never theirs.

When I see a soldier walking toward the food for his third refill, I get up and approach the table. He tells me his name is Dario and that his troop just arrived in the area. I ask him some questions and he is at ease with sharing this information. Dario is tall, handsome, and in his mid- to late twenties. I would have gotten his age but it's a strange question to ask someone you don't know right off the bat and I had not identified myself as a journalist. In fact, he wondered who I was. "Are you one of the managers here?" he asked me. "The orders we got were just that we were coming to guard some people but they didn't tell us who." I told him that no, I was not a manager and turned the conversation to the ammunition he was carrying. He thought I was flirting (and I probably was). That's what I do when I'm confused. "This is an M-60," he tells me. "It's a very good machine gun. Then this here is a Galil and a few grenades here. I also have an additional forty kilos of explosives." He hands me the grenade with a smile. I take it in my hand, hold it for a while; it weighs about as much as a small cantaloupe, or a large apple, and I return it to him with a smile. To hide the pit in my stomach I say "That's a lot of stuff."

"They just killed four of us; we need to get back at them," he says. It's frustrating, he tells me, to see the rebels with their flag hoisted in the *tienda* in town, mediating infidelities. "The assholes were going to kill Álvaro Uribe, the presidential candidate, and Pedro Rubiano, the head of the Church, the other day with a Bible filled with explosives. An *hijueputa* arrived dressed as a seminarian carrying a briefcase but he repented and confessed before doing it."

Dario asked me if I worked here every day and told me he could come visit me again. "I don't live here," I said.

"But you work in this *empresa*, right?"

"I don't," I responded. Preciado walked up to us. Everyone had finished eating and we were ready to go on with the program that my uncle and Preciado had prepared. He reminds me what I had forgotten: The clock is ticking and we are on borrowed time.

In the office I see Luis Peña, who has worked at El Carmen since 1964. It was he who had told me the story about having his own marijuana field while working at El Carmen. He is unhappy, he tells me, about the new El Carmen. He misses the times when he would get invited over for "one of those drinks Don Gabriel called highballs." "What was he like?" I ask him. "He was happy and everything was fine as long as it all went his way. If I wanted to leave and he didn't want me to," he tells me, "he would stare at me and say he would send a bulldozer to flatten my house." He prefers when things were that way. "Too many laws, now," he says. "They're telling me I have to stop working. That this is my last week, that because I'm sixty-five they have to retire me. Who's ever heard of that?"

Agustín introduces me to another worker, a relative old-timer who has lived in the area since the early eighties. He is as shy as Luis is extroverted and wears sturdy leather boots, jeans, and a khaki work shirt with the company's slogan. On the left-hand pocket I read "Wellness and Progress." He says he is willing to speak about the farm's history, but only if I agree not to use his name. Around here, to talk about politics is to risk your life.

He came to La Provincia during the fat years of the cotton bonanza, he says. When the banks started knocking on the doors of the cotton plantation owners to remind them about the unpaid interest on their lines of credit, the *algodo-neros,* men of great pride, could not live with the shame of ruin. When a few killed themselves, a group of worried wives flew to Bogotá to see the president to ask for his help.

Unemployment brought thieves, rustlers, and rebels. They settled, like revolutionaries do, deep in the sierra, up close to the Motilones—the Indians who in calmer days came to El Carmen to sell their game and where I had once been taken to see them. He points to the horizon, showing how the FARC's Front 41 took the hills north of El Carmen and the ELN's José Manuel Martínez Quiroz Front, settled to the south of the farm. "At first, they camped out in the land of the small farmers, up there where it starts to get cold," the employee says, obviously uncomfortable in his role of historian. "They arrive with food and ask if they can use their kitchen. Then they invite them to eat with them and slowly start talking about their beliefs."

To many of the laborers, farmers, and peasants, the revolutionary ideology must have rung true. All they had to do was look around to see the enormous landholdings in the hands of a few. At the beginning, there even was a peaceful coexistence between the landowners and the rebels. Agustín can recall a time when landowners almost welcomed them. "They came in and started doing the work of the absent state," he says, "punishing the petty thief that steals the hen, the pig, or the cow." Many ranchers went up to the rebels' camps with whiskey and accordion trios, and the singing of *vallenatos* would last until dawn. Agustín, who hung up a poster of Che before I did, during his university days, says that "once or twice" he contributed to the rebels, providing medicine, for example, or a credit order slip at the general store. Many requests came in the form of typewritten letters with "lots of revolutionary salutes," not to mention spelling mistakes. What started as requests, however, evolved into something far more menacing. "They became conditions, impositions, obligations," Agustín says.

By 1989, the Soviet bloc may have been dead, but the rebels' takeover of the region was complete. The nice revolutionaries had evolved into threatening guerrillas ready to embark on a full-blown war. They ran rudimentary protection rackets, with landowners paying fees to "vaccinate" themselves against cattle rustling, crop fires, and kidnapping. After a few relatives were kidnapped, six hundred head of cattle were stolen, and an entire prairie was burned. Agustín, who used to stay Tuesday to Saturday with his wife and newborn son, felt it was time to leave.

It all changed for the workers too. "When they destroy your workplace, it feels like they are destroying the work of your own hands." In La Fortuna, a town of about twenty thousand people where he and more than half of El Carmen's employees live, rebels replaced lawyers. If you had a problem

of any type—a debt, a boundary dispute, even a matrimonial problem—
you went to them, and they fixed it. There was a street where you met the
"urban contacts" of the commanders up in the mountains. Everyone went.
There was the time that the father of a young woman who had been
deflowered and abandoned complained to them. After the rebels confronted
the young man in question, he quickly agreed to marry. Often, the rebels
helped squatters, especially those who supported them, acquire a piece of
land. That's when stealing cattle and burning crops until the landowner gave
it up came in. "The family would get the parcel," the employee of El Carmen,
who has turned source, tells me, "but the guerrillas would charge a price, usually paid with the son that was of fighting age." If the rebels wanted a road
fixed or a street paved, they called the local authorities, who complied immediately.

Leaning in close, he tells me that he himself was summoned once. One
morning, a young boy handed him a note, a small piece of paper rolled up and
tied with black twine. A former worker had complained to the rebels about his
severance. The note announced the day, time, and place of the meeting. "They
became experts at calculating severances," he says. "You arrived with your cal-
culations, and they showed you theirs. The meeting ended after the settlement
satisfied them." Before the meeting was over, they always asked for something.
"Boots, radios, batteries, whatever. I'll never forget how violent their threats
could be. Days of much anguish."

"And now?" I ask.

"It is a different kind of anguish."

He is referring to the arrival of the paramilitaries. When he sat down with
me, he had expected questions about palm cultivation, not the political situation. He tries as best he can, but his reluctance to speak grows stronger by the
second as he tells me that while the guerrillas had taken hold of the area by foot,
las autodefensas, the self-defense units, are doing it in fancy four-wheel-drives.
To recruit informants, the AUC often pays more than Colombia's minimum
salary of $140 a month. Then, brandishing lists of suspected rebels and rebel
sympathizers, the paras roll into town, breaking down doors, dragging people
out of their houses, and, often, killing them. And not only with guns but also
with stones, machetes, and even chain saws.

"It was dreadful waiting for what could happen in the middle of the night,"
the employee says, adding in a whisper, "La Fortuna is half empty." Half of the
missing have been killed. The others have left in a panic, especially squatters
who got their land with help from the rebels. In a nearby hamlet, all twenty-
seven families have fled; only a seventy-eight-year-old peasant was left behind.
"Before, saying the word "guerrilla" got you things," he says. "Today, people are
afraid to utter the word."

Like the rebels when they controlled the area, the paramilitaries are now the law and the mediators. They punish the thief, the drug peddler, and the unfaithful husband. In some areas, they forbid men to wear long hair or pierce their ears. Like the rebels' "vaccine," "protection" by the paras comes at a price. "We do it, but we do it with more tender, loving care," Carlos Castaño, the head of the paramilitaries, said during his first televised interview, the one that turned him into an instant sensation. "We negotiate the price with them. They can be a few days late with their payment. They are our friends."

Most Colombians, rich or poor, prefer life under the paramilitaries. The FARC are seen as abominable and arrogant bandits who kidnap and kill without mercy, using children as soldiers and kitchen gas tanks as bombs. This explains why the overwhelming majority of Colombians are getting tired of President Andrés Pastrana's peace process.

I ask the employee why, if the paramilitaries are so effective and the guerrillas so widely despised, we needed the protection of soldiers to make this trip. "Kidnapping," he says of the rebels, "is still their way."

Since the paras arrived, the rebels have been forced deeper into the sierra, and their urban contacts have had to go way underground. This has made it harder for them to get everyday essentials like food and clothing, so they come down from the mountains, set up one of their Miraculous Catches, and stop everyone. If before they grabbed people only with landed last names, today they don't even look at the names on your *cédula*. "Only when they're up in the mountains," the man says, "do they start researching who it is they've got and start investigating what it is they can pay." He told me that sometimes they think they've captured the landowner but then realize thay only have the chauffeur.

AFTER LUNCH, I WALK TO THE MIDDLE OF THE TERRACE. I REMEMBER HOW the front door was always open and people came throughout the day to drop off game, to say hello, or to ask a favor. Don Gabriel sat in his rocking chair, or lay in his hammock, receiving them one by one. This is where he entertained everyone—the politician, the landowner next door, his relatives, or a *trabajador*—for whisky and a cigarette, a game of chess or dominoes. From here, he ordered shoes to be bought for the barefooted children of his employees. The last time I visited, I saw him playing cards with my grandmother until two a.m., guarded only by the light of the moon. His chair still rests against the wall. His hammock is nowhere to be seen.

I walk over to the fence that separated the house from the houses of the workers. They are empty. So is the schoolhouse, its door and windows still painted green. "One of the first things we did," says Preciado, rousing me from my memories, "was to move the town outside of El Carmen." As part of the modernization plan that he and Agustín implemented in the nineties, the workers' barracks were dismantled. The company decided it was better to create housing and transportation subsidies for the workers than to have them live in those squalid conditions. I am surprised to see Alfredo, the handyman and watchman who used to live in my grandparents' house in Barranquilla. My grandparents are no longer here but "where would Alfredo go," my uncle tells me. He owns nothing; he has always lived here. He is illiterate, and he never really learned to do anything other than my grandparents' bidding. "We are all he has." Alfredo, who still carries a machete, does the same thing he has done as long as I have known him. He asks me if he should fetch me a coconut so I can drink the milk. I, like always, say yes.

Two men in their early twenties join us. They are the new tenants of the house, recent college graduates with degrees in agriculture. With Alfredo on one side and the interns on the other, the old and new El Carmen collide. The young men talk with Agustín about organic pesticides and the need for a computer with Internet access. Alfredo hands me a coconut.

More than drugs or the intransigence of the rebels, Colombia's real problem is how to reconcile two incompatible personalities—the feudal, paternalistic side represented by my grandfather and the new, modernizing side, represented by my uncle, Preciado, and the interns. Even if the cocaine labs and the FARC were to disappear tomorrow, this chasm would not.

While I'm chatting with the interns, I'm told that it is time to go. Everyone is keeping time except me. Apart from the scare with the Trooper, everything has gone so smoothly that I don't think they are serious about the deadline. "I think I want to stay overnight," I say.

My uncle seems to feel the same way and glances questioningly at Preciado. "Is it OK?" he asks.

"No!" the interns reply in unison.

BACK ON THE PLANE, AGUSTÍN IS BEAMING, HAPPY TO HAVE BEEN THERE, PROUD of what he showed me. He talks about his plans for the *empresa,* the company; it is no longer *la finca,* the farm. In the next few months, he will plant three hundred more acres in palm and build another reservoir. Despite the chaos and the violence, he sees a country that is moving forward. His optimism is admirable, and I've seen some of what he means.

Yet, I am less confident. For now, Colombians are ecstatic about the new military offensive against the FARC. "This is what we have been waiting for," a friend says. "Without the FARC, Colombia will be fixed. Colombia will be back to normal." But "normal" is exactly where the problem lies. It means life in the days of my grandfather, when the state neither policed nor provided, when local politicos traded favors for votes and justice was dealt from the barrel of a gun. The leaders of the FARC and the AUC are, after all, children of that tradition. And despite the efforts of a few to modernize, this mentality is still alive. During local elections earlier this month, votes were still being bought in cash. "That's the other guerrilla we have to vanquish," Agustín says. "The corrupt politicians."

This is Colombia's schizophrenia; this is the crux of the conflict, how difficult it will be to reconcile these two different and incompatible personalities. Colombia has a democratically elected president but Colombia is far from being democratic. In 2000, I heard President Andrés Pastrana speak in English in front of an international delegation about foreign investment, rule of law, international cooperation to combat drug trafficking, money laundering, and the preservation of human rights. But Colombia, like El Carmen, still has little, if any, of that. For all the desire of 44 million Colombians to have peace, they are at the mercy of men who, like the heads of the FARC and the AUC, are guided by the experiences that formed them in a lawless countryside.

Perhaps El Carmen, as my grandfather's farm, does not exist anymore. A new one is evolving. My uncle sees a country that, despite the chaos and the violence, is moving forward. "The local politicos are not able to get away with the same things they were fifteen years ago," Agustín has told me and I see some of what he means. Even I, during my short time here, have seen glimpses of a way forward. Last week I attended a training workshop for new policemen in Barranquilla given by the Red Cross. They were being taught how to ask questions before shooting, how not to use their *bolillo,* the wooden stick they all carry, at every opportunity. El Carmen doesn't have overseers but managers and supervisors. It doesn't have mules; it has bicycles and scooters. Fernando Preciado drives a brand-new jeep. The farm has 160 workers who work with gloves on, who wear good leather boots and khaki work shirts with "Wellness and Progress" embroidered on the shirt pocket. Still, Alirio, a thirty-three-year-old fruit picker I met today, makes less than two hundred dollars a month. His wife is giving birth to their seventh child and he has not stopped by the office to pick up the education subsidy the company allots as part of its modernization effort, to allow him to enroll his oldest child in school. "It is difficult to change mentalities," Preciado offered when I wondered, incredulous, why he would ignore this benefit.

On the plane, I glue my nose to the round window. The place I knew as a child is now obsolete. Will this new one be able to emerge? My grandmother, who regales me with stories about her days in El Carmen, told me that when the Motilones came from the sierra to her front door to sell their game, she would buy it all and ask them when they would bring more. They smiled, she told me, and simply said they'd be back in a couple of moons. As we leave my grandfather's farm behind, I feel that to bring peace, justice, and safety to El Carmen, if ever it is possible, it will take many, many more moons.

24

BODY LANGUAGE

I returned to the United States in a hurry soon after I got back from my four-hour visit to El Carmen, only to find myself in Barranquilla five months later. I took on Allegra's challenge to do what real *barranquilleras* do: *"Gozate tu Carnaval"* is the city's motto. Enjoy your Carnival. February, the month when Barranquilla is one never-ending Carnival party, found me back in the room at my grandmother's house. I went back to see if, like Allegra, I would be able to dance while people are shot daily outside tiendas, to discover if the spirit of King Momo, the Carnival's Louis XIV, could feel closer than the violence of the rebels in El Caguán and the paras in the region around Córdoba.

When I returned, Pastrana was caught in the worst conundrum. I saw it all, once again living with my grandmother, which meant living like a *barranquillera* during the day and on the street like a journalist-gringa-spy at night. My mother's friend, Dora, had left word with Fanny when I had just been back a few days that I was to be at her house at five for *un té,* one of those tea parties. I was always flattered and amazed by how fast everyone would find out that I was visiting. When I arrive the uniformed maid guides me through the French doors, and inside the air-conditioned room another uniformed maid passes around goblets of chilled white wine and tall glasses of *jugo.* There's a selection to choose from: guava, melon, pineapple, or soursop, fruits that the English could only taste if they fly to the Caribbean for a vacation in their former colonies. These tea parties only qualify in the sense that it is a mid-afternoon get-together of señoras. They rarely serve the hot beverage that the English ladies of the Victorian days would drink at this hour.

Dora's place is two houses down from my childhood home and as I set foot inside I am transported to my teenage years in Riomar when I had to come in and kiss all their cheeks and feel their scrutiny and their affection. I am starving both for the delicious food I see at the table and to be part for the first time of being accepted as one of them. Nothing has changed in the way they sit and the way they serve the food, which always includes the heavy silver tea set, perfectly polished; the teapot always empty.

I have known these ladies all my life. They are my mother's friends and the mothers of my friends. My aunt Luisa is here. If my mother were in Barranquilla and not in Bogotá she would be here too. I bend over to kiss each one of them hello and they kiss back with enormous affection. Unlike Ma Cris, they plaster their lips on my face. They have not seen me in years but they continue with their conversation as if they had seen me yesterday. I am so familiar to them that they will not change the topic of their conversation. They are sitting comfortably, spread out on two leather sofas, their coiffed hairstyles preserved by the welcoming chill of the air-conditioning and their purses right next to them, on the couch, never ever on the floor, that brings bad luck as I am immediately reminded when Celia sees me rest mine on the wood floor. *"M'ijita,"* she says pointing at it. "Money runs away when you do that."

"Ah," I say jokingly. "That's the reason why I don't have it. I keep forgetting to leave my purse off the floors."

"Stop doing it then and you'll see the change." It feels like I'm entering into a comfortable dorm room party and a shark pit all at once. They love me, I know that, but they will also scrutinize me with no mercy from what I'm wearing to what I say. They have always been and will always be an unforgiving combination of Greek chorus, Page Six, and judges for the Miss Colombia pageant.

I turn to the television, surprised to see it on—men in camouflage flashing in and out, like they did that day on Shelter Island. The ladies fill me in: the FARC has just kidnapped a senator, blatantly ignoring the cease-fire it had negotiated just last week with the government. President Andrés Pastrana had told them that if they violated the cease-fire, which included a halt to kidnappings, he would send the army into the demobilized area, no ifs, ands, or buts. And that is what they had just done. The "bastards" had breached the cease-fire. It was up to Andrés Pastrana now, the ladies tell me, "to show some pants." It was time to end the farce of El Caguán, the area the size of Switzerland that he gave to the rebels as a gesture of goodwill and that for the last two years has increasingly become a stone in the president's shoe. The country was starting to lose patience with the way the president was dealing with the armed group, having conceded to them an entire state of their own, with their rules. Whenever I speak to Max, he refers to the DMZ as FARClandia.

When Pastrana's face shows up on the TV screen the ladies boo at the president. When it shows the face of the FARC leaders they scream, *"Mátenlos!"*— they want them dead. They wear medallions of their favorite saints from long gold chains but the ladies are more hawk than dove. I listen to them talk politics, which is interspersed with gossip and humor. Mercedes, the sharpest of

them, says they might all end up tonight like the ladies in *Tea with Mussolini*—
"one of my favorite movies," she says—and tells those who haven't seen it that
it is about a group of women who are trapped in their mansions in Tuscany
when the Second World War begins.

I stay silent as they discuss the situation. They all agree that Pastrana has
been a fool for conceding the demilitarized zone to the guerrillas. They've only
used it "to make fun of the entire nation," says Dora. "Enough talk," says Marta,
"they've been talking for two years. Time for bombs." No one asks my opinion
and I do not offer it. I only speak to ask them if they can point out Simón
Trinidad, one of the seven FARC commanders, on the TV screen.

"I'm not sure I can recognize him," says my aunt. Simón Trinidad's cousin
was married to a Montblanc. I have wondered all these years if he would
explain to me why he decided to join the revolutionary movement.

Simón Trinidad was born Ricardo Palmera in Valledupar, born into a family very much like the families of the ladies at tea. He is exactly Agustín's age; in
fact they knew each other quite well when he was Ricardo, a bank manager and
an economics professor, not Simón Trinidad, who declared that his class background is the only regrettable birthmark in his revolutionary life. From the
moment I found out the FARC had among his commanders someone who was
in so many ways connected to my family's provincial past, I have wanted to
know everything I could about him. Was he at all different? Could they tell that
one day he would turn around and point a rifle at them? Many argue that the
reason the number of kidnappings has increased in the region is thanks to him.
He knows everyone so well that he knows what everyone has. He knows whose
cattle is whose and whose land belongs to whom. He even knows the amount
of money in their bank account. He comes from Valledupar, but married a
woman from Barranquilla and the wedding party was at el Country Club, where
many of these ladies and their children had celebrated their own weddings. But
it seems that I am the only one who finds this fascinating.

I did some research. Simón Trinidad's parents were well regarded and liked.
His father was a distinguished lawyer in Valledupar, an active Liberal and an
elected senator. His mother was an elegant woman from the interior whose
father had been governor of Santander. The couple gave their children the best
education possible. Ricardo went to the fancy schools of Bogotá's elite and
spent years attending universities both in the United States and England.

When Ricardo Palmera returned to Colombia after his time abroad—unlike
me—he worked at the government agency that gave agrarian credits to poor
farmers. It was here, he has said, where he got his first revolutionary thoughts.
As he learned about land ownership and crop cultivation, he started finding
himself on the side of the poor. He quit the development bank to become a

professor and it was at the university that he first started getting involved in politics. In 1982, he joined the throngs of young men and women who had found a new leader in Luis Carlos Galán, a strong speaker with charisma who was running as the presidential candidate for the Liberal Party. Galán called for an end to corruption and drug trafficking but like most opponents and vibrant speakers in Colombia, he was silenced. Galán, like Gaitán was assassinated as he gave a speech. These men are considered Colombia's John and Bobby Kennedy even if they were not blood brothers and died forty years apart.

These were days of suspicion, so Palmera and a bunch of "lefties" were arrested by the army. The president had passed the so-called Statute of Security, an undeclared state of siege. Accused of being part of a rebel movement, Palmera was interrogated for three days without food or water. That experience, he has said, strengthened his resolve and in 1986, three years before Communism in the Soviet Union crumbled, Ricardo joined the Unión Patriotica or UP, the Patriotic Union, the political arm of the FARC. In 1983, negotiations between the government and the rebels had begun. If the rebels dropped their guns, the government promised to grant them amnesty. The M-19 had done it. In elections that year, Colombians elected ten members of the Patriotic Union (UP) to the house and two to the senate. Soon after the elections, however, the members of the UP were dropping dead. With every dead member, Manuel Marulanda grew fiercer and vowed that the FARC would never give up their arms. It was one of these assassinations, Ricardo Palmera says, that turned him into the man with the rifle I'm searching for on the TV screen.

Ricardo had arranged to meet with Jaime Pardo Leal, the head of the UP, a charismatic lawyer, whom he had never met. He was looking forward to it. But the meeting never happened. Pardo Leal was assassinated the day before they were scheduled to meet. Ricardo says that, "afraid for his life," he wrote to the FARC: "I will not run away like a dog from the country. I will stay." A month later he was receiving his military training in the jungles of Meta. A few months later, a trained Ricardo Palmera was back in the land he was born into. This time as Simón Trinidad, commander of the FARC's 41st Front.

I had asked Agustín about Simón Trinidad before our trip to El Carmen. "We had chemistry," he told me. "I liked talking with him." Agustín recalls one day when he went to visit him at his office and they were so involved talking— "philosophizing," he tells me—that Palmera's secretary left and they had to close the office themselves. Agustín missed his plane back to Barranquilla and stayed at Ricardo's overnight. "He is a true believer," Agustín says. My uncle thinks that Palmera was put between a rock and a hard place. His life was in danger after Jaime Pardo Leal's assassination. If he stayed in Valledupar, the chances were high that he would have been another dead UPer. Palmera turned out to be a valuable asset to the rebel organization, this time on the military end of things. He knew La Provincia better than anyone in the organization.

At the tea party, I try to instigate a conversation about him but no one is interested in the rebel that shares the birthmark of their class. To them he is another FARC bandit, which can only mean one thing: he is the enemy that needs to be vanquished.

I COME HOME FROM THE TEA TO FIND MY GRANDMOTHER IN FRONT OF THE television with her cousin Cecilia, but they speak over the news about anything but the news. I call my uncle to see if he is worried about the breakdown of the peace talks but he is at el Country Club having a sauna. I call *El Heraldo*'s newsroom but the reporter answers my question with so much apathy as if I were asking her about the peace process in East Timor. When I ask to speak to someone who might know more, she tells me that no one's there. "Everyone's gone to the stadium to listen to King Momo. He is about to do the reading of El Bando," she informs me. I know enough about the festivity to know this is it. From now on, Barranquilla is by law a party. The King of Carnival reads his decree, announcing the beginning of the festivities and ordering everyone to participate, out in the street. Dancing and drinking are the news of the day, not that the government is ready to send in the army to the demobilized zone. The only attention Barranquilla is giving to the demobilized zone is to use it for word games. As of this moment, Barranquilla is the demobilized party zone.

Once again I feel so terribly lost in the city of my childhood that I decide to do what I always do when I want to understand something: I get involved as a reporter. I dial the number for *Newsweek*'s Miami bureau and offer to cover the breaking news for the magazine. My mind is working fast. This is my chance to go meet the FARC; so many of my American journalist friends have made the trip to FARClandia, stories I hear with envy sitting at a bar stool at the Half King. Maybe I can even interview Simón Trinidad. I am not staying for the bacchanal in Barranquilla. I am off to El Caguán. "Sounds good," says the bureau chief hiring me. If I can file a story about what is going on in the next forty-eight hours, we could still be in time for it to make the magazine's following issue. But as soon as I hang up, I realize I have no idea how to get there.

I call Margarita Martínez at Associated Press in Bogotá to see if she is going. Getting to El Caguán is going to take me at least a day, she tells me. I am to fly from Barranquilla to Bogotá, from there to Florencia, if I am lucky to catch one of the two flights a day and to get a seat, especially now with the breaking news. From Florencia I have to hire a cab to take me to the demobilized area. "It is a bad road and it's the rainy season now, so it gets worst and it's hard to find taxis that want to take you there. Offer them dollars and you might get luckier,"

Margarita says. She gives me the name of a few local journalists to see if they can hook me up with a local driver or a stringer. I call them but they cannot wait for me to get here. They have to fly out as soon as possible. They want to be there right away—what could unfold could be a very big story. The entire peace process is about to end. The government is declaring war on the rebels.

When I find out from one of the reporters that I'll need a Colombian press pass to enter the demilitarized zone, I make up my mind. Sorry *Newsweek* I will not be traveling to El Caguán today. I don't get on the plane, a decision based on self-preservation and self-flagellation, unsure if I decide against it because I am too scared to take the road trip or if I'm punishing myself because I abandoned Colombia and I cannot just parachute in with a plum assignment. Listening to the journalists on the phone, to the way that they are Colombian, and that they do not doubt it, like I do, stops me from moving ahead with my reporting plan. I don't want to interview Colombians like I have interviewed Nicaraguan mothers who lost their children to war.

I have decided not to go to El Caguán, but I tell myself I can still file a story, from here. I start with the standard, an American expert that can put Colombia into American context. Michael Shifter, a fellow at the Inter-American Dialogue, has become the omnipresent quote for American stories about the Colombia situation. I dial his number in Washington, D.C. I ask him what he thinks of the impasse between Pastrana and the FARC. "It's a good thing," he says as I open my empty notepad. "It makes the government be a bit more realistic. A peace process involves more than they thought. It is fine to give concessions but it is important to put pressure when you have to." Shifter thinks like the rest of the nation. Pastrana has been too soft on the rebels.

Shifter explains the details of the three-year-old process and I realize that it is more complicated than I had imagined reporting the story would be. I lock myself in my room, television, radio, and laptop computer at hand. Time to work. In a few hours, this could all turn into mayhem. Aren't you glad you can cope with it now, I keep telling myself. You can stop being Colombian and become the reporter. My brain is operating beautifully, telling my heart to stop pounding and my hands to stop sweating: Just report. Report. Listen. Listen. Take notes. Watch. Watch. Read into it. Interpret. Interpret. Write. Write. File. After the newcasts, I prepare a set of notes to send out to Miami. "Do you think the talks will break?" the bureau chief asks me when I call him to see if he got it and if he needs more. "What can you tell based on their body language?"

I am at a loss. I sit in front of the images on the television screen, steadfast in my refusal to visit El Caguán. When I come out of my room, my grandmother tells me that she is worried. I echo her concerns, surprised that she is mentioning the peace process. "Will you be able to handle it?" she asks. "If you want I can ask one of them to stay." Ma Cris is going to Santa Marta to visit her relatives for the weekend, and it is Fanny and María's weekend off. The only problem right now in my grandmother's life is the fact that her granddaughter will have to spend two entire days without servants.

"I will be fine, Ma Cris," I say.

When Cecilia leaves, I hear my grandmother making her own arrangements. She has decided to ignore the *runrún* and have José take her to Santa Marta for the weekend, to visit her cousin, who had called to say that "the coast was clear." Lucky her, I say under my breath, feeling a little jealous that the road to Santa Marta is safer than the one I wanted to take to El Carmen. I've heard it's thanks to the paras. The leader is a man from Valledupar, who goes by the name of Jorge 40. He is the aristocrat-para; the other side of the coin to Simón Trinidad, the aristocrat-rebel, both men born with silver spoons, destined to be the best and the brightest of Padilla's promise, but have instead turned into armed outlaws.

I watch my grandmother pack her bags. She walks to the linen closet and takes a set of white embroidered sheets. When I try to help, she says no thanks. I realize that I am intruding on her, watching her get ready for her trip. I walk into my bedroom and take to the war on TV. Instead of feeling worried that she is going on a road trip, I am jealous I didn't have the nerve to get to El Caguán.

THE PEACE NEGOTIATIONS ARE MUCH MORE COMPLICATED THAN I COULD HAVE ever imagined when I made the call to *Newsweek*. For three years before I returned to Barranquilla in February 2002, there have been lawyers, politicians, priests, foreign presidents, and diplomats involved. There have been hundreds of drafts, communiqués, secret meetings, and international brokering. In a nut shell, the government and the rebels said in 1999 that they were ready to negotiate peace. Both sides agreed to sit down and negotiate but to do that both sides needed to agree to a cease-fire. As the peace talks moved forward, the FARC continued to attack and kidnap. In November 2001, the government told the FARC that if they continued breaching the cease-fire, they would be forced to leave El Caguán. November with its deadline came and went without an answer from the rebels. So Pastrana gave them a two-month extension that is about to expire as Barranquilla is about to start Carnivals.

The FARC's answer to the deadline came in the form of another kidnapping this week. "Give us back our dignity," all of Colombia asks both sides. The rebels get the usual insults: "Cynics" is the nicest word I hear when Colombians from all walks of life refer to the incident. But they are getting fed up with the president. Their "Andresito," the savior angel, the golden boy who believes in the Divino Niño is becoming Andresito *mariconcito* and Andresito *payasito*, little queer, little Andrés or little clown, little Andrés. Not "President Pastrana" any longer, who was elected with the highest number of votes of any president in the country's history. And this is the legacy he wants to regain before it's too late. He only has a few months left. If Shifter calls him naïve, others call him a self-serving opportunist, accusing him of doing this to get a Nobel Peace Prize. His opponents in *Semana* report that he had gone all the way to Sweden to propose his name as recipient. The people who had seen him as the savior of Colombia now saw a pampered boy with no substance.

It was Pastrana's last chance to act. Colombians were telling him that he had played enough with their patience. The dauphine is being tested. I might not be able to interpret the body language between the government and the rebels; I cannot make out if the way they sit and stand around each other signals a break-up or a reconciliation but I am sure of one interpretation. Colombians are angry, humiliated, fed up. People want revenge. A friend who had worked on Pastrana's campaign summed it up for me when I called him to get a sense of where he was leaning: "It is a question of pride. It's about his image in front of an entire nation. He has to do something now." And then Pastrana, as if he were listening to our conversation, announces on national television that the army is moving in. I have seen him address the nation before and wondered if this time he too would use the strange way he likes to end his remarks, "May God bless Colombia and may God bless me." If Colombians had found his personal religiosity charming, this time he really needed the blessing.

After Pastrana's news, the television moves to El Caguán. I have been surprised to see how much it resembles El Carmen. The room where the government and the rebels negotiate is a kiosk exactly like the ones in the *fincas* I have visited on the coast. A simple open-air structure made out of a cement floor and a thatched roof. And the Negotiation Table, also referred to as the Dialogue Table, is a white plastic table with chairs just like the ones where we were served our lunch in El Carmen. The table with its promise of peace is the garden furniture used by families and friends to sit around a summer barbeque. The table is covered with a white cloth as if a meal is about to be served but there are microphones instead of placemats on each seat and on one side of the table there are a few resting rifles.

I had seen men in fatigues and with guns, the rebels, and men in civilian clothes, the government, pacing around nervously but I have no idea who's who, which one of the men in wrinkled suits is the peace commissioner, which one of the bearded revolutionaries is Simón Trinidad. I suppose that the handful of men in civilian clothes, who look uncomfortable with the heat and with the rifles around them are Pastrana's boys, the boys from Bogotá, with foreign educations and the formality and the mild manners of the Andes, men who seem to have good intentions and little patience with the ways of the jungle and of the intransigence of the men with the guns. The other group is the men in green fatigues and in rubber knee-high boots, men whose rough ways come across the TV screen in clear contrast to the gentle demeanor of the government negotiators. What I notice the most is the lack of interaction between them. The rebels and the government representatives do not chit chat.

I see a different kind of face in James Lemoyne, a United Nations official who serves as the facilitator for the talks is being interviewed, so I carefully focus on his body language, see if I can hone in and read between the lines. Lemoyne speaks as carefully as I am listening to him. He is taking his time choosing his words but I can tell it is more for content and message than for a lack of vocabulary. His Spanish is perfect even if slightly accented. "I hope this can be resolved," he says to the cameras. "We will have a proposal ready today. We have spent the day working, moving forward and hopefully resolve this crisis. It must be negotiated. This country deserves this."

At the table I count five rebels and although I am scribbling what he is saying, I am wondering if one of the men he is sitting with is Simón Trinidad. "I beg of all parts to be flexible, creative, and committed in their search for peace. The future of the country is at play." I wonder if I will be able to recognize Simón Trinidad immediately; can I tell him apart from the rest? The news anchor announces before breaking to commercials that Simón Trinidad will be serving as the FARC's spokesperson. This is music to my ears. I will get to see a lot of close-ups. Will I be able to understand what drove him to take arms against his own people? Could I read his body language? After all he is family, kind of. He has a niece who is a Montblanc.

A handsome clean-shaven face wearing square-rimmed glasses and a shaven head fills the screen. I immediately know it is him because he feels familiar even in his camouflage clothes and the tight brood across his face. Simón Trinidad is arrogant for sure. It is the haughtiness of being male in a macho country and not having grown up in Bogotá. Trinidad's body language is that of a provincial man, regardless of his political position. In either case, be it my grandfather with his bad temper or Manuel Marulanda with his revolutionary conviction I do not want to be on the receiving end of their determination. These are men who do not negotiate. Because that is the way they were raised; because of what is called *la ley del monte,* the law of the mountain. I don't think the peace commissioner or the ten ambassadors or James Lemoyne get that.

As Trinidad gets ready to speak, I see the journalists running around, the long zooms of the lenses, the small tape recorders placed near his mouth, the note scribbling. I'm taking it all in sitting on the edge of the bed; my legs tingle as if telling me that they are happy that I was unable to travel there but I do feel incompetent for not doing what is 90 percent of journalism: showing up. Being there to get the smell, the quotes, the nuances, the descriptions, and the dateline. Trinidad speaks into all their recording gadgets. The FARC, he says, has the best intentions to negotiate and to prove it Lemoyne will spend the night with them and the Red Cross will have more than fifteen vehicles patrolling the zone. And there is more: there will be no FARC checkpoints tonight. I feel pretty stupid for not going but I tell myself it was a good move. *Newsweek* is only mildly interested in the story. The chance of it running is better if the talks break; and for tonight that doesn't seem to be the case.

THE NEXT MORNING I REPEAT MY METHOD. I SET MYSELF IN THE SAME EXACT place I have been doing my cowardly reporting: in front of the television. The government has sent a document to the FARC, which they announce they will analyze over lunch. This is not only a digitalized rebel army with Iridium and satellite phones but a well-fed one too. But by five thirty that afternoon, the rebels have not responded to the government and the plane is ready to take off with the diplomats and the government negotiators back to Bogotá. As the men from the capital board, Simón Trinidad takes out a lighter from the right pocket of his military pants, flicks it, and with the tiny flame he sets on fire the papers he holds in his hand. Neither the reporters nor the pundits comment on the dramatic act of the "aristocratic rebel," as the foreign press has dubbed him.

By six o'clock, the Negotiation Table at El Caguán is empty. The party has ended and by Trinidad's disposition I assume the war is on.

General Jorge Mora, commander of Colombia's armed forces, is ready for it. "My men," he tells the country, "are ready to take over the demilitarized zone. The deadline will not be protracted." A war is being transmitted live, second by second, and I am the only one interested. I call my parents in Bogotá and they are out so they are obviously not watching and in Barranquilla it is Sábado de Carnaval. A grenade explodes in a tiny hamlet, blowing the straw roofs off twelve homes. "Start running," an average citizen interviewed randomly, advises them. "Run," says another one. "Run like rats."

At nine o'clock at night, after nine hours of uninterrupted television watching, the government announces that the president will address the nation. All of a sudden Andresito, the peace president, the privileged boy whom the country was not sure if he was naïve, stupid, or infinitely sly and opportunistic was having his comeback. He had closed his fist in front of 44 million Colombians and was "finally ready to shove it into the faces" of seventy-year-old Sureshot, the senior FARC leader, and his cronies, as a friend explained on his cell phone when he called to make sure I didn't want to go to a "good party."

At the rebel camp, Simón Trinidad has added a green scarf around his neck. As he prepares to read a document, his announcement of the FARC's response to Pastrana, he removes the AK-47 from his shoulder. "Aaay," he says. By now, you'd think he is used to the weight of his weapon. "Let me just put this thing here on the floor." Should I read into this? Does this mean they are disarming? Or does it mean that "the thing" is always by the feet, reachable just in case? Trinidad explains how they've been working "without interruption" to solve this crisis and that they are planning a draft for the government. He is sure they will reach a cease-fire. Before they do that, however, they have a list of demands. Point number five is "the undeniable will of the FARC to justice" and it comes with Trinidad's closed fist in the air. He pauses and tells reporters he will take no questions. The FARC has spoken. Manuel Marulanda grabs his rifle and slips the leather strap on his shoulder like ladies grab their purses when they're getting ready to leave a tea party; he leaves a bottle of Buchanan's scotch behind. I recognize the green bottle because my grandfather had those bottles on his table too. "The last word is Pastrana's," Trinidad says forcefully. He folds the document he has just read in half, passing his finger over the fold. How should I interpret that? Was it a caress of hope or a threat to cut throats?

If for a second this all made sense, if for a second it seemed that they were reaching an agreement, don't be fooled. Trinidad comes back out. They have one more request, he says: The government has two months to put an end to unemployment. This is like asking a lover with a heroin addiction that he has a weekend to clean up. It is unrealistic. It is passive-aggressive. It is hard to know if they bring this up now out of true and honest naïveté or is it that they are just the cynics that Colombians who live here have come to despise? It has been said that Manuel Marulanda is out of touch, that he has been too entrenched in the mountains fighting the army with such hate that he does not know how the world works. To educate him, when the peace process began, he was given a crash course in globalization. He was invited to Europe for six weeks where he met with all kinds of social democrats. Both Richard Grasso, the head of the New York Stock Exchange, and Steve Case, the founder of AOL, flew down to El Caguán to visit the oldest living Marxist guerrilla fighter in the world. The Europeans and a handful of liberal Americans have promised to help them integrate their ideas into today's world. Commandant Andrés Paris studied in the Soviet Union and Commandant Simón Trinidad spent time at Harvard. But it is unclear what the FARC really wants.

As I sit alone with the door closed, I try to make sense of what is starting to confuse the binary preconception I arrived with, my romantic perspective on the rebels. No one can be against people, I thought, who claim they want to "reduce the suffering of the civil population" and "improve the living conditions of our people." The FARC makes it sound like there is a magic wand that is in the hands of the wrong people, like the plot of a fantasy fable of good and evil, and that if it were rescued and put in the hands of the right people, everything would be fixed. The paramilitary and those who support them, a group that is exponentially larger than those who support the FARC, believe exactly the opposite. If it were not for the FARC, "a bunch of bandits who kill the civil-ian population," Colombia would be wonderful, Shangri-la, Middle Earth. If the FARC magically disappeared, even if it takes massacres and death by chain saws, the country would be fixed. According to these ideologies, if Colombia were grabbed from the other, this would happen instantly.

When the clock strikes midnight, Pastrana steps up to the microphone and announces that "only a public manifestation to a cease-fire will be able to stop the clock." If he keeps his word, by tomorrow morning I will be caught in the middle of a war. I look out the window and face the silence on the street and the darkness inside the houses of the neighborhood. Mine is the only room that has the blue light of the TV reflecting on the window. I have sat in front of a TV screen for an entire day, so close to it that I can stretch my arm and touch it, as if that would take me there. I know this is not the way to report a story but I also have a feeling that it will not matter, that concentrating on this stops me from dwelling on why I've decided to come back to Barranquilla for a second time. What is my need to see it again? I find a certain comfort by concentrating on Pastrana's call to war. It keeps me focused instead of altered.

Ten thousand soldiers are getting ready. The army will penetrate five munic-ipalities "by land and by air"; the planes will bomb, the convoys and the boats will attack. "I'm gonna go get them," a very young man screams into the screen. Images of helicopters, boats, convoys of trucks on the way to El Caguán flash inside my room, one after the other. I am in an air-conditioned bedroom sit-ting on a flowered bedspread but I feel the hatred in each image. "We are going to get Marulanda's towel," says another and it feels like he is on the way to the stadium to watch his soccer team take on the rival team.

The televisions reminds us that the president is behind closed doors with "his close advisers" and that the army bases of Tolemaida and Apiay are now "reinforced since Plan Colombia." Men in fatigues jump inside the wide bellies of Hercules planes and twelve helicopters, also supplied by the Americans, are ready to go. Back in El Caguán LeMoyne tells a TV reporter that the people who live in the area surrounding the demilitarized zone are concerned about their safety. He will stay there, he offers, and serve as their shield. This body language is easy to interpret: He is worried. The population around the demobilized area know that the moment the FARC leaves, the AUC comes in. And they know what happens next—the same thing that happened in La Fortuna, the town outside El Carmen. When the rebels leave, the paras come in with one mission, to kill whoever helped them. The people are scared to be labeled FARC sympa-thizers, when their only involvement can be that they just happen to live where they are the law. "I live here," a man wearing a work shirt too big for his scrawny chest tells the TV reporter, "because this is where I have always lived." He was there before the rebels, he continues in an effort to disassociate himself from them. He stayed because "this is his land." Fortune played a bad trick on him he says. "It is not my fault that the small plot of land that feeds my family is located in the same spot where the FARC chose to put up a billboard that reads WELCOME TO VILLA NUEVA COLOMBIA."

SIMÓN TRINIDAD STEPS TO THE DAIS, READY TO SPEAK FROM INSIDE THE REBEL compound, in a room that has a huge mural of Simón Bolívar, clearly the man he took his nom de guerre from, the other Simón with authoritarian ways. He places himself between Bolívar's eyes. "It is Pastrana," the rebel says, "who has brought this to an end." He announces that the FARC will leave the zone. They will leave, he says, but they would like to turn the zone over to the government in a public ceremony. They are not going "to run like rabbits." They will give it back in front of diplomats and cameras and with speeches "as was done when we received it from them." I cannot believe they are being so compliant. And then, the dramatic revolutionary raises his voice. "Once again, the selfish interest of the rich and privileged minority has been placed above those of 40 million Colombians. The same old war mongers have won out, obstructing the chance for peace."

After all the posturing, Pastrana announces that the FARC can stay in the demilitarized zone till April. When the planes and the soldiers are called back there are no cameras to report it.

Morning finds me feeling flustered and hungry. I had not eaten much, too worried to miss an important moment. Foolish me. I am the only one who took what was happening seriously. Perhaps my grandmother and Allegra know better when they turn a blind eye to those who would like to bring this conflict into their lives.

I open the refrigerator and find five bowls on the middle shelf: cut papaya, cut mangoes, cut pineapple, and cut melon and one with a big chunk of white cheese like the kind they used to make in El Carmen but don't anymore. Ma Cris had told me before she left for Santa Marta that they—Fanny, María, and she—had figured out how to feed me while they are gone. Fanny had made arroz con pollo that I can find in the oven. "Go to the kitchen now," she ordered me, "and she will teach you how to turn it on so you can warm it up when you get hungry." I obey, wondering if she finds it normal that she thinks I need to be taught how to do a simple chore like turning on an oven. I think she wouldn't know how to do it. "You're not going to eat it cold. Are you?" I never turn on the oven. I eat the yellow rice with chunks of chicken like I would leftover Chinese food in New York—cold. I feed myself from the pot realizing it's time for me to get back to my life.

Colombia's conflict is a story that I, as a journalist, am not prepared to cover. When García Lorca returned to Granada, unable to run away from what he called "the flowered scent of the knife," he knew who he was fighting, just like Charlie knows who his enemy is, like Manuel Marulanda knows who his enemy is, like Carlos Castaño and General Mora know who they want to vanquish. I have yet to define my enemy. I came here to declare war on Colombia, to tell every Colombian that they have blood on their hands. Today, I realize that I am at war with myself and with my relationship with Colombia, that I came here because I had always felt I had run away from a responsibility when I left. But the truth is that no matter how much I try, this is not a war that I need to fight or to win. No matter how much I try to fall in love with Colombia, I can't. I don't even like our revolutionaries. Simón Trinidad has proven to be nothing more than a bad actor. I was happy to stay away for twenty-five years and I have not liked coming back. It is okay, I tell myself. It's okay not to like it here; and it's okay to explain why. More than one hundred people are killed everyday in this Catholic country and yet not to follow one of the Ten Commandments is not as much of a sin as criticizing Colombia. Thou Shall Not Kill can be broken; to kill your neighbor if he is on the other side is almost a national duty—*por Colombia,* for Colombia—but to say anything critical of Colombia is the only mortal sin.

Upon my grandmother's return, I ask her if she had fun and she tells me that it was lovely. Her cousins have a great house on the beach and she describes every meal in full detail. She takes out some *nísperos* in a brown bag and tells me they are from their patio. "They need a few days for them to be ripe," she says as she walks out of the room. "I will tell Fanny to wrap them in newspaper and leave them outside. That's how they get ripe."

Her bag is left open on the bed and in an effort to make myself useful I decide to unpack the rest of the things. The moment I grab the folded sheets, I notice that they are heavier than they should be, that there is clearly something inside them. I slide my hand in, thinking it's some other edible from her cousin's kitchen or garden but I feel something so cold and hard that it cannot possibly be food. I have just touched a gun, I think to myself. My grandmother packs a gun, I think in disbelief. I pull the heavy piece of metal from between the folded sheets. I am faced with a crucifix, the size of a .45. She grabs it from my hand and places it under her pillow. Neither of us says a word. It's time for me to pack my bags.

Back in New York, I buy the first papayas and mangoes of my life. I usually buy apples, blueberries, or tangerines. I had never wanted to taste a fruit from my childhood that was wrapped in so much plastic, with a sticker and a price. The fruit from my country came without those things. I unwrap the plastic from the slice of papaya, remove the gray seeds, and consider for a second cutting it in squares, the way I've eaten papaya all my life. I choose instead to take a spoon, dig it into the salmon-colored meat, notice how much paler it is than the one José gets for my grandmother and scoop it out as I do with Häagen-Dazs. The chunk melts in my mouth and it is delicious but the exercise leaves me unsatisfied. Will I ever reconcile the two sides of me? When will a papaya just start being a papaya and not a fruit from back home? When will a papaya once again be a fruit in Colombia and not mean danger, fear, these words of hatred and war?

The reconciliation between the rebels and the "oligarchic rich" as the FARC refers to Pastrana's government and to anyone that is not on their side, does not last long. Less than a month after I return to New York, completely readjusted to my American routine, having left the fears and the questions at my grandmother's house, I read in the paper that the FARC hijacked a small plane with another senator on board. This time Pastrana expels them, no ifs, ands, or buts. But in New York the immediacy and the intensity of what would happen does not have the same force. I have little interest in the fight that had consumed me a month ago.

Two months later the *Wall Street Journal* calls, and offers me a chance to go back, and once again I am pulled by Colombia's seductive tug.

BOOK THREE

Santa Fe de Bogotá

Caribbean Sea

PANAMA

VENEZUELA

Pacific

Ocean

★Santa Fe de Bogotá

COLOMBIA

ECUADOR

BRAZIL

| 0 Miles | 200 | 400 |

| 0 Kilometers | 400 |

PERU

© 2007 Jeffrey L. Ward

25

HOW DID I END UP HERE?
MARCH 2002

When Charlie, the young marine I secretly interrogated on the plane, had told me that if someone were to make a movie about his life it would be called *How Did I End Up Here?* I didn't tell him that I would call mine *My Colombian War* and that it wasn't a movie, that I was actually writing a book; and that, like him, I was on the flight from Miami to Bogotá, because I was coming to hunt down some motherfuckers too. I will spend a week in Bogotá, covering the upcoming election, another assignment that works as a cover for my personal inquisition. The difference between us is that Charlie had clearly defined his enemy—those drug dealers that had turned his mother into an uncaring parent and I wasn't sure, especially after my trip to Barranquilla and El Carmen, who my enemy was. I was judging 44 million Colombians guilty; I was accusing them all of having blood on their hands. I had declared war on Colombia.

Plane rides make a good place for confessions to strangers and Charlie had spent three hours talking to me about his life, so it was only natural that we would exchange e-mail addresses. I was the first Colombian he had ever met, and my interest in him was not just as the marine in Colombia—my reporter's greed was mixed with a genuine desire to keep in touch. Charlie is as likable and as handsome as Zack Mayo, the officer and the gentlemen in the eponymous movie. "Bye, *cuidate*," he said as he rushed out the door. "Maybe I'll see you here sometime. I'll be speaking Spanish, *te lo prometo*."

CHARLIE WAS IN MUCH MORE OF A RUSH TO SEE BOGOTÁ THAN I AM, ALTHOUGH I have to admit I am also excited about the trip, my first to Bogotá in a professional capacity. I've come to help a *Wall Street Journal* reporter navigate through his first time in Colombia. American journalists usually get their fixers locally, and I have long since moved on from my fixer days but I took the job offer. I agreed to come from New York and show a staff reporter around. There was something in it for me too, a chance to see Bogotá with my American-trained journalist eyes. Here, unlike in Barranquilla and in El Carmen, I could just be a bystander, a note-taking, question-asking fly on the wall. Reporting for a leading American newspaper opens a lot of doors and I wanted to be let inside them, especially in Bogotá, the center of power.

I had already fought two battles. I had taken on Barranquilla and I had confronted El Carmen. Bogotá was missing. Like all wars, mine was becoming much more complicated than when I had declared it and also much more prolonged than I had expected it to be. But why am I surprised—isn't that true of all wars? I came to Bogota to point out where its responsibility lies in this brutal conflict that happens mostly in the hamlets and towns that are so remote from the life of the capital that they could very well be casualties of a conflict in all together another continent.

AS I RIDE FROM THE AIRPORT TO THE HOTEL WHERE I WILL BE STAYING IN Bogotá, I am pumped to be here, ready to fight my Battle of Boyacá. Hopefully, after this trip I will free myself of my internal war with Colombia just like Bolívar freed the entire country from the reins of Spain. My personal war aside, it is also an interesting moment to be coming to report. In five days Colombians will vote for a new president marking the direction of the country for the next four years. Everything seems to indicate that the war will only intensify. The leading candidate is a relatively unknown landowner from Medellín who has served in various public offices in his state since the early days of Pablo Escobar. Álvaro Uribe, a 48-year-old from Medellín, has promised to never ever talk to the rebels. He promises instead to destroy them militarily. I ask my cab driver and he confirms it. "Yes, war, that is what Colombians want." If in 1998, Colombians had voted for Andrés Pastrana's plan to negotiate peace with the FARC, today, four years later, he will leave office with the lowest popularity rate of a president in the country's history. I had witnessed it myself. Six months before, during the six weeks I had spent in Barranquilla, I could sense the frustration of those who had voted for him.

There has been a plan and a rigor to this journey, or perhaps I should say, I had a theory about Colombia's violence and Bogotá is my last stop on my itinerary. Being able to throw around the name of a big American newspaper will allow me a certain kind of access and distance. I am coming to Santa Fe de Bogotá as it is formally called to indict her too. Just like I proclaimed that the people of La Provincia are guilty of feudalism, so I found plenty of evidence in El Carmen and inside my grandmother's house. The ways of the men who brought progress to Padilla's land by opening the road and taking down the mountain, the method of bulldozing before asking, is great for *vallenato* lyrics, bad for democracy. The *costeños* represented here by my fellow *barranquilleros* have mixed together the feudal way of the countryside with the flawed vibrancy of an incipient modernity brought by a cauldron of immigrant cultures, all male-centric. The mixture is great for carnivals, bad for democracy. I am here now to charge the *bogotanos*. Santa Fe de Bogotá is the distracted king; the cold hearted snob who cannot be bothered with the unsophisticated ways of the rest of the country; all those bloody regions are really not too important or interesting. Let them figure it all out there. They think they are modern here because they dress like the Brits and they have sushi restaurants and theater festivals but they are guilty by proxy. They have been flaunting their disinterest, hiding their distain, hoping to obstruct the ugly visions of poverty and killing in the countryside in their snobbish ways. Let them fight and divide and conquer as much as they want as long as no one bothers and distracts us. That is what the denizens of Bogotá have essentially said since the battle of Boyacá.

Coming to Bogotá is different than going to Barranquilla, in the sense that it is a place where I do not feel I am from. I have no attachment to it. Being here is like going back to a place I went on a family trip a few times as a young girl. The memories are all associated with being here as part of a family of five: my parents, my sister, my brother, and me, without grandparents and cousins and servants around us. Bogotá is the place where I have the most vivid memories of doing things together as a family, *con papi y mami*. These are memories of when I was nine, ten, eleven; when my father, at age thirty-two, one of the up-and-coming leaders of *la costa*, was appointed by the president to head a federal agency. There were weekends when we would come and see him instead of him coming to see us. And once we spent the entire Easter week in my father's two-bedroom suite at the Hotel Tequendama, which housed all the high government officials from out of town—a Watergate Hotel of sorts. Bogotá always felt different. For one, it was colder than Barranquilla, so we had special clothes, *ropa de frio*, cold clothes, what *costeños* wear in the country's capital. My sister and I had matching tweed coats and red sweaters to wear over our *costa* cotton dresses.

My mother took us around to museums, parks, and the planetarium, none of which Barranquilla had. For the first time, the three of us walked around, she in the middle holding my sister and me on either side. In Barranquilla, we were sent to the movies with our uniformed nannies. In Bogotá she sat through *Flipper* with us. One afternoon, she took us to a photographer's studio and on a set decorated with one big white cube we posed with her: Laura sitting on the floor, *mami* on the cube, and I standing next to her or *mami* sitting on the cube and Laura and I cross-legged on the floor. Hernán Díaz, the Richard Avedon of our country, captured a beautiful young mother in those shots but then she wanted to pose alone. The photographer was taken by her looks and after he shot her profile many times in a classic turtleneck, he asked her if she would pose for him wearing a tunic like the women in the Guajira wear. He wanted to make a *guajira* princess of my mother. She politely declined the offer, even if Asunción, her birthplace was in the Guajira, preferring to stick to her style. With her dark hair gathered in a tight low ponytail, thin hoop earrings, and thick fake eyelashes, she looked into the camera, prettier than Natalie Wood.

My parents moved to Bogotá in 1986 and they have been living here ever since. I, of course, have visited but as with Barranquilla my stays were sporadic and short. They prefer being here rather than on the coast. Bogotá is where Dorothy would go if she were to tap her ruby heels in Colombia. My parents love living here and they have been here for more than twenty years but for *cachacos* they are still *costeños* living in the capital. I am not staying with my parents this time.

THE *JOURNAL*'S REPORTER AND I HAVE SPOKEN ON THE PHONE BEFORE BUT WE have never met. As with marines, American foreign correspondents are easily detected and it was not difficult to spot him in the lobby of the Victoria Regia, the hotel that a journalist friend recommended, centrally located to do interviews and walking distance to the many restaurants and nightspots everyone raves about. Bogotá is earning a reputation as a great Latin American capital, sophisticated and modern. He speaks Spanish and is a seasoned reporter, a foreign journalist who takes notes, asks questions, sits at his computer, composes a story, and files it. That is why he is here. His only connection with Colombia is that Colombia's name will appear in the dateline next to his byline—exactly the opposite of why I am here.

This is his first time in Bogotá. Bill has been in the city half a day and already has that love-at-first-sight gaze people develop upon first contact with the city's Republican elegance and red-brick high-rise buildings surrounded by the fertile verdant Andes. Bogotá seduces at first sight and Bill is an easy victim— he refers to Caracas, where he is based, as "the city of cement."

My friend John, a Cuban American lawyer, a classmate from Columbia University, is in the lobby too. He moved to Bogotá as part of a USAID project to build courthouses in small towns in Colombia, efforts of the social agenda of Plan Colombia. As a lawyer, he is rigorous and creative, but most of all, John is always positive. He praises his friends to the point of sounding like a publicist and when he gives himself to a cause he is ready to give it everything. This time the recipient of John's gregarious generosity and his belief in the rule of law is Colombia. John has a book under his arm and he presents it to me as if it were a forbidden item.

"It's unbelievable," he tells me. "I had to go to seven bookstores to find this book." I glance at the cover and recognize the face of the leading candidate. "A biography of Álvaro Uribe," I say. "So he is that popular?"

"Absolutely," says John as we drive to a restaurant with Bill in the backseat. "But it's not that the book is hard to find because it's a bestseller. What is happening is crazy." As I leaf through the book, John tells us what's happening. The country is up in arms over this book's controversial message. Bookstores have refused to carry copies because it presents Álvaro Uribe in a bad light. John, a First Amendment lawyer, could not believe this was happening. He had been so upbeat about the country in the two years he's been here. John has been impressed by Colombia's legal system, telling me how modern the laws of the new constitution are; and that he has met the generation of impressive young lawyers and congressmen who rewrote it. But the bookstores where he has spent hours perusing the shelves are refusing to sell the book, which adds a new layer to the Colombia of lawyers and human rights activists that he has met. I tell him I am not surprised about the ban: The book might ruin the idea of the man that Colombians have chosen to be their savior.

Colombians don't vote for human beings; they vote for saviors, believing blindly that saviors exist. Every four years, they deposit at the ballot box their unquestioning faith in a human being just like they do at altars adorned with the statuettes of the Divine Child, a young boy of golden locks and a pink robe that everyone from presidential candidates and beauty queens to thieves and prostitutes pray to with great devotion.

Four years earlier, Colombians prayed for peace and voted for Pastrana, who campaigned on the premise of sitting with the rebels, of a negotiated solution to the conflict. After the showdown at El Caguán, Álvaro Uribe's cry of war resonated. No concessions to the barbarians, he cries at every appearance. Everyone nods in agreement and with great relief. Finally, a real statesman, they say, someone who wears pants, who doesn't negotiate with assassins. "Colombians vote the same way I choose boyfriends," I say to John jokingly. "They go from one extreme to the other. It's a losing proposition. There has to be something in between."

The banned biography, *Lord of the Shadows,* makes allegations that Álvaro Uribe has ties both to drug traffickers and to the paramilitary. It insists that his father had ties to Pablo Escobar and that, when he served as governor of Antioquia from 1995 to 1997, he promoted the creation of vigilante forces, the massacring paramilitaries of today. To many Colombians this book is just a dirty maneuver by his opponents to bring him down. The bookstores are doing the right thing by not allowing "a book to destroy his election." Bookstores, they claim, are doing "the patriotic thing." I am pleased that John is getting a dose of how Colombia is not as modern as he had thought. "I told you, Johnny," I say.

Because of his position and his work he surrounds himself with the Colombia that can be cataloged as modern, but he is discovering it could just be a thin veneer.

"I know," he says. "The work of the people I meet is so admirable; it's heartbreaking to realize it means so little."

"It's a country of lords," I tell him. "The problem is not that they are lords of shadows but that we are ruled by lords; all kinds of lords, even good ones."

It is a popular consensus in the rest of the country that *bogotanos* are haughty and they have the pretensions of modeling themselves after English lords in clothes and home décor. But the real lords in Colombia are not the men of the capital (as is their conceit), even if they sniff the brandy and wear the right tie and coat better than the *costeños*. The true concept of lord, as owner of the land and of the hands that work it, is more applicable to the men in the provinces. Álvaro Uribe is one of them.

The title of the book would like to stress Uribe's alleged shady past. I choose to focus on his inherited background, that birthmark Ricardo Palmera set out to destroy when he became Simón Trinidad. Uribe might or might not have worked for Pablo Escobar and he might have colluded with abusive vigilante forces. If he did, that makes him the lord of the shadows that the title implies. But the reason he is the leading candidate is because he is a lord, with *fincas* and horses and terraces and serfs.

Colombia, the doll made of broken parts split into regions, is a country of lords, some benevolent, some vicious, but mostly a mixture of both. When Charlie told me he was coming to kill motherfucking drug lords, I could have told him I was fighting the same war he was. He was coming here because those motherfuckers had denied him a caring mother and I was coming back here because some motherfuckers are denying me a country in peace. Except I do not know who the motherfuckers are anymore. The rebels? The paras? The military? The narcos? The *costeños*? The *cachacos*? The Conservatives? The Liberals? The State or rather the oft-invoked explanation of every ill: the absence of it? The Church? The politicos who sell votes or the people who buy them?

Most Colombians have identified their enemy, and have decided that Álvaro Uribe is the statesman that can save them from the paws of the rebels. But Uribe uses the ways of his birthright to do so, forgetting about the classes he took at Oxford and Harvard. He yells at journalists when he doesn't like their questions. He makes statements based on rumors. He grandstands. His ways are not unlike those of my grandfather or any of the men of the provinces. They govern over their landholdings like lords, with methods that have little to do with law, merit, and equality, and lots to do with orders, whims, birthrights, and preferential treatments. Álvaro Uribe's popularity extends all the way from the exclusive circles in Bogotá to the political chieftains of the regions to the individual *finqueros,* small businessmen, and merchants who have been victims of the FARC's violence. On his home turf he parades on his purebred horses with a poncho from Antioquia, but in Bogotá, he dons his blue blazer and red tie. The landowners love Uribe because he is one of them.

I SHOOK URIBE'S HAND AT A PARTY AT THE COUNTRY CLUB IN BARRANQUILLA IN early September 2001, as I waited for Agustín to prepare our trip to El Carmen. Ma Cris had been invited to Alonso Daza's birthday party, the Liberal patriarch of Padilla's province. She had told me how Abuelo Gabriel and Alonso were great friends and that even though Alonso was a Liberal he had dropped by the farm to show his support when the rebels threatened to "come for the tiger." He offered my grandfather his favorite revolver, my grandmother had told me. I asked Ma Cris if I could go with her. I put on a pretty red and white sleeveless cocktail dress and sandals with rhinestones in its high heels and entered the party with my grandmother. Everyone who came up to say hello would see me by her side and without missing a beat would kiss me and then ask "which granddaughter are you?, *¿hija de quien?*" That was who I was for the night, and in that moment that was all I wanted to be.

I ran into Alonso's grandchildren who had lived in New York after their college years, but unlike me never thought of leaving their land behind. As we continued on, I realized that just like no one had forgotten my face, I had not forgotten any of theirs. It was easy to recognize Roberto's mother and Dr. Elias, who fitted me with contacts, and my Montblanc pediatrician. It was fun to sit around and say nothing and just hear them all talk. Guillermo was there too, always soft-spoken and smelling of vetiver. After dinner, a man went to the stage and announced the arrival of Álvaro Uribe, the presidential candidate. The ladies I was sitting with who weren't sure who was being introduced were told he was "Colombia's solution. Listen to him. He is what we need." The ladies continued their chat, but I got up and moved closer to where he was being introduced.

I recall a short man in glasses and a priest's haircut wearing a rumpled business suit and tie but as I did not take notes I don't remember word for word what he said. I do remember, however, the spirit of his speech and the comfort that enveloped the ballroom as he spoke from the microphone. They listened to him like they listen to a priest's eulogy, with respect and faith. The moment he started to talk a pair of familiar faces across the room distracted me: The parents of my first boyfriend, Luis, as elegant a couple as when I had last seen them when their son and I were a pair, and my life was still rooted. My heart skipped as I walked toward them. I kissed his mother, who offered me a warm hug. "Does your mother tell you how much I ask about you when I see her?"

she asked. "Now I recognize you," Luis's father said. We had run into each other at an art opening the week before and he had not recognized me. "Last week you looked like all those American journalists that come to interview me. This is better. Much better."

The candidate spoke, standing in a circle surrounded by the big Liberal men of *la costa*, and a few Conservatives as well. When he finished, everyone clapped. Then he stepped down. I happened to be in the path of his exit and we were introduced by Alonso's son, who was escorting him out. "The solution," he had said, "Alvaro is what we need." By his words I gathered he meant that he promised his plan would end with them all going back, once again able to sleep on their *fincas*.

I had found the entire night a bit anachronistic and a perfect illustration of the theory I came to prove: how the landowners from La Provincia joined forces with the political machinery of the traditional parties in Barranquilla, thereby maintaining an exclusionary system intact. The party had begun with a mass celebrated in the club's chapel. Alonso sat in a special chair, like a king on a throne. His guests filled the pews and accompanied the Daza family while the priest blessed their lives and spoke for twenty minutes about their importance for our society. I walked Ma Cris to the communion line, tempted to take the body of Christ myself, as I would do only when I lived here. The dinner was a spectacular buffet with every possible type of seafood and meats and salads and cheeses. All the typical foods from the countryside mixed in with the fancy food of continental cuisine. The birthday party had soon become a political gathering. There were speeches and mentions of honors and as the big surprise, the appearance of the new savior, flown in for the hour it took to be introduced to coastal politics. Uribe had to know that if he could get on the side of Alonso's guests, this region would be his; and if he went to the other regions and did the same, getting each region to turn their political networks to elect him, then the presidency would be guaranteed to be his. After the presentation, *la costa* had given him their support. As he left, the band started to play, and the couples on the dance floor had smiles of hope on their faces.

JOHN SWERVES AROUND THE STREETS OF LA ZONA ROSA UNTIL WE FIND A PLACE to park near Niko's Café, where we have arranged to meet a group of foreign journalists. Margarita Martínez from AP is there and I am happy to see her. She and I have many things in common: We are both from the coast; we were both educated in the United States; and we both have what I call the journalist gene. García Márquez had said at a workshop in Cartagena that journalism is not a job, it is a gland. Some people are born to tell stories and others aren't. The maestro's theory resonated with me and I took his metaphor further. It's that simple, as simple as genetic coding. I call it the J-chromosome. Just like some people are born with blue eyes and others are born with brown eyes, Margarita and I were both born with it, and it is not much different from the X-chromosome that Alcoholics Anonymous thinks is inherent in some people, making them alcoholics. Journalists are, in many ways, addicts. Instead of being addicted to heroin or to cocaine or to scotch, we are addicted to "the story," and that involves the same kind of rushes and withdrawals. Sitting at Niko's and talking story, I am getting my fix. I order a glass of red wine that comes with most political discussions in New York, and settle into my French bistro chair, feeling as comfortable as I have ever felt in Colombia.

I start up a conversation with Margarita whose insights about Colombia I value. She is in a privileged position, working for a foreign outfit in her native country, I tell her, confessing guilt and envy. Important political actors understand the difference between a story published locally and one that has international reach. She tells me that perhaps in Colombia it's different, sharing a recent experience when Salvatore Mancuso, the paramilitary leader, second in command after Carlos Castaño, came out of his secret lair to tell Margarita what no one in Colombia knew. His organization, he claimed, controlled 30 percent of the country's members of congress. "My legs trembled as he talked. I knew I had huge news but what got me the interview was not the fact that it said AP on my business card," she tells me. "It was my second last name on the card. It's considered an important last name in *la costa*," she tells me knowing that I know what she means. Like most scoops, this one was the result of a mix of perseverance, patience, and luck and that extra talent of knowing how to use ambiguity in your favor.

When the story came out a few days later, everyone in Colombia picked it up. The paramilitary claiming that they controlled one third of the country's congressmen was very important news, but those who read the story about the infiltration of the paramilitary in local politics did not know the details that Margarita is regaling me with now. No one who read the AP story knew that Mancuso had "dressed like an Italian prince" for the meeting, wearing a linen jacket and the latest model Nikes. "As if he had been shopping in Miami," she offers. "Córdoba is very, very poor. Clothing like this is very noticeable there."

Part of the comfort I feel here is exactly this—being surrounded by storytellers. We like to write stories, but we also spend hours sharing the details that never make print, the stuff that explains the human face behind the ideology and politics. That Mancuso has linen clothes and Nikes bought in Miami explains more about the nature of the paramilitary than perhaps the boilerplate stuff of on-the-record interviews.

I tell her that I am jealous of what she is doing. She sighs. She needs to get away every so often, she explains, like R & R for soldiers. In fact, she has just taken a week off, doing nothing. "The hangout," she says, "for the entire foreign press covering Latin America. It's fun." Before getting on the plane back to Bogotá, she goes and has a sauna, the perfect preparation, she says, for coming back. "If you don't do this once in a while," Margarita tells me and flashes her perfect smile, "Colombia will make you go mad. I had to cover Bojayá last month and I couldn't take it anymore." I thought she had mispronounced Boyacá, the name of the Andean savanna, where peasants grow potatoes and where Simón Bolívar fought that decisive battle against Juan Samano, the cruelest of all Spanish viceroys. I have seen pictures of the white bridge with stone edges and a big memorial, the kind with men on horses, the kind the women don't get unless they are virgins. My father loves visiting the Boyacá Bridge and being a guest in his house is a guarantee for a guided tour.

Margarita didn't mean Boyacá, she meant what she had said—Bojayá. "A tiny *pueblito*," she explains, educating me about the tiny hamlet of no more than a couple thousand people, mostly black and mostly poor, in el Chocó. "Nowhere." On the map of Colombia, it is the armpit where Colombia borders Panama, the chopped appendage that did so well for itself after Teddy Roosevelt claimed it to build the passageway that would cut traveling time around the globe in half. Upon my return to New York I will look for Bojayá on my kitchen map where I have started to highlight with a blue marker the names of those towns that were so unknown to me and that I've come to know thanks to tragedies. Bojayá, I will later find out, is so small and unimportant that it is "nowhere" to be highlighted. But after May 2, 2002, everyone in Colombia recognizes the place, and associates it with death.

"What happened in Bojayá can only be called horrible. I can't get it out of my head." Attacks—rebel attacks, para attacks—happen every day in Colombia but there was something about this one, Margarita tells me, that was different. It was the first time that everyone could be blamed. "The FARC, the paras, and the army are all responsible for this one." The images that came out of that place were too much for the country to take in silence or in denial or by shrugging their shoulders as another story that came in through the evening news.

The FARC launched one of their signature bombs, something that's happened so many times before. "It is not the first time the FARC has attacked civilians," I say. But this time, it was launched at a church, killing more than 120 civilians; half were women, the other half children. "The entire town had taken refuge at the church in the square," she explains. "They had been hiding for days."

"Why?" In the past ten days more than five hundred paras had moved into the area. They wanted to make it their territory, to take it away from the FARC. "The residents saw them come in, heavily armed, going up the river. The residents counted seven boats. They alerted the army." There is a huge army base along the river where the boats had to go through to reach Bojayá but they weren't stopped. The army knew that the paras had made the three-day journey up the river. Where was Andrés Pastrana, *el Presidente de la Paz?* The population of Bojayá and the human rights agencies and the church were demanding answers.

What happened in Bojayá, is what happens in rural Colombia: it was being disputed between the FARC and the paras, not because they have different ideologies but because, like so many places in Colombia, it is a perfect location for smuggling. It is on the banks of a river; this one is called appropriately Río Sucio, or Dirty River: it is close enough to a big city, in this case Medellín, and to the lush jungles of the Darién that hide cocaine laboratories so well. The area first belonged to the paras but the FARC had won it over in March 2000. The rebels had destroyed the police station, killing twenty-eight soldiers and destroying an entire para camp. Now the paras wanted it back, so they took seven boats up the Dirty River in broad daylight. The deployment was done so openly that the local representative of the United Nations in the region had notified the government. The answer that the UN official got was they were aware of the situation and "in alert." When the para boats arrived, the rebels surrounded them. The paras had helicopters and planes flying over but the FARC was fighting strong with all of 1,500 men. When the paramilitary realized that they already had lost five hundred men, they took refuge in Bojayá's square. They hid at the clinic, at the school, and inside the church. The rebels defended themselves by saying that the paras took the civilian population as their shield and insisted that they were not targeting the church; that it was a mistake; that the tank went astray. But it's hard to trust their good faith, Colombians say, since they do this every day. Bojayá's priest shows no sympathy for the FARC's mistake. More than three hundred people were inside his church and they knew it. Everyone could hear them praying.

Bojayá is so remote that when the story broke, it took journalists the same three days it had taken the paras to land on the banks of the Dirty River. The first to arrive was a Spanish journalist from *El País.*

Learning about Bojayá, sitting at Niko's, I feel as remote as if I were sitting at the Half King in Chelsea. I could be hearing this story in New York City; that is how remote Bojayá seems from Bogotá and my glass of wine.

I tell this to Margarita, half as a confession and half as a question. "How do you manage to live with this duality?"

She nods her head, gives me another one of her perfect smiles, and tells me she has no idea. "It's not easy."

There is the duality between reporting about her country for a foreign outlet and in English. There is also the duality about living in Bogotá and being from the coast. I want to know if, like me, she feels the tugs of what I liberally call schizophrenia. We laugh and take a sip of wine.

The conversation turns to the election. I have noticed that the main papers and magazines have been critical of Uribe's authoritarian tantrums, like when he shouted at the journalist from *Newsweek* or when he accused human rights lawyers of being on the FARC's payroll. I voice a question that has been gestating in my head: Is it easier for the *bogotanos* to criticize Uribe because they in many ways have much less at stake? Isn't it easier for the media elite here to ponder ideas when they are so far away from the kitchen tanks turned into bombs and the chain saws turned into weapons for mutilation? I find myself repeating the things I've been accused of by my own family. Easy for you in Greenwich Village to criticize what's happening here.

Margarita nods her head vigorously, making sure I get that she agrees with me. She goes further. She tells me that the reason why *bogotanos* are happy with Uribe is precisely because he knows how to talk to the provinces; they don't. Uribe understands what it's like to suffer the consequences of the rebels. Because the rebels have stayed out of the city the *bogotanos* are spared the real horrors of war. Uribe speaks the same language as the other actors of the war. Like Manuel Marulanda and Simón Trinidad on the other end of the spectrum, he does not accept the middle ground.

Uribe's figures of speech, his use of diminutives and his *paisa* accent, the poncho he likes to wear all give goose bumps to the members of the tony families of Bogotá. But they are quite clear that it is exactly what they don't like that they are better off endorsing him. Uribe speaks the language of the countryside so they don't have to. If Uribe has the rest of the country hypnotized with this patriotic cry of war the Bogotá elite can stay put and continue riding their polo horses, not those that Uribe parades in the provinces. They can continue having a glass of nice wine in the city, in peace. The parties in the town's square of Valledupar with their accordion cowboy songs and the bottle of contraband scotch are fun during the Vallenato Festival, but that only lasts a week. And the Flower Battle in Barranquilla with the dancing queens atop the floats with throngs of people dressed in what they are not—men love to dress as women; white women love to become black; thugs are dressed as priests and prostitutes as nuns—are so much fun. But the Carnival that *barranquilleros* take as seriously as raising children, it is an everyday affair, is to the *cachacos* another chance for a quaint party with the crazy fun-loving *costeños*. After both festivities, and with strong hangovers, the *cachacos* thank their hosts with a gentle nod and a distant handshake. "Let me know when you're in Bogotá. Allow me to entertain you," they insist to the *costeños* and the *vallenatos* who have done everything to show them a good time, who've thrown their houses out the window as the popular saying from the coast goes. But the phone calls, the *costeños* complain, go unreturned. And the *vallenatos* are to be played at their parties only.

When I ask Alejandro, a former minister, if he is a *cachaco*, he smiles. He tells me he was born in a small town outside of the capital, surrounded by Andean clouds and not by culture. "Yes, by now I am considered a *cachaco*." And with his impish look of the cat that ate the canary, he continues. "I am from Bogotá because the *bogotanos* allow me to be from Bogotá." I don't ask Margarita if the *bogotanos* grant her that label yet. I decide to enjoy another glass of wine and turn to the volunteer for a European medical relief agency who has been working for the past year in Córdoba and listen to his surreal stories of how he treats the casualties of the war that doesn't exist. One of the main problems they encounter is the lack of blood at the ERs. I look around the table and see Bill, the American journalist, John, the American lawyer, and the French doctor for whom Colombia is so much different than it is for me.

26

MEETING THE REBELS

Bill and I are on our way to Residencias Tequendama, a high-rise building in downtown Bogotá that offers apartments with hotel services, to interview Luis Eduardo Garzón, the presidential candidate for the left. Garzón's press person, a journalist I know, with a few exiles under his belt, got us in to see him. Garzón has allotted us a strict ten minutes. I am kind of dragging Bill to this interview. The candidate with the least possibility of winning is of no interest for the piece that he is preparing, a no-frills "curtain raiser," to use journalism slang, that will give the readers of the paper a very general idea of where the country's political and economic stability stands. I, however, am very interested in meeting the candidate. It is pretty unlikely that he'll get any more than 10 percent of the vote, but Garzón has been able to bring together an interesting coalition, a marriage between the rigid Communist Party members and ex-militants of the M-19, and a good chunk of the intelligentsia and bohemians of the capital. He has the support of prominent columnists, economists, publicists, campaign managers who have defected from the traditional parties and have joined his Democratic Pole. They are the men and women behind the new face of Bogotá, the one that Bill and John fell in love with and the one that *bogotanos* pride themselves on. Álvaro Uribe is running as an independent but he is a product of the Liberal machinery of his region and he finds himself lucky that the Conservatives are also embracing his candidacy. As I understand it, Garzón has no political machinery supporting him, no local politicians buying votes, throwing big parties in the pueblos where the liquor flows free and where there are T-shirts and baseball caps handed out as incentive for a vote to people for whom these things are essential articles of clothing, not just political endorsements.

The Residencias is a known place in Bogotá; it is the residential side of the Hotel Tequendama, the prime hotel of yesteryear before Bogotá grew so much and became the ultramodern city of today with boutique hotels in the north, much like the one we are staying at. But it was here where my father lived in 1969 when he worked for the government and it was here where I stayed as an eight-year-old. It was here that I saw the man land on the moon for the first time. It was here that I discovered the pleasures of room service and better yet, the pleasure of sneaking out to see what people left on their trays after they ordered. My sister and I loved going through the halls on Sunday mornings looking for little jars filled with orange marmalade and white bags of sugar with the hotel logo and five stars surrounding it that to us were precious. We stuffed our pockets with them and took them back to our dolls in Barranquilla. They were perfect because they were small like the dolls and we could serve them when we made them tea.

Bill and I pass by the doors of the Salón Rojo, whose bronze handles have gone opaque and the red carpet smells of old age. My sister and I would sneak out at night in our pajamas and into the weddings and balls being held here. Once we got so disoriented amidst the ladies' gowns and the long buffet table that we huddled in a corner until the maître d' rescued us and took us back to our parents' suite. As we get into the elevator, I wish we were getting into the big one that announced every floor with the sound of a bell. We are taking the small one, the one that comes straight to the floor from the garage for security reasons. Garzón has reasons to be cautious. He is a union organizer who from 1984 to 1999 led nine strikes in the area of Barrancabermeja, a city whose name means "vermillion riverbank." As evocative as the name sounds, Barrancabermeja has seen its share of spilled blood and to be a union organizer is a sure way to increase your chances of being assassinated. Along with teachers, journalists, and human rights workers, to be a union organizer gets you labeled a leftist, a guerrilla sympathizer, or a stone in the shoes of many, especially the paramilitary. In *El Tiempo* last year I read a story of how this city of a quarter-million people located on the Magdalena River, has gone from "one illegality to another one," in this case from being a rebel stronghold to being taken over by the paras, similar to what I heard happened in La Fortuna near El Carmen and what Margarita explained happened in Bojayá. The story quoted the town's priest as saying he was the only safe citizen of Barrancabermeja. "When I am stopped at the checkpoint, no matter from which side, there's always someone who will let me go free. 'You baptized me, father, don't you remember?'"

Garzón lives in a one-bedroom apartment with his mother. He is a stocky man in a turtleneck and a double-breasted jacket that is at least a size too big for him. He is polite, not overly friendly. He sits in a rocking chair while his bodyguards lean on the bulletproof windows that show the green Andes in the horizon straight and regal as a horse's spine. He is the son of a maid; his father never recognized him and he paid his way through college by working as a caddie on the golf courses of Bogotá's country club. He tells Bill and me, the two American journalists, to sit in front of him on the leather couch and that he will give us ten minutes. He is very busy. "I need to do this for her," he says, pointing to the bedroom where his mother watches television. "I owe it to her." I want him to expand on this. I want him to tell me what it was like at the club, I want to understand the condition of servility in the capital, but Bill changes the direction of the interview.

"How would you deal with the FARC?"

"I think we need an agrarian reform," he says. "Don't know if it's the one the FARC proposes. In many things I agree with them but not with their arrogance. There are many things I agreed with Pastrana about when he started the peace talks with the FARC. It was very smart of him to internationalize our peace process. The demilitarized zone was a smart idea but it turned out badly. Today the stage is for negotiations not for insurrection." Garzón thinks that the fact that he is running for president does not mean that the traditional politicos who run the country are ready to open up to the left he represents. "For the last ten years," he says, "they have given the left the ministries of health, agriculture, even labor. But they last in their posts for only a few months. The longest, I think, was minister for an entire seven and a half months. I will feel that we are part of the country when we get the defense or the foreign ministries." After the promised allotted time, he gets up, uninterested in chatting up the gringo journalists. He takes off his ill-fitting blazer and one of his guards passes him a bulletproof vest. The bodyguards walkie-talkie the rest of the security team standing outside the building and alert them that "the candidate is exiting the building." He reads the question in my eyes. "If we arrive alive to election day, great," he says as a way of responding. "If not, others will."

BILL WANTS TO GO BACK TO THE HOTEL TO CHECK IF THEY'VE CALLED US BACK about our interview with Gloria Quiceno. Apart from the curtain raiser he has come here to do, the story he really wants to do is about a frozen juice company in the outskirts of Bogotá that hires rebels who've given up arms as part of a government program to "reinsert them into society." We receive word that Quiceno will see us tomorrow at around eleven but that the location is still undisclosed. Gloria Quiceno, a former rebel herself, is the director of the program. Her job is to make sure that the seven thousand *reinsertados,* as they are called, find jobs in the private sector. She is a sort of social worker and parole officer for rehabilitated rebels. She needs to make sure they are following the rules in adjusting to civilian life. This interview has both of us very excited. Bill because his story is moving in the right direction, and I because she is the first Colombian guerrilla girl I will meet. It's a familiar feeling of excitement, this prospect of getting close to a rebel. I was so infatuated with the dream of revolution that when I met Sonia at a party in Panama in 1979 and another of the girls told me that her parents were "Communists from Nicaragua," I befriended her instantly. I envied her life: Her parents knew the entire directorate of the FSLN and one summer they made her go to an army training camp. I tried to be invited to dinner at her house as often as I could. After being there I would drive home and dream of joining the cause. But I never did. I just danced with my dream with my eyes closed in the darkness of my bedroom.

My infatuation with the romantic ideal of revolution was reignited when I met Hollman Morris, a Colombian journalist, in 2001. I was in Mexico City on assignment, working on an oral biography of Gabriel García Márquez for an American magazine. I was there to interview María Luisa Elió, the Spanish woman who encouraged Márquez to write *One Hundred Years of Solitude* and whom he acknowledges in the book's dedication. Morris was living in exile in Spain. He worked as a TV reporter covering "the armed conflict," he told me, making me feel I finally had met someone who was close to admitting that Colombia was in a state of war. That was the reason he wasn't living in Colombia. After he aired a story about the paramilitary taking over Puerto Wilches, which he calls the "cradle of the paramilitary," he was forced to leave the country. He was able to capture by camera how a para platoon rounded up civilians in the town's square and shot in the air, terrorizing everyone and ordering them all to leave their homes behind. When the story aired that night on national television, "someone" didn't like it and complained by sending a death notice accompanied by a purple funeral wreath with his name on it to his house. As Morris was not home to receive the announcement of his own death, the messenger handed it to his pregnant wife. A few weeks later with the help of Amnesty International, Morris and his wife were given refuge in a Basque town. Their daughter was born there.

When I met Morris he had been away from Colombia for almost nine months. It had not been easy living away from "the story"; as drug addicts can find one another in a crowd, so can we story addicts. When he heard that the Gabriel García Márquez foundation was offering a workshop, he applied. He not only got in but also was offered a full grant to attend. He had been in Mexico City three days and was coming back to life, seeing other Colombian journalists, talking about the homeland, catching up with what was going on. He was even thinking of staying on and trying to get some freelance assignments, having found out that Subcomandante Marcos and his EZLN were going to enter the city in a few days for the first time. Marcos was going to take over the Cathedral's plaza and promised to represent the cause without shedding blood.

Morris and I agreed to go see it together and to meet at the National Museum of Anthropology. I wanted to show him the Rufino Tamayo mural I love so much, with the yellow coyote, the silver moon, and the red crepuscule and he wanted to see the pre-Columbian solar calendar. But we talked more than we saw anything at the museum. He told me about a Colombia I had never heard about. When he entered the military service, he was the only one in his entire platoon who had his own bar of soap. "The other kids bathed without soap. And my bar would get stolen every week." In 1988, he was a journalism student when he read about the Mapiripán massacre and was so outraged he thought it was a story to be discussed in class. No one else was interested. They wanted to discuss the upcoming Miss Colombia pageant. He is now so committed to changing Colombia "through stories" that a life outside of it means nothing to him. He will continue working for a Colombia "where we all fit," paraphrasing Subcomandante Marco's words about why he was entering Mexico City. He misses the rivers and the hamlets, he tells me, all of the ones that I don't know, I tell him. He has explored all of the body parts of the country I barely know. He tells me that maybe one day we can work there together: "I miss those rivers so much it hurts."

On his wrist, Morris wears a bracelet with the colors of the Colombian flag. Unlike the foreign reporters who go to FARClandia, he tells me, reporting is different when it's about your country, which is a strange concept in itself. It's like a doctor being asked to diagnose his own parent or a surgeon to operate on his child. "That's why I need to get going," he told me as we walked around the museum, "I have asked to see Calarcá." He explained that Marcos Calarcá served as the international spokesperson for the FARC. I asked if I could tag along.

The FARC leader was there when we arrived at the outdoor café a few blocks from the museum. The handsome, bearded revolutionary of my dreams was a middle-aged man with a V-neck argyle sweater and a weight problem. He got up to shake my hand when we were introduced and asked me if I wanted something as he waved to the waiter and ordered his second espresso. He expected Morris to explain who I was and why he had brought another Colombian to this meeting, which, after all, was clandestine. When Morris explained that I live in New York, and am a freelance journalist who has written for the *New York Times*, he relaxed and tried to pitch me a few stories. Morris asked his question: "Why can't the FARC be more like the Zapatistas who call for revolution without violence?" And the rebel answered: "Because they are not real revolutionaries like we are." To me it sounded like a canned answer. I didn't think Morris had a scoop, but as I saw him scribbling on his notepad, I realized what he was there for. He was getting his fix.

It was my turn to ask: "Why is it I don't hear about the FARC on American campuses like I did about the Nicaraguan FSLN and El Salvador's FMLN when

I went to college?" He told me that it was because they were concentrating on doing that in Europe, where they had lots of supporters and that in any case the United States was not that important to them. That is perhaps half of the answer because most of the members of the FARC are not allowed into the United States; they are wanted for drug trafficking.

"Here's our magazine," Calarcá says, handing me a copy of *Resistencia*, a very glossy publication, much, much glossier than Cuba's newspaper, *Granma*, or *The Nation*, the standard-bearer of the American left. With a Picasso painting on the cover, it resembles an art magazine and not an ideology-laden rag. It was sixty pages in heavy, shiny paper and a bound spine. Agustín had told me years ago how *Resistencia* had published his name in their list of the people's enemies. "I have never seen it but I think it was issue number 116," he had said to me.

"It's our peace issue," says Calarcá. "That's why we chose this image." It is a painting of a young girl holding a dove close to her chest. Inside I find articles by Chomsky—I wonder if he knows it and if they pay for reprint rights—and by Calarcá himself. Morris insists on getting a better answer to his question. "What is more dignifying," Calarcá asks before taking a bite of his second pastry and a sip from his third coffee, "for a child to die from a bullet wound that he got fighting for a better world or for him to die outside a hospital gate from dysentery because the system cannot take care of its poor?" Shortly after his declaration, he stands up and says good-bye, leaving me with his unpaid bill.

THE MOMENT GLORIA QUICENO WALKS INTO THE ROOM SHE BRINGS WITH HER the tension that she lives with in her daily life. She is an hour late to our meeting and she apologizes but not profusely. To want to meet with her, one must play by her rules. She is a petite and handsome woman of dark skin and formal ways. I can tell she is definitely not a *costeña* but I cannot place where she is from. She gives up very little. She is dressed in a black-and-white suit and unadorned pumps, carefully put together, defying every stereotype I could have had of what a rebel woman looks like. Her style is closer to the conservative look of Condoleezza Rice than that of radical Angela Davis. There is something guarded and regal about this woman who joined the M-19 when she was a sixteen-year-old and right out of high school.

Gloria seems more nervous than anyone else we've met about Álvaro Uribe's possible victory. His motto is "Big heart, strong hand." If he wins, she thinks that her program would suffer financially if it is not simply terminated. She is a former rebel who works with former rebels and Uribe has promised to deal with anything remotely rebel-like with a "strong hand." Gloria is also worried about her security, especially if Uribe turns a sympathetic eye, "a big heart," the

other part of his slogan, to the paramilitary like people are rumoring that he
will. Gloria is a *reinsertada* herself, so she knows how difficult it has been for
society to accept former guerrilla members. Bill has started to interview her
and I have gone speechless again, something that rarely happens anywhere else.
I study her every move, overtaken by the history of what her life must have
been like. She spent more than twenty years as a militant, holding guns. "Did
you ever kill?" I want to ask. Instead she answers Bill's question about how
amazing these two businessmen have been in hiring former rebels for their
company. It is very tough convincing business owners to hire these young men
and women. But, then again, the owners of the frozen juice outfit were *com-
pañeros* themselves, two *combatientes* like her in the rank and file of the M-19.
She also explains how the other problem with the *reinsertados* is relapse, as in
all recovery programs, recovered drug addicts or alcoholics, rebels also relapse.

In 1999, as part of the peace talks, Andrés Pastrana created a program to
"bring back to society" seven thousand rebels who have given up arms, including one thousand children soldiers. The program promised them schooling. In
two years, about 2,500 rebels have voluntarily joined her program, more rebels
than paramilitary.

The reason for this is that rebels are getting increasingly "authoritarian" and
"inhumane." Of every ten *reinsertados,* she says, eight belong to the rebel army
and two to the paramilitary. Another reason that there are more rebel deserters
is that the rebels force families to give up a son or a daughter—sons are
preferred—to the cause. If they don't comply, they pay the price. But some of
the boys are underage and unlike her they didn't join out of a real belief. It is
very difficult for the children to keep up with the training and their lifestyle,
and so they leave. From January to July of last year she had received 264 children who had defected.

Gloria was a top-ranking member of the M-19, one of only two women in
the entire organization. So when the M-19 negotiated an amnesty with the
government in 1990, she entered public life. In 1990 she gave up her rifle in a
ceremony in the mountains of Cauca along with one thousand other militants.
Colombia, a newspaper article has said, had nine peace treaties with different
rebel armies during the last forty years and more than 7,500 rebels have been
"reinserted" into society. The M-19 has mayors and senators, and as Garzón
mentioned, they have been given a few ministers for a few months. When the
M-19 signed its amnesty, the organization had 917 members. A dozen or so
were given room in the government, as congressmen, diplomats, and mayors.
The rest were allocated a pension and many returned to their homes, mostly in
towns located in Valle, Cauca, Tolima, Huila, and Caquetá.

I have read how difficult it is to adjust to life, to be a rehabilitated rebel, to live in "the mountains" for fifteen years and then have the government trade your rifle for a television and a set of cookware. I wonder what made her, not me, and not Imelda, take the steps she took. I want to ask her if she would do it again. I don't ask her, but I know she joined the rebel group in 1974, so I will assume she will respond by saying it was a sign of the times.

27

WRONG MUSIC

Armando, a well-known architect, invites Bill and me to a party that night. He tells me that it is a birthday party for a Bohemian princess of the left. Her guests will not be Uribe supporters. They are the team behind Luis Eduardo Garzón. I was curious to meet the progressive intelligentsia of the country, hoping it would be a place where I would finally be at ease in Colombia. I like the sound of it, especially because it is held at a restaurant in La Candelaria, the equivalent of the East Village if it were all beautiful colonial buildings. It is where the painters, the writers, the scions of fortunes with a bit of a streak have bought houses even if it also has pensions that rent rooms to petty thieves, transvestites, and prostitute boys.

The restaurant is a cavelike group of rooms with a covered terrace serving as the dance floor. Everyone knows one another and as much as Armando tries to introduce Bill and me, we are snubbed almost as badly as Charlie was at the Miami airport. I recognize a few faces; the people I know say hello with an air kiss as they go their own way. They have a lot to talk about among themselves; these are crucial preelection days; lots of internal politicking and strategizing and gossip to share. But the tapas are delicious and so is the *aguardiente,* a Colombian version of anisette firewater served in shot glasses and accompanied with chopped pieces of coconut and *uchuvas*, something like a lichee and an orange-colored grape. Bill sits in a corner, happy to be a fly on the wall, to eat, drink, and observe like all good foreign correspondents. He is still under the Bogotá spell, which increases with every drink of *aguardiente.* I am a bit more agitated, needing to mingle, hear what they're saying, maybe even have fun at a Colombian party.

I spot Salomón Kalmanovitz, the shy and brilliant economist whom I had interviewed a few weeks after I had gone to El Carmen, seeking him out to run my theory by him. Colombia is a feudal country, I explained to him that afternoon. It is not the FARC but our feudalism mentality that we have to vanquish. But Kalmanovitz had calmly rejected my theory. He told me that the FARC were not revolutionaries but a drug-trafficking operation. I was not so convinced by the explanation that he had given me almost six months ago in whispers, while a boom box played The Animals under his desk at his grand wood-paneled office at the Banco de la República. I am happy to see him here tonight. We dance to an old Cuban song, stepping all over each other's shoes.

I join Bill in the dark corner and enjoy a conversation that flows better than it has all night long with my fellow Colombians left-wing or right-wing, *costeños* or *cachacos,* it doesn't seem to matter. I feel very un-Colombian around Colombians. Bill keeps remarking, however, that Colombia is so great and fun.

The truth is that Bogotá is an interesting place. It has been given a new modern face. Bogotá has been transformed to a city with public transportation and public spaces—parks, bicycle paths, and libraries sprouting everywhere. It also boasts a high culture and a hardcore nightlife. It now has a theater festival in April, a fashion week in June, and techno music raves with guest DJs from around the world all year round. The people of Bogotá are happy, the people from all over the country that live in Bogotá are ecstatic, and everyone who comes to visit falls in love at first sight. Wherever you turn, you hear it: Bogotá has changed so much for the better. *Bogotá está preciosa.* Bogotá is so much fun. *Una rumba buenísima.* A great party.

It started about ten years ago with the election of a new kind of mayor. Kalmanovitz had explained it me in his office last year: Bogotá is different because it has a different kind of elected official who was making visible changes to the city, not just pocketing the money. "*Bogotanos* are learning civic pride. They are learning for the first time that they have a fiscal responsibility; and when they see that their money is being used and not stolen, they actually pay taxes willingly," he said. One of Bogotá's main thoroughfares on Sunday mornings turns into a bike path, a jogging track, a Rollerblade rink, or a singles hangout, whatever *bogotanos* feel like doing outside. Cars can only be used on certain days and have to be parked in specifically designed zones, not just on the sidewalk, a very Colombian practice. At first people complained of the new measures that were seen as hassles but now everyone is proud. "I take care of my city now," a well-known actor once told me. "I never really took care of it before."

Why, then, don't I feel completely comfortable in this nascent city, which everyone is convinced will be held as an example not just for other Colombian cities but also around the entire developing world? My mother is right, I am such a *desubicada,* a word that means both difficult and kind of ridiculous, and always out of place. When she invites me to have a coffee at Pomeriggio, which does serve a very good espresso and delicious *tramezzinis,* I cannot stop frowning. When she asks to go see the new stores that have opened up, competing with Madison Avenue—"It is not so necessary to go shopping in New York." All the big names are found in Bogotá now: even Louis Vuitton. The ladies see the new stores as an example of how Bogotá is improving. "Let's go," she invites me. "Let's have a look." I can enjoy the beauty of things, I like to see these stores in New York, but I cannot enjoy them in Colombia. I have to tell my mother that these stores are ridiculous. I just do not know how to keep my mouth shut. Sixty percent of the population in Bogotá makes in a month less than what one of the wallets costs.

BOTH ARMANDO AND I HAVE HAD ENOUGH OF THE PARTY AND HE OFFERS TO give me a lift back to the hotel. The moment I step outside I remind myself of how incongruous this life is and why I prefer to stay away. I had forgotten how heavy the door of his white 4x4 is. Armando's car is bulletproof. I had been in his car many times before. I spent three months in Bogotá, from November 1999 through January 2000. I met him in New York the summer of 1999 at around the same time my friends from Barranquilla were coming back into my life, and the same time I saw the CNN report in Shelter Island. In some strange irony, "the situation" that was driving them out, drove me in.

A friend was throwing a dinner party for him and after exchanging a few words, I was curious about the *cachaco* so I booked myself a ticket and landed at my parents' house in Bogotá. They sure were surprised.

Bogotá had mesmerized me, like what was now happening to Bill. On our first date, Armando and I went to an Italian restaurant that was charming and intimate in a house that resembled a chalet and the owner made sure everyone was enjoying dinner. The second date was in a strange restaurant called Renault, as in the French carmakers. Armando knows Shakespeare sonnets by heart but to hear them in a place displaying the latest cars made it hard to concentrate. I was taking it all in, open to the strange ideas of what passed for cool in the Third World, and feeling the tug of my two sides. After all, I am a child of the developing world.

I was enjoying my time getting to know life in Bogotá with Armando. His friends were involved with changing the new face of Bogotá and I was introduced to many of them. At the parties I met the doers: the Argentine who had started the theater festival; the head of the libraries; filmmakers. I met the woman who served as minister of education and was responsible for building libraries, as imposing as any in a rich neighborhood, in the marginalized barrios. I was offered a tour of the libraries, the crown jewels of the movement.

Bogotá has five new libraries in poor neighborhoods, including one built by Rogelio Salmona, Colombia's architect laureate, in his signature red brick. I found all this both exhilarating and yet somewhat intimidating. Instead of staying away, these people were there building a country, and they had a lot to show for their efforts.

My introduction to the new Bogotá continued. Armando and I went out to dinner frequently and the choices were many. We often went to an area known as the Park of Ninety-third Street, a kind of Restaurant Mile, where each house bordering a green lawn, the so-called *parquesito,* has been turned into a restaurant. The culinary choices are many: Thai, Chinese, French bistro, French fancy, sushi, Middle Eastern, crepes and waffles. They all have great décor, attract a beautiful crowd, and serve pretty good food. The conversation always flowed smoothly until our talk turned to Colombia.

Armando had been a sympathizer of the left-wing movements of the early seventies, but had moved on, describing himself as belonging to the category of mistaken idealistic youth. He had little respect for those who still adhere to those beliefs. At first I just listened, trying to understand the mentality of this new Bogotá, taken by his commitment to build a new country. He and his friends were building libraries and bike paths; they were bringing international theater back to the city; they were eating well and they were partying hard.

At the restaurants he preferred to stick to literary chitchat. But eventually I pried. I knew Armando had finished his high school education in the United States, in a boarding school, and I was surprised that he had chosen to return to Colombia for college. He filled out the story in bits and pieces, reluctantly. Armando was convinced that he would continue his education in the United States, but his father, a successful doctor, would not allow a son of his to become a hippie. There was no way a son of his would grow long hair and start smoking marijuana. So Armando returned to Colombia and enrolled at the Universidad Nacional. Neither father nor son realized that the university was a hotbed for the revolutionary movements that had been getting stronger and that they were recruiting whomever they could to join their rank and file. It was not hard for these groups to find sympathetic ears in the young university students. Even scions like Armando liked what they were hearing. He spent hours discussing the ideas—those that today he calls obsolete—with other students. What no one knew then, I finally found out, is that some of his new friends also believed that everything is valid in the name of revolution, even kidnapping one's buddies.

In a strange twist of fate, Armando, a sympathizer of their ideas became one of the first victims of this now everyday occurrence. I had tried many times to talk to him about his experience, always dwelling in that blurry space between information-gatherer and friend or relative when I'm in Colombia. But each time I would bring it up, his usual response was, "what is there to say," and then he would change the subject. One night over dinner I thought that I would try again, that perhaps this was the time he would say more. All I got was, "it was not like it is now. My father paid, and I was released." I push for more and finally realize he had nothing to say not because he feels guilty that he got out alive, or that he didn't spend years and years being held like the more than three thousand victims of today or that he was lucky not to be killed in a rescue operation. I think that Armando avoids the subject because it really hurts to know that he was taken by someone he trusted.

ONE AFTERNOON ARMANDO TAKES ME OVER TO SAY HELLO TO HIS DEAR FRIEND Enrique, an older gentleman in the true sense of the world, the epitome of an old-style upper-class Colombian. He had a house filled with books, beautiful paintings, sober, elegant, lived in and yet formal. He has impeccable manners and impeccable clothes and I am there to get his approval. I listened to them go about their conversation, which went from Proust to Prague. Enrique had recently returned from a long stint in Europe and he regaled us with stories of the art exhibits and the restaurants he visited there. He was curious about me and smiled enough so that I would feel welcome. Somehow the conversation turns to *boleros* and the two of them, I can see, respect these ballads, an art of equal importance and mastery as poetry. "Do you like *boleros*?" Enrique asks and I feel I am taking an entrance exam. I don't really know how to answer; I don't know what he is asking me. I didn't know what made a *bolero* a *bolero*. As far as I know, a *bolero* is a romantic song with high drama, the ones I like to listen to in Barranquilla when driving around with Allegra but do I like them? I'm not sure. I don't own any *bolero* CDs. I like dancing to Cuban music sometimes and I like those standards like "Bésame Mucho" that even Plácido Domingo and Linda Ronstadt include in their Central Park repertoires; I like the songs now made famous by the charming gentlemen of the Buena Vista Social Club, but am I an expert on boleros? Well, I don't think so. "I like them, sure," I say shyly. I want to be admitted to their club.

"Which?" he asks, "Which ones do you like? Agustín Lara? Matamoros? 'You Are in My Heart'? 'Blue Night'? 'Enchanting Damsel,' which one?" Armando, coming to my rescue, explains that *la nena* was more of the "American persuasion."

"She likes her rock," Armando answers for me.

"Aaah," Enrique says, leaning back. "Ah, now, really? You do? But one cannot be a rock lover and a *bolerista* at the same time."

"Of course not, Enrique," I say. "It seems that that is impossible. I would like to try though." The next day Armando buys me a CD of *boleros* as a gift.

I STARTED TO THINK THIS COULD WORK. I COULD SPEND MY TIME IN BOTH places. Maybe it was time for me to integrate Colombia into my life. But there were moments when I found myself so alone in my thoughts and reactions that blending in was becoming more difficult. Most of the time the feelings of alienation started in front of the television, and most of the time it had to do with how people I knew reacted to the news of the FARC.

Like he did most evenings, my father was sitting watching the newscast when Armando came to pick me up for a Christmas party. And like most evenings, the news reported kidnappings and killings perpetrated by different fronts of the FARC in the remote areas of the country. I consider joining my mother in her bedroom, where she never listens to the news so "she can keep living." However, I stay and listen to another conversation about how Colombia can resolve its problems by getting rid of these bandits.

"You should leave now," my father offers, after the newscast. "You don't want to be late for your party." Armando and my father shake hands and I kiss my father's cheek as he says, "*Adios hijita*, have fun."

We ride in silence to the party, driving on a winding road taking us up to the northern tip of Bogotá that leaves the traffic and the strip malls behind. Rows of pine trees and the smell of eucalyptus welcome us. The air is colder here and I wrap myself tighter in the velvet coat that I've taken from my mother's closet. "Keep going," I tell myself. "Understand them."

At the party I run into a few familiar faces, and I'm happy to see Arturo and Teresa, two *costeños* who run with the Bogotá elite. They are surprised and curious to see me in Colombia, at a cocktail party and as Armando's date. I am relieved to see them and wonder if they notice my unease. I am nervous for two reasons. One, because I never think that I look like people do at Colombian parties despite my mother's borrowed coat, and they only like people who do. And two, because I feel my eyes tear up as I try to smile and tell them I am happy to be here. The hopeful idea that I can return to Colombia is starting to crack.

"Your mother had said you were here," Arturo says, looking at Armando at the other end of the room and wanting to hear some confidential information about the two of us. I wish I could give Arturo good news when he asks me if I will stay long this time. I knew he was a broken man, that he too had lived one of those tragic stories I cannot get used to. He had lost a son but I did not know the details. When I see Teresa I kiss her cheek. She too wants to ask about Armando but I cut her off and ask her to tell me the story of Arturo's son.

"Poor man," she says. His son had been kidnapped and Arturo, like most fathers with the means to do so, had paid the ransom and the young man had been released. Nothing out of the ordinary about that. From that day on Arturo made sure his son never went anywhere without bodyguards. One evening, as Arturo's son left the house to go to a party, his car was intersected in a second kidnapping attempt. I heard stories of rebels not returning captured people despite getting paid a ransom—this had happened with Don Mario Montblanc—but I had not heard of kidnapping the same person twice. The bodyguards shot at the kidnappers and the kidnappers shot back killing the bodyguards and Arturo's young son. Rumor has it that Arturo called the paras.

Colombians who had been victims of the FARC like Carlos Castaño and Arturo see revenge as the only solution. This is not the first time I hear this. A friend had once told me about his friend whose wife had been raped. So he hired hit men to murder the rapist. These aren't movies with Meg Ryan and Jodie Foster. These are the stories that happen to people I know; they are the victims of violence and at the same time perpetrators of violence. These stories feel like kicks to my stomach, making me want to abandon Colombia forever. I cannot dissociate people from the stories they tell and so I am always faced with this conundrum: how to love my family and friends in Colombia and not see them as implicated in the violence. "The thing is," Teresa continues, "the thing is that you have to pay one or the other. And I have to say I'd rather pay the paras than the guerrillas. I cannot tell you why, I just do. And I am someone who sends money to Amnesty International every year. And losing a child like that—I guess you are capable of anything when someone kills your child."

We are called into the room with the nativity scene. The novena is about to begin, when everyone gathers around and the owner of the house reads the passage from the Old Testament corresponding to the nine days before the birth of Jesus Christ. I ask Armando if we can leave. Once in the car, protected by the bulletproof glass and the distance from the party chatter, I burst into tears. Armando does not know what to say. He never knows what to say—I am too much and cannot restrain myself. I tell him that I must be crazy but that I cannot enjoy life here. I cannot live with the news stories but most importantly I cannot live with everyone's reactions to the news stories. I start to tell him what Teresa told me about Arturo and what my cousin told me about his friends and about—but Armando interrupts me. "My father," he offers as consolation, "said the same thing to me." We ride in silence down the winding road.

ARMANDO AND I CONTINUED TO GO OUT TO DINNER OFTEN, AND THIS IS WHERE I started to feel the dreaded disconnect. No matter how different the food and the décor were, I felt I was sitting in the same exact room every time. It was hard to pinpoint but I was getting antsy, irritable just walking in. Was it the way people spoke to the waiters or the way the waiters spoke to the clientele? "I want to have a drink at a bar," I told him. "I want to sit on a stool. I want a juke-box. I want waiters to mistreat me like they do in New York," I say jokingly, "and not say a *sus ordenes* at the drop of a hat." One night as we were leaving Harry Sassoon, I snapped at him because he told a nine-year-old child that he didn't have change to give him and when I took out a two-thousand-peso bill, the equivalent of two dollars, he said, "That's too much" and asked the boy for change. Armando tried as best he could. And I did too. But it wasn't either of our faults. I don't know if it was this moment or the moment at Enrique's house, or thinking that support of paramilitary groups is the only solution, but it was time for me to leave. For some reason, I do not get this claustrophobic in the West Village.

I pushed Armando to tell me what it was like to be kidnapped, but he wouldn't. Sometimes I crossed the line; it is my style, I guess. Armando would get back to me with one line. "To those of us who decided to stay and put in our two cents' worth to make this country, you can say what you want. But no matter what it is, it's never boring here."

I was unable to fit in. Was it me? Was it them? I don't know, but after a month I decided I missed New York. The evening before I was scheduled to leave, Armando called to arrange the time he should come pick me up for my good-bye dinner. "The princess is no longer sad," he said referring to Rubén Dario's "Sonatina," the same poem my grandmother Lili would recite whenever my sister and I were sad: *La princesa esta triste. Que tendra la princesa?* He pointed out that I had picked up the phone in a different voice. "It makes you happy to know you're going back." I sometimes listen to Daniel Santos in New York singing "Dos Gardenias" from the CD of boleros Armando gave me. He taught me that boleros are beautiful ballads of love and that the most beautiful are those written to recall the burn left after the flame of the possibility of love extinguishes. It is so important to know when it's time to leave.

28

CAN'T STAY AWAY
MIAMI, MAY 2003

I could have chosen to fly directly from New York to Bogotá, but I chose to go through Miami again. This is the only way that I can seem to handle going back, a gradual descent. On my way to my gate, I stop for a snack at a place called Café Versailles. As I order a pastry filled with guava jam and a *cortadito* (Cuban for espresso with hot milk), I think that one could argue that American cuisine is influenced by Latin America's political instability. Though Café Versailles is now a fast-food stand at the Miami airport, it started as a restaurant in Hialeah, outside of Miami, a home away from home for all the Cubans who fled the revolution and missed the taste of *ropa vieja* (stripped meat) with *moros y cristianos* (rice and black beans). Forty years later, Cuban food in New York and Miami is as popular as pizza. Will the next fast-food stand at the Miami airport be Colombian? I'm not sure if Colombia will have its own revolution, but the people that left in droves are now starting their lives in America and it won't be long before a hard-working entrepreneur sets up a stand selling *arepas,* a Colombian pancake, at the Miami airport. I've already started seeing them sold for $3.50 at summer street fairs in New York City.

My brother Pedro is thirty-seven years old and must have thought often about leaving Colombia. With his American education and his impeccable English, he is a perfect candidate to become an expatriate. Not only has he chosen not to leave, but on Saturday, he will marry a young Colombian woman and start a Colombian family. As I walk toward my gate, I wonder what my new sister-in-law will be like. Though I am looking forward to the occasion, I find that Bogotá still brings out the worst in me. Wherever I go, I arrive with a stern face and the proverbial big stick that I wave in silent accusation. Twenty-four hours after my arrival, I still don't feel at home, but as the hours pass my apprehension starts to give. It is difficult to hold my stance of constant questioning when all I see is beauty around me: Bogotá, flanked by the luscious green Andes that seem to kiss the sky, is loveliness; my parents' home is charming, and all I receive from family and friends is warmth and tacit acceptance. Over the years, I've become less indignant as I try to reconcile the situation of the country with the comforts of my parents' lives. I am only now starting to comprehend how difficult it must be to live with war constantly at your side. My father raises the volume of the TV set as the evening news begins; the leading story is about a bomb that was detonated by the army in a nearby hamlet. I sit in silence and admiration as I see that even amid the stories of horror and hopelessness that the television flashes, my brother and his fiancée are a couple in love, planning a wedding and a future together. Andrea, my brother's bride-to-be, is finishing a degree in political science, I learn from my father, and I would like to know more about her career interests and her opinions about the way our government and society is run. She sits next to my brother on the leather sofa, his hand on her knee, and I see a bride worried about the things every bride is worried about five days before her big day. As I listen to her talk with my mother about the preparations for Saturday's wedding and her excitement about the honeymoon trip to Venice and the Greek islands, I am simply happy to see that my brother is marrying a beautiful young woman with the face of a Spanish *maja,* a soft-spoken twenty-three-year-old who is excited about the life ahead of her. She wants to be a professional, a mother, and a wife in a country that offers large doses of despair even during happy occasions.

My mother takes out the photo albums with pictures of their engagement party. Pedro and Andrea got engaged in February 2003 in an old-fashioned ceremony that my mother described to me on the phone as she has done every major family event and political tragedy since I left her side. To formalize the engagement, my parents and brother flew to Cartagena, where Andrea is from and where her parents still live. The toast to their happiness was about to begin when the phone rang with bad news. A bomb had just exploded in Bogotá. The rebels had struck the epicenter of elite Bogotá, attacking the capital for the first time. The bomb exploded at Club El Nogal, a private club where families my family knew ate dinner, played squash, and took saunas. Thirty-six people died.

"Remember Luz?" my mother asks when I called to congratulate my brother. She usually begins her stories to me with a preamble, saying "remember" or "you won't remember." She usually is on the mark about this, who I knew and who I didn't meet "before you left," she says, referring to my life outside Colombia.

"Luz, *Mami,*" I say, "of course from *el bus de Luz.*" She was a beautiful woman with black hair and soft manners who ran a car service when she divorced. We used Luz's company to drive us to school, a gray Land Rover jeep where she would pack us like sardines in the back.

Luz's stepson was killed at El Nogal. My mother is always astonished by my memory, as I have been of her reports about what happens to people I know. For every story of family celebration there was also one of tragedy. People die, I know this, but in Colombia so many of the deaths are related to this unnamed war. Even if everyone thinks of the country as Happy Colombia, the best place in the world to live, and magazines dedicate their covers to the irrelevant English study.

It had been four years, almost to the day, since I saw the footage of the rebels marching toward Bogotá as I sat in Shelter Island. I had decided then that I would come back with a mission: I would read Colombians the Riot Act. I would tell them how much I could see from the outside. As I sit today looking at the pictures, with my parents and my brother doing something I never do in New York, spending a relaxing evening surrounded by family, I am happy to have come back to my parents' couch, to have taken off my shoes, and have let my mother hold my hand and caress it the way she likes to do.

As we sit around and I think about how Andrea will soon be part of every family gathering, the newscaster announces in a rather strange coincidence that El Nogal had that morning reopened its doors after a recent renovation. The footage shows many of the survivors, club members, and employees, some still showing scars and walking with crutches, attending a solemn ceremony. Since I knew that the explosion had been on the day of the engagement, I try to talk about it with Andrea, but she just nods her head and turns to my mother, who is showing her a present that has recently arrived. She had also opened presents earlier today, at the bridal shower that my mother's friend organized for her. A bridal shower could not have been more perfect. A house could not have been lovelier. The flowers in the garden were in full bloom; the vases inside the house overflowed with white roses and orange and yellow orchids. The stuffed chicken breasts and the chocolate mousse were exquisite. The ladies were funny, charming, and completely committed to not letting war ruin this wedding. But as I walk by the family den, I notice the title of one of the books on the shelf: *Kidnap-Hijack-Seige: How to Survive as a Hostage.*

No matter how much I try not to get caught in my usual ruminations and judgments, it is hard and soon I am my old Inquisitor self, Colombia's Girolamo Savonarola, angry that everyone seems to be living in Switzerland and not in Colombia. Álvaro Uribe has been in power for a year and the authoritarian *paisa* is still the Loved One. In keeping with the tradition of euphemism, Uribe took power and claimed that Colombia is in a "state of internal commotion," and that the military is the only way out of it. As I stay up in my room enjoying late-night television, I see a public service ad of the Uribe reign.

They are images of young soldiers in combat. "Love them," the voiceover pleads to or demands of young Colombian women, difficult to tell which one. "They are watching over you."

After a couple of days of staying in, absorbing second after second of family life, I decide I'm ready to venture out and experience the hustle and bustle of a regular weekday in the streets of Bogotá. I call Armando, by now my Bogotá comfort guide. He comes to pick me up and after lunch I ask him to drop me off at *El Malpensante*, Colombia's premier magazine. To get there, we have to cross the city from north to south in bumper-to-bumper traffic. (Traffic is so bad that cars have restricted circulation hours depending on their license plate numbers.) But since we had not seen each other for months, the inside of his four-by-four becomes a cozy den where we catch up on life. I ask him to update me on the political situation, to give me his assessment of what has happened since President Álvaro Uribe took office last August and began implementing his "strong hand, big heart" campaign slogan, strengthening the country's military might to fight the rebels. "It seems that they are really hitting them," he tells me. I tell him about the ads I had seen on television and that every day I notice a news story stating the number of rebels killed—a couple of days ago, for example, I heard twenty-something. They're not only being killed, he explains, they're also deserting, and many local leaders are being captured. But the big shots are still at large. It is unclear if this is because they are so adept at hiding in the jungle, or because they are so well protected, or because the government is waiting for the perfect moment to strike. Armando has many theories but none that criticize the president's plan. Like most Colombians, he is behind Uribe, who has almost a perfect 100 percent approval rating.

The traffic moves so slowly that the vendors and the beggars have time to hock their wares. A young woman, perhaps in her late twenties, carries a stack of black garbage bags and a cardboard sign that reads: I AM A DISPLACED MOTHER OF THE COUNTRY'S VIOLENCE. I HAVE TO SELL THESE BAGS TO SURVIVE. PLEASE COLLABORATE. Behind her, two boys, who are maybe twelve and thirteen, raise bags filled with fruit they need to sell. I am about to roll down the window, but my friend reminds me that I can't. Bulletproof windows are too heavy.

Spending an afternoon at the offices of *El Malpensante* is one of my favorite things to do in Colombia. Six years ago, Andrés Hoyos, a cantankerous *cachaco*, remaining faithful to his mission of being a contrarian, decided that he would challenge everything. With the country in shambles and with everyone leaving, he decided he would not. He pushed the envelope further, and invested his own money to publish a thinking magazine in a country of nonreaders (or, more accurately, of readers who like their news magazines to feature the voluptuous bodies of beauty queens). He found a partner in crime in Mario Jursich, his antithesis, an affable, easy-going man. Together they founded (and still run) a stunning literary, political, and cultural magazine, an amalgam of *Harper's* and the *New Yorker* that they call "a magazine of paradoxical readings." *El Malpensante* issues now almost eighteen thousand copies, and in Colombia, where statistics show that the average person now reads less than two books a year, this is quite an achievement. But Andrés and Mario have also created an informal support network for fellow *"mal pensantes."* People call them, as they would a hotline, as an intellectual outlet. They receive self-published novels, one thousand pages long, dedicated to them. Letters to the editor often run to many impassioned pages.

Andrés and Mario prefer to talk poetry instead of politics, but they wear their politics on their sleeves. They are what the Colombian government is not: inclusive, irreverent, fearless, commited to rigor and beauty. The "naughty thinkers" have run a collection of homoerotic photographs of Peruvian matadors by Ruvén Afanador, and an entire issue arguing for the legalization of drugs. They've published both an essay titled "Give War a Chance" by one of George W. Bush's hawks, Edward Luttwak, and a defense of *The Communist Manifesto* by Marcel Berman. Today they are excited about André Gide. Mario has discovered that León de Greiff, one of Colombia's master poets, translated Gide (as did Jorge Luis Borges and Vladimir Nabokov). And that Gide's *La Symphonie Pastorale* was selected as recommended reading when it was published and was reviewed in *Ideas,* a literary magazine published in Barranquilla in 1920 by none other than Ramón Vinyes, the Spanish erudite whom Gabriel García Márquez met, as a young man, and immortalized him in *One Hundred Years of Solitude.* Mario hands me a copy of Borges's translation of Gide's poem "Persephone," published in 1933. *El Malpensante* will publish it in their next issue, he says with the excitement of someone who has just won an arduous battle.

In their own way, Andrés and Mario are fighting for Colombia. The government believes that, first and foremost, Colombia needs to vanquish the rebel army, and that only when this happens will the Colombians be free. *El Malpensante* exists to remind the government that the free flow of art and ideas, of opinions and of beauty, is also essential. To quote from Gide: "Knowing how to free oneself is nothing. The difficult thing is knowing how to live with that freedom."

Andrés cannot drive me back to my parents' house so I ask him to call for a taxi. In Colombia, if you want to take a cab, you are advised that, for safety reasons, it is best to "call for a taxi service." This is a bit like ordering a car service to take you to the airport in New York. But when I call, instead of giving the pickup address, the base operator and I exchange secret information. She gives me a code, 976, which I know is the last three digits of the license plate number of the car the service will send. I know not to get into a car with a license plate that does not correspond with these numbers. She then asks me for "the last two digits," and, knowing she means the last two digits of the telephone number I am calling from, I say 20. Minutes later, a yellow four-door car honks outside. I check the license plate, and, since the numbers correspond, I get in, though admittedly rather reluctantly. When taking a cab involves so many passwords, giving in to the system makes me a bit nervous. I once heard that a band of thieves could intercept calls and send their own cars. Instead of taking you to your desired destination, they took you to various ATMs at gunpoint, while the driver awaited your withdrawals. This is called the *paseo millonario,* or the million-peso ride.

When I get into the car, a very polite man greets me and asks for my code. He radios the base for confirmation, which reassures me enough to start a conversation. I ask him how things are going. He is a bit surprised by my question. "Fine," he answers, "things are pretty normal," which is a very colloquial Colombian expression and one that I have never really understood. How can anyone use a word like "normal" when living in Colombia? I continue with my questioning. I learn that the driver's name is Julio and that he is a thirty-four-year-old father of two. I ask him if he feels the effects of the war when driving his car. He shrugs his shoulders, says yes, offers nothing more. A second later he continues: "Day to day, you cannot think about the war," he says. "You have to think about working to make money to support your family." But, he tells me, there are entire neighborhoods that are guerrilla strongholds, and rebels move through the city with the ease of fish in a pond. He also mentions the explosion at Club El Nogal, adding "many people were happy about that because it was directed to the rich. Not me, but many people celebrated." It seems that the fuel that keeps the rebels strong still exists even under Uribe's mighty hand.

Julio says that the real problem in Colombia is not so much the rebels but unemployment, which is at a record high. If people had work, he argues, they wouldn't join the guerrillas, who pay as well as any job. People would prefer working to kidnapping and bomb throwing, the rebels' signatures. These are the same words that I have heard while being chauffeured by my grandmother's driver, José, in Barranquilla, and Sergio, my father's driver here in Bogotá, who actually had come to the capital running away from the rebels in his area. "My father had eight sons," Sergio told me, "and the rebels came to tell him that he had to sacrifice one of them to the cause, so he sent me away because as the youngest it was going to be me."

Julio started driving a cab eight years ago, when the chrome factory where he worked closed and he was left without a job. To make the daily equivalent of the fifty dollars he needs to make ends meet—twenty to rent the cab, fifteen for gas, fifteen for him and his family—he needs to work twelve hours a day. And things get harder every year, he says. He used to be able to make that same amount of money in seven or eight hours a few years ago. I ask him if it is because of the war, but he says no. It is because the golden days of the Medellín and Cali cartels are gone. "When those guys were around," he tells me, "there was money on the street. Everyone took cabs." But Colombia has not stopped being the world's biggest supplier of drugs, I tell him. "I know," says Julio, "but now they have to be really low key. Before, people showed off their wealth; now people cannot call attention to themselves. The government wants to apprehend them, and the guerrillas want to tax them."

Julio begins to enjoy the interview and starts to volunteer information. He tells me that his main problem is not the guerrillas but the transit police. "They violate our human rights all the time," he says, and I prepare myself to hear about unjustified beatings or a corrupt system of kickbacks, but Julio's story is more an indication of the long road ahead for Colombia. The local government, which in the past eight years has made a tremendous effort at creating civic awareness, is simply reinforcing traffic laws. A few weeks ago, Julio was fined because the passenger in the front seat was not wearing a seat belt. To Julio, the fact that the cop gave him a ticket, and not a break, constitutes a human rights violation. To illustrate his point, he tells me the story of the taxi driver who killed a cop who was writing him a ticket. The driver had financial trouble, and to face a hundred-dollar fine was too much, Julio says.

"Why was a cab driver armed?" I ask.

"This is Colombia," he says. "Here, it is the law of the strongest." I am relieved when we reach my parents' house.

29

NEEDING TO REPORT AGAIN

The addict in me needs to do it again. I have been in Bogotá trying to be a family member, a daughter, a sister, and a member of the wedding party, but after a week I pick up the phone and call Ignacio Gómez. He is a friend and an investigative journalist. This is the phone call every foreign correspondent would like to make. Those lucky enough to know him, call him when they land in Bogotá. Nacho, as his friends call him, gives you the lay of the land reporter style. "What's happening, Nacho?" I say. "I'm here." I invite him over for a drink at my house, late, after everyone's gone to sleep. I tell him to come late purposely. I want to make sure everyone is asleep. That way I feel freer to talk with my journalist's voice, just like I did after my grandmother would go to sleep in Barranquilla, albeit to myself. I take a bottle of scotch from my father's bar, free from the daytime protocol of the house. I plop the bottle on the table and hand him a glass. "Neat," I say. "I'm not bothering with the ice downstairs." I don't want to risk our secret meeting. I don't want the maid to show up with a bucket filled with ice and with cloth napkins for the glasses.

Ignacio takes me by surprise when he tells me he is no longer writing investigative pieces. He is now a television investigative reporter. The reason is that no newspaper or magazine wants to hire him. He has all the credentials, including awards from London's Amnesty International and the New York–based Committee to Protect Journalists, but that is exactly the problem. Every story Ignacio does becomes a headache for his editors. He steps on so many toes that at forty-one he has already lived in exile five times. We met in New York during his last time out in 2000. His investigations of the links between the paras and the army now being trained by the United States under Plan Colombia were not viewed favorably.

"What are you keeping in your refrigerator these days?" I ask him. Ignacio keeps the sensitive documents of his investigations in a blue 1950s refrigerator in his apartment, which he likes to share with foreign journalists. There he has kept the documentation about the killing of union organizers in Coca-Cola bottling plants; six since 1994; and those about the role of British Petroleum in hiring paramilitary forces to guard their pipelines in Yopal. "Not much," he replies. "These are strange days. No one has dropped in. Colombia was on the radar with Plan Colombia. I have proof of Chiquita Banana paying the AUC millions of dollars. But after 9/11, Afghanistan, and Iraq, the Americans are not interested in our news. They don't even want to know about the contractors that the FARC kidnapped last month."

In February 2003, the FARC killed an American and took three more hostages. The four men had been flying over the jungles of southern Colombia, over what had been the demilitarized zone that Pastrana had allowed the FARC and that became known as FARClandia. The three men were employees of a subsidiary of Northrop Grumann, a company that subcontracted them to the United States government to work as consultants, "drug consultants we could say." Their job was to fly over Colombia and identify cocaine laboratories from the air, then notify the Colombian army so that the Colombians, not the Americans, could destroy them. Plan Colombia prohibits direct action from U.S. military personnel, a condition that makes many of the men stationed in Colombia very unhappy, feeling like lame ducks.

ON FEBRUARY 12TH, A SINGLE-ENGINE CESSNA OWNED BY THE U.S. STATE Department, equipped with FLIRS, the spying equipment that allowed them to home in on what was happening on the ground, took off from Bogotá and into the gut of Colombia, to surveil the jungles with four Americans and a Colombian guide aboard. Flying above the dense jungles, the plane's motor failed and the plane hit the ground. Everyone survived the crash but soon they found themselves surrounded by FARC rebels. The American pilot and the Colombian were shot and killed and the three others were taken into custody, as prisoners of war, according to the FARC. That had happened four months ago and had gotten very little press. "You tell me," Ignacio says. "Three American lives held by so-called terrorists and no one has yet to call me about it." Colombia is no longer news but Plan Colombia is still intact.

When he left, I opened the door to my father's office, turned on his computer, and composed an e-mail to the young marine I had met on the plane a little over a year ago on his way to kill drug dealers. "Do you remember me?" I write to the e-mail address he had given me before we said good-bye. I had kept it, thinking that there would be a time when I would want to know what he was up to. It was not every day that you found a talkative marine in times of war. "Where are you?" In a matter of hours I get a response, in Spanish. But the news isn't too encouraging. He is no longer stationed in Colombia. I decide to go for broke. "Did you, by any chance, know them?" I asked, referring to the hostages.

Charlie didn't ask why I wanted to know; he sent two paragraphs explaining how he actually knew and liked one of the men. They had flown together a few times. In fact, he says, "I think it was that same plane." He described him as a "funny dude." However, he did not volunteer much more about himself. Whatever question I sent in my messages—Where are you living? Do you have a phone number?—went unanswered.

Every few weeks I would send him an e-mail to tell him I was waiting to hear from him and would immediately get a response back, telling me that he was working on his notes; that it was taking longer than he thought but that he was "writing it all down" for me. "I realized," he wrote, "that I had lots more to say than I thought."

IN AUGUST 2003, I RECEIVE THE FIRST OF WHAT CAME TO BE TEN INSTALLMENTS from Charlie. The first one arrived with this note:

Dear Silvana,

   When I told you I had some things to say about my experiences in Colombia, I never thought that you would really be interested in hearing them. After all, we only met for a brief time. I remember that flight like it was yesterday. However, after thinking about the things I saw and experiences I had there, I thought that if I write it down to someone who would listen, that maybe it would help me get past the things that I haven't been able to get out of my mind since I returned. If it gets a bit long winded, please be patient; I'm not much of a writer. The only thing that I ask of you is a bit of discretion if you decide to share this with someone else. There are things I will write here that could be considered "questionable." I (to sound like a cliche) have changed all of the names. Not to protect the innocent (there were none of us who were really innocent) but out of respect for the safety of the men I served with and their families. Finally, I will say that being from there, obviously you have a bit of a connection to the situation. You will understand then if at times I seem to get a bit emotional about telling you something. If this happens, please just read on because I'm certain it will all make sense to you eventually. My selfish reason for telling you this story is to get on with my life. The other reason is respect for the sacrifice I saw and for the people who risked everything to protect me. This is not a "whistle blow." It's only the experiences of somebody who ended up in a place doing things that he wasn't supposed to, but did because he learned to love that place. That somebody was me and the place was Colombia. As long as I live I will never forget them and that place forever for me will be like an open wound I tried to forget but I just can't.

I didn't tell Charlie how much his words resonated with me, just like I had not told him on the plane that day that like him I was fighting a war in Colombia and that I too needed to do it so I could "go on with my life." Every ten days or so for the next six weeks, I get an e-mail from him and the moment I receive each message, I call Allegra, who is in New York trying to make contacts with art galleries. I open it only when she comes over. I read it out loud to her just like I would read every book we were assigned in ninth grade. Afterward we walk the streets of the West Village just like we once did in Barranquilla. Summer evenings have turned chilly and one day she shows up wearing Román's Armani cashmere coat that she had kept since he bought it in New York in 1982. These days Allegra is fascinated by street art and I walk with her as she points out the stickers left on lampposts and the spray-painted signs on the sidewalk, commenting and speculating about all that Charlie is writing to me. They are very complicated tales and intricate webs between narcs, feds, suits, embassy people, Colombian police, motherfucking drug dealers, and rebels. For her, it's like trying to decipher a detective story or a Martin Scorsese movie. For me, it's trying to get the scoop about the marine who allegedly went haywire in Colombia.

The intended three months, Charlie explains in his first message, became ten. "I was scared to death getting off that plane," he confesses. "I had heard so many horror stories about Colombia." Kevin, who would become his guide, was at the airport to introduce him to his new life, which included getting used to the heavy doors of armored cars. Kevin took him to his new digs, a luxurious four-bedroom penthouse in the Zona Rosa, a few blocks from the Victoria Regia Hotel and Pomeriggio and the stores my mother likes, that the embassy rented for them. He would have to share with three other volunteers, but still it was pretty fancy; it came with a Jacuzzi and a full-time maid. That night, Kevin took him out to a local *whiskeria* and after a few drinks confessed to Charlie that he needed to get out of Colombia. After fourteen months, he was burned out. Charlie shrugged his shoulders, not really understanding. Kevin seemed to be ranting and he had no idea what could have gotten him so on edge. It all seemed pretty nice: a great apartment, good pay, nice bars, and pretty nice "ladies," lots of Spanish dictionaries with long black hair. "Four hours in and I already have a girl on my lap." His Spanish was going to be perfect and he could tell he was making a good impression on his American colleague.

Kevin explained to Charlie that if he wanted he could take over his job. But Charlie wasn't clear what that meant. He had signed up to work in training; for six weeks at a time he would be managing American soldiers coming to teach Colombian soldiers how to fight. He was also clear about his mission. In official language he was there to "defeat the producer of narcotics," just as he had planned when he was a young, hurt kid who lost his mother's love and care to drugs. He also knew the training would involve rivers. He didn't get why Kevin was so bent out of shape. It all seemed pretty straightforward to Charlie.

The next morning Kevin introduced him to Frank, the American liaison with the Colombian military. The three went to the U.S. embassy, the largest U.S. embassy in the world and certainly the most secure. This fact has always intrigued me because it supports the surrealism of the relationship between my two worlds. Colombia receives more military aid from the United States than most countries; its biggest operation in the world is in Colombia (that's before Iraq), and most Americans still think Colombia is spelled with a *u*, like Columbia University. The embassy sits alone on the outskirts of the city surrounded by empty lots and concertina wire. It is very hard to access. No public transportation lines pass anywhere near it and yet every day at dawn throngs of Colombians go there hoping for a "yes" response to their visa applications, which most will not get. Charlie told me he noticed the line as he entered with Kevin. There Kevin introduced him to everyone he would be working with. He met the FBI guys and the CIA guys. He met the Secret Service, the head of Narcotics Affairs, even Ambassador Ann Patterson. Of all the people he was introduced to, he liked the DEA guys the best. "What a bunch of cowboys. Great guys." He was given a briefing that was very simple. Basically, there are two organizations that control the drug trade: the left-wing FARC and the right-wing AUC. At the bar the night before, Kevin had told him that the FARC murders children and that the AUC double-crosses anyone who gets in the way of their cocaine empire. After that, he got his ID badge and "drew his weapon."

A few weeks after he had settled into his life as a marine abroad, the first team of soldiers arrived from the United States. Charlie flew with them to Puerto Inírida where the United States had set up one of their three training camps. I get up from my chair the moment I read that name and walk over to the kitchen map. Allegra had never heard of the place either. It takes me a while to find it. When I finally do, I notice that half of the name rests in Colombian territory, the other half sneaks into Venezuela. "Puerto Inírida," writes Charlie, "was the Khe San in the old Vietnam War videos: camouflage buildings, sandbags, razor wire."

Puerto Inírida was the pits. The place stank of garbage and had carcasses of dead dogs on the streets. There were no cars. Everyone rode on scooters. Charlie knew immediately it was going to be hard staying there for six weeks. Kevin introduced him to Carlos, an officer in the Colombian military. "This man was a killer," Charlie writes. "Somewhat like a knight who killed for good, with a morally founded mentality that was overall good, but all the same, I would not like to cross him. This man was a killer. I could not mistake the look in his eyes." He then heard from Kevin that the State Department had once denied Carlos vetting, as he was accused of human rights abuses.

Back in Bogotá, Kevin came clean. Charlie's "real" job, if he wanted it, was to gather information, both for the embassy and for the Colombian military. He was to find, through any means he could, the location of cocaine laboratories. Carlos, he told him, would prove to be very helpful with this. He was to take the information to the guys in intel, who would check it out. If the information proved right, then the Colombian military could go and blow up the "target." He was so happy that when Kevin asked him if he wanted "in," he said "yes." It was better than hanging out in the offices. "I figured I might as well do something worthwhile while I'm here."

A week into the job, he got his first call from Carlos. He wanted Charlie to meet him. He had a good tip, not necessarily with a direct connection to drugs, Carlos said, but close enough. It was a counterfeit scam, and because the drug dealers were paying the farmers for the coca leaves with fake pesos, they could still go after them without breaking the rules. It was Charlie's first time so to be careful, he decided to share Carlos's information with a Secret Service agent. "After all," Charlie writes, "I'm no cop. Although I wanted to be successful, I am not stupid. Kevin had told me that if I made the wrong move I could get killed. The informants could go either way. It's a dangerous game." Charlie walked out to get the informant through the preference line at the embassy, not the long line of Colombians applying for U.S. visas standing in front of the building. "Americans don't have to do anything but just show up here," Charlie once told me. He had never realized that so many people wanted to go to the United States, or that the process could be so gruesome. His heart, he says, went out to the Colombians standing in that line.

The informant, however, was "a fat lowlife who smelled bad; not at all like I had imagined an informant to look like." He was ratting on his friends for the equivalent of three hundred dollars. When the informant finished his story, Charlie grabbed him by his collar—"Just to be cool I figured I'd show off a bit and said to him in Spanish: 'If you're fucking with us, they'll need your teeth to identify you.' I guess I had seen too many movies." As I read this in my apartment in New York, I remember how much Charlie referenced the movies and how funny he could be. "The room went silent then erupted in laughter."

The information checked out. Charlie was invited to see the action, but he refused. "I was still playing by the rules." When they were hitting the target that night, they confiscated three million fake dollars. Not only that, for the first time in a counterfeit operation, they got the printing press. The operation made the papers. "I got a nice certificate and a lot of pats on the back. I started to dig my work."

Meanwhile in Puerto Inírida, his team was having problems. The Americans and the Colombians were at odds. The marines felt they weren't being listened to and the Colombian colonel felt the marines had no idea what they were talking about. Charlie sided with the Colombians. The marines were reservists with no combat experience and very little Spanish. "They had came to fuck around, not to fight a war." The Colombian was fed up with one marine in particular who had never been in combat; had never been in combat in a river; had no experience in guerrilla warfare and was giving him attitude about how to do things in his country. *A la mierda.* True, the U.S. marine had never fought in a place with so many rivers but Charlie knew by now that the main problem between them was that to get along with the Colombians, you have to get into "being macho." But Charlie didn't tell this to the marines in Puerto Inírida; he had no time for the personality problems between the Americans and the Colombians. His job in Bogotá was picking up.

Charlie's accounts were proving that the American military in Colombia is more active than Americans realize. There've been a few stories: Two national guardsmen were buying guns from the FARC to sell them to the AUC. The wife of a DEA agent had an affair with her driver and together they were smuggling drugs through the diplomatic pouch. But they were isolated cases, small stories that appeared on the inside pages of *The New York Times.* There hasn't yet been a story about the four hundred miltary personnel who are running around the country.

Charlie's story is the story of another United States war. I read further and try to make sense of his mission as a Marine abroad, but like the U.S. War on Drugs and War on Terror, and Uribe's way with the FARC and the FARC's way with the AUC, and Charlie's war with drug dealers and my war with Colombia, they all turn brutal, sad, incoherent, and are rarely resolved.

In the midst of Plan Colombia, Charlie was on an absolute war high. This is how he explains his war. The system went like this: Carlos would call him on his cell and tell him he had an informant. Charlie would then set out to meet with him. This was his favorite part. He had realized that to get the information he had to get "cozy with the Colombians."

Soon after his arrival, Charlie became Carlitos. He grew his hair long, dyed it black, and grew sideburns. He bought new clothes. He had his suits tailor-made and wore a lot of silk shirts and leather jackets. "Those guys talked better" if he showed up wearing the Arturo Calle suits with the big lapels and the gold-rimmed shades with the yellow tinted glasses. He wore two-inch heels, a gun, and a U.S. Embassy badge. Like the Colombians, he took to smoking Royals—"more macho than Marlboro Reds"—and drank Chivas whisky. He went wherever he needed in the name of his mission. He calls himself a "free agent," implying he took liberties. "If you keep yourself off the radar screen you can be a player and that's what I most wanted to be." The cost was irrelevant. "It all came from my pocket. I was making plenty and I saw it as productive. I don't have a wife and children to support." If the information was in Medellín, the better it was for him. He loved going there. He had a girlfriend, one of many, but his favorite by far. He'd fly there, check in to the Dann Hotel, and have the time of his life. If Charlie felt the information he did get was worth something, he would bring the informant to the embassy and would call the DEA to listen to the story. The informant would normally draw a map to show where the "target," meaning the coke laboratory, was located. There were two kinds of informants, Charlie soon learned. "And they were both pretty disgusting. Those who did it for the money, paid to them only after their tip was verified. Or the lowly that wanted to turn on his boss." If the information checked out, a pilot would take out "the bird," one of the Cessna planes equipped to surveil the jungles. It worked. Information was coming in and when the pilots went out, the leads were checking out. The Colombians were hitting the labs.

Charlie writes about going on a surveillance mission over the Río Mira. The informant was a coca-leaf picker who was turning in his employer for not paying him. The FARC protected the lab and it put out as much as two thousand kilos of cocaine a month. "From the outside it was not very impressive, just a charter Cessna with a single engine, a couple of antennas, and two bubbles on the port side." But the computer equipment inside was pretty powerful. When Charlie walked to the cockpit to help them find the target based on the informant's map, the computer lit up and the imagery came in. "I looked at the hand-drawn map and we decided this was it." Charlie saw the first lab from the air and was told what color of green was a cocaine field and which hue was heroin; the less bright color green was always a legal crop. The bird's equipment could also identify truck tracks in the mud, even the garbage bags used to store the drugs. The FLIR went crazy when it picked up microwave radiation; microwave ovens are used to dry the hydrochloride before it is shipped. Charlie was not allowed to see it being bombed, but they told him that they had confiscated a considerable amount of cocaine, chemicals, and weapons.

This is Plan Colombia in action. I am reading what it's really like. Presidents, senators, congressmen refer to it in grandiose speeches but in reality what they are referring to is a twenty-six-year-old wanting to do what Charlie is doing, for whatever reason he is doing it. Plan Colombia is an American boy with an absent mother, a hungry heart, a bottle of whisky, a gun, a badge, and a lot of balls. "The Americans would set the explosives and the Colombians would technically do the hit," he writes. "This was the most important part for me. When my Colombian brothers on the Riverine Brigade would call to tell me that they had just seized three hundred kilos of hydrochloride, used to process the leaf into paste, I would think of all the stupid fucking crazy heads on the streets of St. Louis and New Orleans; and that the pusher would come up short for a month. Fuck 'em. I loved it. It was a good feeling."

CHARLIE ALSO WRITES ABOUT HOW MUCH HE LOVED EVERY SECOND OF BEING in Colombia. Wherever he looked there was one more "beautiful lady," one more great restaurant, one more bottle of Nectar Azul, one more night out having "this piece of meat called Chateaubriand that cut like butter," escaping the curfew and dancing till dawn at Andrés Carne de Res, or having beers with his buddies Paco and Jordi at the Beer Factory a few blocks from his penthouse apartment. There was always a weekend with Patricia in Medellín, going out on Sunday mornings after a crazy night to Barefoot Park and having a *bandeja paisa* for lunch, the local fare, a platter of everything that is bad for your heart: a huge steak served with beans cooked with pork and eggs over white rice. "I never felt so at home among strangers," he writes.

"I started to really care about Colombia," he continues. He started resenting many of his fellow Americans stationed with him, those who only cared about "their careers" and were there "on a fucking holiday, buying up leather jackets, emeralds for their girlfriend, and getting cheap liposuctions." He preferred hanging out with "the narcs, the spooks, and the Colombians."

The rules of engagement do not allow Americans to get involved in direct action, things like hard hits of labs or prisoner snitches, but they sometimes do, Charlie tells me. This has been a huge issue. Americans stationed there feel that they are lame ducks; that they are there exposing themselves to all the danger and they do not feel protected enough because they are not allowed to defend themselves. So sometimes the rules bend. "I will only tell you that yes, it goes on and that yes rules are broken. However, in the defense of that I will say people who deserve to die, die. And in the minds of most of us, the ends of a peaceful place we all came to love being free from the scourge of this green earth and happy instead of scared was worth some of the shortcuts we had to take." Surprisingly, I find myself less drawn to what Charlie has just told me. I could propose a story about what the American military is doing in Colombia. Perfect for, say, *Rolling Stone.* I could write about how they all get their eyes and their teeth fixed and get BOTOX and staple their stomachs. Colombia, one of the countries most concerned with physical beauty, has a huge and very competent and price-competitive beauty industry so I could also pursue the story about the three subcontractors whose families have been trying for years to get the United States government to do more about trying to find them. Or about how the young personnel stationed there find ways to bend the embassy rules. Charlie, for example, called Bogotá *Bogotraz.* He could not go out to jog; he could not take taxis; he could not go to the best parties in town because they were held in the outskirts of the city. The soldiers were only allowed to ride in embassy cars, armored and with drivers. But it was so hard to book one. They couldn't bring girlfriends up to their penthouse unless they were vetted by the embassy. Charlie took things a step further—he not only invited girlfriends, he had a dinner for Carlos and his wife. Charlie and his buddies had it all figured out—for ten dollars they could bribe the embassy drivers to keep quiet about the girls and the trips to forbidden restaurants. One of the drivers owned a taxi, and for less than ten dollars, he would drive Charlie around all night. The driver's nickname for Charlie was *el diablo.*

The story I am interested in is Charlie's sudden love of Colombia. "The deeper I fell in love with that place and the courage of the young soldiers, the more I could not think about coming home. I was home. I really was ready to die there. Why not? Why in the blue fuck should some animals who just want to sell blow and live by their own rules destroy such a place with such a people?" I wanted to call Charlie and tell him that the fight in Colombia was not really about getting cocaine to the streets of American cities, that the fight in Colombia had started much before cocaine, much before Pablo Escobar. But I wanted to hear the end of his story.

In his fifth installment, Carlitos was drinking all day and all night. His success was going to his head. He pulled a gun at an American officer inside the embassy and did not take it well when told there were things he could not do, that the line had to be drawn. In his mind, he had one mission, "to win this war," and that meant "all bets were off." At one point he writes: "I stopped caring about staying alive and began thinking more about how I could hurt these assholes who were not only killing innocent Colombians but Colombian soldiers as well. I think my downfall ultimately was identifying with these folks. I started making decisions, not thinking about how it would help me but them. That never washed with most of the guys at the embassy because most of them either couldn't care less or had never been out and seen what was really happening."

Colombians became his friends. Charlie couldn't shake the sense he had that a great injustice was being played out, and if he couldn't get at the source, he was damned sure going to help his newfound brethren any way he could. Many of the Colombian conscripts were so poorly equipped that Charlie gave a pair of combat boots to Javier, a Colombian soldier in his brigade. They were a size too big for him but they were better than what he had. "It didn't matter; a few weeks later he was killed in an ambush up the river," Charlie writes. On an outing one morning going to check on a target, the FARC ambushed them and killed five of the thirty guys on the mission using a Soviet grenade launcher. He realized Javier had been hit when he saw his boots. He saw the nine soldiers who had been wounded lying on the open cement floor, no doctors, no nurses, and no medical equipment to take care of them. That's when it became clear to him that his war, the war in Colombia, was a war being fought by Colombians. He was not going to kill drug dealers with his own hands. Javier, and many like him, were the ones who would try to, "with the worst equipment and fighting the toughest fights."

In his time there, Charlie had developed deep feelings for the plight of the Colombians. "Colombians want what every honest person wants," Charlie writes, "a decent job, enough to eat, maybe a car, a place to live, fifteen seconds of fame some day, and to have family in a place where they don't have to worry about getting beat up or killed by some drug-dealing punk who thinks it's funny to blow shit up and ignore the government. All this while in my country everybody was wondering what their next car was going to be or why they have to pay a couple more cents at the gas pump. Kids bitch about having to go to Stanford instead of Yale. The women complain that men only want one thing and are like parking spots—the good ones were taken. The guys bitch they never get paid enough to buy their women what they want and that they hate being married." Charlie was so smitten with Colombia that he tried to buy a *finca* outside of Medellín, but when he asked his bank in North Carolina for a mortgage and they realized he meant Colombia, the country not Columbia, South Carolina, "Well, they politely said fuck no."

Sometime in late 2002, things at the embassy started to change, to "die down." The focus changed. Instead of wanting to hit drug labs, the order came to interdict drug dealers. So Charlie did not have as much license as before. Still, when Carlos called to tell him he knew an informant who was ready to spill the beans on Negro Acacio, Charlie took the next plane, on his dime, to Puerto Inírida. Negro Acacio is the leader of the FARC's Front 16th that operates in Puerto Inírida, and is thought to be the organization's drug baron, connected to Fernandinho, Brazil's main drug lord. Acacio is accused of trading drugs for arms from Brazil. "I had a real hard-on for that guy," Charlie writes.

That was the decision that cost Charlie his beloved Colombia. He not only broke the rules but he learned how nasty fear in Colombia, without the help of a U.S. badge, tastes. Charlie, or better yet Carlitos, was so hooked on his job that he needed it just like his mother needed her drug fix. He wanted it so much that he didn't mind going back to that stinky Puerto Inírida, the place he had called a hell hole, the place where he had felt lucky not to be one of the servicemen stationed there. He hated the smell, "a cross between piss and garbage." He hated the streets, "with stray dogs everywhere; corpses of stray dogs sometimes lying on the streets." Puerto Inírida is a place with dark alleys and no electricity for twelve hours every day. But he went back with an extra plane ticket in his pocket, to meet a source that he thought might have useful information.

Charlie went straight to the military base in Puerto Inírida for some rein-forcement, meaning guards to escort him around town, but they told him they had none to spare. He had a few hours to kill while he waited for his informant, so he checked into the hotel, an open air structure that offered beds with mos-quito nets and candles. Charlie was hoping this guy had something good—the embassy was losing interest in his work and he desperately wanted to show up at the embassy with a GBG—a good bad guy.

When his phone didn't ring after some time, Charlie called a young woman he had met on his previous trip, another dictionary with the long black hair. They hung out at the local disco for awhile and then called it a night. He sprayed insect repellent all over his body and lit a candle. "I sat in the light, smoking, and thinking about the situation." The source had not shown up and for the first time Charlie felt alone. And feeling alone in Colombia made him anxious. "My anxi-ety was the worst it had ever been." When the supposed source did arrive, he whispered in Charlie's ear, "If I ever see you here again, you die." Charlie was real-izing how scary it was to be in a place where, "folks saw death every day, nobody really cared if someone woke up dead." He just wanted to buy time. Enough time so that morning would break and his plane would arrive and take him back to Bogotá. He called the girl again the next night and danced with her again, this time until the place closed down. Back in his room he burned the extra plane ticket. He was not going to show up with anyone for the embassy officials to debrief. His cell phone was dead but, "that didn't matter. I had nothing to say. I lit no candles, just sat against the wall with my pistol in my hand, a smoke in the other, waiting to hear the children in the playground. At least then it wouldn't be dark anymore."

In his last missive, Charlie wraps up his story, describing how he was sent back to Camp Lejeune. When he got there, his friends had all gone to Iraq. He was able to get a job as a reservist in San Francisco and that's where he has been, where he was writing these installments from. He tasted fear in Puerto Inírida but having been forced to leave Colombia was worse. A few months before I contacted him, he had tried to kill himself. He couldn't bear life with-out Colombia. He felt he had left a job undone, he made promises he couldn't keep, and he missed those nights of Chateaubriand and Nectar Azul. He ran huge bills just calling Paco and Jordi, and of course all the girls. He played "that Shakira song" nonstop. Writing to me, he said, had helped him.

"The last thing I will say is that this is an account of a normal person put in an uncommon situation. What I have talked about is true. I have avoided embellishing and elaborating for the fact that I along with other people could get into big trouble if the wrong folks were to know what goes on down there. My only purpose in doing this was to say that I've been there. I know what it means to be tied up in it. The friends I lost and the ones I had to leave behind will be with me forever. . . . When I can return to my second home, look up Carlos and his family, maybe go pick up some shrimp in Tumaco without having to worry about being kidnapped, eat *cazuela* in Cartagena, and fly into Medellín to visit that place and those people I have been away from for so long, too long, call Luis and have him saddle up Abraxis, my favorite horse, for a ride; when Carlos hugs me and looks at me and says 'We did it!!!' I know I will have peace. We pray to God in our time. The answers come in his time. Until that time, Colombia will be a whisper to me that I'll hear when I'm driving or when I'm alone."

What I want from Colombia is not the same as what Charlie wants. What I want is not to go to the farm and water-ski in the reservoir as Agustín tells me we could do if things were different there. I don't want Colombia to be a place where I can go now and defy the rules and buy an *alegría* from the street because I miss its taste and my childhood like my grandmother misses her sugared grapefruit from Asunción. What I want is for my map of Colombia to stop reminding me of a broken doll; what I want is a day where I don't have to read *El Tiempo* and have to walk up to the map and highlight another tiny town because it's been marked by death. I want to see a Colombia where fathers do not give up their children, where their children don't have to serve other children. I want to see a Colombia where kids do not grow up knowing the meaning of the word "kidnap" because they have to use it to explain why their mother or father is absent and not attending parents' day at their school. Charlie, my friend, there is no piece of Chateaubriand and no Nectar Azul that tastes good if it's always mixed with the stench of fear. Remember Puerto Inírida.

30

OUR COLOMBIAN WAR

When I called Charlie to ask him if he would meet me in Las Vegas, he said he would clear up his agenda and drive from San Francisco. Ever since I gave him the dates of my travel, he made sure to keep me posted of his every move. I was to arrive on Tuesday, October 4, 2003, and he had to be in Yemen "on a training mission" until the Sunday before. He called me as soon as he landed in Washington to say he would be back in time for our rendezvous. He was proving to be a very reliable source.

Charlie had been so open in his letters and on the phone when we made our arrangements to meet at the Bellagio Hotel where I am staying, but now that I am here, he sounds a bit less confident. There's an inhibition, a nervousness that I had never sensed in him before. "I'm downstairs; let me give you to the concierge." It felt like he was the private waiting to receive orders.

"Do you want him to come up to your room?" the concierge asks.

"No," I say caught a bit off guard. "I'll come downstairs."

In the elevator with its draped walls, I face the fantastically friendly staff at the Bellagio. The place is overstaffed and it feels like they're all on some kind of feel-good drug, trained to interact with guests and ask them questions that I am frankly not interested in answering. "First time here?" asks the elevator man. "From where?" asks the valet. "Good afternoon," guards in the elevator hall sing on cue. I smile politely. I walk past the domed rooms packed with gambling machines the color of gold, constantly ringing with the sound of coins and wonder if it's really that easy to win. It is three in the afternoon and there are so many customers feeding them that you'd think that everyone hits the jackpot. I wonder if I will hit mine. But it is not clear to me yet what it is I want to get from Charlie. There is something Gonzo in it all. I just knew that I wanted to see him.

Charlie stands in a corner beneath an EXIT sign. I had not thought whether we would recognize each other again and I had to look twice to make sure it was him. Charlie looks so different from the picture I had in my mind, not like a man who did the type of work he described to me in his electronic letters. He looks clean cut, scared, and shy and stands almost in a military stance, like a well-behaved soldier. I smile at him. Eighteen months have passed since I had seen him on the plane. I smile again, wanting the awkwardness between us to go away. We exchange hellos and I lean over to give him a kiss.

"It's good to see you," I say. I get a shy hug.

"I'm at your disposal."

"Thank you, let's find a place to sit and have a drink."

This cathedral of capitalism offers us many choices; no matter where we turn we find a bar and someone willing to make our stay "better." We decide on a bar that looks like a library and sit on a leather couch. "Thank you for listening to me," he says. "Thank you for being my priest. It's been very important to me." I can feel he is tense here, so I suggest we go somewhere else, outside. He chooses the bar of the China Grill across the street. We both order beers. Charlie's shoulders relax for the first time; he leans on the counter and looks at me, "Oh, so you are a beer drinker," he says. "Sometimes," I respond, remembering his smile, and ask him for a cigarette. "I don't smoke," he says. "I thought you did," I say. "You're always talking about smoking in your letters about Colombia."

And that's when the conversation picked up.

"I was smoking there because it was a big part of the machismo," Charlie begins. "It was all about gaining their trust. It was very important that I could show them that I could hang. For the Colombians the important questions were: Do women like him? Can he smoke and drink? Does he have balls? I don't know why they place so much value on those things." I had read Charlie's ten-part story many times, and in it he had told me that he had stopped being Charlie and had turned into Carlitos in order to do his job. In front of me is a charming young man who reminds me of Richard Gere in *An Officer and a Gentleman* and I am here hoping to get into the mind of Carlitos, the hardass guy who smoked, drank, and got into trouble. "Colombians," he says, speaking into his beer and rolling his eyes. It comes out with both respect and affection. Sitting at the bar, Charlie looks like the regular American he is only now "coming back to being." It has taken him more than eight months to adjust to life without Colombia. He tells me that when he first showed up to work, he was still Carlitos. "I showed up wearing a silk shirt and what I call my sexual chocolate shoes, and the two Mexican guys in the office were like 'Whoa, what's up with you?'"

When I ask him to describe Carlitos to me, he shows me two pictures, like a before and after of a makeover—and we both laugh. The first one is of Charlie at the beach in North Carolina before going to Colombia. He is kneeling on the sand, wearing swim trunks and is bare chested. He is flexing his muscles to show off a perfectly sculpted abdomen and engorged biceps. He looks like a harmless young man who spends a lot of time at the gym. The second picture, showing the transformation from Charlie into Carlitos, is almost a parody of a good boy gone bad. He leans against a white wall next to a painting. I recognize the naïf image of an Andean village in a gold frame, omnipresent in Bogotá. Carlitos is unshaven, dressed in black, wearing sunglasses, side burns, and a smooth smile. Kevin taught Charlie the ropes at the embassy and told him who his Colombian main contact was but what Kevin didn't teach him was how to get the informants to talk. "I had to learn the street on my own," he says. To do that, he created Carlitos. "I was playing a part at the beginning, to get the job done, but then Carlitos took over."

IN COLOMBIA, WHERE MILITARY SERVICE IS MANDATORY, YOUNG MEN TRY TO find all kinds of loopholes to get out of it. Their parents call in favors, make special requests through personal connections. Boys who live in neighborhoods in *estratos* five and six are rarely called in. Many arrive to the draft interview with falsified medical conditions: flat feet, drastic myopia, and schizophrenia. Those who don't have the clout to make the correct phone call need to be more creative. My mother recently told me that her housekeeper—my mother makes a point of correcting anyone who uses the word "servant" these days—received a frantic phone call from her sister in the countryside pleading for help. Her only son, who was trying to avoid his service, had been taken in a military raid by the army and they were holding him up in a station in Bogotá ready to deploy him to the jungle to fight. Marta proved to be as resourceful with the military as my mother thinks she is at her job. She showed up with a pregnant young woman and convinced the generals that she was the young man's fiancée. In reality, the two had never met—Marta had offered the pregnant girl twenty dollars to play the part.

Now I'm sitting with a young man from an affluent country who not only joined the military voluntarily, but sought out a particularly risky assignment. Before I can understand Carlitos, I realize I need to understand Charlie. How does a young American man end up in a foreign country, take on an alternate identity, and get so wrapped up in that country that when he is forced to leave it, life loses meaning? Charlie had told me he had volunteered to go to Colombia but I want to know what had made him choose to go fight in the first place.

"Why did you join the marines?" I ask him.

Charlie does not seem to mind telling me anything nor is he taken aback at my questions, which have gone from Colombia to personal. And not once has he flinched at responding. He doesn't really need to know why I am asking all of this and he has not asked me one question about myself. He tells me that he had seen a marine unit jogging on the beach in Florida on a day he was feeling particularly blue and lost, having a hard time handling a heavy load of college courses and work. To make ends meet he worked two jobs, as a UPS delivery man in the morning and as a security guard at night. When he saw the young men running in front of him in perfect formation and following a leader, it seemed to him to be a better life. The order of it attracted Charlie so much that the next day, really unclear why, he walked into their recruiting office. "What can you do for me?" he asked the uniformed marine behind the desk. "You, young man," the marine responded, "go outside, spit out your gum, tuck your shirt in, keep your keys in your pocket, and come back in and ask that question differently."

Charlie loved the marines from the day he enrolled. He trained hard and graduated with honors from his officer course at Quantico. His adoptive parents threw a big party at a Holiday Inn, even his mom showed up. After Quantico, Charlie went to infantry school. "It's so much fun," he remembers. "You blow shit up and shoot and shoot for eleven weeks. One thing is that you starve, because you survive on one MRE (Meals Ready to Eat) a day." Charlie could have chosen to become a pilot but like 60 percent of marines he chose to stay in ground troops. To him, that is what makes him a true marine. The marine philosophy, he explains to me is that the reason everyone is trained as a ground trooper is because they have a motto: Every marine is a rifleman, meaning he has the ability to pick up a rifle and fight in the infantry. "I never want to be the kind of military man who only plays golf."

On his first assignment he was part of an assault platoon in Croatia in the search for Slobodan Milošević. His eyes light up when he talks about being in helicopters and organizing the raids to blow up the "object." Back in Camp Lejeune, Charlie decided to learn a language. The knowledge of a foreign tongue not only gets you send abroad faster, it gets you better pay. Charlie had mentioned in our first conversation on the plane that he had been studying Russian for a few months when he saw the ad for the Spanish course that led to the option to "work in drug interdiction." "I was thinking that there would be a lot of action in this type of work. By that I mean, a lot of operational activity. I was a wide-eyed kid with a new ability, and I wanted to take advantage of it. So I signed up. Up until we got there, the river patrols were not getting involved in drug interception. They just served as civil guards." Charlie explains that this was a huge wasted opportunity; since Colombia is like a giant Venice, due to the lack of roads and the amazing number of rivers, the country moves by water and so the water plays an integral role in drug running. I tell him I didn't know that.

Colombia is a country of rivers but sees itself as a country of cars—ironic, since Colombia is basically undrivable. Colombia has the Magdalena like the Congo has its heart of darkness. I have learned how people in Colombia communicate through all kinds of water vehicles, from oil tankers to fiberglass motor boats to dugout canoes and bamboo planks. I have learned how "riverine" Colombia is, though I had only navigated these channels briefly as a child, when we crossed the Magdalena on the rusty ferry to cross over to Santa Marta to holidays by the ocean. On my kitchen map the many rivers fan out across the country, spilling into the ocean on the coasts.

Nereo showed me a photograph of a mass being held on a river, the pious arriving in their dugout canoes and the priest, in a larger one, preaching from the Bible. Guillermo told me how my grandfather transported cattle up and down the Magdalena River. My grandmother told me how she got to school by steamships, like the ones in Mark Twain's stories. My grandparents took the kind of steamboats as the lovers in García Márquez's *Love in the Time of Cholera.* Hollman, the TV journalist forced to live outside of Colombia for his reporting in the war zones, told me in Mexico City that what he misses the most about living away is "the boat rides through those rivers" that take him to the places where he reports his stories. All that is needed to survive and all that is needed to destroy flows through the country's thousands of miles of navigable water. These arteries of muddy waters move emeralds, coal, and cocaine, the commodities that Colombia was born with; they connect families and friends; they bring doctors, teachers, and priests to the most remote banks so they can spread their aid, their knowledge, and their succor.

FOR THE NEXT THREE DAYS, CHARLIE AND I SPEND A LOT OF TIME TOGETHER. After lunch one day we stand in front of fountains that danced to Andrea Bocelli while hundreds of visitors snap their cameras at them. The next day we lounge at the pool at the Bellagio and talk about Colombian "hellholes" surrounded by guests wearing Versace bathing suits, reading bestsellers and *People* magazine. I show him an article about the Green Berets complaining about the same thing he did: Americans wanting to fight in Colombia. We see *Once Upon a Time,* a Robert Rodriguez film with his characteristic cartoon-type violence and I could tell Charlie loved every time there was stuff being blown up. After the movie, we share a double fudge sundae. We ride in his pickup truck and my mind is jumping back and forth, as I try to make sense of our friendship. He called me his "priest" and I saw him as a "source." When I see a pill bottle in his car, I wonder if I want to know what he is taking, as a friend or as a journalist. There are moments that I feel uncomfortable. Am I his friend, his shrink, or simply a Colombian that understands his Colombian side?

Finally, as I see there is not much of the chocolate ice cream left and that my time with him is running out, I gather strength to ask what I have wanted to ask him all along.

"Do you remember what you told me when we first met?"

"No," he says.

"You told me that you wanted to kill every motherfucking drug dealer with your own hands."

He laughs. "That's what I said? Well, I guess that makes me a crusader, innocent, and maybe stupid. Was I ever naïve—I had no idea what I was getting into. I was an idealist. What took me there was my desire to get involved. I am the sacrificial lamb. Yes, I did questionable things. Kevin saw a wide-eyed guy with ability. I was waiting to be called to be involved in the war on drugs."

Charlie takes the last bite of ice cream. "I would have never believed I could say this but legalization is the only way. I would have never said that before all this. We are telling them to grow crops they can't mass produce, to pick it with equipment they don't have, put it on trucks they don't have, drive them down roads that aren't there, and sell it to people who don't want to buy it."

ON MY LAST DAY, AS I WAIT FOR LUNCH WITH CHARLIE, I DECIDE TO EXPLORE Las Vegas. I walk from the hotel's lobby directly onto an internal boulevard offering the best and most expensive things money can buy. I see women with French manicures, enhanced breasts and lips buying bags at Chanel. I eye a beautiful dress at the Giorgio Armani boutique. I try on a pair of Prada boots. I walk with ease at first, definitely easier than if I were seeing these expensive items in Bogotá. I do not have the instant urge to judge this church of consumerism with frescoed ceilings and water tanks that simulate the depths of the ocean. But two hours spent inside the belly of American consumerism, seeing gilded machines spitting out coins presented as monuments makes me lose my bearings. I want to get out but I cannot find an exit. I bump into a couple, who get very annoyed, and into a blond woman claiming to be Cleopatra with golden dust glued to her hair. "Welcome to Las Vegas," she says and I get so spooked I ask a security guard to help me find my way out. He asks me if I am okay and I tell him that I was having trouble finding a way out surrounded by all these things. He is a retired cop "who escaped New York" to come here. He works a few days a week as a guard and gambles and goes to shows at night. "This is great. Why wouldn't you like it here? Much better than New York." He holds the door open and gives me a big smile and a wave. I breathe the dry air in and turn my face to the hot sun.

Outside there are other things for sale. A Mexican-looking woman in her sixties wearing a Betty Boop T-shirt hands me a yellow business card with the picture of a blond woman with the largest breasts I've ever seen. A block later, a young man, also Mexican-looking, wearing an image of Che on his T-shirt, hands me a card with the phone number for a sex hotline. Inside the hotel, I go for some coffee and bump into an Australian woman who talks about her five-hundred-dollar dress. "A steal," she says. "I just wanted something new for the Excalibur show." Charlie finally shows up with a surprise.

He plans to take me to a Colombian restaurant he found. "They have Néctar Azul and *bandeja paisa*," he tells me to sell me the place. If he only knew I am not a big fan of either. I don't say anything because he is excited to be sharing this with me, with someone who actually "gets it," he tells me. "Miss that," he says. "Finally, someone who is familiar with Colombia, so you know what I'm talking about." He loves talking about Colombia, he tells me. "I can do it for hours." But explaining Colombia in San Francisco is like explaining a color to someone who has never seen it.

This is by no means a classy place. It is a hole in the wall in the back of a strip mall that caters to the tiny community of Colombians living in the area. As we walk in, I pick up a copy of *Colombian Echoes,* a newsletter written by Colombian immigrants, many of whom work in the casinos. Charlie and I read it together. The editorial talks about the need to create a social community and maybe organize a big dance. But it cautions people to lower their expectations at these gatherings. The Colombian community is small and financially limited so they are not able to bring in a Colombian band. The closest one is in San Francisco so the next party would be with a disc jockey. The important thing the editorial says is national unity. Charlie agrees but jokes about going to try to find the band.

Charlie orders a *bandeja paisa* and a bottle of *aguardiente;* he is disappointed when all I get is a café con leche and a plate of fried plantains. He is surprised by my choice but I promise that I will have some of his. When the bottle arrives, he starts taking shots, saying *a la carga* every time, an expression that means take charge, do a shot. It's an expression I'm not familiar with. I am trying to keep up my Colombian front but I am afraid my lack of interest in the *aguardiente* is going to give me up and Charlie is going to discover that I am a fake Colombian. The place has nostalgia food displayed everywhere, things that only a Colombian living here would want. I explain to him the ones he does not know, hoping to keep my cover: the Manimoto bags, peanuts covered in fried dough, which I liked in Barranquilla but have never thought about since I left; Chocolatina Jet, a thin bar of bad milk chocolate that I liked mostly for the drawings of animals that come with it. They are hyperrealistic with weirdly bright colors and now on my refrigerator door, next to the map, I keep one of a marmot, the nickname my father gave me to tease me about my oversleeping. He knows the cups of *arequipe Alpina,* the Colombian *dulce de leche,* a familiar phrase now in the United States where the globalization of cuisine has made a dessert of my past into one of the more popular Häagen-Dazs flavors.

When the food arrives, Charlie asks me to dig into his plate and I take a forkful of rice and beans. I ask the Colombian lady behind the register for a second café con leche and ask Charlie what brought him to San Francisco.

When he was sent back to Camp Lejeune, all of his buddies were in Iraq. His Dodge truck was still in the same parking space where he had left it, so he just drove and drove without thinking until he reached San Francisco, arriving in the dead of winter. He rented an apartment and hung the Colombian flag on the wall. "When I got really homesick, I spent hours looking at photos, playing Shakira tapes over and over and over again, and calling all of my girlfriends back in Colombia. I racked up five-hundred-dollar phone bills." Charlie even bought a plane ticket knowing he couldn't go back but just having it on his dresser helped dull the pain of not being there. "Then sometimes I would lose it and throw all the shit around."

I draw a map of Colombia on my napkin. I have started to get used to talking about Colombia as the doll I see in my mind's eye. I want to tell Charlie a little about my Colombia, so I point at her long swan neck. "This is where I am from," I say, making a circle with my pen where Barranquilla would approximately be on the left side of the neck. "This is where my mother's family comes from." I make another circle on the right side of the neck. "Here very close to Venezuela, my grandfather colonized some land and called it El Carmen. There are some mountains here. That's where the FARC and the ELN took over. Then the paramilitary arrived."

"Yeah, the soldiers say that the paras make their lives easier because it's like having another army."

I realize that Charlie is not interested. To Charlie, this Colombia is as foreign as his is to me. He shows me where Arauca and Puerto Inírida are and I mark a C for Charlie at those spots. "My life was in Colombia," Charlie says, channeling every Montblanc I've heard say that they cannot return to their land. "And all of a sudden it was taken away from me." He keeps repeating "homesick" over and over and looking around the restaurant. I take another mouthful of food so I don't have to say anything.

Could it be possible that Charlie is more Colombian than I am? Charlie searches for Colombia in the taste of the food in this rundown restaurant in the middle of the American desert. There are nights that he needs so much to feel Colombian, he tells me. So he goes out into the San Francico nights looking for them. But there aren't very many Colombians there. "They are mostly Mexicans," he says, "and that is different." Still, he gets to practice his Spanish and he dances even if it's with "shorter ladies." He raises his glass to me and thanks me for being here with him. I tell him that talking to him helps me also. That I too cannot remove Colombia from my life. What I don't tell him is that I am not as enamored of Colombia as he is. Charlie picks up a piece of pork rind, sparkling with grease. "I love this," he says, handing it to me. Not me. My grandfather loved his *chicharrón* and every time he offered me one I would turn my head away and my father would once again remark, "Silvana doesn't eat that—remember, the stork dropped her in the wrong country."

Charlie asks for a coffee using the Colombian word for it—a *tinto,* like my grandfather called it—and drops a shot of Blue Nectar in it. "Oh, I have missed this so much," he says looking straight into my eyes. "Por Colombia." I raise my coffee cup too, "For Colombia," I say.

Jorge Luis Borges wrote only one love story. It takes place over the course of one day, where a man and a woman, who is an architect, meet during a conference in the English town of York. The protagonist, Jorge Otálora, a Colombian architecture professor, introduces himself to Ulrica, a Norwegian woman, who he believes has "a tranquil mystery." Otálora makes it clear that he is Colombian.

> The woman asked him pensively:
> "What does it mean to be Colombian?"
> "I don't know," I replied. "It is an act of faith."

It is undoubtedly a potent phrase and it is understandable that Colombians have appropriated it these days. It strikes a chord in the face of such a sad daily reality for a simple reason: It is a hopeful phrase. I've heard it used by diplomats and by a few of the country's columnists They use it as a prophetic statement of how we should act in the face of the current unrest, as a way to reinforce our patriotism, our love for Colombia. But let's be honest: It is used out of context. Borges meant it as a pick-up line, not as a political declaration that encourages people to believe blindly in a state and a social contract that do not work. To use this phrase is as vacuous as the letters sent by IbelieveinColombia.com.

Borges's story reminds me of Dawn, a young woman whose desperate quest to be Colombian intersected ironically with my own unmoored identity. In the summer of 2003, a few months after I returned from my brother's wedding in Bogotá, I came home to this message on my answering machine: "Hi, my name is Dawn; I am Colombian," said the voice of a young American woman, without a trace of an accent. "I would like you to help me find my mother." I had no idea what this was about but my curiosity won over and I immediately dialed

The Map of War

Caribbean Sea

Santa Marta
Barranquilla
Cartagena
Valledupar

PANAMA

Caracas

VENEZUELA

Ralito

Bojayá
Medellín
SANTANDER
Saravena
ARAUCA

Pacific
Ocean

CHOCÓ

BOYACÁ

Magdalena River

★ **Santa Fe de Bogotá**

Tolemaida

Puerto Inírida

Jamundí

C O L O M B I A

The Andes

San Vicente del Caguán

Mapiripán

Florencia

Quito

ECUADOR

BRAZIL

AMAZONAS

0 Miles 200 400
0 Kilometers 200 400

Amazon

PERU

© 2007 Jeffrey L. Ward

the number she had left for me. When I reached her, Dawn explained to me that she had found my name on the Internet when she was doing research trying to find a journalist who would get interested in her story. She figured a Colombian woman journalist who lived in New York City would be a pretty good bet.

Dawn was born in Colombia, she told me, but was adopted from an orphanage in Bogotá some twenty-three years ago by an Irish couple from Staten Island. In all good faith, they stripped her of her Colombian past and raised her impeccably as an Irish American. She had no real problems fitting in. She looked kind of Irish but then again, "I could pass as anything," she says. "The other day they asked me if I was Albanian." Her cheeks were a bit rounder than the rest of the girls in her neighborhood, she tells me over the phone, and she was a bit shorter but her pale complexion and her straight brown hair blended in with all the others.

Dawn always knew she was adopted from Colombia. Her birth certificate said her name was Edilma. She even knew that her biological mother's name was Claudia; she knew her mother's date of birth, even her *número de cédula,* that very Colombian way of identifying ourselves. But she had no idea what her mother looked like, or what she did or how she lived. Growing up she would look at her belly button and wonder who had it been attached to and why her mother would give her away. It made her sad but she asked no questions. When she started having her own children, finding her mother became imperative. "I don't even know their clinical history," she tells me. "When I go to the pediatrician with them I cannot answer half the questions."

Dawn was on a double mission. She wanted to find her mother to know about her DNA but she also wanted to become Colombian, though she didn't really know what that meant or how to go about recovering her heritage. She wished that she had been encouraged to interact with other Colombians so that she would have learned how to speak Spanish, and dance, she tells me in a wistful voice that exposed a real sense of loss. "I see Jennifer Lopez and I think I want to do that. I, too, am that." So Dawn was now taking a self-taught crash course—trying to style herself like JLo—in how to be Latino. She tells me her husband looks at her and rolls his eyes. "Stop it. You white, girl!" She joined a chat group held by other Colombian adoptees and through them, she learned that there were many Colombians living in the tristate area, so she would drive herself to Colombian neighborhoods in New Jersey and Queens as much as she could, so that she could feel that "Colombian vibe."

"I saw people that looked exactly like me," she says. "I walked on the streets and I felt for the first time Colombian."

I agree to go to Staten Island and meet with her. "How will I recognize you?" I ask.

"Oh, don't worry. It will be really easy. I'll come get you at the ferry stop. My car has a big Colombian flag in the rear window made of beads. You'll see me."

In the afternoon I spent with her I saw a young mother as American as apple pie. Her clothes, her body language, and her attitude expressed in her will and resourcefulness to find her mother were so American. I was happy to hear it when she told me that she was getting fed up with the bureaucracy at the orphanage and the laws in Colombia that say that adopted children cannot know their history. "It is my right," she says to me. "I will find out my story." After a while I could detect some of Colombia seeping out in her thick black hair, in the small roundness of her body. I could see the Andes in her manicured fingers and toes.

Dawn and I talked for hours. She would call to ask me to describe Colombia to her over and over. The more I told her things, the more I understood that Colombia was a place in her mind that had nothing to do with the real Colombia, that she was headed toward disappointment. Yes, there are beautiful emeralds as heavy as apples there, I said, invoking Pablo Neruda. Yes, the music is great, I agreed with her when she told me she loved Carlos Vives and that she had gone to his concert at Madison Square Garden. When she described the food she had eaten at the 20 de Julio celebration, I told her that in Barranquilla where I am from we eat differently than those in the interior. That I prefer fish, fried plantains, and coconut rice to the *bandeja paisa* that she savored. Most of the Colombian community in New York hails from Medellín, not the coast. I insist on educating Dawn on things about Colombia she knew nothing about. Whenever I told her that Colombia has a bloody war and three million displaced people, she would go silent and then say, "So tell me, what does Bogotá smell like?"

I saw a lot of my own doubts in Dawn's search for her identity. She would tell me how she was determined to go to Colombia—just like I had done in 1999—to find her roots. She hired an investigator who promises adopted kids like her that he can find their mothers. But one day, after months of incessant calls, she stopped. I think I had bored her. Whenever she called to ask me about Colombia, I would also tell her that being Colombian in the United States comes with lots of perks: delicious food, good music, great traditions, but that just to embrace that side of Colombia would be selfish. To get the good of Colombia you must also be ready to stomach the entirety of Colombia. I insisted she learn about the displaced families, the threatened journalists, the lack of opportunity, and our obsolete machismo. Perhaps it was too hard for her to confront the reality that, in many ways, the ills of Colombia were what turned Edilma into Dawn.

I checked in with Dawn a few months after I knew she would have been back from her anticipated trip to Colombia. "I cried from the moment I got there," she told me over the phone. "I thought it was going to be immediate that I would love Colombia from the moment I landed but I didn't really feel anything and I missed my family. I felt no connection to Colombia at all."

ON NEW YEAR'S EVE, 2005, I WAKE UP TO BIG NEWS FROM COLOMBIA. PRESIDENT Uribe has scored his first goal: His army, with the help of U.S. intelligence, had captured Simón Trinidad in Ecuador. After less than eight months in office, he was doing what he promised to do, vanquish the guerrilla forces. I e-mailed my uncle Agustín to wish him a happy new year and also to find out what he thought of the news. I tell him that his niece sends him love and that his journalist-niece wants to know about Simón Trinidad. When I receive his reply, the subject line reads: "To my niece, the journalist." "The wings of this little bird have been clipped," he writes, using the word *pajarito* to refer to the captured rebel. "We will talk about this in person, in a hammock, hopefully with a breeze and on the farm."

I am surprised and relieved by his sober and subtle—and poetic—response. There was no showing off, no real celebrating, and no sense of a war-mongering victory. I was comforted not to get the let-him-rot-in-jail attitude that I had learned to expect in every conversation concerning the FARC. But as I continue reading the news story on my computer screen, the calmness of my uncle's message dissipates. "I touched her arm. She was cold and didn't respond so I realize she was dead." These are the words of a four-year-old boy describing what had happened to his two-year-old sister on New Year's Day. "She was still and her dress was filled with blood."

The FARC entered Yellow Flower, a hamlet in Tolima, in the south, to allegedly avenge Trinidad's capture. The young boy jumped out of bed to find more blood and more still bodies on the floor: His father and his sister were dead. His mother and his eight-month-old brother wounded. The attack on Yellow Flower left sixteen people dead. Only five people remained alive, including him, his seventy-year-old grandmother, his aunt and uncle, and his three-year-old brother. The rest of the town, the sixty people who lived there, crossed the river. By noon the entire town had fled. The sixteen houses by the side of an unpaved rode lay abandoned, their doors locked up. When the reporter from *El Tiempo* arrived, the soldiers gave her a tour of the tragedy. She saw beer cans on the dusty patio floor and a huge cauldron on an open fire. It was ten thirty at night when the attack began and the entire town was there celebrating New Year's. Fifteen minutes later, the town had ceased to exist, reduced to a four-year-old left with these memories. What kind of Colombian will he turn out to be?

I am ready to go search for the town on my map, but I do not move from my bed. I have stopped wanting to know, wanting to mark my map with stories like this one. The map of Colombia, issued by the National Corporation of Tourism, a map I had bought thinking that I would like to get to know my elusive homeland by road, has turned into a battleground. I had put up the map, searching, but not really knowing for what, like Dawn yearning to know her mother. "Every night I lay in bed looking at my belly button," she had said to me, "wondering who I was attached to." In my own way, I wanted the same thing she did. To know where I had come from. If I was ever to love, I needed to know this part of me.

I never did take that road trip. My journey with this map ended up being a virtual one. For four years, I have read about every possible way that a person can be killed. After reading each report, I would walk to the map and look for the place of tragedy and highlight it with a blue marker. They are all there—Caguán, Mapiripán, Jamundí, Bojayá, Segovia, Puerto Inírida. Something prevented me from making the actual journey, to visit these towns ruined by years of conflict, wars that blended in one to the next, turning the map into a travelogue of violence. And I am ready to stop now, even if Colombia is no closer to stopping the violence today than it was when I saw the CNN report. One has to know when to stop.

The green leather album of my childhood is exhibited on a table. I take it from the living room and put it with the rest of the many albums I have, albums that depict my life after I left Colombia. For four years I've ignored those in favor of the photos in the green album: my baptism, my first phone call, swimming in the ocean, showing off my birthmark, my sixth birthday, when I wore patent leather Mary Janes, the color of Dorothy's ruby slippers. I see Imelda in the background of most of these photographs. And as I start putting Colombia away, friends and family stop calling to say they are weathering the storm. Ignacio Gomez and Hollman Morris, my father and mother, Armando and Allegra, they are Colombian, no *ifs*, *ands*, or *buts*. For them it has stopped raining even if the war continues. For them, life with the war has evolved into a livable, though uneasy truce. The roads are so safe in March 2006 that *El Tiempo* has printed an interactive system for Easter called Colombia's Routes. Colombians are encouraged to take thirty-one different roads and get to know all the different regions.

I look at how the innocent outline of Colombia in my kitchen became a pockmarked map of war, each highlighted name a wound. Mapiripán, the town where the paramilitary spent two days killing. Bojayá, where the FARC threw a bomb into a church where women and children hid and prayed. Today after educating myself, reading the piles of books that have sat like brick columns all over my apartment, I've stopped shouting about Colombia. I had put up a map of a place I did not know, like the picture of a new love. I am not sure why—it seems like one never is—but it did not work out between us. I am ready to take down the map just like I have taken down photographs of those with whom I once shared love that ended.

I'm ready to step out again, with a new identity, one that includes the Colombian in me, clear now that, even if Colombia is a failed state that scares me to the point of blindness, that angers me to the point of blindness, that hurts me to the point of blindness, it is where I come from.

I remove the piece of tape holding it to the frame and Colombia comes down easily. The map drops, freeing the words that it has been covering.

> Lightning . . . then darkness! Lovely fugitive
> Whose glance has brought me back to life! But where
> is life—not this side of eternity?
>
> Elsewhere! Too far, too late, or never at all!
> Of me you know nothing, I nothing of you—you
> whom I might have loved and who knew that too!

BIBLIOGRAPHY

Álvarez Gardeazábal, Gustavo. *Cóndores no entierran todos los días.* Santa Fe de Bogotá: Plaza y Janés Editores, Selección Cultura, 1984.

Aranguren Molina, Mauricio. *Mi confesión: Carlos Castaño revela sus secretos.* Santa Fe de Bogotá: Editorial La Oveja Negra, 2001.

Araujonoguera, Consuelo. *Escalona: El hombre y el mito.* Santa Fe de Bogatá: Editorial Planeta, 1998.

Arciniegas, Germán. *Biografía del Caribe.* Bogotá: Planeta Colombiana Editorial, 1993.

Arnson, Cynthia, and Robin Kirk. *State of War: Political Violence and Counterinsurgency in Colombia.* New York: Human Rights Watch, 1993.

Apuleyo Mendoza, Plinio. *Aquellos Tiempos con Gabo.* Barcelona: Plaza y Janés Editores, 1998.

Bacca, Ramón Illán. *Maracas en la ópera.* Santa Fe de Bogatá: Planeta Colombia Editorial, 1999.

———. *"Voces* de Barranquilla." *Huellas: Revista de la Universidad del Norte,* no. 69–70 (2004): 60.

Becerra Jiménez, Jorge. *Historia de la Diócesis de Barranquilla a través de la biografía del padre Pedro María Revollo.* Santa Fe de Bogatá: Banco de la República, 1993.

Betancourt, Ingrid. *La rabia en el corazón.* Santa Fe de Bogatá: Editorial Grijalbo, 2001.

Blanco Barros, José Agustín. *El Norte de Tierradentro y los orígenes de Barranquilla.* Santa Fe de Bogotá: Banco de la República, 1987.

Brieva Mariano, Horacio. *Retrato de una generación.* Santa Fe de Bogotá: Orba Management Editores, 2000.

Cantelier, Henri. *Riohacha y los indios guajiros.* Biblioteca Virtual del Banco de la República.

Carrigan, Ana. *The Palace of Justice: A Colombian Tragedy.* New York: Four Walls Eight Windows, 1993.

Castro, Pepe. *Crónicas de la Plaza Mayor.* Santa Fe de Bogotá: Cargraphics, 1998.

Cervantes Ángulo, José. *La noche de las luciérnagas.* Santa Fe de Bogotá: Plaza y Janés Editors, 1980.

Cetina, Eccehomo. *Jaque a la reina: Mafia y corrupción en Cartagena.* Santa Fe de Bogotá: Planeta Colombiana Editorial, 1994.

Christman, Daniel W., John G. Heimann, and Julia E. Sweig. *Andes 2020: A New Strategy for the Challenges of Colombia and the Region.* New York: Council on Foreign Relations, 2004.

Colombia's Killer Networks: The Military-Paramilitary Partnership in the United States. New York: Human Rights Watch, 1996.

Dangond Daza, Jorge. *De Paris a Villanueva: Memonas de un vallenato.* Santa Fe de Bogotá: Plaza y Janes Editores, 1990.

———. *Renacimiento de Valledupar: Asi nació el Cesar.* Santa Fe de Bogotá.

Donadío, Alberto. *Lo que no se ha dicho sobre . . . los hermanos del Presidente.* Santa Fe de Bogotá: Planeta Colombiana Editorial, 1993.

Dudley, Steven. *Walking Ghosts: Murder and Guerrilla Politics in Colombia.* New York: Routledge, 2004.

El Regreso del infierno: Historias de los que volvieron. Santa Fe de Bogotá: Universidad Sergio Arboleda, 2001.

Fals Borda, Orlando. *Historia doble de la Costa.* 2nd ed. Santa Fe de Bogotá: El Áncora Editores, 2002.

García Márquez, Gabriel. *Vivir para contarla.* Santa Fe de Bogotá: Editorial Norma, 2002.

Giraldo, Diana Sofía. *Memorias: Periodistas, guerra y terrorismo.* Santa Fe de Bogotá: Universidad Sergio Arboleda, 2003.

Giraldo de Melo, Diana Sofía, Ismael Roldán Valencia, and Miguel Ángel Flórez Góngora. *Periodistas, guerra y terrorismo.* Santa Fe de Bogotá: Universidad Sergio Arboleda, 2003, and Santa Fe de Bogotá: Editorial Planeta Colombiana, 2003.

Herr, Michael. *Dispatches.* New York: Avon Books, 1978.

Kalli, Leszli. *Secuestrada.* Santa Fe de Bogotá: Planeta Colombiana Editorial, 2000.

Kalmanovitz, Salomón. *Las instituciones colombianas en el siglo XX.* Santa Fe de Bogotá: Alfaomega, 2001.

Kirk, Robin. *Generation Under Fire: Children and Violence in Colombia.* New York: Human Rights Watch, 1994.

———. *More Terrible Than Death: Massacres, Drugs, and America's War in Colombia.* New York: Public Affairs, 2003.

Lara, Patricia S. *Las mujeres en la guerra.* Santa Fe de Bogotá: Editorial Planeta Colombiana, 2000.

Manjarrés, José Manuel. *Rafael Celedón: Estudio crítico-biográfico de tan eminente autor por José Manuel Manjarrés.* Santa Fe de Bogotá, [publisher tk] 1917.

Martínez Carreño, Aida. *La Guerra de los Mil Días: Testimonios de sus protagonistas.* Santa Fe de Bogotá: Planeta Colombiana Editorial, 1999.

Mendoza, Plinio Apuleyo. *Los retos del poder: Carta abierta a los ex presidentes colombianos.* Santa Fe de Bogotá: Intermedio Editores, 1991.

———. *Zonas de fuego. La guernilla en Colombia: reportajes y analisis.* Santa Fe de Bogotá: Intermedio Editores, 1990.

Moser, Caroline, and Cathy McIlwaine. *Urban Poor Perceptions of Violence and Exclusion in Colombia.* Washington, D.C.: World Bank, 2000.

Pardo Rueda, Rafael. *La historia de las guerras*. Santa Fe de Bogotá: Ediciones B Colombia, 2004.

Pastrana Arango, Andrés. *La Palabra bajo fuego*. Santa Fe de Bogotá: Editorial Planeta Colombiana, 2005.

Posada Carbó, Eduardo. *El caribe colombiano: Una historia regional (1870–1950)*. Santa Fe de Bogotá: El Ancora Editores, 1998.

Posso Figueroa, Amalia Lú. *Vean vé, mis nanas negras*. 2001. Reprint, Ediciones Brevedad, 2002.

Reclus, Éliséo. *Viaje a la Sierra Nevada de Santa Marta*. Santa Fe de Bogotá: Biblioteca Popular de Cultura Colombiana, 1947.

Salcedo Castañeda, Lola. *Una pasion impresentable*. Santa Fe de Bogotá: Planeta Colombiana Editorial, 1994.

Saldívar, Dasso. *García Márquez: El viaje a la semilla, la Biografía*. Madrid: Santillana, 1997.

Taussig, Michael. *Law in a Lawless Land: Diary of a Limpieza in Colombia*. New York: New Press, 2003.

———. *The Magic of the State*. New York: Routledge, 1997.

Vargas, Mauricio, Jorge Lesmes, and Edgar Téllez. *El presidente que se iba a caer: Diario Secreto de Tres Periodistas Sobre el 8,000*. Santa Fe de Bogotá: Planeta Colombiana Editorial, 1996.

ACKNOWLEDGMENTS

I was able to write this book thanks to the people who are close to me and who have graced my life—some I've known since childhood, others I met during this journey. Thanks to them I have written the book I needed to write.

My first thank-you goes to my parents. It is their love that makes anything I do possible. As always, they went beyond their call of duty and diligently answered my questions, taking pen to paper and sending their "homework" on time. I am deeply grateful to my maternal grandmother for her patience and her generosity of spirit. To my uncle for always indulging me, even when my requests became risky. It is not easy to have an obsessive journalist in the family.

There is a group of Colombian friends who have coped with my contentious relationship with my country of birth, never once allowing anything to come between our friendships. My childhood friends María Elvira, Roberto, and María Cecilia are my home wherever we are in the world. Margarita, Elizabeth, and Jackie taught me how to be a *costeña* in New York City. Paula shared news, books, and rants. Lourdes helps me decipher my schizophrenia. I am lucky to have Miguel Falquez-Certain always ready to share his vast knowledge of my mother tongue and the history of our native city. I thank Stephen Ferry, an honorary Colombian, for sharing his Colombia with me and listening to mine.

There are also my gringo friends who are really family and who make sure I am well in New York. My thanks go to the late James Chace and the carriers of the Chaceian torch; you know who you are, "dudes." To Sam and Laura, my *rubia* sister. To Daphna and Harvey for letting me be *tranquila*. To Stephen Wilson who let go of his laptop for three weeks. To Kym Canter for wanting Colombians in her life and to Ruven Afanador for finding Colombia in my face. To Michael Vachon for always checking in.

To Kyle Crichton, at the *New York Times Magazine,* who sent me to Colombia with an assignment letter. To my agent, Heather Schroder, who made sure the idea of this war was a book. To my editors at Holt: Vanessa Mobley, who liked the idea and to Supurna Banerjee, who bravely saw it through the difficult moments. To Anton Mueller for reading it early on. To the New School for Social Research for giving me the home of the World Policy Institute and to my fellow fellows.

This book was only possible thanks to those who fought in the trenches, carrying out the battle of my messy office. Ariel Bowman commanded the research ship. There is not a thing Ariel cannot find or do. From turning boring timelines into art work for my walls to understanding the importance of talking before getting to work. *Gracias Doctora!* Thanks to Rebecca Plevin for offering to help out with organizing "my war" for a few weeks.

And from the bottom of my heart, to Mert, who found a frazzled writer on deadline and didn't run away. I am so lucky you go to the deli at midnight.

INDEX

Entries in *italics* refer to maps.

ABOUT THE AUTHOR

SILVANA PATERNOSTRO is a Colombian-born journalist. Her articles and features have appeared in *The New York Times Magazine, Newsweek, TIME,* and the *Paris Review,* among other publications, and she is the author of *In the Land of God and Man,* a finalist for the PEN/Martha Albrand Award. In 1999, Paternostro was selected by CNN/*TIME* as one of Latin America's leaders for the millennium for her innovative voice. She is currently a senior fellow at the World Policy Institute and lives in New York City.